Her Life Historical

THE MIDDLE AGES SERIES

Ruth Mazo Karras, Series Editor

Edward Peters, Founding Editor

A complete list of books in the series is available from the publisher.

Her Life Historical

Exemplarity and Female Saints' Lives in Late Medieval England

Catherine Sanok

PENN

UNIVERSITY OF PENNSYLVANIA PRESS

Philadelphia

Production of this book has been assisted by a grant from
the Medieval Academy of America.

Copyright © 2007 University of Pennsylvania Press
All rights reserved
Printed in the United States of America on acid-free paper

10 9 8 7 6 5 4 3 2 1

Published by
University of Pennsylvania Press
Philadelphia, Pennsylvania 19104-4112

Library of Congress Cataloging-in-Publication Data
Sanok, Catherine.
 Her life historical : exemplarity and female saints' lives in late medieval England / Catherine Sanok.
   p. cm. — (Middle Ages series)
 Includes bibliographical references and index.
 ISBN 978-0-8122-3986-7 (cloth : alk. paper)
  1. Christian hagiography—History—To 1500. 2. Christian women saints—Biography—History and criticism. 3. Christian literature, English (Middle)—History and criticism. 4. Christian women—Religious life—England—History—To 1500. I. Title. II. Series.

BX4656.S33 2007
235'.20820942—dc22   2006044664

For Basil

Contents

PREFACE ix

1. IMITATING THE PAST: EXEMPLARITY AND/AS HISTORY 1

2. FEMALE SAINTS' LIVES AND THE INVENTION OF A FEMININE AUDIENCE 24

3. FICTIONS OF FEMININE COMMUNITY IN BOKENHAM'S LEGENDARY 50

4. EXEMPLARITY AND ENGLAND IN NATIVE SAINTS' LIVES 83

5. HAGIOGRAPHY AND HISTORICAL COMPARISON IN THE *BOOK OF MARGERY KEMPE* 116

6. PERFORMING THE PAST: SAINTS' PLAYS AND THE *SECOND NUN'S TALE* 145

AFTERWORD 175

NOTES 181

WORKS CITED 227

INDEX 247

ACKNOWLEDGMENTS 255

Preface

> At her lyfe historiall example may take
> Euery great estate, quene, duches, and lady
> —Henry Bradshaw, *Life of St. Werburge of Chester*,
> 2.1985–86

THIS BOOK IS ABOUT THE EXEMPLARITY OF female saints' lives: the expectation, voiced in the epigraph by Henry Bradshaw, that women take the legends of female saints as examples for their own ethical and devotional practices. Exemplarity is, on the surface, a regulatory fiction: saints' lives present idealized feminine behavior and encourage female audiences to adopt it. But the ethical address of female saints' lives is not merely or simply prescriptive. This book presents two related arguments. I argue that vernacular legends, understood as exemplary narratives, construct a feminine audience, one which contributed to the increasing visibility of women's participation in Middle English literary culture. I demonstrate, in turn, that this imagined audience was central to the ways that hagiographers and some of their readers used saints' lives as vehicles for historical reflection. By enjoining a contemporary audience to consider their devotional practice as an imitation of ancient saints, vernacular legends provided impetus and occasion for thinking about the aspects of gender identity and religious ideals that had changed and those that had remained constant. The exemplarity of female saints' lives encouraged medieval hagiographers and their audiences to reflect on historical continuity and discontinuity through the category of women's religious practice.

This may seem an unlikely claim for two reasons. First, vernacular saints' lives do not, in general, represent the past in "historical" terms. The genre is notorious for borrowing events from earlier narratives and for confusing, even collapsing, different persons to create largely—sometimes wholly—fictionalized ones. Although there are important exceptions, many vernacular lives of female saints have a formulaic plot that centers on the miraculous integrity of the virgin body: a young girl refuses sexual advances and announces that she is a Christian; she is tortured violently, but her body is restored supernaturally to wholeness before she is martyred. My argument is not that the genre was concerned with the factual veracity of its narratives but that its emphasis on exemplarity could encourage audiences to reflect on historical differences separating the sacred past from the social present. Even the few vernacular legends that do aspire to a substantial and authoritative representation of the past understand it in relation to the present through the exemplary model that the saint provides for contemporary audiences.

The second difficulty is that the idea of exemplarity seems to imply a static cultural context. Exemplarity assumes that ethical practices retain their meaning and social value across time—that is, that they are ahistorical. But ethical practices are not, of course, ahistorical, a fact that is not so much obscured as highlighted by the expectation that the devotional practices of ancient saints can be imitated by late medieval audiences. Reading contemporary behavior and the social codes that inform it against the template provided by vernacular legends inevitably registers the differences between the sacred past and the devotional present, even as it assumes a coherent religious tradition linking them. Late medieval writers took advantage of this apparent paradox to explore questions of cultural continuity and change, sometimes imagining audiences who could, or should, imitate ancient sanctity in their own devotions and sometimes imagining audiences alienated from the example set by traditional saints. The feminine audiences addressed by vernacular lives, that is, figure a model of history in their ability—or inability—to reproduce ancient sanctity. The epigraph from Bradshaw's legend of St. Werburge neatly encapsulates the claim I am making here. The identification of the long poem as a "lyfe historiall" refers to its careful placement of Werburge in a detailed account of Anglo-Saxon political and religious history, but it is also intimately connected to the identification of Werburge as an "example" to contemporary queens, duchesses, and ladies.[1] Indeed, while "historiall" modifies "lyfe" in the first instance, it also points to "example," registering how the poem addresses the relationship between the sacred past and the social present not only through its representational strategies but also through its ethical address.

This book thus seeks to understand female saints' lives from the perspective of the interpretive position they construct. It is broadly indebted to approaches to literary form that stress reception or interpretive practices and insist on genre as a social institution. Critics have come to understand that audiences determine the cultural meaning of a narrative tradition in two ways: through their reading practices and through their own affiliations with the genre. Vernacular hagiography can help us understand better that the constitutive relationship between literary form and social institutions works in the other direction as well: narrative traditions themselves construct a relationship to social practices and particular communities through fictions of address and ideal response. I am interested in both sides of this reciprocal relationship: Chapters 3 and 4 investigate the way that saints' lives construct an imagined feminine audience through their exemplary address, while Chapters 5 and 6 consider how audiences respond to that fiction. Together the final four chapters of the book seek to describe how writers and audiences use the exemplarity of vernacular saints' lives and the feminine interpretive community it constructs to think about ethics and history.

From this perspective, gender is important to an analysis of a narrative tradition with respect not only to the strategies of representation it employs and the cultural practices with which it is affiliated but also to the interpretive position it establishes in the contested field of vernacular literature. Middle English legends of female saints address a feminine audience, often explicitly, identifying the saint as a gendered exemplar. In Chapter 2, I argue that the expectation that women's reception of female saints' lives is informed by their sex encouraged writers to understand gender as a salient category in vernacular hermeneutics. As we will see, this expectation had concrete effects on women's visibility in late medieval narrative culture. The hagiographic fiction of a feminine audience allowed women to surface in the historical record as book owners, patrons, and readers; it is no coincidence that vernacular legends provide the most abundant and detailed evidence of women's role in the production and diffusion of Middle English narrative. I trace some of the evidence that testifies to the central place that saints' lives should have in histories of medieval women's participation in English literary culture. My interest, however, is not to recuperate vernacular saints' lives as women's literature but to investigate the idea of women's literature itself as a fiction of the genre. Women's participation in the production and circulation of saints' lives surfaces so frequently in the historical record because it conforms to the broad cultural fiction that they form a distinct audience for the genre.

I offer evidence of historical women's interest in saints' lives, that is, not as the context for but as a consequence of hagiography's gendered address.

In creating a feminine audience, the exemplary address of vernacular legends also fashions an imagined community. Medieval women were surely too diverse in their personal experience and their social identities to form a single, coherent interpretive community. But saints' lives, although they sometimes also acknowledge differences based on age, sexual status, and class affiliation, generally imagine a collective feminine response. The construction of a feminine community, defined through this response, was crucial to the use of saints' lives to comment on the history and identity of other communities—political and religious, regional and national, contemporary and transhistorical. In particular, medieval authors frequently use exemplarity to define a stable feminine devotional community against the instability of other social formations. The fantasy that contemporary women imitate ancient saints could, for example, mark the differences between the authority of civic institutions in the pagan past and in the Christian present; or it could figure the categories of identity that define Englishness as a coherent term, despite significant changes in the political and ethnic makeup of the country.

My central concern in this book is with the fictional audience addressed by vernacular legends, but I would like to consider the possibility that the medieval women who read or listened to vernacular legends, like the hagiographers who wrote for them, attended not only to the devotional model that saints were thought to provide but also to the implications of this model for the historicity of the communities they inhabited and of the gender roles and religious practices that defined their own place in those communities. We do not know how most medieval women responded to these stories, of course. But if they did sometimes seek to understand their devotional practice as an imitation of ancient virgin martyrs, they had to account for the vast historical distance separating the social world they inhabited from the one represented in Middle English legends, along with concomitant differences in civic and religious institutions and the status of feminine devotion. In the last twenty years we have come to recognize that, in the largely masculine domain of secular literature, medieval narratives of the classical past provided a substantive and nuanced forum for thinking about social identities and institutions as products of history.[2] Female saints' lives, the single genre universally endorsed as women's reading in the Middle Ages, may have served an analogous function—one that reminds us that "negotiating the past" is gendered, with different forms of negotiation available to different audiences. Indeed, while there is evidence that some medieval women were fascinated with classical narrative,[3] they were more often and more widely exhorted to understand their identity and practice in the context of the Christian past, especially as represented in the legends of traditional saints.

* * *

I am not the first to address the relationship between female saints' lives and the audience enjoined to imitate them: it has been a pervasive concern of feminist approaches to the genre. Critics have emphasized, in particular, how inappropriate the most popular hagiographic narratives are as models for the growing audience of late medieval laywomen. Understood as normative, female saints' lives are egregiously misogynist, not only in their representational strategies—their definition of women's goodness in terms of sexuality and sacrifice and their fascination with the young female body as the object of often erotized violence—but also in their putative psychological effect. Incapable of imitating the practices valued in vernacular legends, laywomen—the argument goes—must have been deeply alienated from the sources of spiritual value. The structural misogyny of the genre has meant that it occupies only a tangential place in histories of medieval women's literature, especially when that tradition is defined through the category of authorship but even when the significant role of female audiences is considered.[4]

This dismissal overlooks not only evidence of women's ownership and patronage of hagiographic books but also their use of saints' legends to structure their own, sometimes idiosyncratic, spiritual lives, as well as the rhetorical and political use of female saints to contradict antifeminist stereotype and to defend female virtue. It is important to recognize that hagiography provided a useful discursive and gestural vocabulary for women's resistance to masculine authority, despite—indeed often because of—its representation of idealized feminine spirituality. Margery Kempe provides the best and most familiar example: imitating virgin martyrs, she refuses marital sex and subordination to her husband and insists on her own religious vocation and authority. The challenge that this might pose to prevailing social ideologies is also well illustrated in Kempe's *Book*. The contemporary reception of Margery's religious vocation offers surprising evidence that when laywomen did try to imitate the female saints celebrated in vernacular legends, their practice reads as dissent, even heresy—a violation of social codes, rather than their perfect fulfillment.

The reception and social use of vernacular hagiography can remind us that prescriptive literature, however energetically it is used to constrain and define women's behavior and identity, never fully governs practice and its social meaning. As sociological and feminist theories argue, the performance of a regulatory script inevitably alters it. Michel de Certeau provides a useful vocabulary for this in the *Practice of Everyday Life*: he contrasts the "strategies" of official discourse and the "tactics" of an audience's appropriation of that discourse.[5] The distinction between them, importantly, does not depend on a self-conscious or overtly resistant agenda on the part of the consumer/performer: normative paradigms are altered in performance whether that performance is intended to endorse or challenge their authority. Gender, in Judith Butler's influential work, works in the same way: the practice or performance of the ideological script of gender at once reiterates its terms and inevitably changes them.[6] In Butler's model, that is, gender identity is deconstructed by the very social performances that constitute it, even as those performances are constrained by the ideological script necessary to their intelligibility. Like Certeau, Butler provides a theoretical basis for understanding overtly dissenting or disruptive responses in relationship to ostensibly conservative ones, because even an apparent endorsement of a regulatory discourse must be understood as a "tactical" response that changes or appropriates its terms. If regulatory fictions define women's identity and practice, they also, inevitably, allow them to contest and reshape the social meaning and performance of those fictions.[7]

This theoretical model subtends my understanding of the specific contradictions inherent to hagiographic exemplarity. If the imperative to imitate or perform a scripted ethical paradigm always produces difference, in the case of vernacular legends this difference is magnified by the historical distance between the female saints who embody that ethical paradigm and the feminine audience enjoined to imitate them. The expectation that vernacular legends could or should serve as devotional models is, paradoxically, what made them vehicles for thinking about cultural change and ethical variability, as hagiographers and their audiences sought to distinguish the imitable from the inimitable, the transhistorical from the contingent. The regulatory fiction of vernacular hagiography is precisely what might encourage historical reflection.

Recent scholars have amply demonstrated that the hagiographic tradition is not nearly as monolithic as was once assumed,[8] and this is true of the hermeneutics of imitation as well. Exemplarity could be—and was—used to emphasize the continuity of identity and ethics *and* their variability. Late medieval writers and readers recognized what was at stake in representing or reading the present as a continuation of, or departure from, the past, and they were interested in the way that the feminine audience of vernacular legends could embody either model of history. While my first two chapters explore the consequences of hagiographic exemplarity I have outlined here—how the genre's ethical address might compel its audience to think about devotional practice in historical terms and how it constructs a gendered audience with distinctive interpretive procedures—the four chapters that follow extend this analysis by demonstrating the variable use of exemplarity to construct the relationship between past and present around the category of women's religious practice. Although the texts I examine use hagiographic exemplarity to construct different models of history, they share an interest in the way that feminine devotion, understood in relation to ancient sanctity, comments on social and political concerns of late medieval England.[9]

Two chapters explore vernacular legends in which the exemplary relationship linking a contemporary feminine audience to ancient saints signals the continuity of feminine devotion, imagined in sharp contrast to the instability and change that marked political culture in fifteenth-century England. Chapter 3 focuses on Osbern Bokenham's *Legends of Holy Women*, which provides some of the best and most extensive textual evidence for women's affiliation with vernacular legends. Its careful identification of its feminine audience, through the proper names of Bokenham's several female patrons, presents this textual community as a model for, and fantasy of, cultural coherence at a moment when England was threatened from within by a looming dynastic crisis and from without by an expensive, ongoing war with France. Against the divided political community of mid-fifteenth-century England, Bokenham imagines a feminine audience with shared devotional interests. This community is diachronic as well as synchronic: he uses exemplarity to figure the continuity of feminine devotion from early Christianity to late medieval England, even as the figural nature of the imitation he proposes indexes changes in the status of public religion.

In Chapter 4, I turn to the emerging interest in native identity and history in fifteenth-century legends. I focus my discussion on Henry Bradshaw's verse legend of St. Werburge, a seventh-century Anglo-Saxon princess and abbess, which represents the saint as an embodiment and guarantee of a coherent and continuous English community. Bradshaw's representation of the saint, whose body remains miraculously intact for centuries and protects England from "innumerable barbarick nations," must be understood in relation to another striking feature of the poem: its careful delineation of a variety of female audiences—maidens, wives, widows, and religious women—and how each should imitate the saint. Exhorted to reproduce Werburge's ethical and devotional practices, the feminine audience addressed in Bradshaw's text is made responsible for ensuring the continuity of the English community the saint represents. In its use of a feminine audience to figure continuity against evidence of social division and political change, Bradshaw's legend makes an argument that recalls Bokenham's *Legends of Holy Women*. But while Bradshaw similarly contrasts the stability of feminine devotional practice to the instability of a masculine political world, he represents feminine sanctity not simply as an alternative to this threatening variability—as Bokenham does—but as an antidote to it.

The last two chapters turn to the performance of saints' lives in late medieval cities, as represented in the *Book of Margery Kempe* and in the suggestive, if slight, historical records of saints' plays. Like Bokenham's legendary and Bradshaw's *Life of St. Werburge*, the *Book of Margery Kempe* imagines that the female saints celebrated in vernacular hagiography can be imitated in late medieval England. Indeed, Margery's energetic imitation of virgin martyrs creates an unsettling analogy between the social world depicted in vernacular legends and the one she inhabits. In representing saints' lives as a model for her own religious practice, Margery represents late medieval England, its communities and its civic and ecclesiastical institutions, as an imitation of the pagan world of hagiographic narrative. Her *imitatio* draws attention to the way that both communities persecute religious difference and the public expression of feminine spirituality. But she also charts differences between these two historical moments, as she investigates how the categorical opposition between spiritual and worldly values so vividly demonstrated in female saints' lives challenges the bourgeois fiction of their compatibility developed in other late medieval discourses.

The final chapter explores the use of female saints' lives as civic drama, particularly as pageants and plays sponsored by parish guilds. Plays and pageants representing female saints abounded in late medieval England, but we still know little about their cultural meaning, largely because of the thin archival and textual record documenting the tradition. I argue that the silences of historical sources may reflect the ambiguous relationship that these plays, and the parish guilds that sponsored them, had to secular and ecclesiastical authority. Like Margery's performance of traditional feminine sanctity, parish plays may have represented English communities in analogy to pagan Alexandria or Rome, an analogy that might express the tension between the practice of lay devotion and the institutions that claimed authority over it. I propose that theatrical convention—especially cross-dressing—may have functioned as a limit on this analogy: the disjunction between the sex of the actor and the gender of the character he represented might have been used to register the difference between past and present. Gender, that is, here serves as a mark of historical discontinuity. Though different from the textual tradition in important ways, saints' plays can help us see better how the imitation of vernacular hagiography constitutes a performance of the relationship between past and present, one that relied on the continuities and discontinuities of gendered practices and identities to figure history.

Note: In quotations from the Middle English, thorns and yoghs have been silently modernized. Translations to modern English are my own unless otherwise specified.

I

Imitating the Past: Exemplarity and/as History

THE LEGEND OF ST. CECILIA, one of several virgin martyrs widely venerated in late medieval England, begins with her wedding. Although she has secretly dedicated her virginity to Christ, Cecilia marries in obedience to her parents. But she has no intention of abrogating her earlier vow, and in her bridal chamber she informs her new husband, Valerian, that an angel guards her body, ready to kill anyone who touches her. Valerian is skeptical about the existence of her invisible protector, and Cecilia explains that he would be able to see the angel if he were Christian. She sends him to the catacombs to be formally converted by Pope Urban, who is hiding there from Roman authorities. Valerian's brother soon pays the couple a visit and is amazed by the sweet smell of the roses and lilies with which they have been crowned, but he is unable to see the flowers until he, too, converts. The family is discovered to be Christian, the brothers are martyred, and Cecilia is brought before the pagan judge Almachius, whose self-aggrandizing claims to power she mocks as she professes her own faith in an alternative and divine authority. Almachius orders his soldiers to kill her, but after three attempts to strike off her head with a sword, Cecilia remains alive, and Roman law forbids further attempts at execution. She lives for three days, during which she turns her house into a church and preaches continuously, converting hundreds of people. She dies only when she prays to join God in heaven.[1]

The Cecilia legend is somewhat anomalous in the canon of Middle English virgin martyr narratives. Most of the female saints with widespread cults in late medieval England adamantly refuse to marry, defying their fathers or local judges, even the emperor, in their steadfast devotion to Christ. But the similarities between the legend of Cecilia and the legends of St. Margaret, St. Katherine of Alexandria, St. Agnes, St. Barbara,

St. Agatha, and others are far more striking than their differences: all of these women designate their virginity as the preeminent sign of their faith and openly flout masculine authority in its defense. The pervasiveness of this plot in late Middle English narrative culture has sometimes obscured how radically different the world it constructs is from the one its audiences inhabited. The imperatives motivating Cecilia's virginity, preaching, and martyrdom did not obtain for the Christian community in late medieval England as they had in third-century Rome: the Church no longer needed women to preach and proselytize, virginity no longer served as a warrant for this activity, and familial and institutional authority were no longer in the hands of those hostile to Christianity. Unlike the early Christian community in Rome, late medieval English communities did not require—indeed did not condone—women's heroic virtue, but rather their everyday conformity to a very different set of ethical and religious practices.

This would not be surprising—narrative traditions, after all, rarely offer a realistic depiction of the ethical world their audiences know firsthand—but for the broad contemporary expectation that saints' lives were exemplary. Saints were understood to mediate between Christ and ordinary Christians, not only as intercessors but also as ethical models: the saint imitates Christ typologically and in turn provides a tropological (that is, moral) exemplar to those who hear or read her story. Hagiographers and moralists repeatedly exhorted audiences—and especially female audiences—to imitate saints such as Cecilia.[2] But how was a medieval woman listening to the legend of St. Cecilia—perhaps at a sermon on her feast day, November 22,[3] or as part of a family's evening devotions—to take this saint as a model? She was surely not supposed to refuse her husband's sexual advances: canon law and social custom dictated otherwise. Nor was she supposed to transform her house into a place of public worship and instruct others in the faith: preaching was expressly forbidden to women, and their unregulated religious initiative could lead to charges of heresy. And, of course, she was not encouraged to mock the authority of civic or state officials who insisted that she conform to accepted social or religious practice.

Karen Winstead and Katherine Lewis have shown that one way late medieval writers responded to the awkward example provided by vernacular legends was to emphasize virtues that were appropriate to their growing lay readership.[4] Fifteenth-century lives of female saints present "refined gentlewomen rather than triumphant viragos," just as late medieval images on rood screens and in Books of Hours depict virgin martyrs as demure and elegantly dressed ladies.[5] Winstead attributes this shift to the expectations of a well-born or well-off audience, as eager for literature that models the social virtues they cultivated as they were shy of texts that might seem to promote social unrest or heterodox belief. But as she notes, even hagiographers such as Osbern Bokenham and John Lydgate, whose virgin martyrs exemplify the new "decorous" heroines of fifteenth-century hagiography, present the same narratives as do earlier legends.[6] John Capgrave's courteous St. Katherine still publicly rebukes the emperor Maxentius,[7] and Bokenham's St. Christine, though moderate with her virgin companions, still mocks her father openly: "'Now perseue I ryght well,' quod Cristyne, / 'That thou wantyst wyt and vndyrstondynng'" (2267–68).[8] Despite the new emphasis on the saints' courtly behavior, late medieval legends, like earlier ones, center on the confrontation of the female saint and male authority and institutions, as represented by her father, the local judge, or the emperor. The plots of late medieval legends reproduce those of earlier ones, and the virgin martyrs they depict—however elegant their manners—still challenge the dignity and value of established social hierarchies.

Unfortunately, we do not have much specific evidence for how women understood the expectation that they imitate such figures. But we do have at least one woman's account of her *imitatio* of a saint: Julian of Norwich's *A Vision Schewed [. . .] to a Devoute Woman*, the Short Text of her *Revelation of Love*.[9] Julian, the first woman writer in Middle English and one of the most remarkable theologians of the period, is extraordinary in many respects. In understanding her religious identity as an imitation of a female saint, however, Julian responds to a tradition readily available to most medieval women, in precisely the way they were expected to respond. Her imitation of the virgin martyr St. Cecilia—whose story is recounted above—suggests that exemplarity could be a surprisingly complicated and flexible mode of interpretation. Julian is certainly not constrained by the legend's ethical paradigm, even though she identifies St. Cecilia as a model for her devotional practices. Instead, Julian understands her own religious desire in relation to the saint's life in a way that registers significant differences between early Christian and contemporary devotion.

At the opening of her *Vision*, Julian explains that she heard the legend of St. Cecilia in church, just as any late medieval woman might have heard it, and she claims that the story inspired the desires that preface her visions and vocation:

I harde a man telle of halye kyrke of the storye of saynte Cecylle, in the whilke schewynge I vndyrstode that sche hadde thre wonndys with a swerde in the nekke, with the whilke sche pynede to the dede. By the styrrynge of this I conseyvede a myghty desyre, prayande oure lorde god that he wolde grawnte me thre wonndys in my lyfe tyme, that es to saye the wonnde of contricyoun, the wonnde of compassyoun and the wonnde of wylfulle langgynge to god. Ryght as I askede the othere two [desires] with a condyscion, so I askyd the thyrde with owtynn any condyscion. This two desyres before sayde passed fro my mynde, and the thyrde dwellyd contynuelye. (1. 204–6)[10]

[I heard a man of holy church tell the story of St. Cecilia, in which showing I understood that she was wounded three times in the neck with a sword, with which she suffered unto death. By the inspiration of this I conceived a mighty desire, praying our lord God that he would grant me three wounds in my life time, that is to say, the wound of contrition, the wound of compassion and the wound of willful longing for God. Just as I asked the other two desires with a condition, so I asked the third without any condition. The two desires explained above passed from my mind, and the third dwelled continually.]

Julian desires to imitate St. Cecilia's three wounds, figured as the desire for contrition, compassion, and a deep longing for God. Significantly, this desire is distinguished from the two other petitions that mark the beginning of her vocation: her desire for a more intimate knowing of the Passion and her desire for the experience of a life-threatening "bodelye sykenes." Julian explains that she qualified these two desires "with a condyscion," wanting them only if God wanted them for her, but her triple desire for Cecilian wounds remains unqualified. Although Julian specifically identifies the saint's physical suffering as exemplary, her *imitatio*, curiously, does not require Julian's own bodily pain or deprivation. She considers neither the ascetic practices that formed the daily routine of anchoritic spirituality nor the mortal illness she names as her second desire (perhaps the closest late medieval analog to St. Cecilia's passion and martyrdom) as part of her hagiographic imitation. Indeed, illness is one of the two desires allowed to pass from Julian's mind lest it conflict with God's will, in pointed opposition to her unqualified desire for figural wounds modeled on the virgin martyr. Julian's response to the legend of St. Cecilia, that is, at once confirms the scholarly commonplace that women were expected to imitate female saints and confounds our assumption that such imitation necessarily involved adopting the ethical practices represented in the narrative. For Julian, and perhaps for other audiences, to read the legend as exemplary is to understand it not as a prescription but a *comparandum* for contemporary practice.

Imitatio here serves as an interpretive structure through which contemporary ethical and devotional practices are understood in relation to ancient ones. By identifying her desire as an imitation of St. Cecilia, Julian presents an uneasy equation between the physical pain of ancient martyrdom and the spiritual suffering of late medieval devotional practice: the pain of recognizing one's own sinfulness, the pain of identifying with Christ's Passion, and the pain of desire, even desire directed toward God. The equation is an uneasy one because it both asserts the continuity of feminine devotion—in the exemplary relationship linking the ancient saint and the late medieval anchoress—and marks the discontinuities between them in the conspicuously figural form that imitation must take. Julian's imitation of St. Cecilia, that is, paradoxically serves as an index of the enormous transformation in ethical and devotional practice that distinguishes, or should distinguish, early Christianity from the practice of religion in late medieval England. In the ethical world Julian imagines, there is no place for the experience of martyrdom, the violent differentiation of the saint and her persecutors; it must be transformed instead, she suggests, into the inward violence of spiritual desire, which seeks to overcome, rather than create, difference.

The hallmark of Julian's work is theological, not historical, reflection, of course. Her revision of hagiographic violence is a strikingly appropriate prologue to the visions that ultimately lead to a radical theology of universal salvation, in which the confident, absolute distinction between good and evil, saint and sinner, presented by vernacular saints' lives dissolves in a sophisticated argument that alienation from the divine is not a mark of sin but an occasion for infinite mercy. In its tacit demonstration that the practices defining the saint cannot be reproduced in late medieval England, however, Julian's imitation of St. Cecilia also has implications for history and especially for the historicity of feminine devotion. In comparing her devotional life to that of the saint, Julian marks the differences between early Christian religious identity and her own and between the social worlds that structure these identities.

Julian's *imitatio Ceciliae* shows how the exemplarity of hagiographic narrative could prompt an awareness of historical identity and location, as figured by continuities and discontinuities in women's devotional practice. The best evidence for this awareness comes from the extended meditations on the relationship between the sacred past and the social present in fifteenth-century writers, especially Osbern Bokenham, Margery Kempe, and Henry Bradshaw. In subsequent chapters I show that these writers use female saints' lives as an important forum for thinking about the status and stability of community in the context of the reduplicating crises of fifteenth-century England—uncertainty over the legitimacy of the monarchy, dynastic contests that led to internecine war, the threat (real or imagined) of heterodoxy.[11] Here, however, I want to suggest that some form of the historical awareness I will trace in subsequent chapters was broadly available to the audience of vernacular legends. As recent scholarship has demonstrated, late medieval England witnessed a substantial expansion of literacy and book owning among women.[12] The audience for saints' lives was much broader even than this expanding readership, moreover, since—as the case of Julian of Norwich reminds us—women also had access to vernacular legends in oral performance, as sermons and civic drama. This audience, taught that the lives of female saints were exemplary, was confronted with the difficulty of reconciling the model provided by female saints with contemporary social and religious practices—a difficulty that may have provoked questions about the shape of history: How is the past different from the present and how is it the same? What do differences in women's devotional practices suggest about the cultural specificity of ethical action and political forms? What do the similarities suggest about transhistorical categories and values?

We can see how exemplarity might provoke such questions by turning to moral handbooks that define feminine ethical and devotional practice with reference to saints' lives, such as the *Book of the Knight of the Tower*, a conduct book for women translated twice into English in the fifteenth century. What is striking is that even explicitly prescriptive treatises do not really endorse saints' lives as normative, even as they are identified as exemplary. St. Cecilia, for example, surfaces in the *Book* as an example of charity. The other two saints it names as models for this virtue, St. Elizabeth and St. Lucy, "gaf to the poure & Indygent the most parte of theyr reuenues," as the *Book* notes (147).[13] Cecilia, however, disposes of her property quite differently: she turns her house into a church in which she preaches and distributes alms for three days before her death. The Knight has no interest in encouraging his audience—including his daughters, to whom the *Book* is addressed—to imitate the public nature of Cecilia's charity, much less its close association with her preaching and the use of her home as an open religious forum.[14] Instead, he reimagines Cecilia's public mission as a model for a social practice that accords much better with late medieval secular and religious expectations regarding the proper expression of women's piety. He moderates the example the saint might provide by following it with the story of "a good lady of Rome" who saw a poor woman at mass shivering with cold, an anecdote that not only emphasizes the private nature of the lady's charitable act, but also maps its difference from public preaching: "The good lady had pyte of [the poor woman] / and pryuely called her to her and wente / and had her in to her hows / whiche was not ferre thens / and gaf to her a good furred gowne / And whyles she was aboute this charytable dede / the preest that sayd the masse couthe speke neuer a word vnto the tyme that she was come to the Chirche ageyne / And as soone as she was come ageyne he spake as he dyd to fore" (147–48). The example of the Roman Cecilia, who turns her house into a church, is sharply qualified by the story of this other Roman woman whose house represents the private space of charity, in pointed contrast to the public preaching of the priest. In this remarkable revision of the Cecilia legend, the silencing of the holy woman—now imagined as an almsgiver but not a preacher—is paralleled in the silencing of the priest, who also stands as an avatar of the saint. The story carefully separates, spatially and temporally, house and church, as well as charity and preaching, which are so emphatically conflated in the saint's legend.

The Roman lady's *imitatio Ceciliae* provides a guide for the *Book*'s readers, who are encouraged to understand their own charity as an imitation of the saint despite the quite different form it takes.[15] Of course, we cannot know whether the Knight's first audience, or the wider one he implicitly addresses, recognized the cultural and ethical discontinuities negotiated in his presentation of St. Cecilia's exemplarity. The central fiction of exemplarity is that ethics are transhistorical, independent of their particular historical moment and social context, and it is possible, even likely, that for many readers this fiction overrode the evidence that ethical practice is contingent on historical location that his exhortations to imitate the saints provide. But the moral treatise does make this evidence available, and—more importantly perhaps—it suggests that late medieval women needed to attend to the historical difference separating them from the saints they were encouraged to take as examples, whether or not they did so self-consciously.[16] The rhetoric of exemplarity here—as in Julian's *Vision*—marks and sometimes measures the distance between the everyday ethics and devotional practices of the past and those of the present.

We can see this, too, in the *Book*'s use of virgin martyr legends to address women's sexuality. In chapter 62 the *Book* offers Sts. Katherine, Margaret, and Christine as models of chastity—that is, marital fidelity—a central, even obsessive, focus of the treatise. Though both virginity and chastity involve the containment of sexuality, they are categorically different. The saint's virginity signals her uncompromising and total rejection of active sexuality; the Knight, in contrast, expects his daughters to be sexually available, but only to their husbands. This is a difference in kind, not degree: the virgin saint refuses marriage, represented as a legitimate forum for sexuality, as vehemently as she refuses sex outside the sanction of marriage—often more vehemently since virgin martyrs readily prefer forced prostitution to apostasy.[17] Reading St. Margaret as a model for marital fidelity requires an interpretive leap as large as that required for reading St. Cecilia as a model for private charity.[18] It is a leap that signals historical difference: if only implicitly, the *Book of the Knight of the Tower* teaches its audience not so much that the paradigms of feminine virtue in saints' lives are imitable but that they are subject to the protocols of historical and social location.

Of course, not all of the practices recounted in vernacular legends were inappropriate to late medieval women, and the *Book* endorses a more direct imitation of traditional saints when it does not violate late medieval social norms. It presents Mary Magdalene as an example of the spiritual value of contrition, confession, and dread of God. St. Anastasia, whose kindness to prisoners prompts God, in turn, to deliver her from prison, exemplifies service to the unfortunate.[19] Most interesting is the *Book*'s vigorous defense of women's education and literacy, for which St. Katherine serves as example and authority. The *Book* claims that "the begynnyng and fundument of the knowlege of god she had thurgh the clergye / where as she knewe the trouthe / & the sauement of her self" (121). Against those who argue that it is inappropriate for girls to be taught to read, it insists that reading benefits all women just as it did the virgin saint: "as for redynge I saye that good and prouffytable is to al wymen / For a woman that can rede may better knowe the peryls of the sowle and her sauement / than she that can nought of it / for it hath be preued"

(122).[20] As I noted above, the *Book* elsewhere allegorizes St. Katherine's virginity as marital fidelity, but it encourages a direct imitation of her learning. Endorsing some saintly practices literally while carefully transforming others through figural models of *imitatio*, the *Book* teaches its audience that feminine ethical practice is contingent on contemporary social expectations. This is clearest when *imitatio* requires the substitution of one ethical practice with another (virginity as chastity or public preaching as charity), but it is also suggested by the identification of some saintly practices as fully imitable by late medieval laywomen. It is precisely by distinguishing between St. Katherine's virginity and her learning, between a practice that is not appropriate to laywomen and one that is, that the *Book of the Knight of the Tower* makes visible the historical continuities and discontinuities of ethical practice.

Such discontinuities might seem especially pronounced in the arena of secular ethics, but they exist as well in the arenas removed—in medieval theory, at least—from the temporal world. The early thirteenth-century *Ancrene Wisse*, a handbook for anchoresses, for example, anticipates the *Book of the Knight of the Tower* in using the fiction of exemplarity to mark the historical distance between its readers and their saintly avatars. *Ancrene Wisse* provides an especially interesting case study because of its close philological and codicological relationship with the early Middle English legends of St. Margaret, Katherine, and Juliana (the Katherine-Group legends).[21] It, moreover, refers explicitly to a legend of St. Margaret that the anchoresses have in their "English book"—most likely the very version of the legend that we have—and enjoins them to imitate the saint. But the anchoritic handbook, like the lay *Book of the Knight of the Tower*, presents the legend less as a regulatory fiction than as an allegorical double for practices that are, in fact, quite different from those of the narrative. Tracing what makes the Margaret legend impossible even for anchoresses to imitate directly can help us see how the idea of exemplarity might have taught women not only that ethics are historically specific, but also that they are inextricable from other categories of social practice and identity.

Like St. Cecilia, St. Margaret is a virgin martyr of the early church, and her story, too, centers on a girl's defense of her virginity and her outspoken resistance to pagan authorities. Margaret, a noble girl, is raised by a nurse in the countryside. One day while she is tending sheep, the prefect Olibrius sees her as he rides by. Struck by her beauty, he sends one of his men to fetch the girl, declaring that he will marry her if she is noble and keep her as a concubine if she is not. When ordered to identify herself, Margaret announces not only her name and family but also her faith. Olibrius is outraged, and the girl is tried and imprisoned for her belief. While in prison, she prays to see her tormentor. A dragon appears and swallows her, but Margaret makes the sign of the cross and the creature's body splits open, releasing her. Next a small demon appears and challenges Margaret; she triumphs over him as well, crushing his head under her foot. When led to her execution, Margaret asks to be allowed a final prayer, in which she asks God that she might intercede for those who remember her death, especially women who call on her during childbirth.

The opening of the early Middle English version of this legend suggests that its anchoritic audience might learn from Margaret to "libben i meithhad" (live in maidenhood), but *Ancrene Wisse* shies away from offering the saint as an example of virginity.[22] The anchoresses are rather encouraged to find in their "englische boc of seinte Margarete" an example of devout prayer, which is, in turn, identified as a remedy for desire.[23] This indirection, like the figural imitations we have seen in the *Book of the Knight of the Tower*, points to the difference between ancient sanctity and contemporary devotion. We might expect that anchoresses, who have taken a vow of sexual abstinence, would be able to imitate the saint more readily than the Knight's lay audience would. But while *Ancrene Wisse*'s first readers were probably, like the saint, virgins, virginity has different ethical and political meanings in each historical moment. In hagiographic narrative, virginity establishes the saint's independence from masculine authority and authorizes her public vocation.[24] As if to counteract this model, *Ancrene Wisse* takes care to explain that public roles are unsuitable for an anchoress:

Ne preachi ye to namon. ne mon ne easki ow cunsail ne ne telle ow. readeth wummen ane. Seint pawel forbeot wummen to preachin. Mulieres not permitto docere. Na wepmon ne chastie ye. ne edwiten his him untheaw bute he beo the ouer cuthre. Halie al de ancres hit mahe don summes weis. ah hit nis nawt siker thing. ne ne limpeth nawt to yunge. Hit is hare meoster the beoth ouer othre iset & habbeth ham to witene as hali chirche larewes. Ancre naueth forte hire ane & hire meidnes. Halde euch hire ahne meoster. & nawt ne reaui othres.[25]

[Do not preach to anyone. Let no man ask you counsel or talk to you; advise only women. St. Paul forbade women to preach: *Mulieres non permitto docere*. Do not criticize any man, nor blame him for his vices unless he is over-familiar with you. Holy old anchoresses may do it in a certain way, but it is not a sure thing, nor is it proper for the young: it is the task of those who are set over others and have to guard them, as teachers of Holy Church; the anchoress has only to see to herself and her maids. Let each mind her own task and not take someone else's.]26

Elsewhere the author claims that reading is a great defense against idleness and fleshly temptation, but he does not identify the legends of virgin martyrs as particularly beneficial in this regard, and passages such as this explain the omission. St. Margaret is a young woman who takes it upon herself to censure men, including civic authorities, and to preach her faith to the crowds that gather to witness her persecution. The relationship between the saint's virginity, the moral and spiritual authority it gives her over men, and the public vocation it sustains renders impossible an unqualified endorsement of her as a model for anchoritic practice. Indeed, the anchorhold is designed to prevent precisely the kind of spectacle of feminine sanctity that provides the narrative center of virgin martyr legends.

Ancrene Wisse instead identifies Margaret narrowly as an example of the value of prayer and its efficacy in warding off temptation. If this is a surprising reading of the Margaret legend, it seems to rely on, and anticipate, the same kind of interpretive structure we saw in Julian's *Vision*, in which contemporary behavior is understood as a figural imitation of hagiographic narrative. In emphasizing the power of the saint's prayer, the anchoresses' spiritual director suggests a connection between St. Margaret's sojourn in prison, where her prayer splits open a dragon that has swallowed her, and the lives of medieval anchoresses, enclosed in their anchorhold and dedicated to prayer. The metaphor relies on the similarity between the prison and the anchorhold, both confined spaces associated with privation, and the complicated idea of agency that both spaces represent. Margaret is imprisoned by her persecutors, but she actively, even happily, embraces her persecution. So, too, the anchoresses' ascetic lifestyle is freely chosen, a form of restriction that paradoxically expresses spiritual agency. But the differences between the prison and the anchorhold, and so between the early Christian saint and the late medieval anchoress, are also articulated through this comparison. To take their "English book of St. Margaret" as an example, the anchoresses had to locate virgin martyrhood and their own vocation historically.

* * *

In practice if not in theory, then, hagiographic exemplarity tacitly acknowledges that ethics are not only socially produced but also inextricable from other categories of social identity and experience. This is central to the reading lesson that the Knight of the Tower offers to his daughters: his model of appropriate imitation takes into account their financial and social positions (in the emphasis on charity) and their future sexual status (in the substitution of marital chastity for virginity). The Knight is not alone in offering this lesson. It is also implied in the vernacular legends that provide a taxonomy of the different forms of imitation that various audiences should perform, such as a fifteenth-century prose legend of St. Katherine that distinguishes between the ideal response of virgins and that of other Christians: "Here in this lyf and passion of Seynt Kateryne virgyn and martir lerneth ye alle virgyns and maydens to despyse and flee alle wordly vanyte lerneth myghtly and treuly to loue oure lord iesu crist. And lerneth to be perseueraunt in hys loue vnto the deeth trustynge to that greet counfort and reward that he geueth to hys louers lerneth ye alle cristen puple to be strong and stable in the feyth of crist. lerneth to haue loue and deuocion to seynt Kateryne. And lerneth to knowe what help ye may gete by hire in alle nedes yf ye worschep hir faythfully and do hir seruyse."[27] The exemplarity of the legend depends, the hagiographer insists, on the social identity of the audience. Virgins and maidens (that is, both those who have vowed their virginity to God and those who happen to be sexually inexperienced) should find in the example of St. Katherine a model for the renunciation of earthly values and the spiritual love that might replace them. But this lesson would contradict the social expectations that govern the lives of other Christians, for whom the categorical rejection of worldly vanities—not only active sexuality but also economic and political power—is inappropriate. The early Middle English legend of St. Margaret discussed above also suggests that the narrative's exemplarity depends on the social identity of the audience. While its manuscript setting points to an anchoritic readership, the legend itself addresses a broader, and carefully differentiated, audience of widows, wives, and virgins:[28]

Hercneth, alle the earen + herunge habbeth: widewen with tha iweddede, + te meidens nomeliche, lusten swithe yeorliche hu ha schulen luuien the liuiende lauerd + libben in meithhad, thet him his mihte leouest; swa thet ha moten, thurh thet eadie meiden the we munneth to-dei with meithhades menske, thet seli meidnes song singen, with this meiden + with thet heouenlich hird, echeliche in heouene. (4)

[Listen, all who have ears and hearing: widows and the wedded, and especially the maidens who should listen very eagerly how they should love the living lord and live in maidenhood, which is the dearest virtue to him; so that they might, through the blessed maiden who we remember today with the honor of virginity, to sing that holy maiden's song, with this maiden and with the heavenly host, eternally in heaven.]

The text emphasizes its special appropriateness for virgins, but it also addresses widows and wives, at once creating a collective feminine audience and differentiating it according to sexual status. The legend's multiple address suggests that its exemplary meaning is not the same for all women: the text divides its audience into three categories, creating three interpretive positions from which it might be read. The distinctions in Henry Bradshaw's *Life of St. Werburge*, are finer still, registering overlapping categories of social, sexual, and vocational status. "Swete comly creatures ladyes euerychone," he asserts, should imitate Werburge by rejecting vanity and adopting simple dress (1. 1779–99). But this group is subdivided in a later passage: Bradshaw addresses widows (2. 1990–1), religious women (2. 1992–8), and virgins (2. 1999–2005) as distinct audiences for the legend. In distinguishing between their several feminine audiences, legends such as these acknowledge that ethics are circumscribed by social identity and by the categories—sexuality, class status, vocation, and so on—that define it.

Modern theories of reception, too, recognize that individuals respond differently to narratives depending on their social identities and personal experiences.[29] Interpretive response is not fully governed by the text; it is informed by the interests and experiences of the reader. This insight is also necessary to, and implicit in, hagiographic exemplarity, which demands the careful negotiation of the ethics of the narrative and the cultural expectations that structure the audience's devotional and social lives.[30] Any exemplary narrative does this, but the repeated and specific injunction to women to read these tales and take their heroines as examples made such negotiation especially important, and visible, to audiences. So, for example, the triple address of the early Middle English Margaret legend prompts questions about how lay spirituality and anchoritic spirituality can *both* be seen as imitations of ancient sanctity.

Of course, it also locates this difference within an omnibus similarity: the special exemplary meaning that the saint has for all women. Differentiating between women according to social and sexual categories paradoxically reinforces the broader category that embraces them all. The ethical address of female saints' lives assumes that the behavior of a virgin martyr and that of a late medieval anchoress, or a noblewoman, or a devout bourgeois woman such as Margery Kempe, share some essential factor rooted in their shared sex. Sex is figured as the stable, continuous social category that underwrites the fiction of exemplarity, despite the abundant evidence that imitation produces alterity, not sameness. Hagiographic exemplarity is structured by this productive tension between the assumption that all women—maidens, wives, and widows—inhabit an ethically meaningful category and the acknowledgment that they are divided by other categories of identity. The mimesis implied in exemplarity, that is, works like metaphor: it both affiliates two things and alienates or distances them from one another. In assuming that all women share a fundamental affiliation with the saint, *imitatio* insists on the continuity and coherence of gender identity, but it also registers the differences between the saint and the audience devoted to her, as well as differences between members of that audience, in a way that ultimately challenges the stability of gender as a historical category.

* * *

We have seen that ethical imitation serves in part to define the social context of devotional practice—a community's values and practices, its institutions and sites of authority, the categories of identity that structure patterns of belonging and exclusion—as continuous or discontinuous. I have focused primarily on discontinuities and the difficulty of imitating ancient saints in late medieval England—the way that Julian's allegorical imitation of St. Cecilia, for example, marks the historical distance separating them and the significant differences in the communities they inhabit. But hagiographic exemplarity could also be used to insist on the continuity of communities and the social institutions that define them. The ability to imitate the saint in an immediate, rather than figural, mode suggests that the social context for the behavior remains constant in some important respect: it presents contemporary society as continuous with, or at least structurally analogous to, the world of the narrative.

Medieval writers—orthodox and heterodox—were aware of the utility and implications of this model of history, especially as a reading of female saints' lives. As we have seen, vernacular legends of female saints, especially virgin martyr narratives, are structured by an opposition between the saint and society—in particular between the individual Christian and an institutional religion that is hostile to true devotion—and this narrative paradigm meant that imitating them could serve to challenge contemporary religious and political authorities. Thus while Lollards generally reject the cult of the saints because it lacks scriptural basis, they sometimes cite virgin martyrs and other female saints as authorities for lay preaching, advocating precisely the kind of literal imitation that orthodox hagiographers generally avoid.[31] In the course of his heresy trial, for example, Walter Brut adduced female saints in his argument that women could preach, noting that "women, devout virgins, have steadfastly preached the word of God and have converted many men while priests dared not speak a word."[32] Wyclif himself had used St. Cecilia as authority for a lay priesthood because she had turned her house into a church.[33] These writers overlook their reservations about this narrative tradition most immediately because virgin martyr legends provide authority for Wycliffite practices. But they may also do so because the ability to imitate the female saint implies that the dominant ecclesiastical and political institutions of late medieval England imitate—unwittingly—the persecuting pagan priests and emperors of hagiographic narrative.

The hermeneutics of literal imitation, that is, might at once serve a specific program—the justification of lay preaching—and point to a broader argument about the structure of Christian history.[34] It posits the continuity between the early Christian world and late medieval England, a continuity that allowed Wyclif and others to identify themselves with martyred saints and to identify orthodox authorities with the religious and state institutions that persecuted early Christians. We see this explicitly developed in accounts of persecutions—imagined and real—of the heterodox. Long before official condemnation of his teachings, Wyclif, anticipating that his followers would be persecuted, represented their prospective suffering as an imitation of the martyrdom of early saints.[35] In the fifteenth century the rhetoric of imitation was grounded in the actual experience of violence: so Margery Baxter represents William White, executed for heresy, as a "great saint in heaven" (*magnus sanctus in cello*).[36] Both Wyclif and Baxter insist not only on the exemplary relationship between the ancient saint and medieval Lollard but also on the structural similarity between the religious and secular authorities that persecute true believers in hagiographic narrative and in the late medieval Church and state. They intimate that the social context of ethical action has remained constant, producing a model of history in which the pagan past is not very different from the Christian present after all. If virgin martyr sanctity is reproducible in late medieval England *without* careful accommodation of contemporary social and devotional practices, perhaps the social and institutional structures represented in the legend are as enduring as the models of ethical action that respond to them.[37]

This model of history did not go uncontested, of course. Orthodox writers have at least two strategies for foreclosing the Wycliffite model of history that presented contemporary persecutions as imitations of ancient ones.[38] One was to embrace the idea of cultural continuity but to identify Lollards as the persecuting pagans. Henry Knighton thus includes in his chronicle the story of two Lollards, William Smith and a friend, who discover a wooden statue of St. Katherine in an abandoned chapel.[39] They decide to burn it to make cabbage soup, and they joke that this will constitute a second martyrdom: "This holy image will make a holy bonfire for us. By axe and fire she will undergo a new martyrdom, and perhaps through the cruelty of those new torments she will come at last to the kingdom of Heaven."[40] As Sarah Stanbury argues, Knighton presents historical Lollards as pagan persecutors and the image "first decapitated, then burned, plays the part of a virgin martyr."[41] Through an analogy between the saint and her material image, the story equates Wycliffite iconoclasm and pagan persecution, both represented as gruesome and appallingly foolish violence against a sacred body. Knighton thus uses the idea of *imitatio* to align orthodox institutions with the tortured saint rather than with her persecutors.[42]

Orthodox writers could also foreclose the Lollard analogy between the state-sponsored religion of hagiographic narrative and that of their own day by demonstrating the temporal boundaries and differences that distance the present from the past. Figural readings of virgin martyr legends traced above—in the *Book of the Knight of the Tower*, for example—may sometimes respond not only to the inappropriateness of certain practices for late medieval laywomen but also to the uncomfortable parallels that a more direct imitation would suggest between pagan institutions and contemporary ones. This is one way we might understand the presentation of *imitatio* by Nicholas Love, one of the staunchest defenders of fifteenth-century lay orthodoxy, in the *Mirror of the Blessed Life of Jesus Christ*.[43] This influential devotional book, produced in response to Lollard discourses, transforms a metaphor for Cecilia's faith, found in the most influential and widely disseminated hagiographic compendium, the *Legenda Aurea*, into an allegory of contemporary devotion:

Amonge other vertuese commendynges of the holy virgine Cecile it is written that she bare alwey the gospel of criste hidde in her breste, that may be undirstand that of the blessed lif of oure lord Jesu criste writen in the gospele, she chace certayne parties most deuoute. In the which she set her meditacion & her thouht nigt & day with a clene & hole herte. And when she hade so fully alle the manere of his life ouer gon, she began agayne. And so with a likyng & swete taste gostly chewyng in that manere the gospell of crist. she set & bare it euer in the priuyte of her breste. In the same manere I counseil that thou do. For among alle gostly exercyses I leue that this is most necessarye & most profitable.[44]

He goes on to use the example of Cecilia to explain the value of meditation on Jesus' life:

First I say that bisy meditacion & customable of the blessede life of Jesu, stableth the saule & the herte ageynus vanitees & deceyuable likynges of the worlde. This is opunly schewede in the blessed virgine Cecile before nemede, when she fillede so fully her herte of the life of crist. that vanytees of the worlde migt not entre in to her. For in alle the grete pompe of weddyngis, where so many vanytees bene usede, whene the organes blewene & songene, she set hir herte stably in god, seying & praying, *Lord be my herte & my body clene, & not defilede, so that I be not confondet.* (12)

In the *Legenda Aurea*, the claim that St. Cecilia "always carried the Gospel of Christ in her bosom" is clearly a figure for her continual devotion to Christ. As the *Mirror* emphasizes, this devotion separates her from the pomp of her own wedding. It also structures her subsequent behavior—her rejection of married sexuality and her spouse's authority over her, as well as her spirited defense of her faith in flagrant contempt of the pagan judge who examines her. In the traditional legend, that is, the metaphor of interior devotion is intimately linked to Cecilia's public vocation. In contrast, the *Mirror* reads the figure for interior disposition as a description of daily practice. The image of the Gospel of Christ, carried always in Cecilia's bosom, is taken as a reference to a literal text: the story of the life of Christ presented by the *Mirror* itself.

This passage is found in the *Mirror*'s source, the *Meditationes Vitae Christi*, and in that context it serves primarily to privilege the cloistered vocation of its first audience, a community of Poor Clares.[45] But in the

English translation, addressed to a broad lay audience, it responds more immediately to the competing claims of official and dissenting religion to a sacred past, and perhaps specifically to the use of St. Cecilia as a model and authority for lay preaching in Wycliffite polemic. Indeed, we might identify a special urgency in the hermeneutics of exemplarity that Love employs. By presenting silent reading and private meditation as the proper imitation of the virgin saint, he neutralizes the more literal and subversive model that her legend could provide, not only for women's active and public religious vocation but also for its corollary: a reading of the contemporary Church as a continuation of the persecuting institutions of hagiographic narrative.

This is an important context, too, for the resistance that Margery Kempe encounters to her imitation of virgin martyrs. In an especially charged encounter, the mayor of Leicester asks Margery to identify herself, and when she replies by referring to her father and family, he dismisses her answer abruptly, saying, "Seynt Kateryn telde what kynred sche cam of & yet are ye not lyche."[46] He is right, of course, in ways considered crucial in the late Middle Ages: in particular, Margery is not, like Katherine, a virgin. The mayor emphasizes this, calling her a "fals strumpet," but his rejection of Margery's imitation of St. Katherine is not limited to her sexual status: he also denounces her as "a fals loller, & a fals deceyuer of the pepyl" (112). These epithets make clear that his rejection is categorical, a refusal to recognize Margery's broad imitation of St. Katherine as such, not simply a denial of the married Margery's tendentious status as a spiritual virgin. Margery, like St. Katherine, is an outspoken laywoman who has sacrificed considerable social power in order to witness to her faith and who has succeeded in persuading others of its validity. But the mayor refuses to recognize Margery as "like" St. Katherine—even as he acknowledges a superficial resemblance between them—because he recognizes no continuity in gender roles or religious practice that could place them in meaningful relation to each other. Margery's devotional practice, in contrast, assumes that a late medieval woman can imitate early virgin martyrs and penitent prostitutes. And, in a stunningly clever inversion, the very rejection of her *imitatio* by figures like the mayor confirms her argument: the hostility she encounters, in formal inquiries and everyday persecutions, elaborates her likeness to virgin martyrs further still.

James Simpson has recently argued that legends of female saints were especially useful in the fifteenth century, a period of significant cultural transformation, precisely because they thematize historical change in narratives of iconoclasm—the rejection of the "dead idols of the old order."[47] I would add that these narratives *also* figure cultural continuity: the old order, after all, persists despite this challenge. The saint is unfailingly successful in destroying its idols and often witnesses the death of her persecutors, but new judges—indistinguishable from their forbears—always replace them. So, too, the idea of exemplarity allowed medieval writers and readers to emphasize cultural continuity *or* change, depending on the political context or social meaning assigned to ethical action. The political and religious upheavals of late medieval England prompted interest in the promise and perils of both cultural continuity and discontinuity. Orthodox and heterodox readings of vernacular legends as exemplary, and the arguments about the shape of history they implied, satisfied some of this interest. If a Lollard endorsement of unmediated *imitatio*—lay preachers imitating St. Cecilia's preaching, for example, or persecuted Lollards imitating early martyrs—presents a model of continuous history, the figural or attenuated modes of exemplarity that we find in Julian's *Vision* or the *Book of the Knight of the Tower* or Love's *Mirror* imply just the opposite: that the social and institutional context of early Christianity is substantially different from that of late medieval England and that this difference entails a revaluation of the practice—if not the ideals—of sexuality, sacrifice, and public spirituality. Hagiography and its exemplary hermeneutics did not, that is, provide one model of history but a vehicle for exploring and contesting a variety of such models.

The exemplarity of vernacular legends is closely analogous to that of other discourses in the Middle Ages and the Renaissance. Medieval historiography, of course, generally understood the past to offer examples, good and bad, for the present (as do modern historiographies). Various forms of the exemplum—ranging from the sermon exemplum to the Mirror for Princes and other kinds of literary narrative[48]—similarly cultivated an understanding of the self and community in relation to an authoritative, if often distant and different, cultural moment. A recognition of the gap produced by this distance is often seen as a hallmark of the Renaissance, but I would claim for medieval exemplary narrative—including vernacular legends of female saints—the productive crux of humanist historical thought, "caught between a veneration of the timeless value of ancient models as patterns for action and a sharp awareness of the contingency that divides modern readers from ancient exemplars."[49] For both periods, the urgency of this contradiction comes from the way that "the exemplary makes a claim on the reader's action in the world"[50]: that is, not just how they read, but how they act. It is only a persistent and reductive myth that medieval Christianity insisted on a single temporal frame for worldly existence that has so frequently obscured the period's historical consciousness.

This historical consciousness was not, of course, limited to feminine exemplarity in the late Middle Ages, and it may be helpful to compare it briefly to the two broad historical paradigms that have received the most critical attention: cultural translation and Christian teleology.[51] The first, an important model of secular history, relies on the idea of *translatio imperii et studii*: the translation of political authority and cultural knowledge to new communities (in an ever westward direction). The process of translation involves change, as cultures rise and fall and old social forms are adapted to new circumstances and expressed in new languages. But *translatio* also preserves some essential element of the past as the foundation for a new culture. History is structured, in this discourse, through genealogy (in, for example, the myth of Brutus as grandson of Aeneas) and claims to cultural preeminence (in the identification of London as New Troy). In contrast, the second model of history, Christian teleology, is grounded in typology and eschatology, a model in which the past anticipates the future as history moves toward its perfect fulfillment, to be eclipsed altogether in the static realm of eternity. This model, too, could emphasize continuity or rupture: the first in the typological correspondences linking pre-Christian to Christian events, the second in paradigms of periodization that structured Christian history, such as the seven ages or the more radical disjunction between history and ahistory at the end of time. Hagiographic exemplarity as a vehicle for historical reflection shares with both of these ideas a flexible sense of the continuities and discontinuities of history, but it departs from them in organizing the structure of history around the category of ethics and in using the feminine as a constitutive feature of this structure.

It is perhaps because there were other exemplary traditions addressing masculine ethical practice that male saints are so rarely offered explicitly as examples to laymen. It may also be that as the unmarked gender, the masculine is less visible, more naturalized, and so less available for this kind of symbolic use: the marked relationship between the female saints and the feminine audience that was to imitate her may be harder to emphasize with male saints and masculine audiences. But it was surely also because the exemplarity of male saints is, if anything, more vexed than that of female saints. Male saints are defined by their offices—king, bishop, abbot—and so in their own way present an even more inappropriate and circumscribed ethical model to the growing lay audience of vernacular literature than do virgin martyr legends.[52]

As we have seen, these legends provided an important locus for reflecting on history as readers discovered the difficulties, even impossibility, of unmediated imitation. I have begun to suggest that these limits should be understood as a consequence of—or at least in the context of—the divided political and religious culture of fifteenth-century England. Subsequent chapters develop this claim by showing how specific hagiographic texts comment on urgent questions of civic and national politics. But the limits of exemplarity are also a consequence of the more basic tensions inherent in the very idea of the example, and, especially, in the understanding of narrative as exemplary. Examples always exceed or subvert the general rule they purport or are assumed to exemplify: the particularities of the example will always threaten to qualify the ostensibly universal rule it demonstrates. This tension is further compounded by the nature of narrative. Ethics and narrative are always incommensurate, even if narrative always fashions an ethics. No matter how schematic, narrative posits a relationship between a character and the specific social and historical location she occupies, as well as a relationship to other characters, each again with her own explicit or implied history—particularities that, again, always modify or complicate the general rule that the narrative is supposed to represent. The more elaborate the narrative, the more this is bound to be true. Even in the relatively brief and formulaic narratives of vernacular hagiography, the occasional individualizing detail that makes them memorable as narrative interrupts the translation of exemplary meaning that turns a particular story into an ethical model. The long "romance" versions of vernacular legends, which became increasingly popular in the later Middle Ages, compound this exponentially.

This argument follows a familiar poststructuralist insight, of course, and I am especially interested in the possibility that it was available in some form to medieval audiences too. The original cannot be reproduced; the copy is always haunted by difference, and that difference is magnified in the case of vernacular legends in which the exemplary model is so historically distant. The exemplarity of vernacular hagiography depends on the fantasy that gender ideology and Christian practice are continuous, even transhistorical, but this is clearly not true: Margery Kempe can imitate the virginity and outspoken vocation of an ancient saint, and yet she is not "like" her precisely because she inhabits the radically different world of fifteenth-century England. I suggested in the Preface that we might understand this more specifically in terms of recent sociological theories of consumption. Michel de Certeau's definition of "tactical" responses to dominant discourses is especially useful: he argues that such discourses are inevitably changed through use, whether or not the "consumer" intends to disrupt or alter their original meaning.[53] The act of consumption is always framed by provisional circumstances that determine the social meaning and performance of a scripted identity or cultural code. So late medieval women, in imitating hagiographic narrative, whether by adopting the saint's practices directly or indirectly, did not reproduce but redefined them through the new social relationships they produced.

The complications of *imitatio* run yet deeper than this. Hagiographic exemplarity works something like mimesis as theorized by Michael Taussig, who argues that imitation alienates that which is imitated, rendering its "originality" and the fullness of its meaning suspect.[54] To put this in the terms of vernacular hagiography, the representation of marital chastity, for example, as an imitation of virginity, or of affective piety as an imitation of bodily persecution points not only to the irreproducibility of the model but also to its cultural specificity. Virginity and bodily persecution—though held up as transcendental values—are revealed to be contingent practices. This is an inevitable consequence of the narrative representation of moral ideals: exemplary narrative presents behavior performed and understood in the context of a set of social relations and institutions, not abstracted from them. It thus endows ethical or devotional practice with a specific position within a cultural contest—here, on the side of the Christians or on the side of the pagan persecutors—and so within a specific model of history—continuous with or categorically different from the early Christian past. Ethics, as we see clearly from this perspective, is the local habitation of a larger ideological system.[55]

In subsequent chapters of this book I investigate how late medieval writers explore and exploit the implications of exemplarity to produce models of history and community. First, however, I would like to consider the implications of hagiographic exemplarity for a female audience. One reason that the question of hagiographic exemplarity needs to be revisited is that it gives us a rare window on to the hermeneutics taught to women as they became more visible participants in textual culture, interpretive procedures that I have tried to sketch here with the limited and often indirect evidence available. Hagiography, as Alain Boureau has argued, endeavored to occupy the largest possible narrative field in the Middle Ages,[56] and the way that women were trained to read vernacular legends as exemplary may have influenced how they approached secular stories too. This is difficult, if not impossible, to trace. But there is evidence that the ethical address of vernacular legends created an expectation that there was a distinct female audience and an interpretive position proper to this audience. As I argue in the next chapter, this affected both women's participation in textual culture and the place of gender in vernacular hermeneutics.

2

Female Saints' Lives and the Invention of a Feminine Audience

A RECONSIDERATION OF EXEMPLARITY as a historical, rather than a regulatory, hermeneutics helps to reopen important questions about the status of female saints' lives for women readers and for the place of gender in vernacular literary culture. As we have already seen, the audience of female saints' lives is frequently gendered, often explicitly—as in the thirteenth-century life of St. Margaret addressed to "widows and the wedded and especially maidens" or in the Auchinleck *St. Margaret*, dated more than a hundred years later, which insists that the legend "mirthe is of to here / to maiden and to wiif."[1] Such specific invocations of a feminine audience reinforce the broad expectation, voiced in moral treatises such as the *Book of the Knight of the Tower*, that women read these legends as particularly appropriate to their devotional and ethical behavior. In imagining an audience whose reading is informed by their sex, the idea of *imitatio* produces—if only in theory—a gendered hermeneutics, an interpretive response proper to female readers. Female saints' lives, that is, ask women to read *as* women. They made gender a salient category in the interpretive protocols that late medieval audiences brought to bear on the new and rapidly expanding body of vernacular literature.

They also, as a consequence, helped to make women visible as patrons and readers—that is, as participants in literary history. The lives of female saints, especially the legends of virgin martyrs that occupy so much of the vernacular canon, are usually seen as misogynist—especially in their representation of sexuality and sacrifice—by modern readers, and they are thus often left out of accounts of women's relationship to literary culture, despite the evidence we have of women's interest in and access to the genre. Thinking about gender as a category of response, as well as representation, can help us to negotiate the gap between the evidence of medieval women's interest in the genre and modern critical responses. Saints' lives made a significant contribution to the increasing prominence of women in late medieval literary culture, a phenomenon that registers most strikingly in the records of women's patronage and book ownership but which also surfaces in secular poetry, as we will see at the end of the chapter in turning to Geoffrey Chaucer's *Legend of Good Women*.

* * *

Julian of Norwich's identification of the virgin martyr Cecilia as a model for her devotional practice is easily overlooked not only because it challenges our understanding of exemplarity but also because it is difficult to reconcile her interest in hagiography with her place in our critical histories. Our paradigms for analyzing women's relationship to literary culture are still focused on authorship and the politics of representation, and the reception of Julian's work is very much structured by these categories. There is good reason for this: Julian is the earliest known woman writer in the Middle English tradition and one of its most daring religious thinkers. Her theology, moreover, draws on the vocabulary and imagery of affective devotion, the spiritual tradition most closely associated with medieval women and the "feminization" of Christianity on the grounds that its attention to Christ's suffering flesh allowed women to understand and represent their own bodies as Christ-like.[2] Julian is lauded both as a singular literary and intellectual figure and as a participant in a larger cultural trend that saw a new positive valuation of women's bodies, which is powerfully developed in Julian's discussion of Christ as mother.

Middle English legends, in contrast, were mostly written by men and seem largely impervious to new traditions of women's spirituality.[3] As a result, they are seldom recognized as part of "women's literary culture" but rather as the misogynist, even pornographic, products of clerical culture.[4] The Middle English tradition overwhelmingly prefers the saints of the early Church and especially the legends of virgin martyrs, such as Sts. Katherine, Margaret, Dorothy, Lucy, Agnes, and Agatha, rather than contemporary saints whose lives seem better to reflect the devotional practices associated with women's piety in the late Middle Ages. The mystical and devotional phenomena that have received the most attention as evidence of the "feminization" of Christianity—the increasingly interior forms of devotional practice, the typologies of suffering and illness that were the basis of some women's identification with the humanity of Christ, the interest in feminine symbols, even in a feminized Christ—are only rarely reflected in vernacular legends. They are explored in the legends of roughly contemporary saints found in Bodleian MS Douce 114, which comprises the stories of Elizabeth of Spalbeck, Christina Mirabilis, Mary of Oignies, and Catherine of Siena.[5] But this manuscript is an anomaly in the English tradition, a striking departure from the majority of vernacular legends, which concern saints purported to have lived a thousand years earlier.

Important work, beginning with Bridget Cazelles's groundbreaking *Lady as Saint*, has emphasized the misogyny inherent in this tradition: its idealizing tropes and normative agenda, its narrow definition of feminine spirituality and ethics in terms of sexual activity, and its often sexualized violence. There is no question that virgin martyr legends define feminine goodness in terms of sacrifice and suffering and that they imagine sexuality as a moral category, indeed as the primary arena for women's moral action. At the same time they replay a sequence of events that centers on the saint's desirable and vulnerable body: the girl becomes the object of male desire; she is exposed as a Christian when she insists on her virginity; her body is subjected to violent torments, though it is either miraculously resistant to torture or miraculously restored to health in witness to the special integrity guaranteed by her virginity; she dies finally when she embraces her martyrdom, represented as union with her divine Spouse. It is much easier to associate these legends, with their startling fantasy of the female body as repeatedly violated, and yet inviolable, with their clerical authors than with female audiences.[6]

These are important concerns and they have been well analyzed by feminist critics. I do not address them in detail here because for the most part I agree with the general lines of this argument and do not intend my approach to challenge it.[7] Like other recent scholars, however, I want to broaden our understanding of the genre,[8] and especially its importance for women's literary culture, by recognizing the way that a genre's representational strategies do not wholly determine its meaning. Its affiliation with particular audiences, in fact and cultural fiction, and its reception and use by these audiences also contribute to what a narrative tradition means in a given historical moment. Understanding literature as a social institution is especially important in the case of female saints' lives, which offer the most abundant and detailed evidence of women's participation in literary culture of any Middle English narrative tradition, although this evidence has often been obscured by the critical emphasis on the genre's misogyny. This approach can complement earlier work that privileges the politics of representation, even if—indeed because—it may arrive at very different conclusions. The one line of argument with which my approach is incompatible is that which reads virgin martyr legends as a species of medieval "pornography."[9] Pornography is by definition a genre understood to transgress the moral boundaries of the dominant culture; in the Middle Ages, virgin martyr narratives lay squarely within those boundaries. They are endorsed not only by male moralists such as the Knight of the Tower but also by socially prominent women such as Christine de Pizan, who encourages girls to read saints' lives in the *Book of the Three Virtues*,[10] and Lady March, who commissioned John Lydgate to translate the legend of St. Margaret. This alone renders the definition of saints' lives as pornography specious.[11]

Indeed, from the perspective of social use or reception, female saints' lives are better understood not as a marginal discourse but as a central part of women's literary culture. They were available to the widest possible range of women: as civic drama and the subject of sermons they would have been accessible even to audiences who could not read or afford to own books. Julian of Norwich herself, as we saw in the last chapter, heard the story of St. Cecilia in church. Saints' lives were, moreover, the single genre universally endorsed as women's reading, distinguished from both the false fictions of romance and the obscure truths of theology. Moralists defined hagiography against secular literature in terms of its moral value and its ostensible truth status: so, the Knight of the Tower contrasts the legend of St. Katherine with the "fables / and lesynges / wherof no good ne prouffyte may come" (122).[12] But it was not only its moral "profit" that made hagiography especially appropriate for women readers. In the late Middle Ages, as the rise in lay literacy intersected with concerns about heterodoxy, hagiography was considered free of the subversive or heretical impetus that other religious genres might provide. As early as 1210 the Synod of Paris prohibited the translation of theological works into vernacular languages but made an exception for the translation of saints' lives in deference to women's desire for devotional reading.[13] Similarly, the sweeping reforms of the early fifteenth century that outlawed much vernacular religious writing in England did not limit the composition or translation of hagiography. Nicholas Watson notes that virtually the only religious writers working in English in the fifteenth century whose names we know are hagiographers: Osbern Bokenham, John Lydgate, and John Capgrave.[14]

Concerns about lay access to theology were so acute in late medieval England that even saints' lives might present difficulties, which may have prompted hagiographers to begin to develop a theory of narrative as a distinct mode of representation, one set apart from what Watson calls "vernacular theology." In his *Life of St. Augustine*, John Capgrave informs us that the legend was written for "A noble creatur, a gentill woman" who requested "the lif of Seynt Augustyn, grete doctour of the cherch" with "ful grete instauns."[15] His patron was devoted to St. Augustine because she was born on his feast day, but her interest in Augustine as a "grete doctour of the cherch" suggests that she was also interested in Augustine's intellectual work. Capgrave, however, pointedly refuses to summarize Augustine's theological texts, saying that in works such as *De Quantitate Animae*, "many sotil thinggis ar touchid whech long not to this maner of wryting that is cleped narratyf" (31). This is the first and only use of the word "narrative" cited in the *Middle English Dictionary*,[16] and it is used to define the discursive boundaries between hagiography and theology on the grounds of literary kind and decorum. Of course, this distinction is surely motivated, too, by a concern that such "sotil thinggis . . . long not" to his female audience.[17] The translator of the late fifteenth-century *Lyf of St. Katherin of Senis* is more frank and reminds us that theology was considered inappropriate even for religious women. Addressing his work to a "doughter" and her "gostely susteren," he explains to them that he has omitted Raymond of Capua's two prologues and other material: "I leue of also poyntes of diuynyte whiche passeth your vnderstondyng, and touche only maters that longeth to your lernyng" (33, 34).[18] He is eager to present exemplary narrative—"fructuous example of vertuous liuinge to edyfycacion of thy sowle and to comforte and encrese of thy gostly labour in all werkis of pyte" (33)—not theological discussion, to his female audience.

As the *Lyf of St. Katherin of Senis* suggests, however, it is less the exceptional status of saints' lives than their exemplary value that accounts for women's access to and affiliation with the genre in the social imagination of medieval England. We have already seen several examples, in the first chapter and in this one, of explicit invocations of a feminine audience that follow from the expectation that female saints' lives provide a gendered moral and devotional example. An especially elaborate example can be found in a late fifteenth-century *Lyfe of St. Radegunde,* ascribed to Henry Bradshaw on stylistic grounds.[19] The saint's Lenten practices, for example, are represented as "Example gyueng / of mekenesse and charyte // Unto all ladyes within christente" (26). This gendered exemplarity is the impetus for an extended direct address to an imagined female audience:

> Swete worthy princesses / borne of great rialte
> Duchesses / countesses / ladies euerychone
> Folowyng your appetite / and sensualite
> In worldly worship / and vayne dilectacion
> Diuersite of garmentes made of theyr newe facyon
> With delicat dayntes repastyng euery day
> The body to conserue / in lust and likyng ay
>
> Beholde and considre with your interiour eye
> This humble abbasse / lady and moniall [nun]
> Howe she refused all wordly dignite
> Rychesse / reuerence / and honour imperiall
> Vayne / vestures / garmentes / possessyons withall
> Entred religion / with great humilite
> Truly obseruyng / the essencials thre
>
> Also for sufferyng / in this present lyfe
> A lytell whyle payne / for loue of our sauyour
> Usyng prayer penaunce / and life contemplatyfe
> Nowe she is exalted / in heuenly honour
> Whose glory shall euer encrease / more and more
> Wherfore noble ladies / example ye may take
> At this holy quene / all vice to forsake. (30)

The legend has earlier defined the "essencials thre" of monastic life as obedience, chastity, and willful poverty (20) and has shown Radegund's perfect embrace of these virtues. While her special vocation as abbess and nun frames her position as a lady in the triple title given Radegund in the second stanza, however, it is in turn framed by stanzas that insist on her exemplarity for aristocratic laywomen, who are to learn from Radegund to renounce some of the pleasures and advantages of their rank: social prominence, fashionable clothing, and delicious food.[20]

This address to laywomen is somewhat surprising given the context that has been adduced for the legend's production. Bradshaw's legend is the first Middle English account of Radegund's life, and it probably had some association with the Benedictine nunnery dedicated to the saint at Cambridge. In 1487 John Alcock, bishop of Ely, had appointed a new abbess, having declared the nuns unfit to elect their own, and in 1496 he disendowed the nunnery to found Jesus College.[21] The legend may have been composed in response to the nunnery's failing fortunes, which, as F. Brittain, the poem's modern editor, suggests, would have been of interest to Bradshaw, a Benedictine monk. The legend provides textual evidence for its affiliation with religious women and, more specifically, with religious women accused of misbehavior. Chapter 11 tells "How this holy abbasse vsyng meditacyon refourmed her syster neglygent" and opens with a long description of her virtues and practices as an abbess (28). At the end of the legend, Bradshaw may allude directly to the nuns' precarious situation: "a person religious / May lerne at this lady to kepe pacience," Bradshaw writes,

> To be humble in soule / gentyll and vertuous
> Obseruyng chastite / and true obedience
> With wilfull pouerte / without concupiscence
> And euer content be with what Iesu doth sende
> Yeuyng [Giving] humble thankes vnto your lyues end. (53)

Brittain notes that passages such as these concerned with Radegund's exemplarity are original to Bradshaw's version of the legend,[22] providing further evidence for both its topical reference and the pressure of a broad expectation of the gendered exemplarity of female saints in Middle English narrative culture. For, as we have seen, if the legend was intended in the first instance to provide guidance or consolation to the Benedictine nuns of St. Radegund, it expands this audience to include laywomen as well. So the stanza preceding the one above that outlines how Radegund provides a specific model to nuns insists again that:

> Euery great estate / empresse / quene / and duchesse
> Example may take at this moniall
> To encrease in vertu / and proued mekenesse
> In churche to be deuout / and courtesse in hall

And to the poore people for to be liberall
Euery true matrone her doctrine folowyng
In heuen may be sure to haue a wonnyng [home]. (53)

Oscillating between secular social categories and religious ones, the legend alerts its readers to the prevailing and unifying significance of the sex shared by its subject and audience.

Exemplarity is the primary, but not the exclusive, impetus behind the gendered address of female saints' lives. It is sometimes also a consequence of the saint's special intercessory role. This is most obviously true for St. Margaret, who was widely celebrated as the patron of women in childbirth.[23] John Lydgate's version of her legend, at times specifically addressed to aristocratic women, specifies a broader audience when reminding women to call on the saint for succour when they are in the throes of childbirth:

alle wymmen that haue necessite,
Praye this mayde ageyn syknesse and dissese,
In trayvalynge for to do yow ese (523–25).[24]

The life of St. Margaret in the *South English Legendary*, rather than addressing childbearing women directly, imagines the scene of reading in which they become the legend's privileged audience: "Wymmen that with other were . wanne hi child bere / Hit were god that hi radde hure lyf . the sikerore ye seoth it were" (317–18) (Women who are with other women when they give birth / It would be good if they read St. Margaret's life, the safer you see it would be).[25] This advice follows from Margaret's prayer that she be granted the grace to protect laboring women who call on her or read her life:

And yif eny womman to me clupeth . in trauail of childe
Other biuore my lif rede . Louerd beo hure milde
Ne lete hure noght therewith spille . ac bring that child to sighte
And al sauf of is moder wombe . with al is limes righte
Moder and child saue bothe . Louerd for loue of me. (283–87)

[And if any woman calls to me in the labor of birthing
Or reads my life before, Lord, be merciful to her

Nor let her die because of it. Rather bring that child to sight
And all safe from his mother's womb, with all his limbs right.
Save mother and child both, Lord, for love of me.]

It perhaps also recalls the implicit promise of physical release in the story of the saint's escape from the belly of a dragon. But this intercessory role does not account fully for the legend's gendered address: as we have seen, maidens and widows—not just wives—are named as the audience of other versions of the legend.

* * *

The gendered address of female saints' lives, whether a function of the saint's exemplary or intercessory role, insists—implicitly and explicitly—that women read as women, that their response is or should be informed by their sex. As in the last chapter, however, my claim here is not that medieval women—and certainly not all of them, always—read in the way that hagiographic exemplarity demands. That is why I have referred to the audience constructed by female saints' lives as feminine rather than female: it is an imaginary audience that defines and is defined by cultural codes of gender identity and practice, one with an important but not determinative relationship to historical women. Even if or when women did read saints' lives as exemplary, they may not have privileged gender as a category—in the narrative or in their own interpretive position—in the way that the hermeneutics of exemplarity generally anticipates. The gendered address of female saints' lives is a fiction of the genre, which surely had variable effects on individual readers. It is also important to recognize, however, that such fictions shape readers' expectations, even if they do not wholly constrain them. If an investigation into the gendering of vernacular hermeneutics and the invention of a feminine audience cannot tell us how women read or how they understood their relationship to other women readers, it does tell us something about the cultural system within which they participated in narrative culture. Female saints' lives are—or should be—central to women's literary history not because women read them, or read them as women, but because they helped to create the very category of women's literature, and they helped to inscribe female readers in the discursive—and so in the historical—arena of late medieval England.[26]

Lydgate's "Legend of Seynt Margarete" provides unusually direct evidence for this in the close relationship between its gendered address and the naming of a historical woman as literary patron. We have already seen how the legend's envoy addresses women in childbirth. A few lines earlier, it addresses a feminine audience defined by class:

>Noble princesses and ladyes of estate,
>And gentilwomen lower of degre,
>Lefte vp your hertes, calle to your aduocate
>Seynt Margarete, gemme of chastite. (519–22)

This generic address in the envoy forms a frame for the legend with the prologue, which more specifically identifies Lady March as the poem's first audience:

>Remembre, O virgyne, vpon that other side
>On hir that caused, oonly for thi sake
>Thyn holy lyf me to compile and make,—
>My lady Marche I mene, whiche of entent
>Yafe firste to me in commaundement
>
>That I shulde considre welle and see
>In Frensshe and Latyne thyn holy passyoun
>Thi martidam and thi virginite,
>And thereof make a compilacyoun. (66–74)

Lady March stands as a synecdoche for the aristocratic women addressed in the envoy who are encouraged to identify themselves as the poem's audience, a community linked by their shared interest in and response to the legend. Conversely, the gendered address of the genre makes the inscription of Lady March's name more likely and more legible: her proper name takes the place of the generic address to "maidens, wives, and widows" or to "ladies of estate" that we find elsewhere. The identification of the poem's female patron, rare and important evidence for women's participation in vernacular literary culture, is both a consequence of and a contribution to the fiction of the genre's feminine audience.

I would read other evidence of women's active role in the production and transmission of hagiographic narrative, long documented in the studies of literary patronage and book ownership,[27] as further witness to the way that the gendered address of female saints' lives contributed to the inscription of women in medieval literary history. Karen Jambeck's study of women's patronage finds that of the thirty-one works dedicated to women in England between the thirteenth and the late fifteenth centuries, twelve (almost 40 percent) are saints' lives, and of these, eight are of women saints.[28] In addition to Lady March's "Legend of Seynt Margarete," John Lydgate addressed an "Invocation to Seynte Anne" to Lady Anne, countess of Stafford.[29] The most extraordinary evidence comes from the work of Osbern Bokenham, whose *Legends of Holy Women* records the names of six patrons: Katherine Denston (the legends of St. Anne and St. Katherine); Katherine Howard (the legend of St. Katherine); Isabel Hunt (the legend of St. Dorothy); Agatha Flegge (the legend of St. Agatha); Elizabeth de Vere (the legend of St. Elizabeth of Hungary); and Isabel Bourchier (the legend of Mary Magdalene).

Evidence for laymen's patronage of vernacular hagiography is sparse in comparison. Most men who commissioned Middle English saints' lives were religious men in positions of institutional authority: John Capgrave's *Life of St. Norbert* is dedicated to the abbot of Derham, John Wygnale;[30] his *Life of St. Gilbert of Sempringham* was written for Gilbertine nuns, but at the request of the "maystir of the order of Sempyngham," who is identified as Nicholas Reysby in the margin of the holograph manuscript.[31] Lydgate wrote the double *Life of Sts. Edmund and Fremund* at the request of William Curteys, the abbot of Bury St. Edmunds, and the double *Life of Sts. Alban and Amphibalus* at the request of John Whethamstede, abbot of St. Alban's. Bokenham's legend of St. Margaret is dedicated to a fellow Augustinian friar, Thomas Burgh. There are a couple of legends written for guilds: Lydgate's *Legend of St. George*, composed for the London armorers,[32] and an anonymous legend of St. Anne, perhaps written for a confraternity at Bury St. Edmunds.[33] But aside from Alexander Barclay's *Life of St. George*, addressed to "Prynce Thomas duke of Norfolke tresorer & Erle marchall of Englonde," I have found no evidence of patronage by laymen.[34] Lay patronage of vernacular hagiography seems largely to have been the preserve of women.

Evidence of women's ownership of hagiographic books is as striking as the evidence for their patronage. Some of this evidence comes from extant books that record ownership or patterns of transmission on their flyleaves and colophons. A manuscript of the 1438 *Gilte Legende* contains a note in which the owner, John Burton, a London mercer (d. 1440), leaves the book "callyd Legenda sanctorum" to his daughter Kateryne Burton for use during her lifetime; it was to be given to the prioress and convent of Halywelle upon her death.[35] Katherine Babington, an Augustinian nun at Campsey priory in Suffolk, owned British Library MS Arundel 396, which contains a copy of John Capgrave's long *Life of St. Katherine*, her name saint.[36] Anne Harling owned British Library MS Harley 4012, which includes lives of her name saint, Anne, as well as lives of Katherine and Margaret.[37] There are also records of hagiographic books owned by nunneries: the nunnery of Kilburn owned two manuscripts of an English translation of the *Legenda Aurea*,[38] and the single extant manuscript of Bokenham's legendary of female saints was produced for a house of nuns.[39]

More abundant, if often cryptic, evidence comes from testaments. Although as household or chapel items, only seldom as sumptuously produced as psalters and Books of Hours, hagiographic books are less likely to be specified in testaments,[40] we have strong evidence of women's ownership from both their own wills and those of testators who left books to them. In 1319 Margery de Crioll left her "little book of martyrs and common of the saints" to Johne Petche.[41] Elizabeth de Burgh, Lady of Clare and foundress of Clare Hall, Cambridge, left to the college a "bone legende" and a "legende sanctorum" in her 1355 will.[42] In 1358 Edward III's queen, Isabella, left a book of French saints' lives to her daughter, Joan, queen of Scotland; Joan, in turn, bequeathed the book to Abingdon Abbey in 1367.[43] Evidence of women's ownership of hagiographic books increases in the fifteenth century.[44] To her daughter-in-law Joan, Elizabeth de Juliers, countess of Kent, left "unum magnum legend" in 1411.[45] In the same year Phillipa de Coucy, widow of Robert de Vere, earl of Oxford, bequeathed a book that included "la vie des sainz Peres, les voiages que saint Antoine fist en la terre d'outremer, l'estorie de Balaam et de Josaphat, l'avenement Antecrist, and l'assumption Nostre Dame."[46] Sibilla de Felton, abbess of Barking Abbey in the early fifteenth century, seems to have come into possession of this book or to have had a similar one.[47] Agnes Stapleton of Yorkshire left "meum librum de ffrensshe de vita sanctorum" to her friend Elene Ingelby in 1448.[48] Margery Carew left an incomplete copy of the *South English Legendary* around 1450.[49] Elizabeth Sewerby bequeathed a *Revelations* of Bridget of Sweden in 1468;[50] another copy was left by Margaret Purdaunce of Norwich in 1481.[51]

Margaret, Lady Botreaux and Hungerford (d. 1478), left to Salisbury Cathedral a *Golden Legend*;[52] she had inherited from her father-in-law, Walter Hungerford of Heytesbury, his "legendam auream de vitis sanctorum in Gallic script."[53] An English legendary was willed by the duchess of Buckingham in 1480;[54] Anne Neville of Stafford left another to her daughter-in-law, Lady Margaret Beaufort, in the same year.[55] Cecily, duchess of York, left her granddaughter Brigitte a *Legenda Aurea*, a life of St. Catherine of Siena, and "a boke of Saint Matilde," probably the *Liber specialis gratie* of Mecthild of Hackeborn, in 1495. To another granddaughter, Anne de la Pole, the prioress of Syon abbey, she left a "boke of the Revelacions of Saints Burgitte."[56] Elizabeth Knevet inherited a book of saints' lives from her grandmother Thomasin Hopton in 1498.[57] Isabel Lyston mentions an "englyssh boke of saynt margarets lyfe" in her will (undated).[58] Eleanor Bohun, duchess of Gloucester, owned many books and left a detailed testament, in which she left to her daughter Anne, Lady of Stafford, "un liure beal et bien enlumines de legenda aurea en frauncois"; to her daughter Isabel, a minoress at Aldgate, London, "un liure de vitas patrum"; and to her daughter Joan a psalter and "autres devociones," which may also have included saints' lives.[59]

Many other women received hagiographic books as bequests. Thomas Berkeley, Lord Berkeley, left his volume of saints' legends "in Anglicis" to the sisters of the hospital of St. Mary Magdalene near Bristol.[60] Robert de Roos, knight of Ingmanthorp, left to his daughter Eleanora a "legendam sanctorum de gallico" in 1392.[61] His kinsman Thomas de Roos of Ingmanthorp left a "legendam sanctorum" to Lady Elizabeth Redeman seven years later.[62] William Phelip, Lord Bardolph, made a special provision in his will, dated 1438, to ensure that his wife Joan would have use of his "nova legenda" during her life, after which it was to be given to the parochial church of Denyngton, Suffolk for the souls of William, Joan, and their family and friends.[63] Thomas Hornby bequeathed a *Life of St. Katherine* to a nun of Swine in 1485.[64]

Such anecdotal evidence for the important place of hagiographic books in women's libraries is corroborated by Anne Dutton's statistical analysis of women's ownership of religious literature. Dutton shows hagiography to be the most abundantly attested category by far: of the 103 texts owned by women in the testamentary evidence she surveys, 31 are hagiographic, more than twice the number of books in the next most popular category, meditative literature.[65]

The evidence offered here is not transparent. I use the term "patron," but we know little about the mechanisms of literary patronage in the Middle Ages and in most cases cannot specify the transactions—financial, social, aesthetic—that occurred between patrons and poets. Evidence of book ownership may seem more straightforward, but as Kate Harris reminds us, it, too, is difficult to assess. The claims that can be made about it are limited by the nature of the evidence, which is incomplete and not necessarily representative, and by the fact that ownership is not a sure sign of "initiative."[66] I provide evidence of women's participation in the hagiographic tradition not so much as proof of their agency in the genre but as witness to the association between women and saints' legends in the late medieval cultural imagination. The poststructuralist critique of historicism has taught us that even the most transparent "fact" recorded in an archival source is part of a larger ideological construct. References to women patrons, book owners, and readers of hagiography surface in the historical record because they respond to, even as they create, a broad cultural fiction of women's access to the genre, one that is corroborated and extended in poetry and moral literature.

A reminder that women's interest in female saints' lives is not an inevitable or natural consequence of their sex, and so also indirect evidence for the force of this cultural fiction, is provided by the Anglo-Norman tradition. Anglo-Norman women were, in an earlier period, also active patrons of hagiographic texts, but they are more often identified with male saints' lives than female ones. Benedeit wrote the *Vie de Saint Brendan* for Adela, Henry I's queen.[67] Isabel de Warenne, countess of Arundel, commissioned Matthew Paris's *Vie de Saint Edmond*;[68] his *Life of St. Edward*, translated from Latin prose, was dedicated to Eleanor of Provence, Henry III's queen.[69] Peter de Peckham translated Ralph of Bocking's *Vita Sancti Richardi* at the request of Isabel, countess of Arundel.[70] A nun of Barking abbey—who declined to record her name because it is an unworthy companion to the saint's—wrote a *Life of Edward the Confessor*.[71] Alice de Vere probably commissioned the *Life of St. Osith*, a female saint's life, but this is an exception.[72] Women's patronage of Anglo-Norman hagiography was much less concerned with gender as the category organizing their literary and devotional commitments; instead, as this list suggests, they were interested in the cultural authority of the Anglo-Saxon past, often as part of their families' claims to political right.[73]

Gender is a primary organizing category for the Middle English tradition, but it does not preclude other points of identification. As Jocelyn Wogan-Browne has written, "there are many possible relations between audience and saint other than shared gender."[74] Some male saints' lives are addressed to women readers: John Capgrave, as we have seen, wrote his legend of St. Augustine at the request of a woman, and Symon Wynter directs his legend of St. Jerome to Margaret, duchess of Clarence.[75] Conversely, men can, of course, be interested in female saints, as Thomas Burgh, mentioned above, seems to have been. Bokenham, too, claims special devotion to his "Valentines," Sts. Cecilia, Faith, and Barbara (8277–78). Hagiographers sometimes even encourage male readers to emulate female saints: a copy of a fifteenth-century prose version of the legend of St. Katherine, mentioned briefly in the last chapter, first identifies its exemplary value for virgins and maidens but then imagines a much broader audience of "alle cristen puple."[76] Bradshaw's *Lyfe of St. Radegunde* addresses laymen more directly:

> [Radegund] had suche wysdome / and singuler grace
> Transcendyng other ladyes / of memory
> Dukes / erles / and barons / and all theyr progeny
> Example may take / at this quene ryall
> To encrease in mekenesse / and vertuous morall. (14)

The point here, however, is that Radegund was a model to her husband, King Clotaire, and so might be a model to other male leaders. The passage continues:

> By her great prudence / and exortacion
> The kyng was moued / to grace and pitie
> Merciable to the pore / in all his region
> Hauyng compassion / lyberall / and fre
> To execute Iustice prompte with mercie
> A good benefactour / to places religyous
> By the instant mocion / of his quene vertuous. (14–15)

Radegund, that is, presents a model of wifely religiosity whose mercy, compassion, justice, and generosity are imitated by her husband. She stands as a model to male readers, but the model is mediated by Clotaire, whom laymen imitate in imitating Radegund. That the association between female saints and feminine audiences was not exclusive does not, in any case, diminish its importance. As Pierre Bourdieu's work suggests, consumption may have symbolic value and be constitutive of the social identity of a particular class even if it characterizes that social identity in only a partial way.[77]

If the genre's gendered address makes women part of literary history, as I have argued, by making their affiliation with saints' lives legible, why did this affiliation—one might ask—not change the hagiographic canon, which is notoriously resistant to new devotional trends? I would suggest that it did, but in ways that have not been readily perceived, and this, too, can be explained by critical approaches that privilege representational practices over social use. Narrative form remains the defining category in literary taxonomy, and from this perspective saints' lives are strikingly conservative and predominantly concerned with male figures. Less than 20 percent of the saints' lives in the *South English Legendary* are dedicated to female saints;[78] the portion is similar in the *Gilte Legende* of 1438.[79] These collections, both strongly influenced by the *Legenda Aurea*, a pastoral collection based on the Dominican liturgical calendar, reflect older patterns of veneration enshrined in this conservative tradition.[80] These expansive compendiums of saints' lives have largely determined our understanding of the genre and have confirmed its supposed imperviousness to the so-called "feminization" of late medieval religious culture, an argument first made about saints' lives by social historians who used statistical analysis of the earliest versions of hagiographic texts for evidence of changing patterns of sanctity.[81] But a different picture emerges if we examine all vernacular versions of saints' lives and, especially, if we distinguish between pastoral legendaries and legends that exist singly or in small clusters. From a modern critical perspective, such a distinction is warranted by their different textual contexts, but there is also evidence of contemporary awareness that legends that circulated independently of large legendaries form a separate category, sometimes with different narrative emphases. An early fifteenth-century hagiographer acknowledges in the preface to his *Life of St. Katherine of Alexandria*: "After I had drawe the martirdom of the holy virgyn and martir seynt Kateryne from latyn into englesshe as hit is wryton in legendis that are compleet ther was take to me a quayere. Where yn was drawe in to englesshe not oonly hire martirdom but also hir birthe and lyuynge to fore hir conuersion."[82] The passage reveals an awareness of the discursive differences between legendaries ("legendis that are compleet"), which include short narratives focused on the saint's martyrdom, and individual legends, which sometimes offer a more comprehensive account of the saint's life, like the Katherine legend mentioned here that circulated in a single quire.[83]

The percentage of female saints' lives that circulated outside of "legends that are complete" is significantly higher than those found in pastoral legendaries.[84] There are twenty-nine male saints and twenty-eight female saints whose legends are found outside of the large legendaries; a virtual tie.[85] But the parity here between the numbers of male saints and female saints is misleading because the legends of female saints were far more likely to exist in more than one vernacular version. There are a total of fifty-seven legends of the twenty-eight women saints, compared to thirty-six legends of the twenty-nine male saints: over 60 percent of the vernacular legends that exist outside of the large legendaries are of female saints. This is a consequence of the popularity of a few female saints, which far exceeds lay devotion to any male saint, to judge by the number of vernacular legends composed in their honor: there are three legends of St. Ursula, four of St. Anne, five of St. Dorothy; six of St. Margaret, and eight of St. Katherine of Alexandria. In sharp contrast, only one male saint, St. Alexis, is the subject of more than two vernacular legends that circulated independently of the large hagiographic collections. Interestingly, his legend is strongly reminiscent of the lives of early female saints: he first manifests his vocation when he leaves his family home in order to avoid the marriage his father has arranged for him. It should be noted that the female saints whose legends circulated outside of the pastoral legends are the same ones celebrated in them: here, too, virgin martyrs of the early Church predominate and more contemporary models of feminine spirituality receive little attention. This is, no doubt, a consequence of the influence of liturgical and pastoral sources. Those sources made few female saints available to lay audiences, but these became the most popular in late medieval narrative culture. We might surmise that they were popular not because they were about virgins, sacrificial and sexualized, but because they were about women. Having few female saints from which to choose as objects of particular devotion and literary interest, the audience of vernacular legends chose the ones at hand.

The prevalence of female saints' lives outside of pastoral legendaries may also be a consequence of their gendered address. Like the evidence of women's patronage and book ownership, that is, it may be part of the piecemeal construction of a gendered canon or the formation of what might now be called a "women's literary tradition," as the expectation that female saints' lives were appropriate to women readers informed patterns of production and ownership. One extraordinary example of this is a beautiful book made for Mary de Bohun, Henry Bolingbroke's young wife: Copenhagen, Royal Library MS Thott 517, which comprises the legends of Mary, St. Margaret, and Mary Magdalene (in French)—a small cluster of saints' lives intended specifically for a female reader.[86] I have already given other examples, including Katherine Babington's book, containing Capgrave's *Life of St. Katherine*, and Anne Harling's, containing three female saints' lives. Tellingly, most explicit references to a feminine audience—whether a general invocation or the proper name of a patron—are found in legends that exist independently of pastoral legendaries:[87] Lydgate's *St. Margaret*, Bradshaw's *St. Werburge* and *St. Radegunde*, the prose Katherine, and especially Bokenham's *Legends of Holy Women*, which, as I will argue in the next chapter, is an effort to establish a gendered canon in a single collection, a distillation and extension of the broader cultural fiction we have discerned here. The case of female saints' lives offers a strong demonstration, first, that the idea of a gendered literary tradition is not natural or inevitable but produced and, second, that it is no less significant for that. If it is historical in the sense that it is contingent, it is also historical in the sense that it affects the shape and meaning of vernacular literary culture and the possibilities for women's participation in it.

It is important to acknowledge that hagiography was not the only genre that contributed to the idea of a gendered response or a feminine interpretive community. Although Middle English romance, as Carol Meale has argued, rarely considers or constructs an audience by gender, preferring class as the organizing category for its audiences and points of identification,[88] other narrative and non-narrative genres do insist on gender as a central category of response. Courtly allegory is one of these: *The Floure and the Leafe* and the *Assembly of Ladies*, for example, in their conspicuous segregation of the sexes and the explicit and implicit *demande d'amour* they each formulate, point to the different priorities of idealized feminine and masculine audiences. Conduct literature also genders its audience, and it does so—like saints' lives—through its ethical address: the *Book of the Knight of the Tower*, as we have seen, imagines the Knight's daughters as its primary audience. The more generic address of the *Good*

Wife Taught Her Daughter genders its audience even more overtly than does the Knight of the Tower's fiction of familial advice.[89] The distinction between masculine and feminine audiences in antifeminist literature and the texts written in response to that tradition also contributed importantly to the construction of a feminine audience: indeed, as we will see in the next section of this chapter, it is in large part the shared importance of an imagined feminine audience—absent in one, acknowledged by the other—that makes antifeminism and hagiography so often antitheses of one another.[90] To these we must, of course, add Books of Hours, many of which include patron portraits, a visual representation of their anticipated audience.[91] But none of these was as insistent or as systematic in imagining a feminine audience as female saints' lives were, and none was as widely available to a broad range of lay and religious audiences. More importantly, no other genre makes gender identity a constitutive part of its hermeneutics.

* * *

I have sought to understand how the expectation that women read saints' lives as women shaped medieval literary history, making women legible as participants in literary culture through the genre's gendered address. I would like now to consider how this expectation might have shaped medieval literary theory by making gender a salient part of vernacular hermeneutics. To do so, I turn to a different kind of evidence: imaginative literature, and in particular Geoffrey Chaucer's *Legend of Good Women*.[92] The *Legend of Good Women* is—notoriously—unconcerned with the ethical agenda of hagiography: its saints are devoted to Love and to the active sexuality this allegorical figure represents. It is, however, very much concerned with the feminine audience created through hagiography's ethical address. This audience, and the specific feminine interpretive position it represents, provides one of at least two—and surely many more—positions from which to read the poem. The polyvalence celebrated in other Chaucerian poems has seemed lacking here; it resides not in the multiple voices of the *Canterbury Tales* or the layered histories and textual traditions of the *Troilus*, but in the divergent audiences it imagines.[93] A crucial one of these is the feminine audience affiliated with the poem's form, a legendary comprising the lives of female "martyrs" of Love.

The *Legend of Good Women* draws together several strands of this chapter around this formal vocabulary: the creation of a gendered canon or tradition; its association with a female patron who stands metonymically for a broader feminine audience; and the construction of a distinctively "feminine" response. It also advances them by showing us how that imagined audience and the formal allusions that point to it can stand for a specific interpretive position—not the "correct" interpretation but one possible interpretation in the contested field of vernacular narrative. Chaucer's poem begins to suggest, that is, the ramifications of the gendered address of saints' lives for late medieval literary culture and interpretive practice more generally. Indeed, in its use of hagiography's feminine address, the *Legend of Good Women* provides striking, if indirect, evidence of the crucial role that female saints' lives played in thinking about the place of gender in vernacular hermeneutics.

The prologue to the *Legend of Good Women* explores the poet's relationship to nature, prior textual traditions, his own oeuvre, and his audience. Geoffrey professes a deep commitment to reading, second only to his love of the spring-time daisy, which draws him out of doors and away from his books. While in his rapt devotions to the flower, he is confronted by the God of Love, who is furious to see the poet of *Troilus and Criseyde* and the translator of the *Roman de la Rose* in such close proximity to a flower associated with his own cult: the marguerite of medieval love poetry. Love's anger is tempered by his mythological consort, Alceste, who catalogs Chaucer's other work and sets for him a new, penitential one, a "glorious legende / Of goode wymmen, maydenes and wyves" (F 483–84, G 473–74),[94] which the poet is to present to Queen Anne.

Alceste, tellingly, is interested in form only. She asks for hagiography, not for Christian saints, and the narrator provides her with stories drawn from her own pagan literary milieu: the "legends" of Cleopatra, Thisbe, Dido, Hypsipyle, Medea, Lucrece, Ariadne, Philomela, Phyllis, and Hypermnestra. The collection omits the classical stories with the greatest ideological affinity to the cult of saints: Chaucer reserves the story of Virginia, for example, for the *Canterbury Tales*, though its emphasis on virginity and sacrifice is far closer to the concerns of most vernacular lives than are the thematics of the "legends" of Love's martyrs.[95] But, however odd the disjunctions it produces, Alceste's interest in hagiography conforms readily to the gendering of narrative traditions in late medieval England. Like Criseyde's flippant assertion that she should read saints' lives rather than celebrate May Day with Pandarus,[96] Alceste's request corresponds so completely to cultural expectations for women's reading that the religious difference hardly registers. That is, in asking the poet for a "legend" of good women, Alceste not only articulates the formal structure of the work but also points to the feminine audience affiliated with this genre, which she then represents and embodies in the person of Queen Anne.

In reading the formal references as a mark of the feminine audience addressed by vernacular saints' lives, my approach departs from earlier analyses of the poem that rely, often implicitly, on a formalist understanding of genre as a category defined by a fixed set of conventions and themes. From this perspective, Chaucer's recourse to hagiography for the stories of classical women constitutes a breach of poetic and ideological decorum: the imposition of Christian form on classical matter produces irony or burlesque, or, in a strong feminist rereading of this model, a representation of the feminine so radically reduced to exemplary goodness that it becomes terminally boring.[97] This approach has taught us a great deal about the poem's representational strategies, but it accounts for them almost exclusively in terms of authorial control. Criticism of the poem, that is, parallels the critical response to hagiography itself. Here, too, we may arrive at quite different conclusions if we understand form in terms of the audience it designates in the late medieval cultural imagination.

To understand this audience, however, we must first turn to the literary problem staged in the prologue—the problem of antifeminist literature and, especially, its totalizing hermeneutics—because the place of hagiography's feminine audience is defined against the (absent) audience posited by antifeminist discourse. Antifeminism is introduced in the prologue through the person of the God of Love, who embodies the hermeneutics proper to that tradition. That Love places Chaucer in the antifeminist tradition is obvious—he castigates the poet for writing a poem about an unfaithful woman and for translating another that exposes the coercions of seduction—but I would argue that he does so less by accusing Chaucer of heresy against the religion of love than by imposing an antifeminist hermeneutics on Chaucer's poetry. Love's own relationship to literary antifeminism has sometimes been obscured by his apparent sympathy for women and eagerness to defend them, but his interpretive method, in which any example of feminine vice redounds to the sex as a whole, clearly derives from that tradition. Indeed, Love is a creature of perhaps the most complicated articulation of medieval antifeminism: Jean de Meun's elaboration of Guillaume de Lorris's *Roman de la Rose*. In a paradox allowed by medieval allegory, Love criticizes the very text from which he derives.[98] It is the *Rose*'s tyrannical God of Love who details the "commandment" that Chaucer transgressed in writing the *Troilus* (which I quote in the Middle English translation once attributed to Chaucer):

> And alle wymmen serve and preise,
> And to thy power her honour reise;
> And if that ony myssaiere
> Dispise wymmen, that thou maist here,
> Blame hym, and bidde hym holde hym stille.
> And set thy myght and all thy wille
> Wymmen and ladies for to please,
> And to do thyng that may hem ese,
> That they ever speke good of thee,
> For so thou maist best preised be. (2229–38)[99]

Love's origin in the *Roman de la Rose* and the antifeminist tradition it represents is clear both in this compositional imperative and in the totalizing hermeneutics with which he reads the *Troilus*. Love paradoxically exemplifies the antifeminist tradition that threatens his own procreative rule.[100]

In his reading, any poem about an unfaithful woman fits neatly into the ideological parameters of misogyny, regardless of the larger claims it makes or more subtle meanings it achieves.[101] In accordance with the logic of antifeminism, Love assumes that a single example can establish the lust, deception, or dereliction of the female sex as a whole. It is the misogynist tradition that reduces Criseyde to an example of an unfaithful woman whose infidelity implies the moral inferiority of women as a class and thus threatens the erotic imperative of Love's rule. It is not surprising, then, that the male god, rather than his female companion, accuses Chaucer of defaming women: although Criseyde predicts that her story will anger women, it is Love, trained in the interpretive protocols of the antifeminist tradition from which he derives, who responds with fury to Chaucer's poem.[102] Love, that is to say, is not simply a "bad" reader; he is a figure for a particular hermeneutic position. That his objections are rooted in literary antifeminism is clear from the fact that the depiction of false male lovers elicits no objection from him: in the absence of a discourse that reads a man's behavior, or even the behavior of several men, as paradigmatic of their sex, Alceste's desire for stories of "false men" poses no threat to him whatsoever.[103]

Like the tyrannical Love whose reading cannot be "countrepleted" by authorial intention,[104] the antifeminist hermeneutics he represents establishes its interpretive hegemony in no uncertain terms, not only rendering a flawed woman as representative of the sex but turning even praise of women into its satiric inverse through the trope of antiphrasis, in which one understands a statement to mean its opposite. Antiphrasis appears in its boldest and most simplistic formulation in the lyric tradition, in poems whose ostensible celebration of women in the vernacular is wholly undermined by its disavowal in a Latin refrain.[105] The best-known example, printed by Robbins as "Abuse of Women," is prefaced with the burden, "of all Creatures women be best: / Cuius contrarium verum est" (The opposite of which is true). This refrain is signaled between each stanza praising women, tellingly, by "Cuius"—the first word of the line announcing the reversal of meaning—rather than by the opening word of the couplet, as one might expect.[106]

In Chaucer's work, the antiphrastic strain of medieval antifeminism surfaces most famously in the *Nun's Priest's Tale*, when Chanticleer glosses "*Mulier est hominis confusio*" (VII. 3164) as "Womman is mannes joye and al his blis" (3166). As in the *contrarium* lyric, the absolute contradiction here is ostensibly obscured by linguistic difference. The *Nun's Priest's Tale* dramatizes the gender dynamic implicit in the trope through the figure of Pertelote: like a feminine audience of the *contrarium* lyric, she is to be cajoled by the compliment, the real significance of which is unavailable to her because she is illiterate. Chanticleer's use of Latin, the prestige language, points to the "correct" adverse interpretation of the claim that woman is man's joy, even as it excludes a feminine audience from this meaning. Antifeminist antiphrasis depends on the absence—often figured by linguistic inaccessibility—of a feminine audience.[107]

Alceste's request responds precisely to this feature of antifeminist hermeneutics. We might expect that she turns to hagiography because it defies the satiric inversions of antifeminism as a religious genre,[108] but vernacular saints' lives also disrupt an antiphrastic reading through their feminine address. The presence of hagiography's feminine audience, represented in the prologue by both the allegorical Alceste and the historical Anne, opens, or keeps open, a reading free from the ironic inversions of the antifeminist tradition, which, as we have seen, generally depend on the exclusion of this audience.

The narratives evince a remarkable awareness of the separate and potentially contradictory claims of a genre's representational strategies and the interpretive community with which it is affiliated. The very features that identify the poet's stories of "good women" as secular saints' lives also expose them to devastating irony. Chaucer's use of abbreviation, the freedom with which he excised anecdote that does not contribute to the development of a narrowly defined ideal, the single focus on one narrative line, and the repetitive thematic similarity between the narratives—however antithetical to modern canons of narrative—all find ample precedent in vernacular legends of female saints.[109] These features are easily read as a response to the (comically) recalcitrant nature of Chaucer's material: the brevity of the stories is attributed to the narrator's boredom, and the excision of narrative detail is seen to point to the difficulties—laughable in their proportions—of transforming women such as Cleopatra into "martyrs," even in the religion of love. But the extreme abbreviation of the narratives and their repetitive similarity must also be set in the context of Alceste's generic request: they are not merely the idiosyncratic practice of the narrator or his inevitable response to intractable material. Framed by the generic vocabulary of the prologue, they are also a response to the exigencies of form, and they herald an affiliation with female saints' lives in a way that would have been clear to a contemporary audience for whom that genre was among the most familiar narrative discourses and one insistently associated with a feminine audience. As generic markers of this audience, these features authorize a hagiographic reading of the poem that is precisely opposed to the satirical reading encouraged by the distortions of the textual tradition necessary to make them conform to the genre's narrative form.

As continuing critical debates about the poem's basic strategies and gender politics suggest, the stories do not point simply toward one of these readings. Certain features of individual legends (the pathos of Cleopatra's dying apostrophe to Antony, for example), of the legendary as a whole (the inclusion of Lucrece),[110] and of Chaucer's authorial persona (his perennial interest in and sympathy for Dido) provide authority for a sincere or "hagiographic" reading. Other evidence points differently, however, as critics have argued since Elaine Tuttle Hansen revived the ironic reading in the early 1990s. The reader is not constrained, as the narrator is, by Alceste's generic request, and many have found an antiphrastic reading more historically or tonally congruent with the poem—interpreting it through the lens of irony as a tacit, but obvious, condemnation of women who fail utterly to live up to the standards of hagiography. The poem cultivates such interpretive flexibility in its formal disjunction, left unresolved—perhaps strategically—by the poem's incompletion.[111]

This irresolution mirrors the divergent interpretive positions that the prologue presents in the figures of the God of Love and Alceste: an antifeminist hermeneutics associated with a male audience and a hagiographic one associated with a female audience. Of course, although these interpretive protocols are gendered in late medieval narrative traditions and in the poem, they can be adopted or resisted by audiences of both sexes. As the work of scholars such as Anne Clark Bartlett and Roberta Krueger reminds us, the hermeneutic position that a text defines for a particular audience, however coercive, is always merely a fiction, one that cannot prevent a reader from adopting other positions.[112] It may bear emphasizing that my argument is not that medieval women and men actually read the *Legend of Good Women* differently, but that the interpretive position that could withstand the hegemony of an antifeminist reading is articulated through the category of the feminine, in the poem's citation of the affiliation between women and vernacular hagiography in the late medieval cultural imagination. The *Legend of Good Women*, that is, provides a searching and complicated example of how the gendered address of female saints' lives opened vernacular hermeneutics by imagining a feminine audience.

In this chapter I have argued that the gendered address of female saints' lives has important implications for medieval literary history—especially women's growing visibility as patrons, owners, and readers—and medieval literary theory—by imagining that a reader's response was, or should be, informed by her sex. These are consequences of the way that female saints' lives constitute women as a distinct interpretive community through their exemplary address. In the chapters that follow, I explore how late medieval writers used this imagined community to think about the structure and priorities of other social communities. If the exemplarity of female saints' lives asks individual readers to consider their own devotional practices in relation to the models provided by the saints, it also asks them to consider their practices as part of a gendered identity that they share with other audiences. Gender here is a crucial category in the construction of a communal identity and so—as we will see in the next two chapters—to an exploration of the historicity of communities, past and present. Where Chaucer uses hagiography's feminine audience to think about the status of vernacular literature and to extend the possibilities of its meaning, Osbern Bokenham and Henry Bradshaw use it to investigate the status of English community and to offer alternative forms of affiliation. On the one hand, members of the feminine audience enjoined to imitate the saint connect the present to the past through their ethical practice: their imitation of female saints is the ground of a historical comparison between ancient and contemporary communities. On the other hand, they represent a community defined by devotional literature and practice, and so as an alternative to communities organized by fictions of inherited identity (whether dynastic, royal, or national) or by the fantasy of a continuous political structure—a fantasy impossible to sustain in fifteenth-century England.

3
Fictions of Feminine Community in Bokenham's Legendary

IN THE LAST CHAPTER I argued that the *Legend of Good Women* must be understood in the context of the feminine audience produced by the gendered address of vernacular saints' lives. Alceste, however, first frames her intervention in terms of political, not religious, discourse. She constructs a hypothetical situation in which she serves as the consort to a tyrannical king swayed by court rumor, rather than as the companion of an omniscient god: "And yf ye nere a god, that knowen al," she says to Love, "Thanne myght yt be as I yow tellen shal" (F 348–49), and she proceeds to offer political instruction relevant to an earthly ruler, if not, as she has quietly acknowledged, to a divine one. When Alceste turns her attention back to the poet Geoffrey, she retreats from this fiction of political advice and returns to the language of religion. The legendary she requests is a penitential text designed to atone for "heresye" and sacrilege against Love's "relyk," not to counter the accusations that court flatterers might make against the poet to Alceste's fictional tyrant. While Alceste briefly imagines a place for herself in political discourse, then, her literary activity and interests are aligned firmly with devotional practice. The prologue sets the question of women's role in politics in close proximity to their role in literary culture—and specifically their interest in female saints' lives—but it does not investigate the relation between these two arenas. They are segregated by representational level: the difference between the fiction of the prologue, in which Geoffrey must find a new way to represent women that will not offend the God of Love, and, within that fiction—at still another remove from the social world—Alceste's own fantasy in which she plays counselor to an earthly king.

This difference is symptomatic of a more consequential one between Alceste's singular privilege and the collective identity of the feminine audience produced by the ethical address of female saints' lives. Even in the realm of hypothesis, Alceste can intervene *politically* only by virtue of her queenship, her special position as consort to a male leader,[1] not as a member of a female community linked by literary and devotional interests.[2] There is no attempt in the *Legend of Good Women* to imagine the place of the feminine audience produced by hagiography's gendered address in a political context. This is, however, precisely the project of Osbern Bokenham's *Legends of Holy Women*. Like Chaucer, Bokenham uses women's association with hagiography to construct an alternative narrative tradition, but he presents his individual patrons in the context of the larger community formed by their shared narrative desires. He does so, I will argue, in order to imagine this feminine literary community as an alternative to the contentious political world of fifteenth-century England.

* * *

Bokenham's *Legends of Holy Women* presents the fullest, if also the most idiosyncratic, development of the association between saints' lives and a feminine audience traced in the last chapter. The collection is unique in two respects: it is the only Middle English legendary organized by the category of sex, and it is the best single witness to women's literary patronage in late medieval England. These two remarkable features are closely correlated in the long "prolocutory" to Bokenham's life of Mary Magdalene, which recounts how the legend was commissioned by Isabel Bourchier, countess of Eu and sister to Richard, duke of York. At a Twelfth Night party in 1445, as the countess's four sons dance around them, she and Bokenham discuss the legends of female saints that he has translated, many at the request of other prominent East Anglian women. Bokenham informs her that he has recently begun the legend of Elizabeth of Hungary for Elizabeth Vere, countess of Oxford; Isabel Bourchier responds by requesting that he also translate the legend of Mary Magdalene, to whom she has a particular devotion. The passage is, to my knowledge, the only narrative representation of a woman's commission of a Middle English text—certainly the only one that specifies in such detail the social context for the request, its relationship to the literary activity of other women, and the patron's personal intentions and interest.[3]

The passage describing Countess Bourchier's commission also heralds the collection's formal innovation, its invention of a distinct canon of female saints:[4]

> wyth me to talke
> It lykyd my lady of hyr ientylnesse
> Of dyuers legendys, wych my rudnesse
> From laytn had turnyd in-to our language,
> Of hooly wummen, now in my last age,
> As of seynt Anne, to blyssyd Marye
> The modyr, of Margrete & of Dorothye,
> Of Feyth & Crystyne, & of Anneys ther-to,
> And of tho Eleuene thowsend uirgyns al-so,
> And of that holy & blyssyd matrone
> Seynt Elyzabeth. (5036–46)[5]

As A. S. G. Edwards has shown, this passage structured the order of the single extant manuscript of Bokenham's legendary, British Library MS Arundel 327: quire signatures indicate that two legends, those of Faith and Dorothy, were moved in the course of the book's production in order to precede reference to them here. As Edwards argues, this confirms the text's own account of the piecemeal composition of individual legends at the request of several patrons.[6] But the passage also constitutes the legends as a compositional whole, setting the legends in relation to one another and gathering them into a collection of legends of holy women. These lines link the legends in the first half of the book not only with the legend of Mary Magdalene but also with the rest of the legendary, through reference to the legend of Elizabeth of Hungary, which ends the book. The medieval evidence for the constitutive force of this passage has a modern analog in the standard edition, for which it supplies the title, the *Legendys of Hooly Wummen*.[7] In both the medieval manuscript and the modern edition, Bokenham's representation of a woman's devotional and narrative desire organizes a distinct and conspicuously gendered canon.

The omissions from this canon are especially telling. Bokenham had previously translated the lives of legendary kings and bishops of England,[8] and Isabel, as an aristocratic woman whose brother could make a claim to the throne, might well be expected to identify with powerful native saints such as these who authorize aristocratic privilege and political power. But Bokenham defines her literary and devotional practices by sex, not class or national identity or some other social category. She stands in the prolocutory as an exemplary *female* reader, and her exclusive interest in female saints there confirms what the legendary as a whole tacitly argues: that women are interested in these narratives *as* women, that their reading is informed by their sex. Bokenham constructs a feminine interpretive community for his legendary not through a generic invocation of "maidens, wives and widows" but through the proper names of historical women. The Magdalene prolocutory represents this community in careful metonymy in the figures of Isabel Bourchier and Elizabeth Vere, who are linked by their shared religious and literary interests. This image is magnified over the course of the legendary, which altogether names six patrons: Katherine Denston, Katherine Howard, Isabel Hunt, and Agatha Flegge join their aristocratic neighbors Isabel Bourchier and Elizabeth Vere as the "cause princypal" (5744) and primary audience for legends of holy women. By naming his patrons, Bokenham produces a feminine interpretive community that is at once historically particular and representative of a larger, more imaginative, collective identity.[9] It is no coincidence that the single manuscript of the legendary was copied expressly for a house of nuns, the most iconic form of feminine community in late medieval England.[10] The manuscript, that is, can be understood not only as a witness to but also as a product of Bokenham's representational strategies. Although the female patrons named in the text are all laywomen, often represented explicitly in terms of their marriages and role as mothers, together they figure a feminine community defined by sex, regardless of differences in vocation and sexual status. Bokenham—in a single text—creates something like the fiction of a women's literary tradition. He offers a distinct canon, in whose production women figure prominently and which is understood to have a particular interest to women readers, whether they are religious or lay, virgin or mother, bourgeois or aristocrat.

The gendered audience that Bokenham constructs through reference to his patrons and readers elides more divisive categories of identity—most conspicuously, the partisan affiliations that would soon erupt into open violence over the rightful monarch. Although Bokenham had significant ties to York family members and was attentive to their political interests, as Sheila Delany has demonstrated,[11] the legendary is not a straightforward partisan project. Indeed, it imagines the feminine devotional community formed through a shared interest in female saints' lives as an alternative to the factional politics of mid-fifteenth-century England. Here, too, the Magdalene prologue is paradigmatic: Isabel Bourchier is Richard of York's sister, and Elizabeth Vere is a member of a prominent Lancastrian family, but in Bokenham's legendary this difference is obscured by the similarity of their literary patronage and devotional practice.[12]

* * *

The first section of this chapter argues that the legend that opens the collection—the life of St. Margaret—frames those that follow with an emphasis on the danger and disorder of the political world. While the dynastic conflict we call the War of the Roses was still more than ten years off when Bokenham was composing the legendary, there were already urgent concerns about the stability of political community under the weak kingship of Henry VI. Ultimately, I want to suggest that this is a crucial context for Bokenham's representation of women's literary activity in general and the feminine audience addressed by his legends in particular. As Gail McMurray Gibson's pioneering work on the legendary first showed, women's experience and the social expectations that shape their lives—especially their role as mothers—are given particular attention in the legendary.[13] In the *Legends of Holy Women* we see an incipient discourse of domesticity as characteristic of women's literature. This is not an inevitable result of women's interest or even of their prescribed role in late medieval aristocratic and merchant class life. It is rather part of Bokenham's attempt to imagine an alternative to the political engagement of other kinds of texts and the communities they posit or create—an alternative necessary to his own career in a politically volatile decade.

The *Legends of Holy Women* thus anticipates the exclusion of "women's literature" from public discourse, but it also constitutes women—their patronage and reading preferences—as a subject of literary history.[14] This is quite literally true, as attested by the place of Bokenham's collection in histories of medieval patronage and, recently, in studies of women's literary culture.[15] The specific historical information Bokenham provides—the names of his patrons and, on occasion, the names of their spouses, the date and place of the commission, and even an indication of the patron's intentions in Katherine Denston's commission of the St. Anne legend—has led most scholars to read reference to the patrons as social history. It is, however, impossible to identify, let alone quantify, their influence on the text, and the debate about it has come to an impasse.[16] This chapter seeks to change the terms of the argument, by recognizing that Bokenham's legendary can be read in the company of other fifteenth-century poems that present what Seth Lerer calls "fables of commission and reception" in which "the making of the literary text becomes the subject of its fiction."[17] Rather than asking how much influence Bokenham's female patrons had, we might ask what purpose this fable serves.[18] I propose that it creates a feminine community at a time when English political community was deeply divided.

Imagining Communities: Geography and Gender

Bokenham's broad concern with English political community is demonstrated by his only other extant work, the *Mappula Angliae*, a geographical treatise describing the topography and towns of England, translated from Ranulf Higden's *Polychronicon*. In the prologue to the *Mappula*, Bokenham tells his audience that he intends it as a companion text to the legends of Anglo-Saxon saints—Cedd, Felix, Edward, and Oswald "and many other seyntis of Englond"—that he had translated from the *Legenda Aurea* and from other "famous legendes" (6).[19] The *Mappula*, he writes, will make these legends more accessible by clarifying their obscure references to the ancient towns and political topography of England. Bokenham's "englische boke" of native saints is no longer extant, and the brief description that prefaces the *Mappula Angliae* is not necessarily a comprehensive representation of its contents.[20] But on the evidence of the geographical treatise offered as a companion text, it seems most likely to have been a collection of native saints.[21] As such, it testifies to a concern with constituting a national community, defined by a shared religious history, at a moment when England was threatened by weak political leadership, the widespread breakdown of public order, and an expensive, ongoing conflict with France. By identifying the geographical references in the legends with contemporary England, Bokenham establishes an "imagined community" in which both the Anglo-Saxon saints and Bokenham's fifteenth-century readers participate—a stable, continuous English identity that promises to persist in spite of current political instability and a long history of ethnic and cultural change.[22] In translating the "dyuers partis, plagis, regnis & contreis of this lande Englonde" from their ancient names to their more familiar late medieval ones, Bokenham literally maps the identity of the English community for whom he writes.

The *Legends of Holy Women* also addresses the problem of a fractured political community, but it does so through gender, not geography: by naming its several female patrons, it creates a feminine audience as an alternative community, associated with both a static devotional realm and a private domestic one. The interpretive community represented in Bokenham's *Legends of Holy Women* embraces women whose political fortunes would shortly define them in sharply opposed ways. Isabel Bourchier and Elizabeth Vere, paired in the Magdalene prolocutory, both accompanied their husbands to Rouen in the retinue of Richard, duke of York, in 1441, but the aristocratic community they shared then would divide along lines of dynastic affiliation in the decade following the production of Bokenham's legendary. While Isabel and her husband, Henry Bourchier, benefited from the patronage of Isabel's brother, Richard of York, and later Edward IV, Elizabeth's husband, the earl of Oxford, and her son Aubrey were executed in 1462 for an abortive plot to restore Henry VI to the throne.[23] A second pair of patrons, Katherine Howard and Katherine Denston, named together in the prologue to the legend of St. Katherine (6366), also represents opposing sides of the coming dynastic conflict. Katherine Howard, Elizabeth Vere's mother, saw her husband John rise in prominence under Yorkist rule to become the duke of Norfolk. Katherine Denston, on the other hand, the only woman to whom two legends are dedicated, came from a family with strong ties to Lancastrian institutions such as Bury St. Edmunds, where Katherine's father, William Clopton, and brother, John Clopton, were lay members.[24] John Clopton, like Elizabeth Vere's husband and son, was accused of treason for his Lancastrian commitments, although he avoided execution by switching allegiance. The two sets of patrons paired by Bokenham—Isabel Bourchier and Elizabeth Vere in the prologue to the Magdalene legend, and Katherine Denston and Katherine Howard in the prayer to St. Katherine—cross boundaries of genealogy and family loyalty that would shortly become much less permeable.

In their frequent representation of women acting together, often across boundaries of religious affiliation, the narratives in the *Legends of Holy Women* provide a guide for reading the feminine textual community figured by Bokenham's patrons. In the legend of St. Christine, for example, the girl's suffering at the hands of her father registers in the response of the women who witness the assault:

> whan wommen seye
> Thus cruelly tretyd this feyre mayde yinge,
> Among hem was meny a wepyng eye,
> And wyth a grete woys thai thus dyde preye:
> "O god of this mayde, hir help, preye we,
> And thus shamefully ne suffre hir for to deye,
> Wych in tendyr age doth to the fle." (2444–50)

The scene opposes Christine's father, who is enraged at his daughter's devotion to Christianity and committed to his own "gods," to the "women" who witness her torture with gendered sympathy and call upon her God to protect her. The general category "women" is supplemented by the synecdoche of a single "great voice": the women so fully constitute a collective identity that they speak as one. In this representation of a gendered community, Bokenham provides an image of the audience of his legends, similarly unified by their gendered response. We find a similar scene in the legend of St. Katherine, as the girl is led to her martyrdom:

> Many a matrone of hy wurthynesse,
> Many a wedwe, & many a maydyn ying,
> Aftyr hyr folwyd, ful sore wepyng
> For sorwe that she this wys shuld deye. (7280–83)

Katherine comforts this group of women but insists that they not hinder her passion, reminding them that she is going to join her divine spouse.[25] Sex supersedes distinctions between virgin, matron, and widow as the women respond to Katherine's suffering as a group. More striking, sex supersedes the difference between pagan and Christian that separates them from the saint. In this instance, the representation of female community has an even more pointed relationship to Bokenham's imagined audience: it provides a thematic parallel and an interpretive guide to his references to the legend's patrons, Katherine Denston and Katherine Howard. Their shared devotion to the saint obscures the dynastic difference that separates them—soon to become violent in ways that would affect each intimately—just as sympathy for the saint obscures the differences between the women who witness her suffering in the legend dedicated to them. This pairing echoes the pairing of Isabel Bourchier and Elizabeth Vere in the Magdalene prolocutory, a doubled image that points to a larger audience of women joined—like the women depicted in the legends—in their devotion to female saints.

English Political Community in the 1440s

The sharp polarization of Yorkist and Lancastrian commitments was still in the future when Bokenham composed his legends of holy women and his friend Burgh had them copied in Arundel 327. Richard of York was still well supported by Henry VI in the 1440s: T. B. Pugh notes the "exceptional marks of royal favor" he enjoyed in the middle of the decade, the years in which Bokenham composed the legendary.[26] Concern about the Lancastrian dynasty had already surfaced, however, and it was newly urgent in these years. The young Henry VI was still without an heir, as was his uncle, Humphrey of Gloucester, who was next in line for the throne. Although there is no evidence that affiliation with York or Lancaster already at this early moment signified in the way it would after St. Albans, the instability caused by Henry VI's weak kingship and the lack of a clear line of succession was already evident. Political community was threatened from within, especially by the factional politics in Henry VI's court, and from without, by England's waning fortunes in France.

The effects of this threat were felt not only within elite aristocratic circles but throughout the countryside. Henry's blindness to the behavior of his favorites encouraged—or at least failed to prevent—egregious abuses of power. A range of sources, from the commons' petition to the king in 1449 to the Paston letters, testifies to aristocratic disregard for the rule of law, rampant criminal activity, and the perversion of legal process through maintenance and livery in this period. William de la Pole, marquess and later duke of Suffolk, the most notorious of the fifteenth-century magnates who took advantage of their military force and their influence on local courts, controlled both Lincolnshire, Bokenham's birthplace, and East Anglia, where Bokenham resided at Clare priory. Suffolk was widely feared by both small landholders such as the Pastons and more prominent figures such as John Mowbray, duke of Norfolk, who was twice imprisoned in the Tower of London through Suffolk's influence.²⁷ In 1449 the commons petitioned the king for more substantial efforts against baronial abuse of power. Their complaint stated that in the absence of vigorous attempts to conserve the peace, uphold justice, and execute the law, "many Murdres, Manslaughters, Rapes, Roberies, Riottys, Affrayes and othur inconvenientes, gretter than afore, nowe late have grown within this your Roialme."²⁸

The king took no action, and the next year saw a more direct expression of widespread frustration with the government's inability to maintain law and order in both the murder of Suffolk and the successful, if short-lived, rebellion led by John Cade, who called himself "John Amend-all." An English chronicle represents Cade as protesting the injustice and tyranny of the powerful—"forasmuche as thanne and longe before the reme of Englond hadde be rewlid be untrew counselle, wherfore the comune profit was sore hurt and decresid"—a complaint that, as we will see, broadly echoes Bokenham's concerns. The action was undertaken, Cade claimed, "forto redresse and refourme the wrongis that were don in the reme, and to withstonde the malice of thayme that were destroiers of the comune profit; and forto correcte and amende the defautis of thaym that were the kyngis chief counselours; and shewde vnto thaym the articles of his peticions concernyng and touchyng the myschiefs and mysgouernaunces of the reme."²⁹ Both the commons' petition and Cade's revolt make it clear that aristocratic abuse of power, misuse of money, and misgovernance threatened not only regional interests—like those so vividly detailed in the Paston letters—but the very idea of public order and political community. History proves them right: the fissures in social structure caused by political favoritism, an ineffectual king, local alliances, and increasing factionalization would soon break into open war.

In the 1440s, the decade in which Bokenham wrote the *Legends of Holy Women*, the most visible symbol of political instability was the falling fortunes of Humphrey of Gloucester, which began with the public humiliation and trial of his unpopular wife, Eleanor Cobham, for treasonous use of witchcraft—an event to which Bokenham may allude in his St. Margaret legend. Eleanor had been a lady-in-waiting to Jacqueline of Hainault, Gloucester's first wife, whom he abandoned when his territorial ambitions in the Low Countries were thwarted by Jacqueline's imprisonment by Philip of Burgundy. Gloucester's marriage to Eleanor was widely criticized: Delany recounts the story, recorded in the annals of St. Albans, of women from London and Stokes who marched on Parliament to protest Gloucester's treatment of Jacqueline.[30] Eleanor came in for reproach as well: she was perceived as ambitious and manipulative; her birth and position made her marriage to a peer of royal blood seem a travesty. When the duke of Bedford died in 1435, Gloucester was in line to succeed Henry VI, who at fourteen had not yet married. R. A. Griffiths argues that the accusations brought against Eleanor in 1441 stemmed from the fear that she would be made queen if Gloucester acceded to the throne: she was accused of using witchcraft to divine when the king would die and her husband would assume his rule.[31] Apparently to ensure that neither Eleanor nor a child born to her would sit on the throne, her marriage to Gloucester was annulled.[32] Propelled by a concern about royal succession, Eleanor's trial must have produced yet more anxiety about it since it now seemed certain that the last of Henry V's brothers would not produce an heir. Griffiths calls the trial the "cause célèbre of the age," and he notes that it is recorded in every extant fifteenth-century chronicle.[33] The long, detailed narrative one finds in the written sources no doubt pales in comparison to oral traditions: the chronicle cited above, after its quite thorough account, adds sententiously, "Othir thyngis myghte be writen of this dame Alienore, the whiche atte reuerence of nature and of wommanhood shul not be reherced."[34]

The event was significant for Gloucester's political standing as well as his prospects for dynastic procreation. Although Eleanor was formally divorced from him, her humiliation was Gloucester's as well. The trial was itself an index of his ebbing influence in Henry VI's court. He was the most senior member of the Lancastrian family in the 1440s, the protector and adviser who had seen Henry VI through his minority, but he had rapidly lost influence as the king came to rely on new favorites, including the earl of Suffolk. Gloucester was soon further marginalized by his support for continuing the war with France, as the king's closest advisers urged him to negotiate a truce to be sealed by royal marriage to a French princess. When Bokenham began the first legend of the collection, the legend of St. Margaret, in 1443, this change in policy had recently become public knowledge. The *Chronicle of London* records the negotiations begun in 1442 and concluded the following year at which it was decided that Henry would marry the French princess Margaret and cede the duchy of Anjou and the earldom of Maine (155). Gloucester adamantly opposed ceding territory, and the public support he still enjoyed, and especially his authority in this matter as someone who participated in the war against France during its time of greatest success, made him increasingly obnoxious to the king's most influential advisers. In 1447, the year in which the manuscript of Bokenham's legends was produced, Gloucester was summoned to Bury St. Edmunds, where he was imprisoned on suspicion of treason. His sudden death five days later was probably due to natural causes, but rumors circulated widely that he had been murdered, despite a public viewing of his apparently untouched body—perhaps smothered between two featherbeds or disemboweled so that the corpse would not betray the violence. Three years later the scandal of his death was still a potent force: William Aschoghe, bishop of Salisbury, was killed by his own parishioners who accused him of "assentyng and willyng to the deth of the duke of Gloucestre."[35]

I think that there is good reason to read the first legend in Bokenham's collection, the *Life of St. Margaret*, in the context of Gloucester's fall, as I will show below. Bokenham is very likely to have followed the duke's declining fortunes with interest: he eagerly modeled his poetic identity on those of John Lydgate and John Capgrave, two clerical hagiographers who enjoyed Gloucester's patronage.[36] Moreover, Henry Bourchier, husband of one of Bokenham's most important patrons, seems to have been allied with Gloucester through his personal interest in French territories.[37] Bokenham's odd remark about Lydgate's mortality in the St. Margaret legend—that he "lyuyth yet, lest he deyed late" (418)—may well be a morbid joke about the likelihood of sudden death at Bury St. Edmunds. At the moment, however, I want to emphasize that Gloucester's personal history also stands as broadly emblematic of the fate of political community in the 1440s, a decade in which old verities were suddenly called into question as Henry VI reached his majority and the memory of Henry V's military success, and the political confidence it provided, receded with the deaths of his brothers. Gloucester's fate is symbolic in this retrospective way, as well as in the prospective one already mentioned: his death, before Henry VI produced an heir, left no Lancastrian in the line of succession. York, closely tied to Gloucester in his last years, could now imagine a claim to the throne.[38]

Outlawry

The pervasive concern about the stability of Henry VI's government, the justice administered in his name, and the dangerous vacillation of the political fortunes of figures such as York and Gloucester registers in Bokenham's representation of the social world as a place of "outlawry." This is Bokenham's distinctive metaphor for worldly existence, and it is often the theme of the extensive autobiographical passages in the text. The idea of social existence as an "outlaw" realm surfaces most insistently, and apparently innocently, in the prayers that frame the legends. Bokenham contrasts the "outlawry" of the social world to the heavenly regions occupied by the female saint. In a prayer to St. Christine, for example, he prays that all those who are devoted to her have the opportunity to repent and confess their sins "Ere thei depart from this outlaurye, / And aftyr wyth the in the heuenly regyoun / Eternally god to preyse & magnyfye" (3136–38).[39] In a prayer to St. Katherine, the opposition lies between "this wrechyd owtltaurye" (7371) and "that gloryous place" (7374) inhabited by the saint. The metaphor is used in prayers to St. Faith (4026), to Mary Magdalene (5364), to St. Cecilia (7447 and 8283), and to St. Agatha (8941). The figure surfaces most poignantly in a prayer to Elizabeth of Hungary on behalf of his patron, Elizabeth Vere, which must have taken on new significance for her after the execution of her husband and son in 1462 for their loyalty to Henry VI: "And syngulerly helpe, thorgh thi specyal grace, / I the beseche, to dwelle wyth the there / Aftyr this outlaury, dame Elyzabeth ver" (9534–36).

A prayer asking to join a saint in heaven is commonplace, as is the idea of worldly existence as a time of exile. But Bokenham's metaphor of "outlawry" is, as far as I have been able to determine, unique in Middle English devotional literature.[40] If it invokes a general allegory of postlapsarian existence, it also echoes contemporary complaints about the lack of order and respect for the law in the English countryside. The metaphor, that is, has two tenors: first, the world as an outlaw region because of its difference from heaven; and second, the more contingent outlawry of a political or social order that allows injustice and unnecessary violence. This second tenor may rely in part on a specific category of outlawry that would have been familiar to Bokenham and his first audience: anyone who failed to respond to an appeal to the King's Bench was declared an outlaw. The financial and legal consequences of this declaration were considerable: the outlaw's property was subject to forfeiture, and he was prevented from bringing cases to court.[41] In the fifteenth century the procedure was often grossly exploited: one could appeal someone in another county, where the defendant would likely remain ignorant of it, and thereby secure the fine imposed or bar him from advancing other legal suits. Bokenham's metaphor takes advantage of the semantic range of "outlawry," between exile from a (heavenly) realm and subjection to an unjust legal procedure in this one. The two meanings are conflated in the legends as well, in which the female saint finds herself in an outlaw community—at least one outside the law of Christianity. The girl's eagerness for martyrdom both expresses a categorical rejection of the world and responds to the specific political conditions under which she lives.

Bokenham first introduces the metaphor of outlawry in the autobiographical matter in the prologue to the St. Margaret legend. This is the only narrative addressed to a male readership—it is written at the request of Thomas Burgh, a fellow Augustinian and friend of Bokenham, and Bokenham imagines the Cambridge house where Burgh resides as the text's primary audience—and the one that demonstrates the instability and danger of the social world most extensively. This legend stands in marked juxtaposition to the set of twelve legends that follow, fully half of which name female patrons as their first audiences. Against his initial emphasis on the disorder of the masculine political and social world, conspicuously associated with a male readership, Bokenham in the subsequent legends presents a private devotional and domestic world, figured through and by female saints' lives and the feminine audience with which they are affiliated.

The first anecdote concerns St. Margaret's miraculous intervention in Bokenham's own life. Bokenham had once touched his ring to a relic of the saint, part of her foot bone owned by an "old pryory / of blake chanons" (136–37) not far from his birthplace. The ring proved helpful when Bokenham, traveling in Italy, encountered sudden danger:

> Not mykyl past, yerys fyue,
> Whan lytyl from venyse me dede dryue
> A cruel tyraunth in-to a fen
> Owt of a barge, and fyue mo men;
> Where I supposyd to haue myscheuyd [perished],
> Had not me the grace releuyd
> Of god, be the blyssyd medyacyoun
> Of thys virgyne, aftyr myn estimacyoun. (159–66)

The mysterious Venetian tyrant and his five men vanish (or at least stop chasing the hapless friar) once Bokenham remembers his ring, after which, he tells us, "I was releuyd ryht sone certeyn" (170). Bokenham offers this miracle, along with a general desire to increase devotion to the saint, as the impetus behind his translation of the legend. His physical contact with St. Margaret and its manifest efficacy are intended to establish the special authority of Bokenham's work, but the miracle addresses more than Bokenham's status as translator and devotee of the saint. "Tyrant" can mean any person who tries to oppress another with force, and in the context of a virgin martyr legend, it recalls the persecuting pagan officials who torment the saint. Margaret's miraculous ability to resist a tyrant, the central concern of her legend, is reproduced in Bokenham's own life. Even the location of Bokenham's adventure—somewhere in Italy—approximates the geography of traditional hagiography (though it is much closer to England and a more probable site of travel for an English friar than is Margaret's own Antioch). The miracle insists that the social structure of the virgin martyr legend still holds in broad outline: the external world is still filled with persecutors not unlike those in hagiographic narrative. It reiterates the central narrative dichotomy of the virgin martyr legend, between a chaotic social world and the serene security to which the Christian virgin has privileged access and which protects her (and those devoted to her) from violence. It suggests, that is, that the "outlawry" of pagan antiquity, the outlawry that endangered the virgin saints of the early Church, still threatens the innocent and devout even if it cannot ultimately triumph over them.

The legend that follows further glosses Bokenham's metaphor of outlawry through the saint's representation of the pagan judicial system as false and oppressive, in comparison to what she represents as the true judgment of Christianity. When Margaret turns to address the sympathetic crowd who begs her to give in to her tormentors, she warns them of the "last assyse," the "hard iugement," which will happen at the end of time, and she offers them "counsel" in order to prepare them for the trial that awaits them (599, 602, 611, 624). In a later prayer to God, she calls him "iuge," asking him to "deme ryhtfully" between herself and her tormentor, against whom she makes a formal complaint—"On hym I pleyne that hurt am y / And woundyd also ful greuously" (680, 681, 683–84)—in a heavenly court to which only she has access. From the perspective of this divine court and its proper domain, the court presided over by Olibrius—indeed, social existence itself—stands as a kind of outlawry, an arena outside of the transcendent law of Christianity. The saint appears subject to this outlawry, but only to those who persecute her. A familiar hagiographic dualism divides body and spirit just as it divides the earthly and heavenly courts. In the course of the judicial violence to which Margaret is subject, her body and her soul are represented as increasingly separate. The difference between them is mapped in narrative shifts between the external description of the physical tortures she experiences and an account of her prayer, which seems to happen altogether elsewhere: "And whil she thus ocupyed was in preyer, / The tormentours hyr shorgyd so cruelly" (575–76). Margaret's suffering body and her serene prayer inhabit separate arenas: a social space in which violence reveals the vulnerability of the body and a devotional space in which torture marks joyous union with God. The radical difference between them is stated explicitly when Margaret refuses again to follow Olibrius's law: "if I of my flesh shuld haue mercy," she declares, "My soule perysh shuld" (664–65). Margaret's suffering body—which later protects Bokenham from a different tyrant—guarantees her access to a divine judge.

Bokenham's long account of translation miracles, appended to the legend of St. Margaret, develops the theme of political instability and its converse, the miraculous statis of the female saint. This is a significant and distinctive part of Bokenham's legend. While the story of the saint's translation is a standard feature of hagiographic literature, it is not traditional in Middle English lives of St. Margaret, and Bokenham draws attention to his addition by marking it off from the rest of the legend with a nine-day vacation he requires before he is able to continue the story. The translation narrative that follows this hiatus occupies almost as many lines as does the legend proper.[42] Bokenham retains the usual argument of such narratives—the saint's continuing presence—but it is secondary to his interest in a long history of political disruption and urban decay, evidence of the transitory nature of the polis. The cities that house St. Margaret's body fall to tyrants or to civil unrest, and translation—conventionally represented as an act of devotion or divine will—is represented here rather than as an act of rescue. The enduring promise of Margaret's grace is developed against a narrative of political instability, the change of regimes, and the cultural amnesia that attends these dislocations. Bokenham first recounts the fall of Antioch, occasioned by the "dissencyoun" between the city's patriarch and its tyrannical prince (949). In a long *occupatio*, he tells us that it would be too long to explain "how gret wrong / This prynce dede, & to what myschaunce / The cyte he brouth thorgh mysgouernaunce, / And be what treytourye his sone-in-lawe, / Sinward, be nyht he brouth a-dawe" (962–66). Nor will he tell what action the prince feigned in order to pursue the patriarch or how and by what deception he drew many people to his favor (967–70). The ensuing destruction of the city prompts the abbot of the church of St. Margaret to return to his own country, Lombardy, and to take the saint's relics with him. They make it only as far as Souters, where the abbot, who has fallen ill, dies. The relics are solemnly dedicated at a convent of black monks, but after a few years this place, too, is rendered desolate by "grete werrys that sone aftyr fel / In thylk cuntre, thorgh stryf & debat / Of sundry cytees" (1186–88). The narrator makes the moral explicit: "for-as-meche as nothyng perpetuel / Is in this werd, ne stabyl in oo staat" (1184–85). The relics are moved again, this time to Ruyllyan, which is destroyed in turn and becomes a wilderness. The third translation—prompted by the saint, who appears to a hermit, John, in a vision to complain that she has been neglected—takes the relics to Mount Flask, where Bokenham, so he tells us, had copied out the source text for his translation. The story insists on the contradiction between Margaret's durable identity and the fragile political communities that house her body, a contradiction that Bokenham draws ironic attention to in the concluding prayer to the saint, in which he imagines the joy "where thou doost dwelle" (1399): though her relics are housed in earthly cities, subject to tyranny, political division, and war, Margaret dwells in heaven, free from the wild vicissitudes of social existence that still endanger her body—and Bokenham's as well.

The Fens of England and the Fens of Italy

Bokenham prefaces the legend of St. Margaret with an elaborate request for anonymity and a carefully coded representation of his identity that together define England, too, as a dangerous and unjust place. He relates how his own interest in honoring St. Margaret was strengthened by the request of his friend and fellow Augustinian Thomas Burgh for a translation of her legend. In spite of this, Bokenham claims, he "durst not hastyly assente hym to / Weel knowyng myn owyn infyrmyte / Tyl I had a whyle weel auysyd me" (184–86). He is especially concerned that his work will be badly received at Cambridge, where Burgh was in residence. David Lawton has taught us to read this sort of modesty topos as a canny response to the uncertain political situation of fifteenth-century England, a self-conscious strategy to diffuse authority in order to speak in volatile times.[43] It is an especially marked trope here: Bokenham had achieved the title of "master," an advanced academic degree that would have distinguished him among Augustinian friars.[44] His specific claim to fear reception in the Cambridge house, the environment in which the authority conferred by his academic credentials was most likely to be recognized, highlights the trope's artificiality and suggests perhaps that the claim to limited authorial control and the desire for anonymity are the consequence of specific events.

Bokenham's fears about complying with the commission are, moreover, elaborated in excess of the standard humility topos. He carefully dates the decision to undertake the translation, claiming to remember the request on the vigil of the Nativity of Mary in 1443,[45] implying a long delay during which he could not even contemplate it. He worries about those who will be "euere besy and eek diligent / To depraue priuly others trewe entent" (197–98). "Deprave" here may mean "vilify," but it can also mean "corrupt" or "misinterpret": Bokenham worries that his true devotional intent will be misread as something else, especially in the Cambridge friary, "where wyttys be manye ryht capcyows / And subtyl" (where there are many crafty and subtle wits) (208–10). He therefore asks that Burgh keep the legend private for a while and to hide the author's identity when he makes it available. Instead of naming Bokenham, Burgh should offer a riddle:

> If ye algate shul it owth lete go,
> Be not aknowe whom it comyth fro,
> But seyth, as ye doon vndyrstand,
> It was you sent owt of Ageland
> From a frend of yourys that vsyth to selle
> Goode hors at feyrys, & doth dwelle
> A lytyl fro the Castel of Bolyngbrok,
> In a good town wher ye fyrst tok
> The name of Thomas, & clepyd is Borgh
> In al that cuntre euene thorgh & thorgh;
> And thus ye shul me weel excuse,
> And make that men shul not muse
> To haue of me ony suspycyoun. (213–25)

As I mentioned above, Bokenham had close associations with the house of York,[46] but he here identifies himself with Bolingbroke Castle, a key Lancastrian property and the birthplace of Henry IV. With this association, Bokenham suggests, Thomas Burgh will "make that men shul not muse / To haue of me ony suspycyoun" (224–25). Clearly political liabilities, rather than literary ones, are at issue—the latter less likely to be resolved by disguised identity.

The political reference is difficult to read, and intentionally so. It seems to me unlikely that it is designed to obscure Yorkist sympathies: there would be no reason that Bokenham would have to disguise his affiliation with York from a Cambridge house of Augustinian friars. Richard of York had become the earl of Cambridge in 1425[47]: the Augustinians there would have no reason to be critical of Bokenham's affiliation with their own lord.[48] Indeed, in 1443 affiliation with York was not a cause for so much indirection anywhere—as noted above, the king himself was still notably generous to York. Rather it seems to point to more topical concerns. Bokenham suggests that he fears the legend's current relevance: he asks only that Burgh keep it "cloos as ye best kan / A lytyl whyle" (211–12). A cluster of references here—and the themes of the legend to follow—suggests the recent sensational trial of Eleanor Cobham for treason. The reference to Bolingbroke may point not only to the house of Lancaster but also to the cleric Roger Bolingbroke, who first identified Eleanor Cobham as a traitor and who was executed for assisting her in prophesying the king's death. Bolingbroke's name was known throughout England but would have had special significance in Cambridge, where a quarter of his body had been sent after execution (interestingly, both "Bolingbroke" and "Cambridge" are underlined in the manuscript). If the Augustinian friars in Cambridge had applied their "capcyows / And subtyl" wits to Bokenham's legend, they might have noted differences—and similarities—between St. Margaret, the most popular saintly intercessor for childbearing women, and Eleanor's most notorious associate, Margaret Jourdemain, known as the Witch of Eye. Jourdemain had testified in Eleanor's trial that she had long been in the duchess's employ, and Eleanor confessed that she had hoped to conceive a child through the intercessions of Jourdemain and the other conspirators.[49] The Witch of Eye, that is, is represented in the trial and in chronicle accounts as a kind of perverse St. Margaret, offering magical assistance to help Eleanor become a mother.

Bokenham's version of the legend gives the two Margarets a shared fate as well: state-sponsored execution as a witch. Jourdemain was burned at Smithfield after she had testified against Eleanor.[50] It is in the context of this, and the commission formed after Eleanor's trial to investigate the use of necromancy against the king, that we should read references to witchcraft in Bokenham's legend of St. Margaret. They are striking in part because they are not traditional to the story: they are not found in other Middle English versions of her legend, in the *South English Legendary* or the 1438 *Gilte Legende*, for example, nor in the widely influential *Legenda Aurea*, on which Bokenham generally relies.[51] In Bokenham's legend of St. Margaret, however, the saint's resistance to political and religious authority is labeled as witchcraft several times by her persecutors. The henchmen of the local prefect, Olibrius, flee from her "as from a wycche" (496), when they overhear her praying to Christ. A devil, who appears in her prison chamber to torment her, complains that she has killed his brother Ruffyn with "wycchecraft" (726). Most telling, Olibrius refers to her as a witch when, frustrated that she will not obey him, he orders her burned (795). The theme is not confined to this legend: it pervades Bokenham's legendary and is given particular attention in the legend of St. Agnes, in which accusations of witchcraft intersect with official fears of sedition. But the Margaret legend, with its onomastic parallel, would have especially recalled the most famous witch of the day and her role in the downfall of Eleanor Cobham and the political ruin of Gloucester.

If this is the topical allegory that Bokenham fears in the prologue, we need to ask what happened shortly after Bokenham wrote this legend that allowed it to appear under his own name some four years later. Already in 1443 there was discussion of a marriage between Henry VI and Margaret of Anjou. Bokenham may have wanted Burgh to hold the legend close until one potential queen had eclipsed the other and a witchy Margaret had been displaced in the popular imagination by a royal one.[52] Once the treaty arranging for the marriage of Margaret of Anjou was signed and became public, Bokenham's legend of her name saint would be more likely to have been read as flattery to her than as sympathy for the duchess of Gloucester. This is, admittedly, conjecture: Bokenham points to the contemporary relevance of his legend and the malicious and dangerous readings it might inspire, but that relevance is carefully coded. What is clear is that Bokenham represents his literary enterprise, like his travels in Italy, as dangerous to himself: in the current climate, he suggests, even the translation of traditional hagiography is risky.[53] The careful dating of the legends is perhaps the most subtle aspect of this representation. In the context of the rapidly shifting policies and favorites in Henry VI's court, interpretations of the text as a kind of topical allegory inevitably shift as well. Bokenham conspicuously locates his Margaret legend in 1443, signaling its potential relationship to news of Henry's engagement, not so much to limit as to register the legend's volatile topical reference. If some readers understood it as flattery to the woman who would become queen and thus as an endorsement of the king's new advisers, others might remark how this endorsement is sharply qualified by the narrator's anxiety. These readers might further note that the riddle Bokenham gives in place of his name identifies him with "Ageland," an ancient and rare place name for a district in Lincolnshire covered mostly by fenland.[54] In a political climate in which established favorites such as Gloucester can fall so precipitously, the fens of England might be just as dangerous as the tyrant-ridden fens of Venice.

It is feminine spirituality—in the form of St. Margaret's talismanic power—that rescues Bokenham from his Venetian tyrant. I want to argue that feminine spirituality—in the form of the feminine address of the subsequent legends—also protects him from the more local dangers he fears as a poet writing in mid-fifteenth-century England. As we have seen, the insistence on the dangers of the social world in the legend of St. Margaret corresponds to and is shaped by the representation of the story as part of masculine discourse, directed to a male audience. The second legend, the life of St. Anne, is a transitional text: it presents polarized representations of Joachim and Anne, of public obligation and private devotion, that link the emphasis on the disorder and divisiveness of political community in the Margaret legend to the new emphasis in the rest of the legendary on the shared devotional and literary interests that produce a feminine interpretive community. This alternative community is figured by Bokenham's female patrons—by Katherine Denston in the legend of St. Anne and ultimately by five more named women—from whom the poet need not disguise his identity. Bokenham's affiliation with a feminine audience, the careful location of his legends in a world of private devotion and domesticity, protects the legendary from the "suspycyoun" (225) he fears in the prologue to the legend of St. Margaret. That fear, however, resonates throughout the legendary, as the poet repeatedly prays for release from the outlawry of contemporary social life. Bokenham's representation of the devotional and literary activity of the feminine community addressed by female saints' lives—to which I now return—is developed against this echo of the first prologue in the collection.

Women's Literature: Procreation, Private Devotion, and Literary Production

The virgin martyr legends that occupy most of Bokenham's legendary generally begin with a threat to the saint's chastity; the legend of St. Anne begins instead with the threat of childlessness.[55] Her husband Joachim abandons her after being expelled from the temple because of his barren marriage. This is the narrative crisis, and like the crisis in virgin martyr legends, it is the context for Anne's declaration of her religious devotion. Here, however, that declaration occurs in a private lament for her barren and broken marriage, not in the public rebuff of an unwelcome suitor or a hostile judge. Anne's trials are far less violent than those of the virgin martyr, but they are—perhaps for that reason—represented with much greater emotional depth. In place of the confident prayer and triumphant faith of the virgin saint, Anne struggles to resign herself to God's will. Remarking that God has punished her twice, first by making her childless and then by taking away her husband, she at first oscillates between earnestly seeking to reconcile herself to God's will and mildly reproving his inscrutable behavior. When she sees a sparrow feeding its young, she begins her prayer again in a more desperate accent:

> O lorde almyhte, whiche hast ouere al
> Souerente, & to euere creature,
> Fyssh, ful & bestis, bothe more & smal,
> Hast grauntyd be kyndly engenderrure
> To ioyen in the lykenesse of ther nature,
> And in ther issue, iche aftyr his kynde,
> To worshyp of thy name wyth-owten ende!
> And I thank the lorde, that thu to me
> Hast don as it is to thy plesaunce,
> Fro the yefte of thy benygnyte
> Me excludynge, swych is my chaunce.
> Yet if yt the had lykede me to avaunce

> Wyth sone or dowgter, in humble wyse
> I wolde it han offrede to thy seruyse. (1763–76)

Anne here submits her will to God's, but her prayer reveals a heavy emotional cost. Seeing the sparrow with its young, Anne is at once reminded of the goodness of God and her own exclusion from taking joy 'in the likeness of her nature.' Although she thanks God for doing with her as he will, she remembers that his will is to keep from her 'the gift of his benignity.' The line break separating her acknowledgment of that gift and her exclusion from it is especially poignant, its emotional weight registering in the lapse from the elevated rhetoric of prayer to the more colloquial, "swych is my chaunce." The line expresses at once Anne's comfortless resignation to divine will and a quiet reproach against its arbitrariness. This passage, with its compelling psychological portrait, is the emotional and narrative center of the legend, the personal trial that, like the trial of the virgin martyr, merits special reward. St. Anne's prayer is thus immediately answered with an angelic message announcing the conception of a child who will be held in reverence and honor until the "werdys ende" (1790). The miracle promises to resolve at once Anne's personal crisis of faith, the domestic drama of Joachim's absence, and the public humiliation of childlessness. Bewildered and grateful, Anne remains in prayer for a day and a night, fasting and denying herself all bodily comforts.

Anne's deeply felt devotion stands in sharp contrast to Joachim's. His participation in the religious life of the family is restricted to his public role at the temple, and when that is compromised by his childlessness, Joachim withdraws from his wife and the wider community. As is traditional to the story, Joachim retreats to the fields where his flocks graze, but in Bokenham's version this represents spiritual as well as social isolation. Anne's prayer, with its difficult attempt to resign her will to God's, differs markedly from the arrogance and self-pity with which Joachim details his grievances, his disappointment at remaining childless and the humiliation of being refused at the temple. Even after an angel commands Joachim to return to Anne, explaining that they have been granted a child, Joachim seems unaffected by the revelation, unable to understand its import for himself or for humanity, and he fails to do as the angel bids him. His servants encourage him to return without delay, but Joachim—absurdly indecisive given the angelic command—still ponders "what best was to do" (1932). Only after the angel appears to him in his sleep once again and reiterates that Joachim must return to Anne "in hasty wyse" does Joachim at last obey (1941).

Joachim remains as emotionally removed from the miracle announced by the angel as he is from the anguished devotion through which Anne merited it. So at the conclusion of the narrative, as the three-year-old Mary ascends the temple steps, leaving her parents for a life dedicated to God, Anne alone prays in thanksgiving for her daughter. Her prayer, a paradoxical meditation on the singularity of her experience and its repercussions for humankind, leaves Joachim out altogether:

> And not only from shameful bareynesse
> I am delyuerde thus singulerly,
> But eke hys peple which was in dystresse
> He hathe vystyted so marcyfully,
> That thoroghe my fruht, lord, gramercy,
> Not I alone but al mankynde
> Shal comforth fynde wyth-owten ende. (2057–63)

The legend establishes distinct spheres for Anne and Joachim, a space of private, domestic devotion and a space for the public practice of religion, and even the final image of their farewell to their daughter does not collapse these. Although they both stand at the foot of the temple steps, Anne's devotion is still represented primarily through private prayer and Joachim's is still represented through his presence in public ritual. If this is a familiar binary, gendered in the expected way, Bokenham revalues its terms: the legend makes an implicit case for private space as the proper, and most efficacious, place of devotion. Public ritual is associated here—in a concatenation of anti-Jewish stereotypes—with Joachim's inability to comprehend the divine revelation that he receives when alone or its meaning for mankind.

The prologue and prayer that frame the legend similarly stage the devotional activity of women—here, the devout patronage of religious narrative—as private and separate. Bokenham uses the exemplary relationship linking the saint and the female audience to present women's patronage as an imitation of the saint's own devout language. As we learn in the closing prayer, Katherine Denston asked for the legend in order to secure St. Anne's help in conceiving a son, just as Anne's own fervent prayer issued in the conception of her child. Like St. Anne, Katherine Denston acts largely alone in her devotion: in the prologue she is represented as independently responsible for the production of the legend. Moreover, Katherine's role, like St. Anne's, is figured by prayer: her prayer to the Virgin is to earn Bokenham the "specyal grace" necessary to its composition (1465–80; Denston is named at 1466).[56] Katherine's husband John is mentioned, but only at the end of legend, when Bokenham prays that the couple will be granted a son (2092–98). He is necessarily included in the prayer for conception but, like Joachim, not in the devotional acts—Katherine's patronage of the legend and her prayer to the Virgin for its successful completion—meant to secure it.

As I argued in Chapter 1, *imitatio* implies a certain cultural continuity: it depends on the assumption that a specific practice can be reproduced in another historical moment, that the social context of that action has not altered so much as to change its value or render it meaningless. Bokenham's representation of Katherine Denston's patronage as a kind of imitation of St. Anne should be understood from this perspective. Following the elaborate representation of the variability of the political world at the end of the St. Margaret legend, the continuity of feminine desires and devotions that link St. Anne and Katherine Denston marks them as outside of history, as an alternative to the instability of the political sphere. We will see in the next chapter that the exclusion of the female saint from history enables some hagiographers to use her as a model for national identity. Enjoined to imitate the saint, the feminine audience can perform—or reproduce—the identity she embodies through their ethical practice. When hagiographers such as Henry Bradshaw turn their attention to English saints, this performance guarantees the continuity of national community. In Bokenham's legendary, the exemplary relation between saint and patron figures the continuity of feminine devotional practice more generally. Private devotion, domestic space, the production of religious language, and procreative work join St. Anne and Katherine Denston in a stable feminine community, unbound by historical or geographical location and sharply contrasted to the unstable and outlaw regions of the masculine world of politics and social life, symbolized in this legend by the wilderness in which Joachim wanders.

The prolocutory to the legend of Mary Magdalene extends the association between procreativity and literary production inaugurated in the legend of St. Anne, as well as the importance of this association to Bokenham's fantasy of feminine community. We have already seen that the prolocutory presents Bokenham's most direct and elaborate account of women's patronage and the interpretive community that creates, and is created by, a canon of female saints' lives. In tracing how the prolocutory also reiterates some of the themes of the St. Anne legend, we can see better how the relationship between patronage and motherhood in Bokenham's legendary constructs a specifically feminine literary tradition that forms the ground of this community. But, as we will see, the Magdalene legend also complicates the matter, since the identification of Isabel Bourchier's commission with a domestic space and a maternal role distances it from the model Mary Magdalene provides of public preaching, which is closely associated with her renunciation of active sexuality. If the Magdalene prolocutory elaborates the image of synchronic community by developing a poetics of literary procreativity and feminine devotion, it also unsettles the image of a diachronic community, defined by the exemplary relationship between the saint and the woman devoted to her, so carefully constructed in the legend of St. Anne.

The Magdalene prolocutory establishes a gendered difference between procreativity and political pedigree through the different implications of family history for Isabel Bourchier and her brother Richard of York. After an astrological introduction, Bokenham recounts Richard's ancestry, which is also his patron's since Isabel "Hys sustyr is in egal degre" (5008). Genealogy means something quite different for Isabel and for Richard, however, as two notably awkward passages suggest: first, Isabel, duchess of York, is said to be Isabel Bourchier's "fadrys graunhtdam" (5010), a phrase that means here not her great-grandmother but her paternal grandmother; and, second, her sister, Constance, is said to have died barren—in Bokenham's conspicuously emphatic phrase she "yssud noht / But deyid baren" (5014–15). The latter has baffled scholars since Constance did not, in fact, die barren: she and John of Gaunt had two children—John, who died in childhood, and Catherine, who survived. Both locutions, however, reveal Bokenham's partisan interpretation of a political issue. As early as 1412 Edward of York had claimed a right to the Castilian throne on the grounds that Constance did not produce a living male heir.[57] His claim seems to have been made specifically with his nephew Richard's prospects in mind: Edward proposed that Richard marry an Aragonian princess. This argument is the likely source of Bokenham's mistake: it is either a garbled or a very careful version of the Yorkist position on the Castilian crown, one which would be repeated in clearer terms by other Yorkist writers a decade later.[58] At the time of the poem's composition, Richard was already actively pursuing this claim.[59] Hence Bokenham's careful reference to Isabel of York as Richard's paternal grandmother: his right comes from a male heir. It is a useful reminder that the Yorkist insistence that succession could be transmitted through the female line was a political expedient, not a broad social vision. Like the Lancastrians, who based their claim to the English throne on the exclusive legitimacy of male succession even as their claim to France rested on female succession, so Yorkists tailored theories of legitimate political inheritance to fit particular claims.

If the genealogy speaks to Richard's political ambitions, it also speaks to Isabel Bourchier's fertility. Pictured with four of her own sons dancing around her, Isabel is represented as the proper heir to her grandmother's procreativity. Like Isabel of York, she provides male heirs to an aristocratic lineage that Bokenham represents as directly relevant only to masculine political interest. The presentation of Richard's genealogy, that is, efficiently intertwines masculine politics and feminine procreativity, even as it effectively positions Isabel outside of the political dynamic that has been invoked in order to define who she is.

In gendering politics as masculine and procreativity as feminine, Bokenham is hardly innovative, of course. What is interesting about his use of these categories is that it subtends his presentation of motherhood as a warrant for women's participation in literary production, which is represented throughout the legendary in terms of the private, devotional, and domestic. Bokenham highlights this with a telling metaphor that distinguishes feminine devotional literature from masculine—specifically secular—traditions, which he repeatedly dismisses. He compares the colorful clothing worn by Isabel's children to the colors of rhetoric:

> I saye, whyl this ladyis foure sonys ying
> Besy were wyth reuel & wyth daunsyng,
> And othere mo in there most fressh aray
> Dysgysyd, for in the moneth of may
> Was neuyr with flouris whyt, blewe & grene,
> Medewe motleyid freshlyere, I wene,
> Than were her garnementys; for as it semyd me
> Mynerue hyr-self, wych hath the souereynte
> Of gay texture, as declaryth Ouyde,

Wyth al hire wyt ne coude prouyde
More goodly aray thow she dede enclos
Wyth-ynne oo web al methamorphosyos. (5023–34)

Minerva is imagined as his patron's rival, incapable of providing "more goodly array" than Isabel does even if the goddess could spin a textile representing all of the *Metamorphoses*. This rivalry stands in for another, of course: the audacious, if only implicit, claim is that Ovid's poetic colors cannot equal Bokenham's. This literary contest is displaced onto Isabel and Minerva in a fantasy of a feminine competition over the capacity for figuration that parallels the agonistic relationship between Bokenham and his poetic predecessors. The conceit specifically recalls other passages in the legendary in which Bokenham dismisses conventional rhetorical tropes and the work of other writers. So in the prologue that prefaces the Margaret legend and the book as a whole, Bokenham declares:

The forme of procedyng artificyal
Is in no wyse ner poetycal
After the scole of the crafty clerk
Galfryd of ynglond, in his newe werk,
Entytlyd thus, as I can aspye,
Galfridus anglicus, in hys newe poetrye,
Enbelshyd wyth colours of rethoryk
So plenteuously, that fully it lyk
In May was neuere no medewe sene
Motleyd wyth flours on hys verdure grene. (83–92)

The description of the children's clothing in the Magdalene prolocutory echoes—and displaces—the rhetoric tradition represented by Geoffrey of Vinsauf's *Poetria Nova*, which is invoked only to be summarily dismissed: "But for-as-meche as I neuere dede muse / In thylk crafty werk, I it now refuse" (97–98).[60] In the metaphors that link Isabel's children with poetic and rhetorical tradition, Bokenham identifies an alternative source for the color of his own rhetoric by associating his writing with his patrons' procreativity. Of course, like any metaphor, this one works both to affiliate two terms and to distinguish them: his poetry might parallel the procreativity of his female patron, but Isabel's proper role is as mother to her motley children.[61]

The representation of patronage as maternal must be seen, at least in part, as an attempt to supplant the model that the legend provides of a woman's unmediated public voice. Isabel Bourchier announces her "synguler deuocyoun / To that holy wumman, wych, as I gesse, / Is clepyd of apostyls the apostyllesse" (5066–68): she is interested in Mary Magdalene not as humble penitent but as public preacher, with authority even over Jesus' chosen apostles. Bokenham here stages the problem of exemplarity traced in Chapter 1: the fact that vernacular legends do not offer easy models for late medieval devotional practice, despite the rhetoric of *imitatio* that insisted that women take them as examples. The rest of the legendary—with the exception of the final legend, the life of Elizabeth of Hungary—presents virgin martyrs who, like Mary Magdalene, assume a very public voice, proclaiming their faith and preaching to the hostile pagan communities in which they live. For Bokenham's readers to imitate central aspects of these legends—the Magdalene's preaching or St. Katherine's theological debate, St. Christine's rejection of her father's authority or St. Cecilia's rejection of her husband's sexual advances—would violate basic social norms.

As we have seen, exemplarity in Bokenham's legendary serves not only to identify the saints as a moral template and authority for women's religious practice but also to establish a feminine community defined by the shared devotional practices that link ancient saints to contemporary women. The fact that the saints present such inappropriate models presents a significant challenge to this fantasy of a static, transhistorical community of women. In the next section I argue that Bokenham responds to this challenge by constructing a new exemplary relationship around the category of literary production. He figures his female saints as muses, whose role in the creation of the text is a model for that of his patrons. Through the trope of the saintly muse, literary production is made the ground of a diachronic feminine devotional community, just as—through the proper names of Bokenham's patrons—it is figured as the ground of a synchronic one.

Saintly Muses

Bokenham's extraordinary references to his literary patrons are echoed in another distinctive feature of his work: his references to the saints as agents of poetic production. Imagined as Christian analogs to classical muses, the saints provide a mystified authority for his legendary that elaborates the identification of the text as "women's literature," gendered through the process of production as well as reception.[62] Bokenham, for example, prays to St. Margaret:

> and specyally
> Vouchesaf of thy singuler grace, lady,
> My wyt and my penne so to enlumyne
> Wyth kunnyng and eloquence that suffycyently
> Thy legende begunne I may termyne. (332–36)

Calling upon Margaret to assist in the composition of her own legend, Bokenham identifies the saint as a poetic, as well as a spiritual, intercessor. He similarly asks St. Katherine to help him in both "wurd & werk" as he undertakes the translation of her legend (6343). After remarking the danger of "prolyxyte, / Wych oftyn of heryng causyth werynesse" (4089–90), he prays with wry self-consciousness to St. Agnes to help him make an end: "Me wyt purchase, lady, & language / Thy lyf begunne wyth to termyne" (4097–98).[63] The figure of the saint as a muse draws on the saint's capacity for salvific language, demonstrated in the legend through her public profession of faith. But it also provides a alternative to this public voice, one in which the male clerical author is the necessary medium of the saint's language. Rather than speaking openly in the pagan court or the city square, the virgin martyr now inspires the poet, who speaks for her. Bokenham, that is, circumscribes the dangerous or impossible model for women's verbal agency precisely by celebrating it.

His invocation of virgin martyrs as muses thus reestablishes their exemplarity for Bokenham's female patrons. He makes this exemplary relation explicit in the prologue to the legend of St. Agatha, in which the narrator prays that the saint's ability to facilitate language be extended to the legend's patron, Agatha Flegge. The saint's access to "perfect" language is explained in the etymology that Bokenham, following Jacobus de Voragine, offers for her name:

> of "aga," wych "spekyng,"
> And "Thau," wych betoknyth "endyng,"
> Thys wurd "Agatha" seyd ys, quod he;

> And wurthyly, for pleynly she
> Fyrst & last in hyr spekeyng
> Perfyht was, as shewyth hyr answeryng. (8305–10)

Having answered her tormentors so perfectly, St. Agatha is a source of verbal authority, which Bokenham calls upon in asking the saint to do her "besy cure" to guarantee that those who love and worship her "haue in speche swych perfeccyoun / That alle here wurdys mow sowe uertu" (8332–33).[64] Most prominent among her devotees is Agatha Flegge, named seven lines later when Bokenham asks that the saint "specyally . . . attende" to her (8339–40). The saint's ability to "perfect" the language of others is confirmed by Flegge's commission of this very text, which will in turn "sow virtue." The doubling of muse and patron is further developed in the prayer to Mary in the legend of St. Anne, discussed briefly above. Bokenham calls on Katherine Denston to pray to Mary to inspire him and to guarantee the "leyser & spaas" necessary for him to finish the legend of her mother, St. Anne:

> I wyl not blynne,
> For your sake, my frende Denston Kateryne,
> Lyche as I can this story to begynne,
> If grace my penne vochesaf to illumyne,
> Preyth ye enterly that blyssed virgyne,
> Whiche of seynt anne the dowter was,
> That she vouchesaf som beem lat shyne
> Vp-on me of hyr specyal grace,
> And that I may haue leyser & spaas,
> Thorgh help of influence dyuyne,
> To oure bothe confort & solace
> This legende begunne for to termyn. (1465–76)

The hagiographer's access to divine "grace" in the composition of his legend depends here on both his female patron and the saintly muse whose attentions she secures. The saint in turn supplies not only inspiration to the poet but also precedent and authority for the patron's role in the production of devotional literature. The trope allows Bokenham to celebrate his patrons as agents of the work—the "cause princypal," as Bokenham calls Isabel Bourchier—even as their literary interests are mediated by a clerical author: like muses, they speak through Bokenham.

The parallels between Bokenham's saints, imagined as muses, and his patrons provides the exemplary relationship linking past and present on which the legendary's fantasy of a transhistorical feminine community depends. This community, defined by shared devotional practice and literary interest, serves—as we have seen—as a kind of bulwark against the variability and violence of the social world. Bokenham's interest in constructing an exemplary relation between his patrons and the saints to whom they are devoted is, I would argue, less to regulate women's literary and devotional activity than to imagine a stable community that contrasts with the unstable political community of mid-fifteenth-century England as it is evoked in the collection's first legend. It is for this reason, I think, that the ethical imperative in the legendary—as figured by his patrons' imitation of the saints—is literary production, the creation of a devotional text produced by and constitutive of a feminine community. Importantly, Bokenham imagines his patrons imitating not only the muse-like saints but also one another: as we have seen, Bokenham represents Isabel Bourchier's commission as an imitation of Elizabeth Vere's. The ethics of the legendary, as defined by the exemplary relationships between the saint and the patron and between one patron and another, is to produce saints' lives that form the basis for a feminine community that elides synchronic and diachronic differences.

I would like to emphasize that the feminine community constructed in the *Legends of Holy Women* does not always or only refer outside of, or beyond, itself to the contemporary political world, even though it is defined in opposition to that world. Gender is not merely an allegory for a more consequential political concern in Bokenham's collection. Here it may be useful briefly to contrast Bokenham to John Capgrave, a fellow Augustinian, whose legend of St. Katherine was known to Bokenham. As Karen Winstead has demonstrated, Capgrave's *Katherine* offers a pointed topical allegory exploring the relationship between religion and politics, specifically the danger that a devout ruler such as Henry VI might inadvertently pose to his people.[65] Capgrave uses the saint's sex as a veil that allows him to offer a mirror for princes and to comment on the practices of the reigning sovereign. Bokenham, too, uses female saints' lives to comment on the social world. He constructs a feminine literary tradition, characterized by its domestic and devotional aspects, as the ground of his own public voice and literary authority, a position from which to address the divisiveness of political life in fifteenth-century England. But Bokenham refuses the kind of allegorical use of female saints' lives that we see in Capgrave. He offers a feminine textual tradition as an alternative to—not an allegory for—a masculine political arena. Defined against this arena, this devotional tradition is, as Bokenham represents it, nevertheless an expression of a specifically gendered sanctity and a specifically gendered literary authority. As we have seen, his legendary founds women's patronage on the saint's salvific language—both the saint's speech in the story and her role as its muse—and it associates feminine devotional community with groups of women that form around the saint in the legends, as well as with historical women joined by their interest in female saints' lives. While Bokenham's representation of feminine devotion echoes other attempts to restrict women's activity to arenas carefully controlled by male clerics, this is presented in the legendary as a response not to the threat that women pose *to* the social order but to the threat posed *by* that order itself.

4

Exemplarity and England in Native Saints' Lives

LIKE OSBERN BOKENHAM, Henry Bradshaw uses the feminine audience addressed by vernacular legends to figure a stable community, in contrast to the divided political community of fifteenth-century England. His long verse *Life of St. Werburge*, written at the end of the century after the dynastic crisis had been resolved, is, however, less concerned than Bokenham's collection is with imagining a contemporary community of women whose shared devotional interests transcend differences of lineage and political affiliation.[1] In the wake of that crisis, the poem is concerned instead to represent the transhistorical continuity and coherence of English identity, and it does so through the exemplary relationship linking a native saint and contemporary women. Bradshaw represents the patron saint of his own abbey, a seventh-century Mercian princess and abbess, as a figure for the continuity of English community, most conspicuously in the miraculous preservation of her body, which remains intact for hundreds of years. When it disintegrates during the Danish invasions—to protect it from infidel hands—Werburge's body no longer just symbolizes the integrity of the community she represents: she actively protects it, warding off invasion by "innumerable barbarike nacions" (2. 758). But Werburge's ability to guarantee cultural continuity also depends on her exemplarity and on the ability of the legend's contemporary feminine audience to reproduce her example. Enjoined to imitate the saint, they too are made responsible for the continuity of English devotional identity and the religious community it defines.

The nature of that community will be one of the central concerns of this chapter. Werburge is, on the one hand, a regional saint, probably not well known outside of Cheshire. When she wards off attack, it is the walls of Chester that she makes impregnable. Part of Bradshaw's purpose in composing the legend, moreover, is to insist on the privileges of his monastery, the Benedictine abbey of St. Werburge, which were challenged throughout the late fifteenth century as misrule and scandal plagued the house. The legend, then, has specific local institutional and regional concerns.[2] But Chester is a border town, and Werburge's talismanic force thus protects the boundaries of England too. The legend oscillates throughout between a local focus and a national one, as we will see, in a way that represents Chester as a metonym for England itself.[3] Certainly it was read that way by Richard Pynson, the king's printer, who published the legend in 1521 for a metropolitan audience. If the printing of the text makes it a national text in its material circumstance, this is facilitated by its ethical address to contemporary women, an audience that significantly extends the local reference of the legend.

Before proceeding I would like to clarify my use of the term "nation." Early modern scholars, most influentially Richard Helgerson, have argued for the validity of using "nation" to address the interest in English cultural identity in the sixteenth century, despite important arguments for the advent of the nation and of nationalism in the nineteenth century.[4] My goal here is not to claim that late medieval hagiography fully anticipates early modern "forms of nationhood": the discourses of national community and the political and cultural practices with which they are affiliated in the two periods are distinguished by significant differences. But as recent work has shown, the idea of the English nation was already an active concern in the late Middle Ages.[5] Vernacular legends of native saints such as Bradshaw's *St. Werburge* take up this concern by imagining a transhistorical national community that finds its origin in England's early Christian history. Like other native saints' lives, Bradshaw's legend develops an idea of Englishness that is not limited to and does not depend on dynasty: by turning to the saintly past of England before the Norman Conquest, it imagines an English Christian identity that bypasses the crisis in dynastic authority and lineage of fifteenth-century England and creates an idea of Englishness independent of the legitimacy of the current monarch. The legend thus creates an "imagined community" of national identity that transcends current political configurations.[6] This community shares some features with the modern nation, as described in Benedict Anderson's influential formulation: the nation in the legend of St. Werburge is a community larger than any one person's acquaintance, understood as "the expression of an historical tradition of serial continuity"

(195). Unlike Anderson's modern nation, however, it is a specifically religious community,[7] and it is imagined through the legend's exemplary address: hagiographic *imitatio*, linking Werburge's sanctity to the devotion of late medieval women, simultaneously constructs a transhistorical national identity and a synchronic community of English women.

One of the most striking aspects of Bradshaw's use of the exemplary relationship between saint and audience is how it parallels Homi Bhabha's analysis of the representation of the nation as a temporal process in "Dissemination." The idea of the nation, Bhabha argues, is split between two temporal perspectives: the "pedagogical" and the "performative." The first represents "the pre-given or constituted historical origin *in the past*"; the second represents cultural practice "as that sign of the *present* through which national life is redeemed and iterated as a reproductive process."[8] So Englishness in vernacular legends of native saints depends on both the monumental embodiment of national identity figured by Anglo-Saxon saints and the iterability of this identity in the devotional practice of late medieval audiences. Bhabha's paradigm gives us a way to read Bradshaw's use of the ethical address of vernacular lives of female saints in terms of community formation. The legend's elaborate representation of a contemporary female audience and its exhortation to that audience to imitate the saint presents a vivid image of the "vigorous contemporary expression" of community identity, an important supplement to the mystified way in which the body of St. Werburge represents England.

In its presentation of Werburge as a guarantee of English identity and its extended address to a contemporary feminine audience, Bradshaw's legend is unique. But it participates in an important but overlooked trend in Middle English hagiography: a growing fascination with native saints. The *South English Legendary*, compiled in the late thirteenth century, originally devoted less than a quarter of its sanctorale texts to native saints.[9] The number increases substantially, however, in some later manuscripts: so, for example, British Library MS Egerton 1993 adds seven native saints to the few who had been represented in the earlier versions of the collection.[10] English saints' lives are also added to some manuscripts of the fifteenth-century *Gilte Legende*,[11] as well as to some late medieval English manuscripts of the *Legenda Aurea*: the text in London, Westminster Abbey Chapter Library MS XII, adds Chad, Cuthbert, Dunstan, Austin, Mildred, Kenelm, Sampson, Sabina, Frideswide, Edmund Rich, Hugh, and Edmund the King.[12] A manuscript of John Mirk's *Festial*, a collection of saints' legends for liturgical use on feast days, is supplemented with a series of native saints and a legend of Katherine of Alexandria, discussed below, that links her lineage to Britain.[13]

More striking is the emergence of national identity as a formal or organizational category for manuscript collections. This happens first in Latin hagiography: British Library MS Lansdowne 436, associated with Romsey, a house of Benedictine nuns, comprises forty-seven English saints' lives prefaced by a short chronicle of the kings of England from Hengst to Egbert.[14] The *Sanctilogium Angliae, Walliae, Scotiae et Hiberniae*, compiled by John of Tynemouth toward the end of the century, is a more influential example, with Latin and vernacular descendents.[15] It is a primary source for the *De sanctis Anglie* and the *Nova Legenda Anglie*; the latter (wrongly ascribed to Capgrave)[16] is the basis for the *Kalendre of the Newe Legende of Englande* printed in 1516 by Richard Pynson, who—as we will see—had a particular interest in nationalist hagiography. With 168 legends of native saints, the *Kalendre* is the largest medieval legendary in English organized by national affiliation.[17] It was probably not the first vernacular collection of native saints, however: as I argued in the last chapter, Osbern Bokenham had translated a series of Anglo-Saxon saints' lives, for which his *Mappula Angliae* was to serve as a companion text.

Independent legends of native saints—often in long, detailed narrative versions—also proliferate in the fifteenth century. John Lydgate wrote lives of Sts. Edmund and Fremund; Sts. Alban and Amphibalus; St. Augustine of Canterbury; and St. George. The legend of Wulfric of Haselbury in British Library MS Harley 2251 was once attributed to him as well. Other anonymous legends include those of St. Edith of Wilton and St. Etheldreda found in British Library MS Cotton Faustina B iii (c. 1420).[18] A prose legend of St. Ursula survives in Huntington MS 140,[19] and one of Edward the Confessor is found in Oxford Trinity 11. Several new Middle English legends of Thomas Becket appeared in the fifteenth century. Capgrave wrote an English life of Gilbert of Sempringham, and Barclay translated a life of St. George.

The vernacular corpus tilts still more strongly in the direction of native saints' lives in the age of printing. While the manuscript tradition favors widely venerated saints such as St. Margaret of Antioch and St. Katherine of Alexandria,[20] early books favor English saints, some of whom—like St. Werburge—must have been entirely unknown to much of their new audience.[21] Caxton printed the *Lyf of the Holy and Blessid Saynt*

Wenefryde in 1485 and the pseudo-Capgrave *Nova Legenda Anglie* in 1500. Lydgate's *Life of St. Alban and Amphibalus* was published by J. Herford in 1530. Wynkyn de Worde printed the *Lyf of Saynt Ursula* (undated), the *Lyfe of Saynt Brandon* (1520?), and the *Lyfe of Saynt Edwarde Confessour and Kynge of Englande* (1523). Pynson printed Alexander Barclay's *St. George* (1515) and a legend of St. Thomas Becket (1520?), in addition to the encyclopedic *Kalendre of the New Legende of England* (1516) and Bradshaw's *St. Werburge* (1521).[22] The corpus of early printed hagiography—including Bradshaw's legend—is part of a larger project by Pynson and other earlier printers to establish a canon of native saints, a project that drew on a fascination with a specifically English sanctity that had already surfaced in the manuscript tradition.

The exemplarity of female saints' lives may have made their national affiliation all the more important: such is suggested, at least, by the convoluted genealogy constructed for St. Katherine of Alexandria in fifteenth-century prose versions of her legend. In some late Middle English legends, St. Katherine is identified as the stepgranddaughter of St. Helen, who was known in the fifteenth century not only as the mother of Constantine but also as a British princess. The convoluted history and genealogy linking Katherine and Helen in the prose legends unfold as follows: a Roman general named Constantius is sent to Armenia to quell a rebellion and is married to a local princess; their son, Costus, is Katherine's father;[23] after the death of his wife Constantius is sent to Britain, again in response to political unrest, and he there marries Helen and begets Constantine. Through this elaborate history, St. Katherine is associated with Britain, by marriage if not by blood, through a Roman imperial paradigm that is—in the person of Constantine—ultimately identified as British. The legend sums up the significance of this history by insisting on Katherine's affiliation with both the empire and Britain: "Whiche holy maydon, as ye may her and vndyrstond, was of the noble kynred of themperour Constantyne, and of the nacyon of Brytayne the mor."[24]

The unlikely genealogy transforming Katherine of Alexandria into a British saint prefaces three different prose versions of the legend, which together have seventeen manuscript witnesses.[25] Its wide diffusion testifies to the expectation that the saint's English affiliations are salient to the audience and to the spiritual ideal she represents. Made part of English history, St. Katherine becomes a model not only for devotional practice but for national identity as well. Her exemplarity is addressed explicitly in one version of the prose legend that begins with her British genealogy. The "d" version, represented by Harvard University Library, Richardson MS 44, concludes with a direct statement of how the saint should be imitated by two distinct audiences, virginal women and all Christians, a passage discussed in Chapter 1. St. Katherine is identified as a model for all, but the audience is encouraged to remember its own identity in interpreting and imitating that model. By specifying the divergent responses expected of virgins and all other Christians, the text signals its concern with the way that exemplarity is framed by contemporary social categories—including, as the prominent account of Katherine's British connections suggests, national affiliation. The legend, that is, constructs St. Katherine as British in order to construct national identity as part of devotional practice.

The female body can ground social categories and national identities because medieval understandings of female sexuality conflate physiological and ethical status by assigning moral significance to physical integrity. In Bradshaw's legend, this is elaborated in the concatenation of the physical wholeness of Werburge's virginal body, its incorruptibility in the grave, and its talismanic powers to ward off the threatened invasions from external forces, such as the Danes, and more proximate ones, such as the Welsh. But this is not, as we might expect, based on a facile equation of the saint's intact body and the integrity of national identity. Indeed, Werburge's body disintegrates during the Danish invasions to protect it from infidel hands. Rather, Bradshaw recognizes virginity—understood as both a social practice and a spiritual identity—as an enabling *metaphor* for national identity, which he represents as both manifest in history and transcending it. That is, to return to Bhabha's terms, virginity in Bradshaw's legend is, like nationalism, both pedagogical and performative, both transcendent essence and ethical practice. The legend illustrates how the fantastic representation of the female body becomes at once a monumental symbol of a national past and the basis for ethical behavior that is represented as part of contemporary national identity—a concern still relevant to modern nationalisms in which feminine virtue is seen as part of cultural identity and transgression against sexual morality, in particular, is seen as an affront to national community.

Bradshaw establishes St. Werburge as both a physical and a transcendent embodiment of national identity by representing her both as outside of English history and as exemplary of it, as I argue in the next section of the chapter. The vacillation constructs England as paradoxically historical and ahistorical, at once subject to the contingencies of history and yet persisting in spite of them. As we will see in the subsequent section of the chapter, the shifting nature of national identity has implications not only for the status of the saint but also for that of the feminine audience enjoined to imitate her, whose ethical practice is crucial to the continuity of national identity.

England Embodied: History and Genealogy in the *Life of St. Werburge*

Bradshaw's legend begins with a theoretical prologue that contrasts the instability and contingency of human history with the ahistorical and transcendent identity of St. Werburge. The first is a devotional and philosophical commonplace in the Middle Ages, and Bradshaw introduces it here as the rationale for undertaking the translation:

> I called vnto mynde / the great vnstedfastnes
> Of this wretched worlde—/ not by cours of nature—
> How there be brought / some men to busynes,
> Oppressed with pouerte / langour / and dyspleasure,
> Some other exalted / to felycyte and pleasure. (1. 8–12)

The unsteadfastness of the world is not natural, for nature itself is steadfast in its obedience to God: the firmament, the sun and moon, with all the planets and stars "kepe theyr cours / bothe to and fro" (1. 18); so, too, the four elements "obseruen theyr duty" (1. 24). Even the birds demonstrate a faithful and obedient stability. Human existence alone is marked by variability—a consequence of original disobedience and cause of the enormous variation of late medieval social practice:

> Dyuers people / haue dyuers condicions:
> Comynly proued / it is euery day:
> Some set to vertu / and good disposycyons,
> In penaunce / prayer / all that they may,
> Some in contemplacyon / the sothe to say,

Some in abstynence / to chastyce the body
And make it subget / to the soule perfytely;

Some other reioyce / in synne and ydelnes,
Some seruauntes to Venus / both day and nyght,
Other to couetyse / and worldly besynes,
Some to deceyue / by subtylte in syght,
Some vnto marchandyse / & wynnynge full ryght,
Some ferefull and tymerous / without audacyte,
Some sadde and sobre / and of great grauyte. (1.36–49)

Bradshaw's catalog goes on for another stanza, listing ribald speech, brawling and martial activity, flattery, blasphemy, backbiting, extortion, and robbery, before he returns to his larger argument that "after fraylte and sundry compleccyons / Dyuers men dyuers in lyuynge there be" (1.57–58). Bradshaw here associates a Boethian insistence on the instability of human life, which vacillates "Now in great langour / now in prosperyte" (1.68), with diversity in social condition and ethical practice. He speaks of the "mutabylyte" not only of fortune, but also of "worldly people" who are engaged in such a bewildering array of activity, from the devout to the criminal (1.65–66). By associating worldly mutability with social diversity, Bradshaw suggests a close relation between the larger forces of history in a Boethian cosmos and individual ethical choice and social practice, a relation that extends the usual role of exemplarity in historical narrative. Here individual action is not simply the cause of historical change; nor is historical narrative valuable as a storehouse of ethical exempla. Instead historical change is *the same as* the diversity of social practice; they are diachronic and synchronic manifestations of the same mutability.

Bradshaw presents St. Werburge as the alternative to both: "replete with vertue," she stands as a saintly and static plentitude, the antithesis of historical change. As Bradshaw protests, "Longe before the conquest by deuyne grace, / Protectryce of the Cytee she is and euer was" (1.102–3). The history that Bradshaw proceeds to narrate develops this theme by tracing the enormous changes in England's political and ethnic identity against the durable permanence of Werburge's body, from its prehistory in the elaborate genealogy he traces for her to its afterlife as relics enshrined at Chester abbey. Her ancestry links her to the Anglo-Saxon invasions, the conversion to Christianity, and the establishment of religious houses; after her death, her body does not disintegrate for hundreds of years, its physical integrity testifying to her continuing presence on earth. It turns to dust, finally, as the Danish invasions begin, to protect it from infidel hands, but her shrine represents her continuing presence, warding off the Welsh and "innumerable barbarike nacions" that threaten Chester (2.758), just as in life Werburge, in a rare moment of comedy, protects the city from a destructive flock of geese.

Her enduring presence is charted against a detailed history of England, beginning with the Anglo-Saxon migrations. Citing Bede as his authority, Bradshaw recounts Hengst's arrival in 494, accompanied by the Angles, Saxons, and Jutes, at the invitation of Vortigern. He details the displacement of the Welsh, the "Brytons" who were "expulsed . . . with great wretchydnes" to Wales in the seventh century (1.143–4). He provides the political geography of Anglo-Saxon England, explaining the heptarchy and naming the early kings. Bradshaw gives special attention to Mercia—its boundaries and topography, its major cities and the abundance of its natural life, its people and their various "commmodytes / pleasures and proprytes" (1.239). This emphasis is, implicitly, due to the fact that Mercia is the kingdom of Werburge's father, Vulfer, but it is carefully framed by the broad scope of the historical disquisition that precedes it. Similar elisions of a national paradigm and a regional one pervade the legend, initiating a tacit argument that the saint and the territories she miraculously protects represent all of England.

The historical narrative points, as well, to the legend's authenticity: the level of detail makes this a credible story, one based not only on the Latin *vita* of St. Werburge, but also on corroborating sources such as Bede, William of Malmsbury, and Ranulf Higden.[26] More importantly, it suggests the way that Werburge, first through her genealogy, then through her life, and ultimately through her continuing relationship with the people of Chester, both organizes and transcends history. She is at once the point of reference for historical change and the unchanging essence that stands outside of history. Indeed, Werburge's saintly essence recuperates a history of political change and conversion, along with their attendant violence, that poses a serious challenge to the fantasy of the seamless development of English Christian identity. Bradshaw's narrative moves between genealogical chapters, which assert the linear continuity of Anglo-Saxon royal identity and the progress of English history,[27] and historical chapters that threaten this narrative with accounts of the difficult, often violent, process of religious conversion and political struggle among the Anglo-Saxon kings who are, in Bradshaw's legend, the royal forebears of English identity. Not simply the background or historiographic authority for the legend, this narrative of the recursive and violent history of the Anglo-Saxon kingdoms proves the necessity of St. Werburge's sustaining presence as the embodiment of a stable Christian Englishness. Her life stands as the culmination and retrospective unification of a history marked by disruption and change.

The multiple genealogies provided for St. Werburge, demonstrating her descent from four kings of England as well as the royal blood of France, constitute the legend's most elaborate evidence for the consolidation of English identity.[28] Bradshaw devotes a chapter to each lineage, tracing Werburge's descent from the kings of Mercia, Northumbria, East Anglia, and Kent, each complementing the historical outline he has already offered. Werburge's familial history presents in effect a surprisingly full history of Anglo-Saxon England. The intimacy of saintly genealogy and political history is emphasized in Bradshaw's particular attention to the introduction and development of Christianity, by which he represents English history as the history of English Christianity. This premise—that Christian teleology organizes history—is most famously developed in Bede's *Ecclesiastical History*, a frequently cited source in Bradshaw's legend. Bradshaw, however, is less interested in Christian eschatology than in designating Werburge as the culmination of a long history of Anglo-Saxon devotion and thus of a prototypical English religious identity that subsequent generations need only to reiterate. Marking the convergence of four illustrious Anglo-Saxon lineages, as well as the French royal line, Werburge stands as the virginal end-point that retrospectively transforms the kings of Mercia, Northumbria, East Anglia, and Kent into the fathers of English identity.

If Werburge is the singular culmination of the early history of English conversion, she is far from the only saint. Her genealogy is a veritable litany: from the Mercian line alone, Bradshaw mentions St. Marcell and St. Merwald; St. Keneburge and St. Keneswyde "the vyrgyn"; three virginal sisters, St. Mildred, St. Milburge, and St. Milgide; and Werburge's brothers and sisters, St. Kenred, St. Wulfade, and St. Ruffin (1.280–301). The effect is multiplied by the subsequent genealogies of Werburge's Northumbrian, East Anglian, and Kentish affiliations, which demonstrate her relationship to St. Edwin, king of Northumberland, St. Hild, abbess of Whitby, and St. Sexburge (in the Northumbrian line); the martyred Egnicius, St. Anna, and his four holy children, St. Audry of Ely, St. Ethelburge, St. Withburge, and St. Jurwine (in the East Anglian); and St. Edburge, St. Ethelburge, St. Enswyde, the martyred Ethelbert and Etheldred, and four sisters, St. Ermenberg, St. Ermenburg, St. Adeldrid, and St. Ermengyde (in the Kentish line) (1.301–99). In one extended passage the legend of Werburge offers a layered legendary of female saints: short lives of St. Audry, abbess of Ely and Werburge's great-aunt, and St. Sexburge, her grandmother, interrupt the story of Werburge's life.[29] The genealogies represent Werburge at once as part of a remarkably extensive network of royal sanctity and as its singular fulfillment.

Genealogy is also a relevant—indeed essential—category of nationalism, for it grounds both the fantasy of an inherited identity and the narrative of linear progress.[30] Both of these, emphasizing as they do the transmission and continuous trajectory of identity, are important to the construction of Werburge as the stable alternative to an unstable world. The legend sets the genealogical narrative against the recursive and partial history of Christian conversion, which remains incomplete for generations despite the coercive measures undertaken to accomplish it. Werburge's grandfather Penda, who had "graunted without contradyccyon, / Vnder a fre lycence his people were at lyberte / Within all his regyon baptysed for to be" (1.453–55), is followed by Peada, under whom the middle part of Mercia is baptized. The partial and temporary nature of this conversion is betrayed later, when Bradshaw recounts that Wulfer, succeeding to the throne after his brother's murder, promises "Errours to correcke by his wysdome and myght, / Clerely to expell all sectes of ydolatrye / Frome his realme and fulfyll by his auctoryte / The promyse truely made at the fonte of baptyme: / The chyrche to conserue and saue it from ruyne" (1.668–672). Wulfer's military achievements allow him to extend Christianity even further, as he conquers the Isle of Wight and promises it to the king of East Anglia on the condition that he, too, be baptized. The process is still incomplete in the next generation, however, and Bradshaw must admit, in telling the story of the conversion of Wulfer's sons, that Mercia was still not free from idolatry (1.1140–41). Indeed, the young princes find it necessary to disguise their visits to St. Chad "Vnder colour of Huntynge" (1.1148), and they are martyred by their own father, now an apostate, who is persuaded by a false steward to murder them for refusing the "auncyent lawes and sectes" (1.1171). The legend represents Wulfer's violence as the tragic consequence of the tenacious presence of idolatry, which is always already there as the earlier system of belief and a continuing threat, in the possibility of apostasy and heresy. When he promises for the third time (after vows at his coronation and his marriage) to eradicate idolatry as penance for martyring his own sons, the iterability of the gesture as well as its violent premise point openly to its inherently partial and reversible nature.

Conversion is not the only aspect of Anglo-Saxon history that demonstrates the instability of the world in Bradshaw's narrative: political formations are also subject to violent change. The political geography of Anglo-Saxon England, divided into seven kingdoms traced carefully at the beginning of Bradshaw's narrative, begins to break down as Bradshaw embellishes Werburge's genealogy. The military success of Penda, the Mercian king from whom Werburge descends, includes victories over five kings, including St. Edwin of Northumberland and St. Egnycius and St. Anna of East Anglia, who are also Werburge's forefathers. Internal violence threatens English identity at its origin. Bradshaw rewrites this narrative of political loss as a narrative of consolidation through St. Werburge who, as the culmination of four royal lineages, comes to embody the separate kingdoms they represent and so to establish them as a single national community. As in the history of religious conversion, St. Werburge here, too, provides a linear narrative that overrides the persistent memory of England's religious and political variability that registers elsewhere in the legend. She does so by standing as the single point of fulfillment to which all the genealogies—even those of warring kings—lead. In his attempt to dissolve the discontinuities of history in the continuities of lineage, Bradshaw again narrates genealogies that he has already given: he presents the genealogy of St. Sexburge, Werburge's grandmother, for example, after having detailed the same family history for Werburge herself. Tellingly, Bradshaw does not stop with Sexburge but, again, with her granddaughter, "The gloryous Werburge" (1.2051). Bradshaw confirms St. Werburge's position as telos of the several strands of Anglo-Saxon royal families through natural metaphor: he compares her to other "naturall thynges" such as a "royall rose" which proceeds from the briar, "Passynge the stocke with pleasaunt dylectacyon," and the sweet river that rushes past its head and fountain (1.722–28).[31] Bradshaw's images of natural teleology—the rose bush producing a flower, its natural end, or, even more emphatically linear, the river as it runs its course—resist the memory of the historical forces of conversion and political consolidation, dissolving the contingent, recursive, violent narrative in the river of Werburge's royal blood.

Cloistered from History

If the historical and genealogical narratives that open the legend emphasize Werburge's stable identity against—and as an antidote to—the vicissitudes of history, the narrative of her life that structures the rest of book 1 explains her privileged position as a consequence of her religious vocation.[32] Cloistered inside the abbey, Werburge is removed from secular history, a separation that Bradshaw demonstrates in the most vividly descriptive passage of the legend: the festivities celebrating the saint's marriage to Christ.[33] As we will see, the wedding is a festival of history, from which Werburge—already ensconced in the monastery—is conspicuously absent. Excused from the order of secular history, Werburge figures transcendent values that link past and present, providing an ethical model for late medieval English women and so creating a national community that spans several centuries. This representation of St. Werburge as separate from history and thus as the transhistorical ground of ethical action is crucial to Bradshaw's later representation of Werburge's reliquary as a sacred talisman that protects both the territorial boundaries of Chester and the more imaginative boundaries of English identity.

As is conventional to virgin saints' legends, much of the *vita* is concerned with St. Werburge's attempts to preserve her chastity. The sacred stability she represents stands in contrast to the dynamic forces of desire. Although the Latin legend already included one episode with an unwelcome suitor, the false Werebod, Bradshaw adds a second episode, with a far more acceptable, but still rejected, suitor, the prince of the West Saxons, as well as two scenes of threatened rape. These chapters stress Werburge's spiritual devotion and her miraculous resistance to assaults on the chastity she has vowed to God, but more importantly, they contrast the secular world of marriage and sexual desire to the cloister that Werburge later inhabits, no longer subject to the historical forces figured as desire in this section of the legend. Indeed, the narratives of seduction serve to link the virgin's physical integrity with her separation from the social variability that Bradshaw had represented as the corollary of historical change in the prologue.

The first scene follows a standard hagiographic narrative: the prince of the Westsaxons promises Werburge that as his queen she will have

> rychcs / worshyp / and honour,
> Royall ryche appareyll / and eke the sufferaynte,
> Precyous stones in golde / worthy a kynges tresour,
> Landes / rentes / and lybertees / all at your pleasur,
> Seruauntes every houre / your byddynge for to do,
> With ladyes in your chambre / to wayte on you also. (1.821–26)

Werburge refuses him, explaining that she has already chosen Christ as her spouse. The scene aligns Werburge with well-known virgin martyrs such as St. Agnes and St. Katherine of Alexandria, who reject marriage to aristocratic suitors on the same grounds. More importantly, it allows Bradshaw to identify Werburge's virginal body with her constancy, as physical and moral manifestations of her stable presence, figured—significantly—in territorial terms. "So constaunt, fyrme & stable" is Werburge that "A mountayne or hyll soner, leue ye me, / Myght be remoeued agaynst the course of nature / Than she for to graunte to suche worldly pleasure" (1. 851–54). Less changeable than a mountain or a hill, Werburge is the antithesis of ethical vacillation and historical variability.

Feminine constancy is so important to late medieval gender ideology that it may be easy to overlook the crucial role of Werburge's desirability to the legend's larger argument about the community and national identity she represents. The conventional travails of the virgin saint as she struggles to resist the cultural imperative of active sexuality here demonstrate the variety of desires she produces:

> So lyke-wyse some came / to her of her vertue,
> Some of her sadnesse / and prudent dyscrecyon,
> Some for her constaunce / so stable and true,
> Some of her chastyte / and pregnaunt reason,
> Some for her beaute / and famous wysedome;
> And some, that were borne / of kynges lygnage,
> Desyred yf they myght / haue her in maryage. (1.792–98)

In describing social variety through the diverse desires different people have for a singular and saintly woman, this passage recalls the multiple interpretations that define Margery Kempe's audiences.[34] Where that variety in Kempe's *Book* challenges the fiction of a unified, homogeneous community, as I will argue in the next chapter, it works here to entirely different ends. Margery Kempe exposes the myth of a coherent social body, but Werburge *creates* such a body: the variety of responses to Werburge is underwritten by a fundamental agreement on her desirability. She figures a social plenitude, a community formed around and by her desirable person, even as her stable and full meaning reveals the partial, various, and divided nature of that community, fractured by differing commitments to ethical, physical, religious, and political values. Just as she organizes event into meaningful history in the genealogical chapters that open the legend, so here Werburge stands as a fixed center that organizes community.

This is true diachronically as well as synchronically: Werburge's most persistent—and therefore perverse—admirer is the false steward Werebode, who convinces Wulfer to consent to his marriage to Werburge. Her mother and brothers are outraged at Werebode's presumption, and he plans to take vengeance on them in some way. The familiarity of the "false steward" trope here provides evidence for the ethical and political continuity between seventh-century Anglo-Saxon culture and contemporary late medieval practice. Werebode ingratiates himself "by crafte" into Wulfer's favor with false flattery "as now is in custome" (1.1037–38). The narrator extends this aside, remarking "Some please theyr mayster and that is ryght nought; / So dyd this Werebode by subtyll polycy" (1.1039–40). The continuity of an ethical practice (or rather an unethical practice) fashions a continuous identity linking the Anglo-Saxon past to the late medieval present. It does so, significantly, through the story of desire for the constant, unchanging, virginal Werburge.

Both stories recounting the courtship of Werburge, by the noble prince and the false steward, are interleaved with accounts of Werburge's own awareness of the transitory nature of secular life. It is this, rather than a desire to preserve her virginity, that motivates her vocation:

> She well consydered / with due dyscrecyon
> Of this present lyfe / the great wretchydnesse,
> How dredefull it is / full of varyacyon,
> Deceuable / peryllous / and of no sykernesse;
> The tyme vncertayne / to be knowen, doubtlesse;

> For here is no cytee / nor sure dwellynge place,
> All thynge is transytory / in short proces and space. (1.1338–44)[35]

Bradshaw here represents Werburge's religious vocation as an alternative to the transitory, contingent existence of the secular world. This might seem commonplace enough, but it becomes clear in the festivities marking her profession—and the vow of chastity central to it—that Werburge's virginal life excuses her from history itself. Much of chapter 16 of the first book, which recounts the festivities celebrating Werburge's spiritual marriage, describes the extraordinary arras hung in the hall for the event. The long ecphrasis is especially marked here, for Bradshaw's poetry is only rarely visually descriptive. The sumptuous tapestries, decorated with scenes from biblical and classical history, are the iconic center of the marriage, and, as I want to argue, of the legend's representation of Werburge's relationship to history.

After Werburge's vow initiating her into the community at Ely under the abbess Audry, her father celebrates her "ghostly spousage" with a royal feast, "as custome is of maryage" (1.1548, 1.1550). Bradshaw declares that "It were full tedyous to make descrypcyon/ Of the great tryumphes and solempne royalte/ Belonynge to the feest" (1.1569–71). But he describes at length the cloth of gold and arras hanging in the hall "Depaynted with pyctures and hystoryes manyfolde, / Well wrought and craftely with precyous stones all / Glyterynge as Phebus and the beten golde / Lyke an erthly paradyse pleasaunt to beholde" (1.1577–80). The tapestries are remarkable not only for their rich materials, however, but also for their elaborate imagery: in an extended ecphrasis, Bradshaw describes the bibilical history depicted on one of them, which shows Adam and Eve, the offering of Cain and Abel, the crafts invented by Tubal and Tubalcain, Noah sending out the raven, Abraham and Isaac, the twelve sons of Jacob, the betrayal of Joseph, and so on. A second tapestry, hanging over the high dais where the three kings sit, represents the categories of religious identity that make sense of this history: it depicts the angelic orders, Mary, the twelve apostles, the four evangelists, the disciples, then martyrs, confessors, and the virgin saints.

These two tapestries are clearly appropriate to the "ghostly spousage" being celebrated; the third is far more interesting, with its "Noble auncyent storyes" (1.1661) ranging from Sampson's triumph over his enemies to Hector of Troy "slayne by fals treason" (1.1663) and King Arthur. This kind of secular history is also represented by song: "A synguler mynstrell" (1.1695) who surpasses all others entertains the guests by singing "Of myghty conquerours the famous vyctory / Wherwith was rausshed theyr spyrytes and memory" (1.1698–99). He tells the story of Alexander the Great, of the Roman state "Ruled vnder kynges by polycy and wysedome" until Tarquin oppressed Lucrece, of Rome's rule over "all regyons of the worlde" under the triumvirate, and of how Julius Caesar "toke the hole monarchy / And the rule of Rome to hym-selfe manfully" (1.1698–1713) until the conspiracy of Cassius Brutus. The spiritual wedding is a festival of history, biblical and secular, in both lyric and visual text, and it thus stands as an epitome and extension of the historical impulse of Bradshaw's own legend.[36]

Werburge is conspicuously absent from this scene: "As for the sayd moynes was not them amonge / But prayenge in her cell as done all nouyce yonge" (1.1581–82). As a professed virgin, St. Werburge is isolated from the narratives of change that are the inevitable consequence of a transitory and variable human existence. In the static and ahistorical realm of prayer, Werburge is an alternative to history and the epic narratives that represent them—not only the narratives of Alexander the Great's victories or Julius Caesar's reign, but even biblical history. While her genealogy identifies Werburge as the culmination and thus retrospective ground of the historical changes in the first centuries of Anglo-Saxon England, in her holy life and after her death she becomes the stable essence that informs—and ultimately prevents—the kind of political and national change charted in the minstrel's, and Bradshaw's, epic poems.

The Virgin's Body and National Identity

The clearest expression of Werburge's exemption from history is the miraculous preservation of her body for hundreds of years after her death. The incorruptibility of her body is evidence that she transcends the ordinary processes of decay—the most intimate and devastating manifestation of historical change and the contingency of human identity. As is conventional in virgin narratives, miracles confirm the supernatural, as well as moral, quality of her chastity even when she is alive. Rapists pursue her on two occasions: the first relents when he sees her discarded veil hang on a sunbeam and recognizes it as a sign of sanctity (1.2774–87);[37] the second persists until Werburge's prayer for deliverance is answered when an oak tree opens to receive her (1.2788–815).[38] Her body is as incorruptible after death as these miracles show it to have been in life. A long tradition had related virginity and physical preservation causally: Bede, for example, claims that St. Etheldreda (Audry) can be confidently identified as a virgin—despite her two marriages—because "the miraculous evidence of her body from corruption in the tomb is evidence that she had remained untainted by bodily intercourse" (4.19).[39] So, too, Bradshaw insists on the close relation between the incorruptibility of Werburge's body and her ethical status: her body remains "Both hole and sounde from naturall resolucion, / As her soule was clere from vice and corruption" (1.3327–28). He reiterates this in more explicitly causal terms some lines later: "No doubt therof for she, with synne nat maculat, / Vsyng all her lyfe in clennes and virginite, / From bodily corruption by grace must saued be" (1.3396–98).

An even older trope surfaces in the death scene, which establishes St. Werburge's continuing physical presence as a sign of her exaltation in heaven.[40] As Werburge ascends through the spheres, accompanied by a multitude of angels, and joins her divine Spouse, "In meane tyme and space," her body lies "whyte, streyght, and colde" (1.3119–20), surrounded by the fragrance of spices and herbs: "The place was so pleasaunt full of delyce / Lyke as it had ben an erthly paradyce" (1.3124–25).[41] Her body, Bradshaw suggests, is the site of paradise, where heaven and earth most resemble one another. The miracles that it produces represent, if only metaphorically, the spiritual grace in which Werburge's soul now dwells. Her body, unchanging and incorruptible, is the central sign that Werburge is now outside history because she is in heaven. It serves as a "mediatrice" (1.3320) not only between devout suppliants and God but also between historical change and heavenly statis, between contingency and eternity.

As a sign of transcendent meaning, her body comes to have tremendous social meaning, as the earthly contest over its resting place makes clear. Although Werburge has commanded that her body rest in Hanbury, those at the monastery at Trentam, where she dies, will not relinquish it. They raise a company "by power Marcyall" (1.3192) with which to defend the corpse and lock the doors and gates. Divine providence, however, intervenes to uphold Werburge's wishes: sleep miraculously overcomes those in the convent as they watch one night, and the locks fall free of the gates (1.3203–16).[42] Those from Hanbury take the body and bury it in their own abbey. Bradshaw's interest in monastic privilege—here of Hanbury—seems to contradict Werburge's otherworldliness. Separated from historical change in the scene of her spiritual marriage, Werburge is, after her death, very much a part of the institutional histories of the monasteries with which she was affiliated in life. The contradiction reflects the paradoxical nature of the transhistorical value that Bradshaw assigns to Werburge, who embodies history (as we see in the genealogical chapters) and is exempt from it (as the poem insists in the story of her spiritual marriage).

This contradiction comes to a head at the close of the first of the legend's two books, when Werburge's body, whose miraculous resistance to physical change has symbolized her transhistorical status, suddenly becomes vulnerable to historical circumstance. After remaining incorrupt for some two hundred years, her body finally disintegrates in advance of the invading Danes to protect it from contamination by pagan hands. Bradshaw offers a partial explanation for this in identifying the Danish invasion as part of a divine plan, not contingent history: the pagan invaders come "by sufferaunce and dispensacion / Of almyghty god for synne and iniquite / Punysshed vnpiteously all this region / with a wofull plage of great crudelite" (1.3463–66).[43] God also orchestrates the disintegration of Werburge's body so that it will not be touched "With pollute handes full of corrupcion" (1.3473). This tidy explanation is supplemented with a more extended, and significant, one. Bradshaw argues that the "resolution" of the body is itself sometimes a sign of grace, to assure "the greater glorie / Of their resurrection for the tyme, truly" (1.3487–88). This is the promise of Werburge's "dissolved" body:

> Great was the respect of diuyne grace
> In the body of Werburge / without resolucion,
> Shewed by her myracles / for mannes helth and solace;
> But greatter was the hope of the eterne renouacion,
> In her body resolued to naturall consumption,
> Whiche for her merites to this present day
> Helpeth all her seruantes that to her wyll praye. (1.3505–11)

The integrity of the body is an extraordinary sign of God's grace, a reward for exemplary virtue, but its dissolution is a greater sign yet, one that points to the eventual exultation of the body in the Last Judgment. Intact, that is, the body is a mark of the ethical; dissolved, it is a sign of the eschatological.

This promise of continued, essential identity, to be reclaimed in the resurrection of the body, underwrites Werburge's ultimate role in stabilizing national identity. In a striking anticipation of Anderson's analysis of the temporality of nationalism, Bradshaw seems to recognize that nationalism is a secular analog to the "homogenous," divine temporality of eschatology.[44] Although—as the Danish invasions demonstrate—Werburge is finally unable to withstand the historical events that challenge national identity while her body remains intact, she wards off invasions that would challenge that identity after her body dissolves.[45] The importance of the dissolution of Werburge's body to the legend's representation of sanctity and national identity is highlighted by the two-book structure of the poem: the first book ends with the disintegration of her body, and the second repeats the narrative of miraculous incorruptibility followed by the divine dissolution of the saint's body. Rather than a division between her life and her exemplary death, or between her *vita* and her posthumous miracles, as is traditional in late Middle English legends, Bradshaw's poem is divided between Werburge's intact body and her dissolved body. This division structures and parallels a shift in English communal identity as well, from the cyclical, recursive history of the Anglo-Saxon kings, continually converting their people and warring over territory, to the static and self-evident Englishness that persists through historical change. Although for the next 230 years—from the reign of Adelwulfe to the Norman invasion—England is threatened by invasions as if from a "swarme of bees from dyuers nacion" (2.172), including Danes, Geats, Norwegians, Scots, Picts, and unnamed others, Werburge's talismanic presence keeps the "innumerable barbarike nacions" (2.758) at bay.

Before turning to these narratives and the static cultural identity on which they insist, it is important to acknowledge that book 2 of Bradshaw's legend has a more regional focus than the first book does. Werburge's shrine is brought to Chester during the Danish invasions as a protective measure, and Bradshaw provides a history of the city at the beginning of the second book, much as he had provided a history of Anglo-Saxon England in the first.[46] The rest of the second book continues to emphasize local concerns, especially the rights and privileges granted to the abbey, a concern that culminates in Bradshaw's repeated plea in chapter 22 that his aristocratic readers from the palatine of Chester "be neuer vnkynde" to the institution.[47] The legend here registers increasing tension between the monastery and the city and the threatened loss of some of the abbey's most significant privileges.[48] But as in early modern chorography, Bradshaw also implicitly and explicitly offers the region as a metonym for the nation. In protecting Chester, Werburge protects the much larger, if more imaginative, space of England. The figural relationship between them is largely a consequence of Chester's strategic military position near the border with Wales: the city represents the territorial boundary of English identity. The poem establishes this relationship through its two-book structure: the parallel histories that begin each section of the legend point to the metonymic relation between England and Chester. This relation is further developed through the narrative. So, for example, in a miracle given particular prominence, Werburge's saintly presence at the monastery cures six people who come from "diuers partes" (2.908) of England. Their collective cure fashions them as a community, one that figures the nation rather than pointing back to their individual homes. As a miracle that produces community as well as health, it enacts not only Werburge's sacred identity as an intercessor and dispenser of heavenly grace but also her status as the figure that unifies English identity, just as she reunifies diseased or injured bodies.[49]

In representing Chester as the urban metonym for England, Bradshaw draws on the already-familiar trope of Troy and Rome as antecedents for English identity.[50] In doing so, he challenges the place of London as the acknowledged metropolitan center. When fire threatens Chester, Bradshaw asserts its place among the great cities of earlier empires:

> Alas, great heuynes it was to beholde
> The cite of Troye all flamyng as fire;
> More pite of Rome cite was manyfolde,
> Feruently flagrant / empeiryng the empire:
> As to the quantite, the cite of Chestire
> Myght be assembled this tyme in like case
> To the sayde citees, remedeles, alas! (2.1626–32)

Like Rome, the city of Chester stands for a larger cultural and political body. Hence Bradshaw's account of the saint's protection of the city replays scenes of siege, in which the saint's ability to protect the walls of the city suggests her ability to protect the less visible (and far more permeable) boundaries of England. In the first of these stories, the citizens protect Chester from a siege led by the Welsh King Griffinus by mounting Werburge's shrine on the city walls. A Welshman who throws a stone at the shrine is killed by a vengeful spirit, and the entire army is blinded (2.688–722). The Welsh turn back, and their king resolves never to attack the lands protected by the saint again (2.723–29). But the story of siege and saintly protection is reiterated as "innumerable barbarike nacions" attack Chester (2.758). These include Harold, king of the Danes; the king of the Geats, and Malcolm of Scotland. Again, the saint's shrine protects the city: a warrior casts a stone at it but—like his Welsh forerunner—is vexed with a spirit and dies, and the kings recognize the saint's power, beg her mercy, and vow never to return again. After a third attack, again thwarted by the saint's protective presence, no nations dare to threaten Chester (2.1031–37).

This reiteration of Werburge's prophylactic power to save the city frames a more personal but similarly iterated miracle that glosses the significance of the stories of siege: the triple healing of Eadgida, a woman made lame by a long illness. She is first healed through Werburge's grace but soon falls ill again, having broken her vows by indulging in "her appetite and carnall lustes" (2.743) when she marries for pleasure. It is, evidently, far too happy a marriage by Bradshaw's standards: she endures her ailment three times and is cured three times. Her devotion to St. Werburge ensures a stable identity, despite her own moral instability and the physical punishment that registers it. This story, mirroring the triple attacks on the city, comes between the narrative of the abortive Welsh siege in chapter 5 and the closely parallel siege by the several barbaric nations in chapter 7, and this careful imbrication establishes the key thematic parallel between them. They share the promise of stable identity: protected by the presence of the saint, Chester, like Eadgida, is attacked but not really threatened.

The single challenge to Werburge's role as the guarantee of stable English identity is the Norman invasion. Bradshaw attempts to mitigate this challenge to the fantasy of Werburge's omnipotent protection through the miraculous deaths of Richard, count of Chester and prince of England, and his perfidious wife Matilda. They attempt to rededicate the abbey to "a nother religioun" (2.1539)—presumably simply a different monastic affiliation, though the language intimates that they are not fully Christian—but are drowned in the river in another demonstration of Werburge's saintly protection of the city and the abbey. Bradshaw insists that the saint's intercession secures a static cultural identity, preventing the city's thorough translation into a wholly new religious or political paradigm. Werburge, "holy abbasse and lady imperiall," has endured as the "defence speciall" for seven hundred years already, he asserts, and "so shall continue, by grace of god almyghty, / To the worldes ende in hie magnificence" (2.1746–51).

Ethical Imitation and English Identity

Bradshaw's poem imagines Werburge's continuing role as protector of England and English Christian identity as an effect not only of her physical presence but also of the iterability of her devotional practice. We have seen how the false steward Weremode's behavior stands as a point of continuity between the Anglo-Saxon past and the fifteenth-century present; so, too, Werburge's ethical practice has implications for a contemporary audience. In a passage that follows soon after the account of Werburge's spiritual marriage, for example, the aristocratic saint is held up to aristocratic women as an example of humility in dress:

> Swete / comly creatures / ladyes euerychone,
> Sekynge for pleasures / ryches and arayment,
> Blynded by your beaute / and synguler affeccyon,
> Consyder this vyrgyn / humble and pacyent:
> A spectacle of vertue / euer obedyent;
> Beholde how she hase / clerely layde away
> Her royall ryche clothes / and is in meke aray.
>
> Your garmentes now be gay and gloryous,
> Euery yere made / after a newe inuencyon,
> Of sylke and veluet / costly and precyous,
> Brothered full rychely / after the beest facyon,
> Shynynge lyke angels / in your opynyon,
> Where lesse wolde suffyse / and content as well
> As all that great cost / folowynge wyse counsell. (1.1779–92)

The emphasis on the sumptuous fabrics of aristocratic dress in this passage—the rich cloth, the bright embroidery, the precious materials—pointedly recalls the extravagant description of the historical tapestries that decorated Werburge's spiritual marriage. Women who wear expensive and fashionable clothing inadvertently show themselves subject to the contingencies of history that the tapestries represent, giving the lie to aristocratic fantasies of essential privilege. The passage also holds out the possibility of escape from this temporal order, however, if women imitate Werburge by dressing more simply. As we have seen, the saint's spiritual marriage exempts her from history: the example she provides to women who live some eight hundred years later is both a consequence of, and evidence for, this special status. Werburge's virtue, passages such as this insist, can be excerpted from the local historical circumstances—the context of Anglo-Saxon conversion and religious practice and the specific relations between aristocratic and monastic life in seventh-century England—and imported into the radically different historical context of late fifteenth- and early sixteenth-century England. Together the saint and the women devoted to her form and figure a transhistorical community, one that supplies England with a continuity that its political history cannot.

The exemplary rhetoric of the legend, then, is essential to its creation of an imagined community linking Anglo-Saxon saints and contemporary readers through the continuity of devotional practice. It perhaps does so most forcefully in passages that collapse the two communities, as happens with Werburge's death-bed prayer. The beginning of the prayer is uncharacteristically lyric, structured by the joyfully anaphoric "Welcome" with which the saint greets her God:

> "Well-come my lorde / well-come my kynge,
> Well-come my sufferayne / and sauyour,
> Well-come my conforte / and ioy euerlastynge
> My trust / my treasure / my helpe and socour,
> Well-come my maker / and my redemptour." (1.2963–67)

These lines and the profession of the creed that they introduce would be fully imitable by Bradshaw's late medieval audience, just as Werburge's subsequent exhortation to the nuns in her charge outline an ethical position appropriate to them, instructing them to forgo "worldly royalte" (1.3012). Indeed, Bradshaw has already encouraged his late medieval audience on these points. The dual address here to the audience *in* the poem and the audience *of* the poem registers the transhistorical nature of Werburge's exemplarity. Direct discourse allows for the collapse of contemporary and future audiences.[51]

Even as he imagines a transhistorical community linking Anglo-Saxon and late medieval laywomen, however, Bradshaw insists on a hierarchy within that community determined by economic class and social position. The performance of Werburge's saintly and English identity, he suggests, depends on—and so reinforces—these categories. Like modern nationalist discourse, the legend imagines the participation of the whole community. But it does not create a fiction of social homogeneity that interpellates all members of that community equally.[52] In the passage discussed above regarding humble dress, after Bradshaw has offered Werburge as a "playne exsample" to contemporary ladies (1.1793), he criticizes women "of lowe byrthe excellynge theyr degre" who dress "As they were ladyes by lyne of nature" (1.1800–1803). This criticism of sartorial display is the corollary of the earlier injunction to dress simply, but it also serves to make categorical distinctions between the aristocratic and non-aristocratic audiences that Bradshaw addresses, distinctions that Bradshaw grounds in the saint's identity and ethical practice. In decrying how non-aristocratic women falsely imitate ladies in their fine clothing, Bradshaw indirectly reminds us that they cannot not perform a true imitation of the saint by adopting humble dress. Their access to sumptuous goods is always already wrong, a violation of social and legal codes,[53] and so they cannot virtuously reject them, as aristocratic women can, in imitation of the saint.

The "breue conclusion" to the poem (book 2, chapter 24) distinguishes even more carefully between its women readers based on social class and sexual status. The story is, first and foremost, addressed to aristocratic women: "At her lyfe historiall example may take / Euery great estate, quene, duches, and lady" (2.1985–86). Within this social category, Bradshaw identifies separate responses depending on sexuality or religious vocation: "If thou be widowe," Bradshaw explains, imitating the saint's life will bring you to bliss (2.1990–91); "If thou be religious," Werburge demonstrates monastic practice (2.1992–98). In only one case does Bradshaw explicitly address a non-aristocratic audience: he encourages virgins "of hie or low degree" to take the saint as a model (2.1999): here—exceptionally—class does not signify, since it is fully subordinated to sexual status. In this passage, as elsewhere, the legend vacillates between an idea of radical purity that excludes women from historical contingency—including the social category of class—and an insistent claim for political privilege, rooted in history. The legend insists on the transhistorical value of an array of contingent categories—economic class, social position, and gender expectations—by representing Werburge's virtue and behavior at once as imitable across the centuries and as restricted to women who share the saint's class or sexual status.

Indeed, throughout the poem Bradshaw represents mimesis itself as properly aristocratic. The commons' imitation is always mediated by the aristocracy: they imitate the ladies of estate who imitate Werburge, and so they often imitate the wrong thing, as in Bradshaw's lesson about excessive luxury. The mimetic behavior of the commons, even when laudable, is faintly absurd. When the religious men and women present at Werburge's translation begin to sing praises to God for the miracle of her incorrupt body, the commons join in, but their song is not the "melodious" sound of the "celestiall songes and hymnes full of blys" (1.3409–11) of the religious class:

> With that the comon rude people euerychone
> In the sayd churche-yarde standyng without,
> Heryng the clergy syng with suche deuocion,
> Towarde heuen they cried / and busely dyd shout,
> The space of .iii. houres / or nere there-about,
> Worshippyng our lorde / with voice shrill and loude
> In hert, wyll and mynde / as well as they coude. (1.3414–20)

The unveiling and translation of Werburge's immaculate and intact body frame this representation of the derivative, comically mimetic behavior of the commoners. The saint's spectacular self-presence, her miraculously incorrupt body, is set off by the secondary status of the ordinary people, even as it cures countless of them, who regain physical and psychological wholeness when they come, for illness or "interiour tribulacion" (1.3253), to her tomb. Bradshaw's representation of Werburge as free from historical contingency works in part to naturalize categories of class and gender. It offers an aristocratic audience—whom Bradshaw hopes will honor the privileges of Chester abbey—ethical proximity to religious culture, measured by the comparative distance of the common people from the virtues that Werburge represents. The legend does, however, address those of "low birth." The national community imagined by the legend includes a full range of social classes, even as the central figure of that community—St. Werburge—also organizes the differences between them.

The poem, that is, highlights the social categories that frame ethical imitation in order to ground those historically contingent categories in the person of the saint, even as she is represented as a transhistorical ideal. In this way it folds contemporary social hierarchies into the legend's ideal Englishness. In its address to women readers—of low and high birth—the poem thus figures the iterability of Werburge's ethical practice, that is, her transhistorical identity, *and* the continuing significance of contemporary social categories. In the fiction of Werburge's exemplarity, late medieval women who imitate the saint ensure both the English identity that the saint so insistently represents throughout the legend and, within that, the social hierarchies that configure late medieval English social practice.

It is important to note that despite the care with which Bradshaw identifies the various feminine audiences for his poem, he does not enjoin any of them to imitate the more strenuous or miraculous aspects of Werburge's behavior: even the virgins are not explicitly told to imitate her sexual abstinence. Instead, Bradshaw defines ordinary ethical practice (such as humble dress or repetition of a prayer) as an imitation of the saint and thus as a reiteration of her saintly identity—an identity, as we have seen, that embodies Englishness. Rather than holding Werburge up as a model for specifically national behavior (whatever that would be), the legend represents her as the origin and authority for standard late medieval social practices, and in doing so it identifies these as part of a specifically English identity.

As we have seen, Bradshaw understands historical change and the diversity of social practice as two intimately connected manifestations of "mutability." Werburge's status as the figure and guarantee of a transhistorical realm of Englishness is just as intimately related to her role as the exemplary model for the noblewomen whom Bradshaw addresses throughout the legend. By providing a stable ethical model, Werburge offers an alternative to ethical and historical variability: late medieval women, in imitating her, perform a devotional identity linking the social present to the sacred past, and they do so within a clear framework that limits the bewildering array of ethical practices cataloged in the prologue. By participating in the transhistorical pattern, reproducing the ethical categories that the saint represents, Bradshaw's feminine audience, like Werburge, ensures the continuity of an English Christian identity that stretches back to the Anglo-Saxon era.

Englishness and Exemplarity in the *Kalendre of the New Legende of Englande*

In 1516, five years before he published the Life of St. Werburge, Richard Pynson printed another volume that juxtaposed national identity and feminine spirituality. The book presents the *Kalendre of the New Legende of Englande*, a collection of 168 abbreviated lives of native saints, to which Pynson appended a legend of Bridget of Sweden, praising its exemplary value "for euery maner of persone" (46).[54] As representatives of English religious identity, the saints of the *Kalendre* also have a marked relationship to the ethical status of the collection's audience, but they do not offer an immediate exemplary model, since their mythical presence is too removed from late medieval social contexts to have clear relevance. Indeed, in its brief accounts of Anglo-Saxon saints, accounts that are at once iconic and "historical," the *Kalendre* threatens to represent English Christianity as part of a remote past. Englishness, defined by Pynson as an ethical category, requires contemporary practice, and Pynson thus includes—however unlikely—a Continental mystic and tertiary as exemplary of that practice. The volume, with its odd inclusion of St. Bridget in a text otherwise comprising Anglo-Saxon and British saints, points to the complicated relationship between the categories of exemplarity, gender, and nationalism in late medieval hagiography. Because Pynson's 1516 book does not resolve this relationship, it may clarify both the representational strategies of Bradshaw's poem and Pynson's interest in making it available to a national audience a few years later.

Pynson offers the *Kalendre* as an education in national history. It is translated "for theym that vnderstande not the Laten tonge" (43), and it seeks to teach an ignorant audience about the missionaries who converted England or turned them back from renewed idolatry and about the kings receptive to this mission:

And neuerthelesse ryght fewe of this realme of Englande, specyally of the commen people, haue harde of any suche men, in soo moche that the oonly herynge of theyr names wyll be a lernynge to most men; and so it wyll be of dyuerse other blessyd men and women that were borne in this realme, whiche haue done many notable thynges for the comen welthe of the people therof as well profytable for this lyfe as for the lyfe to come . . . by which gloryouse sayntys with other borne in other countreys, as before apperyth, the fayth of our Lorde hath ben preched, receyued & greatly prosperyd in this realme so that many of oure auncestours, neyghboures and frendes by the mercye of our Lorde be now in the ioyes of heuyn to praye for vs, and for all the people, & we also by the grace & goodnes of our Lord be heyrys apparaunte to the kyngedome of heuyn. (44)

Although the unfamiliarity of the English saints and the desire to commemorate them are emphasized first, the idea animating the legendary is that the English people are heirs to the glory of the English saints from whom they descend. This formulation conflates genealogical and intercessional causes: they pray for us, and we inherit from them. Pynson implies here that social or national affiliations organize saintly favor, as they do political favor. Indeed, heaven is like a nation, inherited by subsequent generations, the heirs apparent of a kingdom inhabited by their forebears. Pynson's English readers should know about Anglo-Saxon saints because they are the basis for their claim to that region, as well as to the earthly one.

One of the striking features of Pynson's introduction is the way that its interest in native history leads to an acknowledgment of the non-Christian world, suggestive evidence that the nationalism of this collection—and perhaps of other late medieval hagiography—responds in part to the increasing awareness of the Islamic world in the late fifteenth and sixteenth centuries.[55] English audiences should feel grateful to the saints who converted the island during its remote origins because they would otherwise have continued to live "in error" to this very day, as other communities still do:[56] "And if the lawe of God had nat ben knowen in theyse parties both we & our auncestours myght parcase haue lyued in erroures as other do, wherfore we be moche bounden to loue theym & honoure them & in lykewyse to do that is in vs to helpe other, as they dyd to helpe vs, our auncestours and frendys" (44). The hagiographic past, the Anglo-Saxon saints so unfamiliar to English audiences, speaks to the existence of other unfamiliar *contemporary* communities. The ancient native saints are the origin not only of English Christianity but—more subtly—of the audience's difference from the non-Christian world. Significantly, this organizes the ethical imperatives of the volume, for the prologue proceeds to argue that if the virtuous behavior of these saints were still practiced, so, too, would the process of conversion they represent: "And veryly if there were nowe in thyse dayes the hygh charyte & parfyte loue to almyghty God & to oure neyghboure that was in theyse blessyd seyntes, or at leest a desyre therto with loue of iustyce & zele of the comen welthe & lyke desyre to brynge the people to good lyfe with hole truste & sure faythe in our Lord as was in theyse blessyd men & women, it wolde renewe the face of this worlde and brynge a newe lyghte among the people" (44). The English legendary, then, works not only to consolidate the idea of specifically English sanctity, but also to establish the ethical responsibility of its readers in the context of an international program. If they became more recognizable as avatars of an ancient national sanctity—became, that is, more authentically English—they would continue the project of conversion and proselytizing that structures their own history, their own national origin. Pynson decries the fact that the English are singularly unaware of their conversion history, the story that might provide a mythical foundation for the continued expansion of Christianity mentioned so wistfully above. Whereas the Irish commemorate St. Patrick for their conversion, the Scots St. Nynian, and the Welsh St. David, the English do not even know who converted them. Reminding its English readers that their Christianity is contingent on the process and geography of conversion, the legendary seeks to make this process iterable, and so "renew the face of this world."

The colonizing agenda of the legendary is local as well as global. The preface justifies the inclusion of saints from Ireland, Scotland, and Wales under the rubric "England" because they "of veray ryght owe to be subiecte & obedyent to this realme of Englonde" (46). The earlier claim that emphasized the specificity of English identity defined against its neighbors who more diligently celebrate their Christian forebears here dissolves in the claim that Englishness encompasses all within its contemporary political borders. The dual temporalities of nationalism conflict here again, as current political institutions define the practice of Englishness and thus the scope of the legendary, but not the category of Englishness understood from the originary moment of conversion This oscillating representation of national identity serves the undercurrent of Christian imperialism: if England could now replicate its earlier devotion, and could carry it throughout the world, then the *New Legend of England* would encompass a far greater geographical range than the British Isles.

The overtly nationalist concerns addressed in Pynson's prologue highlight the extraordinary inclusion of the life of St. Bridget of Sweden in this expansive collection of native saints. Pynson does not acknowledge the abrupt shift from nationalist concerns as he introduces the final legend of the collection: he merely insists on its exemplary value for a broad readership.[57] It is a telling supplement to the English legends, which the compiler hopes will inspire his audience but which he cannot expect them to imitate. The exigencies of lay life in the late Middle Ages have little in common with the concerns of conversion, kingship, and monastic foundation characteristic of the native legends, which exist here, in any case, in such abbreviated forms that they could provide little moral example. The devout practice that defines Englishness, then, paradoxically finds its "ryght expedyent" example in St. Bridget, whose life can serve as a model for all audiences, especially married or widowed laypeople, "that they may se what grace and vertue was in this blessyd woman which lyued in the same degre as they do, and the rather to be encouraged to desyre to haue lyke grace and vertue" (46). The "expediency" of this legend is hardly transparent, however. Pynson does not explain either why a female saint provides the best example to his lay audience of men and women or why a Continental saint is an appropriate model for a devotional program that he has defined in terms of national identity.

The first may be explained by the fact that male saints invariably represent significant religious or political authority; they are bishops, abbots, or kings, and their ethical practices depend on their offices and cannot therefore provide a model to Pynson's broad readership. Only a female saint, whose devotional practice does not depend on ecclesiastical or monarchical authority, is exemplary for ordinary lay readers. Having defined Englishness as an ethical practice available to—indeed demanded of—these readers, Pynson must turn to a female saint to find a figure who lived in the "same degree" as they do. Late medieval saints such as Bridget spoke to lay audiences of men and women precisely because they were excluded from the forms of authority represented in male saints' lives.

The second concern finds a preliminary answer in contemporary theories of nationalist discourse. In the turn to a Continental model of exemplarity for its English audience, the book seems to demonstrate Homi Bhabha's contention that contemporary ethical practice necessarily displaces the nationalist ideal rooted in the past: as "the 'subjects' of a process of signification that must erase any prior or originary presence of the nation-people to demonstrate the prodigious, living principles of the people as contemporaneity."[58] Pynson hopes that his audience will be able to reproduce the English identity represented by the native legends, but they can do so only by reproducing the devotional postures represented in the legend of St. Bridget. Paradoxically, the audience can become more closely identified with the sanctity of their forebears—that is, perform the saintly ideal of Englishness embodied by native saints—by following the more historically and culturally proximate example of the Swedish Bridget.

Figure 1. Woodcut from the title page of *Here Begynneth the Holy Lyfe and History of Saynt Werburge* (London: Richard Pynson, 1521). Reproduced by permission of the British Library (C.21.c.40).

This negotiation of exemplarity and Englishness is not, however, quite as unlikely as it might first seem, for Bridget was also, by this time, an "English" saint in a more subtle way as the patron saint of the Bridgettine abbey at Syon, which enjoyed considerable royal patronage since its foundation by Henry V. Pynson's St. Bridget may in fact reflect the institutional affiliations that make her "English" if his legend is, as John Henry Blunt suggests, the one that Thomas Gascoigne translated for Syon nuns, as mentioned in his *Theological Dictionary*.[59] Pynson's choice of St. Bridget, then, preserves a complicated institutional location of English nationalism: the sponsorship of the Bridgettine abbey by Henry V as part of a program consolidating his political authority.[60] It is perhaps significant in this regard that the woodcut of St. Bridget used in Pynson's 1516 book is recycled in his 1521 edition of Henry Bradshaw's *Life of St. Werburge*, a tacit visual identification of the two saints that suggests a particularly close relationship between the two printed books.[61] Woodcuts were expensive, and Pynson's reuse of one is not in itself remarkable. But in this instance such recycling, associating a late medieval tertiary with a seventh-century abbess, required an unusual imaginative leap. That leap is accomplished, I think, by the agenda that the two books share: providing a national identity that can be reproduced by contemporary readers. While it returns to the concerns of the 1516 book, the *Life of St. Werburge* establishes a more coherent representation of national identity by providing a bridge between the mythic past and the ethical present in the figure of the feminine audience repeatedly instructed to imitate Werburge. If in this later volume Pynson gives up his prior interest in providing an ethical model for all lay readers, male and female, he gains a seamless category of Englishness not divided even by gender.

5
Hagiography and Historical Comparison in the *Book of Margery Kempe*

> Damsel, yf euyr thu be seynt in Heuyn, prey for me.
> —*Book of Margery Kempe*

IN THE LAST CHAPTER, we traced how Bradshaw's legend represents Werburge's religious practices at once as historically specific, placed in and produced by the historical context that Bradshaw abundantly details, and as exemplary, to be imitated by late medieval women who thus guarantee the continuity of the English religious community that Werburge embodies. Imitating female saints, however, does not always work to confirm such fictions of community. It can also contest them, sometimes by pointing to disconcerting similarities between the past and the present and sometimes by revealing the contingency of ethical and religious ideals represented as transcendent. We find examples of both strategies in the rare cases of medieval women who imitate traditional saints without fully accommodating their example to contemporary social protocols. Often read as an attempt to "authorize" a woman's devotional practices or a spiritual identity, imitation of a traditional saint can also serve to criticize the community she inhabits by comparing it to the social world depicted in traditional legends. The *Book of Margery Kempe* presents the most sustained and self-conscious example of this, and it thus serves as the central focus of this chapter. Margery insists on the reproducibility of ancient feminine sanctity and faces considerable resistance from civic and ecclesiastical authorities as a result. Refusing to acknowledge her *imitatio* of virgin martyrs and other holy women of the early Church as such, these officials inadvertently demonstrate the similarities between the pagan persecution of female saints and the hostile reception of a woman's public spiritual vocation in late medieval England. While Bradshaw insists on the reproducibility of ancient devotion in order to imagine a continuous, coherent English community, Kempe does so in order to represent that community as incoherent, divided by the ideal of feminine sanctity it extols in vernacular legends and its commitment to a social order that forbids precisely the kind of active, articulate feminine devotion that these legends model.

This chapter marks a shift in focus. I have been primarily concerned in the last two chapters with the feminine audience constructed through the ethical address of female saints' lives and how hagiographers present this interpretive community as an alternative to other forms of community and the histories they organize. In this chapter and the next, I investigate the way that the idea of exemplarity allowed, perhaps even encouraged, medieval writers and readers to explore the historicity of women's devotional practice and the cultural contexts for its performance, especially the social ideals and institutions that regulated women's spirituality. We can see this in the twelfth-century *Life of Christina of Markyate*, which provides a somewhat more straightforward example than does Kempe's wonderfully idiosyncratic *Book* and so serves as a useful introduction to a more extended analysis of that work. Like Kempe, Christina's hagiographer is interested in the holy woman's *imitatio* of a virgin martyr and in the way it provokes energetic resistance from social and ecclesiastical authorities, reproducing the opposition between feminine spirituality and the social order that structures most lives of female saints. But the *Life of Christina of Markyate* has a more conventional subject and form than the *Book of Margery Kempe* does: it concerns a woman who adopts a recognizable religious vocation and is voiced by an anonymous male cleric rather than the would-be saint herself—both of which make its exploration of *imitatio* clearer, if also perhaps less resonant, than the *Book*'s.

Christina of Markyate's *Imitatio Ceciliae*

The *Life of Christina of Markyate* begins, as do most virgin martyr legends, with social and parental pressure to submit to the cultural imperative of heterosexuality. Christina has vowed to remain a virgin, a vow first tested when Ralph Flambard—the "justiciar of the whole of England, holding the second place after the king" and the future bishop of Durham—propositions the girl while a guest of her aunt Alveva, his close friend.[1] Christina manages to escape his advances, but the scorned bishop encourages Burthred, a young nobleman, to request her hand in marriage, a match welcomed by Christina's parents. Christina insists on her prior vow of Christian celibacy, but after a year of pressure from family and friends she reluctantly agrees to the betrothal, a state tantamount to marriage.[2] When Burthred tries to consummate the engagement, however, Christina resists. Her parents encourage Burthred to assault Christina in her sleep, but when he enters her chamber at night, he finds her fully dressed and awake. She delivers a pillow sermon on the theme of St. Cecilia:

And sitting on her bed with him, she strongly encouraged him to live a chaste life, putting forward the saints as examples. She recounted to him in detail the story of St. Cecilia and her husband Valerian, telling him how, at their death they were accounted worthy to receive crowns of unsullied chastity from the hands of an angel. Not only this: but both they and many others after them had followed the path of martyrdom and thus, being crowned twice by the Lord, were honoured both in heaven and on earth. "Let us, therefore," she exhorted him, "follow their example, so that we may become their companions in eternal glory. Because if we suffer with them, we shall also reign with them."[3]

The story stops Burthred's attack, and Christina promises to live with him, albeit chastely, so that he will not be publicly humiliated. But when he informs others (the text does not specify whether these are friends or Christina's family) of what has transpired in the bedchamber, he is ridiculed and convinced to return again, this time not to be feminized (*effeminetur*) by her endless subterfuges (*infinitis ambagibus*) or her holy words (*candidis sermonibus*). Christina continues to refuse him, and the couple finally take their case before Robert, bishop of Lincoln. The bishop initially upholds Christina's original vow to Christ but, bribed by her parents, soon reverses his decision and hands the girl over to Burthred. Christina again defends her virginity through imitation, this time implicit, of the Cecilia legend. She asks Burthred what he would do if another man abducted her, and when he responds that he would kill his rival, Christina informs him that God is an equally jealous lover: "Beware then of taking to yourself the spouse of Christ," she says to him, "lest in His anger He will slay you."[4] The exchange parallels Cecilia's warning to Valerian that he will be killed by her angelic protector if he tries to touch her. Extending the *imitatio* of Cecilia that she had earlier proposed as the structure of their marriage, Christina here uses the threat of vengeance, rather than the promise of spiritual reward, to protect herself from Burthred's sexual assault.

Although Christina's imitation of Cecilia as a model for secular marriage serves primarily to demonstrate her chastity, it also indexes larger narrative parallels between Christina's *vita* and the Cecilia legend. Christina's enemies never question her holiness;[5] they readily acknowledge the piety of her words and the sincerity of her devotion. But the validity or importance of feminine spirituality is categorically rejected, not only by her parents but even by the two bishops who collude with them to force Christina into a sexually active marriage in place of the spiritual one she prefers. The *vita* presents a sharp indictment of the close relationship between aristocratic and ecclesiastical authorities, and especially their shared investment in ensuring women's circulation in a sexual economy that frequently serves to align the interests of secular and religious elites. The narrative, that is, uses Christina's *imitatio* of St. Cecilia to suggest a further parallel between the social institutions and religious authorities of third-century Rome and twelfth-century England, both of which are threatened by a virgin's holy words and her resistance to active heterosexuality.

In contrast to the corrupt ecclesiastical hierarchy, monastic and eremitic practice is represented in the *Life of Christina of Markyate* as the context for true spirituality, an opposition that also resonates with the Cecilia legend. In the legend, the fugitive pope Urban hides in the catacombs, forced—like Christina—to live an eremitic life in order to escape persecution from a state-sponsored religion that amounts to little more than a fraudulent spectacle of devotion and spiritual authority. This opposition between hermits and socially powerful clerics, in turn, structures the representation of ethnic and political difference in the *Life of Christina of Markyate*, specifically the tensions between Anglo-Saxon monastic culture and the newly arrived Norman ecclesiastical hierarchy that C. H. Talbot has identified as one of the text's pervasive themes. Talbot notes that most of the people who help Christina to pursue her vocation have Anglo-Saxon names: Sueno, Alfwen, Eadwin, Loric, Ulfwine, and Godescalc.[6] Her primary spiritual adviser Roger seems an exception, but if his name identifies him as Norman, his speech identifies him as English: he speaks the single vernacular phrase in the Latin *vita*, addressing Christina as "myn sunendaege dohter" (my Sunday daughter).[7] Throughout the *Life*, the holiness of Roger and other English hermits contrasts sharply with the behavior of the Anglo-Norman bishops, not only the bishop of Durham, the would-be rapist, but also Robert, bishop of Lincoln, who is so easily bribed by Christina's family to reverse his endorsement of her original vow. The broad narrative parallels between these Norman authorities and the Roman judges who persecute St. Cecilia might have pointed, with sharp irony, to Anglo-Norman myths of cultural identity: the Normans claimed Roman ancestry and political authority through the trope of *translatio imperii*, a claim here turned back against them in the suggestion that, like their Roman forebears, they persecute devout Christians and manipulate true spirituality for crass political ends.[8]

Christina's *imitatio* of St. Cecilia culminates—and abruptly ends—when she makes her formal monastic vow. Released from her engagement to Burthred at last, Christina suddenly worries that she is not worthy of the profession to which she has so long aspired. The *vita* signals divine approval by returning to images from the virgin martyr legend: Christina sees herself surrounded by beautiful young men (*iuvenes eximii decoris*) who greet her on behalf of Christ and set upon her head a crown that He has sent. Christina recognizes that the crown signifies the virginity of her body and mind (*mentes et corpore virginem*, 128–9). The passage completes the *imitatio Ceciliae*, initiated by Christina's promise to Burthred that their chastity will be rewarded in precisely this way. Of course, Burthred—who imitates Cecilia's husband only until mocked by his friends the next day—is not privy to this miracle. The most significant difference, however, lies in the vocation prefaced by Cecilia's crowning and Christina's. In the Cecilia legend, the lilies and roses signal two separate but related virtues: the angelic crowning both confirms her sacred virginity and anticipates her martyrdom. It marks a transition from the initial domestic context of Cecilia's religious practice to the public role that will lead to her death. In the *vita* of Christina of Markyate, in contrast, the crown symbolizes only virginity, which does not authorize a public role: she is cloistered in the small community of anchorites at Markyate, and the largest arena for her influence is the monastery of St. Alban's, whose abbot, Geoffrey, becomes her spiritual companion. Returning to Christina's first invocation of Cecilia as her model, we see that her account of the legend anticipates this narrowing in its careful exclusion of Cecilia's public vocation. Christina tells Burthred that Cecilia and her husband are crowned at their deaths, but in the standard versions of the legend they are crowned as soon as they agree to a chaste marriage and Valerian converts to Christianity.

Christina, that is, elides the public professions of faith that follow Cecilia's commitment to a chaste marriage: she forgets both Cecilia's spirited confrontation with the judge Almachius and the transformation of her house into a church where she preaches for three days. Christina's *imitatio* parallels her truncated account of the legend: the second half of the *Life* ceases to allude to St. Cecilia and insistently associates Christina with a retreat from, rather than an engagement with, the social world.[9]

In the *Life of Christina of Markyate*, then, *imitatio* and its limits help to define both the holy woman's spiritual profile and that of the communities she inhabits. Christina's ability to imitate St. Cecilia points simultaneously to her spiritual authority and to the failings of the social and ecclesiastical institutions that oppose her. Nevertheless, the challenge her *imitatio* presents is finally contained, as her disruptive desire for God is carefully cloistered in the anchorage at Markyate, where she no longer resembles the outspoken virgin martyr who had provided her with an alternative to the accepted protocols of heterosexual marriage. The difference between the two sections of the narrative invites readers to consider which aspects of women's religious practice remain constant across considerable historical and cultural distance and which do not. While Cecilia's public vocation is evidently not imitable in twelfth-century England, other ethical and devotional expectations persist: sexual purity remains a necessary precondition for a spiritual vocation; the pursuit of that vocation in its purest form requires a removal from centers of social and religious power; and the holy woman has divine sanction to reject the authority of her family, spouse, and religious leaders if they threaten these imperatives. The implicit corollary to this, the substance of the *vita*'s social criticism, is that certain institutions—marriage, the patriarchal family, state-sponsored religion—have also remained static or at least stand as close analogs to those in traditional legends.

There is little evidence of an active cult of Christina of Markyate in late medieval England, but her *Life* circulated, if in a limited ambit, into the early modern period. It was copied into a volume containing John of Tynemouth's *Sanctilogium Angliae* in the mid-fourteenth century (British Library MS Cotton Tiberius E 1), where Nicholas Roscarrock read it in the early seventeenth century and redacted it for his encyclopedic collection of native saints' lives.[10] Excerpts from the *vita* were included in Thomas of Walsingham's *Gesta Abbatum monasterii Sancti Albani* (c. 1390) as well. But while the *Life of Christina of Markyate* does not seem to have been well known in the late Middle Ages, its exploration of the challenge that feminine spirituality can present to both social order and religious authorities resonates deeply with a fifteenth-century biography of another woman who struggled to change the terms of her marriage in order to pursue a spiritual vocation: the *Book of Margery Kempe*. Both narratives imagine their protagonists as avatars of St. Cecilia, and in both, this *imitatio* structures not only the spiritual life of the holy woman but also the texts' criticism of social and religious institutions.[11] Unlike the *Life of Christina of Markyate*, however, the *Book of Margery Kempe* does not confine the holy woman's *imitatio* to sexual practice: Margery adopts the public, as well as the virginal, persona of the virgin martyr, standing trial for her religious identity and practice, preaching in public arenas, and embracing the humiliation and persecution that attend her spiritual vocation. As a result, Margery Kempe's *Book* provides a much more thorough and challenging analysis of its protagonist's community than Christina's *vita* does.

If Margery's *imitatio* of traditional saints is more extensive than Christina of Markyate's, it is also, paradoxically, more difficult to identify as such. The very similarities between Margery's spiritual practice and those of early virgin martyrs or other female saints obscure, even as they define, the relationship between them. Christina of Markyate is readily recognizable as a holy woman, to her hagiographer and to his audiences, precisely because her imitation is limited: rejecting the sexual economy of aristocratic marriage and even the authority of bishops too deeply enmeshed in the secular world in favor of a cloistered life of prayer and privation is readily identified as part of a very specialized religious vocation. But while a few of Margery's contemporaries identify her as someone who might someday be "a saint in heaven," her refusal to adopt the social or religious practices considered appropriate to her sex and the hostility this engenders in some of those around her—though these are precisely what affiliate her with the virgin martyrs so popular in vernacular legends—strangely make it harder, rather than easier, to see how similar she is to them.

The sincerity and validity of Margery's spirituality remain remarkably durable critical concerns, but they rest too readily on the assumption that Margery herself is the *Book*'s single subject. As Lynn Staley's important work has shown, the representation of Margery as a holy woman is inextricably—even formally—related to the *Book*'s social criticism.[12] To be sure, Margery's capacity for *imitatio* offers only uncertain evidence of her sanctity, but it offers quite clear parallels between the world inhabited by virgin martyrs and her own late medieval world. I would like to extend Staley's analysis by thinking about how Kempe's social criticism is also a kind of historical thinking. Like Bokenham's legendary and Bradshaw's *Life of St. Werburge*, the *Book of Margery Kempe* explores the relationship between the sacred past and the social present through the exemplary relationship linking a contemporary feminine audience—Margery herself—to ancient saints. But Margery's full embrace of traditional female sanctity exposes how partial and attenuated the *imitatio* proposed by writers such as Bokenham and Bradshaw really is. The contrast with Bokenham, Kempe's East Anglian neighbor and near contemporary, is especially sharp: as we have seen, Bokenham represents literary patronage as an imitation of the saint's role in producing salvific language, acknowledging the significance of women's devotion for a larger textual community but also restricting it to private arenas, in pointed contrast to the public ones represented in the legends. Margery, however, occupies these public spaces in flagrant disregard of the social ideologies and interpretive practices that ordinarily denied them to female readers of hagiography. Those practices—the careful modification of potentially subversive precedent, the subordination of the narrative to contemporary expectations for women's behavior, the attention to the historical difference that separated Mary Magdalene or St. Katherine from a late medieval woman—are upset, exposed, and analyzed in Margery's performance. Refusing to read and imitate hagiographic narrative through the filters of contemporary devotional discourses and secular gender ideology, Margery demonstrates the considerable distance between the ethical paradigm of traditional legends and late medieval expectations for laywomen's religious and social practice. The *Book*, that is, uses the exemplarity of female saints' lives to develop a striking analysis of the historical specificity of feminine devotion.

Vernacular legends provide Kempe with an especially productive framework for this analysis because the model of feminine spirituality they develop is radically different from that of other late medieval religious discourses, especially devotional and mystical discourses that advocated inward and private forms of religious practice.[13] While lay readers were repeatedly encouraged to turn their devotions "inward" by most of the vernacular religious texts they read, saints' lives represent female spirituality as a very public phenomenon. St. Margaret or St. Katherine's private devotions are rarely the focus of vernacular legends, and late medieval saints' legends, as Karen Winstead has shown, frequently eliminate whatever prayers and meditations are found in earlier sources.[14] Instead, the spirituality of traditional female saints is almost invariably expressed in public forums, most often in trials in which they proclaim their faith and challenge that of their pagan persecutors. And it is in martyrdom, always attended by crowds of onlookers, that their sanctity receives its fullest and final expression. In imitation of vernacular legends, Margery's religious practice is insistently, conspicuously public. Instead of praying silently at mass, perhaps with the aid of a devotional book,[15] Margery weeps before the altar like a late medieval Magdalene, transforming the parish church into an open forum for a laywoman's spirituality. Transformed, as well, are Continental pilgrimage routes, the hostels, and the passenger ships—even the Via Dolorosa, which becomes the site of Margery's own, emphatically social, suffering. Upon her return to England, her spirituality finds expression, once again, in institutional settings—mayoral courts, chapterhouses, and archbishops' chambers—as Margery is brought before a series of civil and religious authorities to explain her irregular behavior. In defining her spirituality in relation to communities and civic institutions, Margery relies on a definition of female sanctity most fully explored in, and most familiar to her audience from, vernacular legends of female saints.

Hagiography has long been considered an important influence on the *Book*, even the genre to which it aspires. For the most part, however, late medieval Continental *vitae*, the lives of mystics and holy women such as Mary d'Oignies and Bridget of Sweden, have received more critical attention from Kempe scholars than have traditional legends.[16] Both explicit textual references and relative historical proximity have made the Continental tradition an obvious and important context for the *Book*. But Margery's spiritual life is also populated by figures from popular vernacular legends, especially Mary Magdalene, St. Katherine, and St. Margaret: they attend her mystical marriage to the Godhead (87), they speak to her and instruct her how she should love God (215), they will be present at her death (51), and, so Christ tells Margery, they will array the chamber of her soul with many fair flowers and sweet spices so that he might rest with her there (210). Critics have, moreover, remarked scattered but marked parallels to these and other traditional saints in Margery's spiritual identity and devotional practice: Margery at times recalls St. Margaret, her name saint and perhaps a model for Margery's assistance to women in childbirth;[17] St. Katherine of Alexandria, noted for her eloquent and witty defense of her faith in public trial;[18] St. Cecilia, who compelled her husband to accept a chaste marriage;[19] and Mary Magdalene, whose penitent tears and itinerant preaching provide perhaps the closest model for Margery.[20] Margery's *imitatio* does not offer one sustained identification, as Christina of Markyate's imitation of St. Cecilia does, but rather a series of temporary affiliations with several traditional saints, which together signal the *Book*'s deep engagement with vernacular legends, an engagement we have identified but only begun to analyze.[21] If, as recent critics have suggested, traditional saints provide Margery with key components of her devotional style, vernacular hagiography—and in particular the exemplary relationship it posits between the saint and those devoted to her—is crucial to Kempe's exploration of the historical and cultural frames that structure gender identity and devotional practice.

Although we classify both late medieval Continental *vitae* and traditional vernacular legends as "hagiography," they constitute distinct discourses: that is, they have different social, linguistic, and institutional associations. The lives of late medieval holy women were largely restricted to Latinate readers in late medieval England. The English translations of the lives of Mary d'Oignies, Elizabeth of Spalbeck, and Christina the Astonishing are attested in just one manuscript, Bodley Library MS Douce 114.[22] The vernacular lives of Bridget of Sweden and Catherine of Siena had only slightly wider currency. The fourth work in Douce 114 is "a letter touchynge the lyfe of seint Kateryn of Senys" (184), and Wynkyn de Worde printed the *Lyf of Saint Katherin of Senis*, originally translated for a community of religious women, at the close of the fifteenth century.[23] There are also only two legends of Bridget of Sweden—one in a fifteenth-century manuscript of her *Revelations* and the other printed with the *Kalendre of the New Legende of Englande* by Pynson in 1516—both originally associated with Bridgettine nuns, a small and specialized audience.[24] Even Elizabeth of Hungary, whose story was included in the *Legenda Aurea*, did not become the subject of vernacular legends until the middle of the fifteenth century, with Bokenham's legendary and the *Gilte Legende* (1438).[25] The lives of St. Katherine of Alexandria, Margaret of Antioch, Cecilia, and Mary Magdalene, in contrast, were part of a vernacular narrative culture that was broadly available to lay audiences in books, sermons, public art, and civic drama.

The discursive difference between these two traditions registers in Kempe's *Book*. As many critics have demonstrated, the Continental *vitae* establish two kinds of authority—Margery's spiritual authority, supported by these accounts of contemporary devotional practice, and the textual authority of her *Book*, grounded in their narrative conventions—both of which are crucially related to their affiliation with Latinate clerical culture. Saints from the vernacular tradition cannot provide the same kind of authority that this specialized and spiritually elite tradition provides. Indeed, Margery's implicit and explicit claims to model her spiritual identity on figures from the vernacular canon are often roundly rejected by civic and religious authorities. When Margery tells the mayor of Leicester that she is the daughter of the sometime mayor of Lynn, he tells her flatly: "Seynt Kateryn telde what kynred sche cam of & yet ar ye not lyche" (111). A more subtle, but no less categorical, rejoinder comes from the second scribe, who reluctantly agrees to transcribe and continue the illegible narrative of Margery's life begun by an earlier amanuensis. Although Margery is repeatedly associated with Mary Magdalene in the *Book*, the scribe fails to recognize her tears as an *imitatio* of the saint's penitent weeping, locating the precedent for Margery's practice in the *vita* of Mary d'Oignies instead. As an audience inscribed within the text, the scribe offers important testimony to the issues at stake in Margery's imitation, and we can best begin to understand the *Book*'s unsettling exploration of the continuities and discontinuities of religious identities and communities by turning to his refractory reading of Margery's imitation of Mary Magdalene as an imitation of Mary d'Oignies.

Reading Mary Magdalene

The *Book of Margery Kempe* begins, quite literally, with Mary Magdalene. The second scribe commences his transcription of the *Book* on the day after the saint's feast, when he is at last granted the "special grace" required to decipher the original text of Margery's story (4). This "lytyl tretys" of how a "synful caytyf" (1) was stirred unto the love of Christ is pointedly associated with Mary Magdalene, the penitent *pecheresse* of medieval legend and drama. We learn from Christ himself in the long colloquy that closes the first part of the *Book* that Margery has a particular devotion to the saint, and that Mary Magdalene is, in turn, Margery's patron and advocate: "I wot wel a-now what thu thynkyst," Christ says to Margery, "Thu thynkyst that sche [Mary Magdalene] is worthiest in thi sowle, & most thu trustyst in hir preyerys next my Modyr, & so thu maist ryth wel, dowtyr, for sche is a ryth gret mene to me for the in the blysse of Heuyn" (210). Margery's relation to Mary Magdalene is not limited to veneration and intercession, however: her own story imitates the large outlines and local details of the saint's late medieval legend, though that imitation is sometimes obscured by the wealth of contemporary reference that gives the *Book* its remarkable feeling of autobiographical and social reality. The Magdalene legend offers precedent for Margery's sexual temptations, her dramatic conversion and personal relation to Christ, her weeping and itinerant preaching.

More broadly, it provides a rare model for the kind of story that the *Book* announces itself to be: a story of conversion. Most legends of female saints, both virgin martyrs of the early Church and late medieval holy women, feature women whose lives are marked from the beginning by their sexual purity. The central importance of sexual renunciation to medieval definitions of female sanctity is too familiar to need rehearsing here, but it is worth remembering that it surfaces even in the late medieval *vitae* to which the *Book* is most often compared. The lives of women such as Bridget of Sweden and Elizabeth of Hungary who were wives and mothers before taking up their holy vocation often emphasize that they marry only in obedience to their parents. Then, once their marriages are consummated, after a miraculous delay of several years, they chastise their bodies with fasts and vigils to atone for sexual activity, to which they submit only in wifely obedience. In its narrative of early sin and sexual pleasure, only later rejected as part of religious conversion, the *Book of Margery Kempe* departs sharply from the conventions of most female saint's lives, traditional and contemporary, with the important exception of the Magdalene legend.[26]

Margery's *imitatio* of Mary Magdalene is elaborated throughout the *Book*.[27] The parallels begin with Margery's early biography: like the Magdalene, she is the daughter of a rich burgess, and her social position leads to vanity and a fondness for extravagant dress. Her conversion from a life of self-regard and active sexuality is occasioned by her personal and direct relationship with Christ. Margery is granted full remission of her earlier sins, a blessing closely associated with Mary Magdalene.[28] She compares herself to the woman taken in adultery of John 8:3–11 (65), who was often identified with Mary Magdalene.[29] Margery is devoted to Christ's humanity, a devotion represented through her imitation of Mary Magdalene's iconographic association with Christ's feet: in one of her more bizarre visions, Margery fondles his toes (208).[30] More pointed still, Margery participates in Mary Magdalene's place during a Passion vision, "crying & rorying" and comforting the Virgin (193).[31] Even Margery's miracle working recalls the saint, especially her repeated association with divine protection at sea and interventions in childbirth.[32] That Margery's spiritual life is modeled on Magdalene's is addressed explicitly in a conversation with Christ. With characteristic frankness, Margery informs him, "I wolde I wer as worthy to ben sekyr of thy lofe as Mary Mawdelyn was"; Christ responds obligingly, "Trewly, dowtyr, I loue the as wel, & the same pes that I gaf to hir the same pes I geue to the" (176).[33]

The most conspicuous feature of Margery's *imitatio* of Mary Magdalene is—or should be—her weeping. Early in Margery's Jerusalem visions, the Virgin Mary instructs her not to be ashamed to cry for God, for she and Mary Magdalene were not ashamed: "yf thu wylt be partabyl in owyr joye," Mary tells her, "thu must be partabil in owyr sorwe" (73). Although her weeping imitates both Marys in the Passion sequence, the tripartite taxonomy with which Margery classifies her tears elsewhere finds its more specific model in Mary Magdalene, who cries tears of compunction for her own sins when she washes Christ's feet, tears of compassion at Christ's death, and tears of devotion at his Resurrection.[34] But the *Book*'s scribe—and following him, most modern scholars—identifies Mary d'Oignies, rather than Mary Magdalene, as authority and exemplar for Margery's tears. Though privy to the conversations in which Margery and Christ discuss her affinity to the Magdalene, the scribe cannot imagine Margery's weeping—and the public vocation it represents—as an imitation of the legend of a first-century saint.

We can understand this failure broadly in terms of the discursive differences between Latin *vitae* and the legends widely available in the vernacular discussed above. The life of Mary d'Oignies, still associated with Latinate textual culture, offers a distinctly clerical authority for Margery's practice that the legend of Mary Magdalene, accessible to lay audiences in sermons, civic drama, and vernacular poetry, could not. But the scribe's inability to acknowledge Margery's *imitatio Magdalenae* also, and perhaps more importantly, marks the historical distance that separates Mary Magdalene and her late medieval avatar; it registers, that is, the scribe's belief in the difference of the hagiographic past. Like the mayor of Leicester, Margery's amanuensis assumes that she is not "like" Mary Magdalene in some essential way, despite the similarity between their abundant tears for Christ. He identifies Margery's practice, instead, with the more proximate example of a late medieval holy woman.

Margery's literal reading of the Magdalene legend and her imitation of it in her own devotional practice confound other audiences as well. Kempe details this confusion repeatedly in the *Book*, cataloging the several responses that Margery's weeping elicits, in passages such as this one: "summe seyd it was a wikkyd spiryt vexid hir; sum seyde it was a sekenes; sum seyd sche had dronkyn to mech wyn; sum bannyd hir; sum wisshed sche had ben in the hauyn; sum wolde sche had ben in the se in a bottumles boyt: and so ich man as him thowte. Other gostly men louyd hir & fauowrd hir the mor" (69). Her tears are read variously as evidence of possession, illness, intoxication, insanity, or—conversely—holiness. The community's inability to agree on a reading of Margery's behavior points to the absence of a consensus on whether it should be read through the categories offered by moral, medical, social, or spiritual discourses and to the considerable differences between these discourses in the representation of normative or acceptable feminine behavior. With the exception of a few "ghostly men" who recognize the legitimacy of her devotion, however, most privilege contemporary discourses in which Margery's public vocation violates expectations about laywomen's religious practice.

As we saw in Chapter 1, hagiography and moral literature often respond to the historical difference between the sacred past and the social present through figural models of imitation, in which the saintly example is made to conform to such expectations. Osbern Bokenham's version of the Mary Magdalene legend, for example, written within ten years of the composition of the *Book of Margery Kempe*, shifts the emphasis from preaching to private devotion. Lady Bourchier, in Bokenham's narrative of the commission, is interested in Mary Magdalene as the "apostless of the apostles," that is, as a figure of articulate, active, authoritative sanctity.[35] In a passage we have already seen, however, Bokenham redirects his patron's interest in public female spirituality by promising her full remission of sin—the reward that Mary Magdalene merited—for *private* reading:

To hyr [Lady Bourchier's] goostly confourth in especyal,
And of them generally wych it redyn shal;

> By wych redyng that thae may wynne
> Fyrst remyssyoun here of al here synne,
> Lych as Mary Mawdelyn dede purchace,
> And that aftyr this lyf they may thorgh grace
> To that blys comyn wher-yn is she. (5255–61)

A narrative centrally concerned with a woman's public preaching is here brought into line with contemporary expectations for women's participation in religious culture, as Bokenham suggests that Lady Bourchier, and future readers, seek the grace that Mary Magdalene enjoys, not by imitating her extravagant weeping or her itinerant preaching nor even by embracing a life of chastity, but through the far more socially acceptable practice of private devotional reading. Bokenham reinforces this lesson by rewriting Mary Magdalene's public devotions as private ones in the legend. So her weeping at Simon's house is glossed as private confession, communicated wordlessly to Christ:

> And thow wyth hir mouth outwardly
> To hym no wurde she dede expresse
> In al this tyme wych so besyly
> She shewyd this meke obsequyousnesse,
> Yet, of hyr wepyng by the grethnesse,
> Of hyr herte she shewyd the corage,
> As thow she had vsyd this language:
> "O moste meke lord, wych knowyst al thinge,
> And art of hertys the inward knoware,
> Wych, as it semyth by thi techynge,
> Desyryst not the deth of a synnere
> But that he be conuertyd & lyue lengere,
> Thou knowyst wele, lord, as I do wene,
> What my wepyng, my syhyng & my sorwe doth mene.
> Y am a synnere, & of euery cryme
> Wyth spottys defoulyd ful horrybylly,
> And so haue I contunyd ful long tyme
> Syth wyt & dyscrecyoun fyrst had I;
> Reforme me now, lord, for thi mercy,
> And in this greth nede by my socour,
> Wych oonly consydryst sorwe & labour." (5437–57)

Bokenham acknowledges the "greatness" of Mary Magdalene's weeping only briefly, devoting far more attention to the silent prayer it represents. Rendered as a private communication with Christ, rather than public contrition, Magdalene's tears can stand as a model for the legend's patron, Lady Bourchier, ensuring that she does not follow her countrywoman Margery Kempe in a more literal imitation of the story.[36]

While late medieval women such as Isabel Bourchier were taught to filter hagiographic narrative through the lens of contemporary devotional discourses and social practice, and thus to observe the historical difference that separated them from the saints to whom they were devoted, Margery Kempe's *imitatio* adopts a far more literal reading of the narrative and its moral imperatives.[37] She does not do so, however, as a Lollard might, to establish the authority of unorthodox behavior. Wycliffite writers pointed to Mary Magdalene as authority for women's preaching,[38] but when a clerk reminds her of the Pauline prohibition against it, Margery famously claims that she does not preach. "I come in no pulpytt," she notes, "I vse but comowynycacyon & good wordys" (126). By respecting the discursive boundaries of preaching established by the Church, represented in metonymy by the pulpit, Margery eludes the attempt to control and limit her practice. It is a course that refuses both the homologies of past and present in Lollard discourse and the alterity that structured more orthodox readings of vernacular literature. Her *imitatio* constitutes rather a complex historical comparison, one with implications not only for the status of feminine devotion but also for the spiritual profile of the community.

This is even more clear and urgent in Margery's imitation of virgin martyrs—especially St. Cecilia, her model for chaste marriage, and St. Katherine, her primary model for religious debate and the public proclamation of her faith—to which I turn in the next section of the chapter. Located in a vividly imagined representation of fifteenth-century England, Margery's improbable *imitatio* of virgin martyrs involves a pointed rejection of the categories that sustain important social and religious institutions. She upsets the institution of marriage, which under canon law guaranteed the spouse's right to conjugal relations,[39] and she confuses the categories of wife and virgin, both of which are ostensibly founded on physiology. Most dangerously, she blurs the difference between orthodoxy and heterodoxy in trial scenes that align archbishops and mayors with the pagan persecutors of holy martyrs, as Lollard representations of late medieval heresy trials do. As the last demonstrates most clearly,

Margery's *imitatio* does not simply borrow the opposition between saint and society that characterizes hagiographic narrative; it uses that opposition to investigate the relationship between the age of martyrdom and fifteenth-century England. From this perspective, the scribe's desire to find a more contemporary authority for Margery's weeping, to distance Margery from the canon of traditional saints, may register his resistance not only to reading Margery's practice as an imitation of vernacular legends but also to so reading the community around her.

Before proceeding let me clarify my reading of Margery's use of exemplarity as an argument about history by distinguishing it from her representations of mystical or liturgical time. Carolyn Dinshaw has argued that in moments of mystical contemplation Margery "exists in some sense out of her world's time, in a spiritual time frame (the everlasting *now* of the divine) that is radically separate from the secular chronology governing others around her."[40] So, as Dinshaw notes, for Margery, Jesus' death is as "fresch" to her as the day he died. For Margery, liturgical ritual often provokes the collapse or rejection of chronology that Dinshaw notes: she understands almost too well the way in which rituals such as Holy Thursday processions or the rites of Purification signify not as representations but as fully present repetitions of the events they commemorate. In her visions, especially those prompted by liturgical and sacramental commemoration of the life of Christ, Margery slips from the historical and geographical place she inhabits—Bishop's Lynn in the fifteenth century—to participate in the event itself. But this is only one way in which the *Book*, as Dinshaw says, "tells us about the status of history itself" (223), and one which is perhaps less challenging to the temporal order of fifteenth-century England. If mystical contemplation or liturgical ritual removes Margery from history, her imitation of female saints places her firmly back into it. The *Book of Margery Kempe* provides an extraordinary case study of how exemplarity serves as a mode of historical comparison, as Margery's behavior recalls the saintly past and insists that the social present be understood in relation to it.

Margery as Virgin and Martyr

If Margery's sexual identity links her first to Mary Magdalene, it later associates her with the virgin martyrs whose resolute chastity brings them into conflict with civil authorities. Mary Magdalene's sexuality ceases to be an issue once she repents, but Margery's chastity becomes, like that of St. Margaret or St. Katherine, part of the public expression of her spirituality. Despite her marriage and fourteen children, Margery dresses in white clothing that identifies her as a virgin.[41] Her tendentious virginity provokes official hostility and thus provides the opportunity and the legal arena for her public teaching, just as Margaret's defense of her virginity secures a forum for proclaiming her faith. The intricate marital negotiations that occupy so much of the first part of the *Book* are finally only a prelude to these more public, and more difficult, negotiations of Margery's sexual and spiritual identity. Margery's sexuality is at once a catalyst that transforms her personal devotion to Christ into a social identity and a crucial sign, which, like her weeping, is read and misread by her several audiences.

Before she takes up the role of public virgin, however, Margery must first redefine her marriage as celibate, and she does so through a careful, and sometimes comic, *imitatio* of St. Cecilia. Christ himself—filling in for the angel who guards Cecilia's body—offers to slay Margery's husband so that she may live chastely:[42] "Another tyme, as this creatur prayd to God that sche myt leuyn chast be leue of hir husbond, Cryst seyd to hir mende, 'Thow must fastyn the Fryday bothen fro mete & drynke, and thow schalt haue thi desyr er Whitsonday, for I schal sodeynly sle thin husbonde'" (21). In the meanwhile Margery is, like St. Cecilia, miraculously and invisibly protected from her husband's desire: "Than on the Wednysday in Estern Woke, aftyr hyr husbond wold haue had knowlach of hir as he was wone be-for, & whan he gan neygh hir, sche seyd, 'Ihesus, help me,' & he had no power to towche hir at that tyme in that wyse, ne neuyr aftyr with no fleschly knowyng" (21). It is difficult to judge the tone of this passage, to decide whether the awkward humor we might sense in the image of John rendered impotent when Margery cries "Jesus, help me" and perhaps even in Christ's casual promise to kill the inconvenient John Kempe would have been available to contemporary audiences. At least one fifteenth-century reader tried to mitigate the awkwardness by emending God's promise to slay Margery's husband to read: "I schal sodcynly sle the flesshely lust in thin husband."[43] Both the ambiguity of tone and the emendation that attempts to resolve it are effects of the temporal disjunctions of Margery's *imitatio Ceciliae*—a disjunction that, I would argue, should be read as a complex narrative representation of the *Book*'s investigation into the relationship between the sacred past and the social present.[44] Margery's husband-slaying God is hard to interpret precisely because he is a figure from the early Christian world of vernacular legends, making an oddly anachronistic appearance.

The conflation of these two historical moments and the tensions it produces become increasingly evident as the *Book* progresses. The climax of Margery's *imitatio* of St. Cecilia, for example, is located precisely in the geography and practical concerns of fifteenth-century England. Returning with his wife from York on Midsummer's Eve, John recalls—and cleverly rewrites—the Cecilia legend by imagining the saint's sword-wielding angel as a figure whom they might encounter on the road and who enforces marital sex rather than chastity. "Margery," he asks, "yf her come a man wyth a swerd & wold smyte of myn hed les than I schulde comown kendly wyth yow as I haue do be-for, seyth me trewth of yowr consciens—for ye sey ye wyl not lye—whethyr wold ye suffyr myn hed to be smet of er ellys suffyr me to medele wyth yow a-gen as I dede sum-tyme?" (23). Margery's *imitatio Ceciliae* is transformed from the miraculous fact of Cecilia's angelic protector to a hypothetical fantasy of highway dangers on the road from York.[45] So, too, her imitation of Cecilia's chaste marriage is finally accomplished not by divine violence (as Christ foretold) but through detailed and conspicuously legalistic negotiations with her husband. John is unmoved by the spiritual rewards that Margery initially offers in exchange for a vow of chastity—that he be saved through Christ's mercy and have more meed in heaven than if he wore a hairshirt or habergeon (23)—but he is interested in having his debts paid off. He at last agrees to remit her marital debt if she repays his financial ones, as long as she also promises to maintain the companionate and social roles of wifehood, continuing to sleep in his bed and eat with him on Fridays. Rewriting Cecilia's angel as a fictional highwayman and Valerian's conversion as a financial deal, Margery's *imitatio* is presented in a richly detailed and realistic late medieval world.

Recent scholarship has emphasized the cultural energy devoted in late medieval England to reconciling secular ideology and spiritual ideals. Much of the active production of vernacular devotional texts and elaborate religious spectacles in the period, especially in the prosperous towns of East Anglia, can be broadly associated with a mercantile class eager to maintain and increase its social and real capital, yet also anxious about the implications of this pursuit for its spiritual status.[46] As Theresa Coletti has shown, a range of texts, from dramatic works such as the *Digby Mary Magdalene* to spiritual treatises such as *A Talking of the Love of God* and moral handbooks such as Hilton's *Epistle on the Mixed Life*, reassured audiences of the spiritual value of their engagement in the secular world and the fundamentally economic structure of salvation. In contrast to biblical and monastic representations of material goods and family ties as impediments to a spiritual life, lay religious culture emphasized wealth as the basis for charity, family as the context for devotional practice, and both as components of a divinely sanctioned social order. Kathleen Ashley reads the *Book of Margery Kempe* as an important contribution to this effort, a form of "social praxis" that offers an imaginary solution to the contradictions between secular bourgeois commitments and the religious discourses that challenged those commitments.[47] The scene of Margery's marriage negotiations offers strong support for this reading: the story assumes that money is not an obstacle to her spiritual vocation but precisely the means by which to secure it.[48]

A different reading emerges, however, if we recognize this scene as an imitation of virgin martyr legends and, in particular, as a comparative analysis of ancient and contemporary forms of feminine devotional practice. Margery's imitation does as much to question as to contribute to what Ashley calls "bourgeois ideology," the cultural representations that allow a late medieval layman or laywoman to "achieve spiritual validation while remaining an active member of mercantile society."[49] On the one hand, Margery's likeness to St. Cecilia points to some important similarities between the social contexts they inhabit: in both third-century Rome and fifteenth-century Lynn a woman's religious vocation is threatened by, and finally incompatible with, the protocols of marriage and family, which deny her sexual and spiritual agency. On the other hand, this agency is no longer secured by angels but by money. The bathos of this substitution, as Cecilia's divine protector is replaced by the "cash nexus" of mercantile community,[50] offers a devastating reading of the confident accommodations of secular and religious priorities in late medieval lay culture. This criticism is elaborated as Margery's subsequent attempt to live a holy life in this community provokes confusion and hostility in those around her, at once extending her imitation of virgin martyrs such as Cecilia and Katherine and revealing the fissures in the ideological fantasy of congruence between worldly and spiritual categories that the *Book* elsewhere seems to support.

The most pervasive category confusion that attends Margery's attempt to pursue a spiritual vocation and retain her social identity is, of course, between virgin and wife.[51] Her trial at York begins with the archbishop's questions about her sexual status: "Why gost thu in white? Art thu a mayden?," and Margery responds, "Nay, ser, I am no mayden; I am a wife" (124). In response to Margery's ambiguous identity, the archbishop orders her fettered as a heretic, and Margery, like an imprisoned virgin martyr, prays to God to help and succor her "ageyn alle hir enmyis, gostly & bodily" (124). In the most striking parallel to vernacular legends, Margery's sexuality allows her to occupy the classic arena for the sanctity of the early saint, the trial for heterodoxy, at which she proclaims and defends her faith.[52] Margery takes full advantage of this public forum: she cries so loudly "that the Erchebischop & his clerkys & meche pepil had gret wondyr of hir"; she recites the Articles of Faith, chides the archbishop, and argues for her right to speak of God, calling on the Gospel as authority for her practice (124–26). This is so characteristic of Margery's extraordinary behavior that its close echo of virgin martyr narratives can easily be overlooked. Like St. Katherine, Margery is here opposed by learned clerks, one of whom challenges her claim that the scripture authorizes her to speak by adducing St. Paul as a counter-authority. Despite the challenge, Margery emerges in the course of the trial as a spiritual authority, and the interview concludes with Margery preaching a parable about a worldly priest that reforms at least one clerk who recognizes himself in the story. Like a virgin martyr who converts others in the process of defending her faith, Margery improves the spiritual and moral status of those who listen to her.[53]

As in her imitation of St. Cecilia, Margery's imitation of the virgin martyr trial involves an elaborate weaving of hagiographic topoi and a realistic portrayal of late medieval life, and again the conjunction of the two is the most provocative aspect of her performance. If the *Book* models the trial narrative broadly on virgin martyr legends, the subjects broached in its course refer rather specifically to late medieval England. The parable she tells of a bear that eats the flowers of a pear tree and defecates is a case in point. She glosses the bear as an immoral priest, whose good works are contaminated by his sin. As Ruth Sklar has demonstrated, her reading treads dangerously close to Lollard arguments that sacraments are affected by the moral profile of the officiant, but it does not go quite so far: the flowers are good works, not sacraments, after all.[54] Its proximity to Lollard concerns highlights the currency of the issues that the parable raises: concerns about the efficacy of the sacraments, the moral and spiritual profile of the clergy, and the status of fiction. Here, then, as in Margery's *imitatio Ceciliae*, we see a careful rewriting of hagiographic paradigms in a vocabulary of contemporary life. Margery is on trial for her belief, like a Roman virgin martyr, and like a virgin martyr, she is given divine assistance to answer her accusers; but the trial is also a verisimilar late medieval heresy examination, addressing current theological and ecclesiological issues. Past and present again converge here in an unsettling synchrony.

Most provocative is the way that the trial scenes suggest that the officials imitate the pagan judges of hagiographic narrative, the necessary corollary to Margery's imitation of the virgin saint. As Margery is questioned before a seemingly endless series of religious and civil authorities, the *Book* establishes a clear comparison between Lancastrian England and the earlier age of persecutions. The *Book* also echoes Lollard representations in this regard, finding an especially close analog in the *Testimony* of William Thorpe. As Anne Hudson has argued, Thorpe presents his confrontation with Archbishop Arundel through the narrative pattern of vernacular legends, with Arundel in the place of the foolish persecutor, outwitted again and again by his innocent interlocutor.[55] But, just as Margery finally maintains her orthodoxy, following church teaching on the sacraments and embracing ecclesiastical authority, the *Book* departs significantly from Thorpe's hagiographic representation of contemporary trials in ways that speak directly to its strategies of historical comparison.

Thorpe's account of the "enemyes of truthe" (25) in the prologue readily calls to mind the pagan judges of vernacular legend: "But, thorugh her olde and her newe vnschamefast synnes, these tirauntis and enemyes of truthe schullen be so blyndid and so obstinate in yuel that thei schullen gessen hemsilf to don plesyng sacrifice to the lord God in her malicious and wrongful pursuyng and destroiyng of innocent men and wymmens bodies, which men and wymmen for hei vertues lyuynge, and for her trewe knowlechyng of truthe, and for her pacient, wilful and glad suffrynge of persecucioun for rightwisnesse, deseruen thorugh the grace of God to ben eiris of the eendles blis of heuene" (28). Introducing this claim as one of the central reasons for writing the story of his trial, Thorpe presents Arundel as stupidly evil, haplessly earnest in his own religious devotion and his pursuit of others who deviate from it, mistaking good for evil and evil for good. The implicit corollary is that orthodox Christianity is as false as paganism, an entirely inadequate framework for recognizing "virtuous living" and "true knowledge of the truth." The final scene of the trial, which I quote at length, illustrates the argument as it juxtaposes the senseless malice of the archbishop and his men and Thorpe's own stable faith:

> Theese wordis and manye moo suche greet wordis weren there spoken to me, manassynge me and alle other of the same sect for to ben poniyschid and distryed vnto the vtmest. . . . And than cam in to vs dyuerse seculers, and thei scorneden me on eche side, and thei manasseden me gretli, and summe conseileden the Archebischop to brenne me anoon, and summe other counseileden to drenche me in the see for it was nyghhonde there. . . . And thanne I was rebukid and scorned and manassid on ech side. And yit after this dyuerse persoones crieden vpon me to knele doun to submytte me. But I stood stille and spak no word. And thanne there weren spoke of me and to me many greete wordis; and I stood and herde hem curse and manasse and scorne me, but I seide no thing. . . . And so thanne I was led forth and brought into a ful vnhonest prisoun where I cam neuere bifore. But, thankid be God, whanne alle men weren gon forth thenns from me, schittinge faste after hem the prisoun dore, anoon therafter I, beynge thereinne bi mysilf, bisiede me to thenke on God and to thanke him of his goodnesse. And I was thanne gretli confortid in alle my wittis, not oonly forthi that I was than delyuered for a tyme fro the sight, fro the heeringe, fro the presence, fro the scornynge and fro the manassinge of myn enemyes, but myche more I gladid in the Lord forthi thorugh his grace he kepte me so bothe amonge the flateryngis specialli, also amonge the manassingis of myn aduersaries that withouten heuynesse and agrigginge of my conscience I passid awei fro hem. For as a tree leyde vpon another tree ouerthwert on crosse wyse, so weren the Archebischop and hise three clerkis alwei contrarie to me and I to hem. (92–93)

The similarity to Margery Kempe's self-presentation is notable: each is the object of scorn and threat of harm, which establishes not the authority of the archbishop but the innocence and sincere faith of the accused. But the cruciform image that closes Thorpe's testimony is more absolute than anything in the *Book of Margery Kempe*: Thorpe and the archbishop are like a tree laid athwart another, at clear, categorical cross-purposes. They are particular instantiations of an allegorical contest between the enemies and the lovers of truth that Thorpe outlines in the prologue: "And thus sumdel bi this writyng mai be perseyued thorugh Goddis grace how that enemyes of truthe, perseuerynge boldli in her malice, enforsen hem for to withstonde the fredom of Cristis gospel, for which fredom Crist bicam man and schedde oute his hert blood ... men and wymmen that louen truthe, and heeren or knowen of this pursuyng that now is in the chirche, owen herethorugh to be the more moued in alle her wittis, to ablen hem to grace, and to setten so litil pris bi hemsilf that thei withouten tariinge forsaken wilfuli and gladli al the wrecchidnesse of this liif" (25–26). Thorpe specifies the current moment—"nowe"—as a time of persecution, but the passage as a whole folds this moment into an ahistorical paradigm in which "enemies of truth boldly persevere in their malice" against "men and women who love truth." On the one hand, these terms are tropological: persecution is not a function of a particular historical moment but an individual's own moral failings. Thorpe claims that if Christians do not willingly take on penance for their sinfulness, God, in his mercy, arranges for the purifying violence of persecution: "And, but we enforsen vs to don thus wilfulli and in couenable tyme, the Lord, if he wol not lese vs, wol in dyuerse maneres moue tyrauntis agens vs, for to constreynen vs violentli for to don penaunce, whiche we wolden not don wilfulli. And, certis, this doynge is a special grace of the Lord, and a greet tookne of loue and of merci." On the other hand, the terms are those of an eternal antagonism between the world and the spirit: "the louers of this world haten and pursuen hem whom thei knowen pacient, meke and mylde, sobir, chast and wilful pore, hating and fleyng alle worldli vanitees and fleischli lustis—for, certis, these vertuous condiciouns ben euene contrarie to the maners of this world" (26–27).[56] Both modes eschew history. Thorpe's *imitatio* of the martyred saint, as it is presented in his *Testimony*, is unmediated by historical difference: ancient persecutions and present ones all participate in the same timeless contest between good and evil and the equally timeless context of God's vigilant grace.

The *Book of Margery Kempe* does not end, as Thorpe's *Testimony* does, with the protagonists still at odds, still representing the narrative categories of tyrant and saint or the allegorical ones of enemy and lover of truth. Margery ultimately uses the trial scenes to proclaim her orthodoxy and to secure institutional sanction for her practice: thus the archbishop of York ultimately approves of Margery's story, "seying it was a good tale" (127), and provides her with an escort. In recognizing the legitimacy of Margery's religious identity and practice, he is himself redefined as a spiritual authority rather than a cruel persecutor. Here, too, we see that Margery's *imitatio* is finally more complicated than either Lollard imitation or the kind of hagiographic exemplarity developed in Bokenham's legendary: it relentlessly confuses the binary opposition of historical continuity and difference. Like Lollard polemic, the *Book* insists on continuity: Margery imitates ancient saints, and her persecutors thus inadvertently imitate ancient ones. The narrative structure of traditional legends, Kempe suggests, is easily reproduced in England, where sincere devotion, uncompromised by conformity to accepted social roles, is readily interpreted as heresy. But the civic and religious authorities do not in fact martyr her, because they eventually recognize—if often only grudgingly—the legitimacy of her religious identity. The point of the *Book*'s criticism, then, is not simply that contemporary mayors or archbishops are "enemies of the truth" or "tyrants," as it is in Thorpe's *Testimony*, but that English community does not form a coherent interpretive community, one that can confidently and consistently recognize a holy woman, united—as Lancastrian ideology would have it—by one orthodox faith, defined against a dangerous religious other.[57]

Reading Margery

The differences within English community are emphasized, as we have already seen, by the divergent interpretations of Margery's behavior. During the proceedings at York, for example, "the pepil" cannot define the religious identity or agree on the ethical status of the woman before them: "Sum of the pepil askyd whedyr sche wer a Cristen woman er a Iewe; sum seyd she was a good woman, & sum seyd nay" (124).[58] The variable response challenges the fiction of shared belief and practice on which social and political institutions, local and national, depend, and it is given extensive thematic attention throughout the *Book*. It is represented broadly in the contrast between the narrative emphasis on the scorn and reproof she endures—represented as a kind of social martyrdom[59]—and the catalog of spiritual authorities who acknowledge the validity of her vocation: a friar in Lynn; Philip Repyndon, the bishop of Lincoln; Richard Castyr, the vicar of St. Stephen's Church; William Southfield, a white friar of Norwich; and Julian of Norwich—as well as those who take her as a spiritual mother.[60] It is given more focused attention in the series of inquiries into her religious practices and beliefs: Margery is first examined in Leicester before the mayor, and then in the Church of All Hallows, before the abbot (111–17); in York, before a doctor in the chapterhouse and before the archbishop (121–28); in Beverley, again before the archbishop of York (131–35), until she finally secures a letter and seal from the archbishop of Canterbury that guarantees her vocation (136–37). Throughout the *Book*, Margery is represented as the subject of civic, ecclesiastic, and social interpretation. But the several attempts to define her reveal less about Margery than about the community she inhabits, which is so fractured by the different commitments to social and spiritual value that it is unable to read Margery correctly or consistently.

The difficulty of interpreting Margery's spiritual status may at first seem to be a consequence of the perpetual changes in her devotional practices.[61] She adopts and then discards distinctive eating practices; she adopts and then discards the white clothing that identifies her as a spiritual virgin; she abandons but finally returns to her wifely role; God gives but also sometimes takes away her gift of tears. The *Book* addresses this changeability in the voice of Christ, who explains why he sometimes withdraws her tears through analogy to the sun: "Sum-tyme thow wetyst wel the sunne schynyth al abrod that many man may se it, & sum-tyme it is hyd vndyr a clowde that men may not se it, & yet is the sunne neuyr the lesse in hys hete ne in hys brytnesse. And rygth so far I be the & be my chosyn sowlys" (31). Margery, like other chosen souls, is an eternal and unchanging element, but the great grace she has been granted is sometimes obscured from view, as the sun is sometimes hidden in clouds. Its social expression is variable, but its ontological status is not. This, too, is borrowed from the narrative conventions of vernacular saints' lives, which present the saint as the fixed moral center of the narrative, the focus of interpretation, read variously by the other characters in the story. In the legend of St. Katherine, for example, Emperor Maxentius is enraged by the girl's faith, but his queen is inspired by it and goes to her martyrdom before Katherine does. Margery's spiritual status, like that of a virgin martyr, is a cipher for the status of the communities and institutions around her, as an early conversation with Christ makes explicit. In response to her fear of becoming vainglorious, Christ promises that he will take the sin from her: "Drede the not, dowtyr, I xal take veynglory fro the. For thei that worshep the thei worshep me; thei that despysyn the thei despysen me, & I schal chastysen hem therfor. I am in the, and thow in me. And thei that heryn the thei heryn the voys of God" (22–23). Margery is not incapable of vainglory—a sin to which she certainly seems vulnerable—but the category is simply irrelevant to her spiritual status, which is here rendered neutral by her full and uncomplicated identity with Christ. Instead of registering her own moral stature, the *Book* insists, her behavior helps to index the moral stature of others, whose reactions—whether of veneration or opprobrium—are not responses to Margery at all but to God, for whom she stands as surrogate.

We can see how Margery indexes the moral profile of the community in her first miracle, her unlikely survival when a stone and beam fall from the roof of the church and strike her. The miracle traces Margery's conversion from private to public spirituality, as her personal devotion, represented by the prayer book in her hand, gives way to the spectacle of the miracle. The importance of the event is precisely its public nature and the disparate interpretations it produces: "mych pepyl magnyfied mech God in this creatur. And also mech pepyl wold not leuyn it, but rathar leuyd it was a tokyn of wreth & veniawns than thei wold leuyn it was any token of mercy er quemfulnes" (22). The opposing responses reveal the spiritual state of Margery's audience in a simple way: some recognize it as a sign of divine grace; others read it as a token of vengeance. The *Book* elsewhere offers more elaborate accounts of the response to Margery's behavior in which the variety of interpretations reflects disjunctions between social and spiritual systems of meaning. It details, for example, the several ways that the "pepil" understand Margery's decision to accompany her daughter-in-law to Germany without her confessor's permission:

Sum seyd it was a womanys witte & a gret foly for the lofe of hir dowtyr-in-lawe to putte hir-self, a woman in gret age, to perellys of the see & for to gon in-to a strawnge cuntre where sche had not ben be-forn ne not wist how sche xulde come a-geyn. Summe heldyn it was a dede of gret charite for-as-meche as hir dowtyr had be-forn-tyme left hir frendys & hir cuntre & cam wyth hir husbond to visityn hir in this cuntre that sche wolde now halpyn hir dowtyr hom a-geyn in-to the cuntre that sche cam fro. Other whech knewe mor of the creaturys leuyng supposyd & trustyd that it was the wille & the werkyng of al-mythy God to the magnifying of hys owyn name. (228–29)

The catalog testifies to the number of different ideological lenses through which Margery's behavior can be read. The first is an antifeminist reading: that "womanys witte" and "foly" motivate Margery and that the story is simply an illustration of the foolishness of an old woman. This seems corrected by the charitable interpretation that follows, which reads Margery's behavior from the perspective of social ideologies of hospitality and family obligation, as the service a woman should render her daughter-in-law.

But this reading, too, is corrected by that of those who know Margery better. Her behavior has nothing to do with social or moral discourses of any kind: it is simply a reflection and expression of God's will. At the same time that these divergent responses define Margery as a saintly cipher, they expose the fractures in English community and, especially, the bourgeois fiction that spiritual and social priorities can be reconciled.

It is significant that the variable interpretation of Margery is diachronic as well as synchronic. In the passage that most explicitly claims future sainthood for Margery, Christ promises, "In this chirche thu hast suffyrd meche schame & reprefe for the gyftys that I haue gouyn the & for the grace & goodnes that I haue wrowt in the, and therfore in this cherche & in this place I xal ben worschepyd in the. Many a man & woman xal seyn it is wel sene that God louyd hir wel. Dowtyr, I xal werkyn so mech grace for the that al the world xal wondryn & merueylyn of my goodnes" (156). Christ later foretells that this reformed community will one day be the recipient of Margery's grace (212–13). The church and community, now hostile to Margery, will one day honor and worship her, just as virgin martyrs, once reviled, are now honored. The change is attributed here to Christ, who will work his grace to change the social reception of her spiritual status, but this passage also—with remarkable complexity—restates the question of historical continuity and discontinuity that marks her imitation of traditional saints. On the one hand, it implies a massive social change that will provide a new ideological framework for understanding Margery's religious practice—like that of the wholesale Christianization of Europe, which made saints such as Cecilia and Katherine worshipped where they had once been martyred. On the other hand, it indexes the continuity between past and present under the current framework, at least with regard to the social rejection of holy women, which is shown to be the consequence not of a pagan blindness to Christian truth—since holy women continue to be persecuted under a Christian regime—but of women's social status and the fundamental incompatibility between social and spiritual pursuits. The passage is also, of course, a fantasy of future consensus. It imagines a community united in its devotion to a sainted Margery, who will—through God's great grace—become agent and evidence of the community's wholeness, no longer divided by the incoherence of its spiritual and social priorities.

This incoherence is the central subject of the *Book of Margery Kempe* as it develops a searching analysis of late medieval community, not only through the structural opposition between saint and society found in vernacular legends but also through the exemplary relationship between traditional saints and the late medieval woman who imitates them in her own devotional practice. By conflating past and present, Margery's imitation offers vernacular legends as *comparanda* for fifteenth-century institutions and ideologies. In doing so, she challenges important fictions of community: the possibility of reconciling spiritual and social priorities and the existence of a community defined by shared religious ideals. But the *Book of Margery Kempe* is less a polemical work than an exploratory one, primarily concerned not with defining the present, but with imagining and performing its complex relationship to the past.

6

Performing the Past: Saints' Plays and the *Second Nun's Tale*

"IN THIS YERE WAS THE PLEY OF SEYNT KATERINE": so reads the entry for 1393 in the *Chronicle of London* contained in British Library MS Cotton Vitellius A.xvi, the first of the *Chronicle*'s two references to St. Katherine pageants. It is a tantalizing record for the scholar of medieval drama or vernacular hagiography, pointing to a public representation of the saint but in its formulaic syntax omitting reference to the civic institutions, urban geography, and theatrical conventions that informed the performance.[1] Unfortunately, in this it is representative of the historical record of saints' plays and pageants, a tradition amply documented, but in so fragmentary and incidental a way as to make clear only its prevalence.[2] The problem is compounded by the even sparser textual tradition, witnessed only by the Digby manuscript plays of Mary Magdalene and the Conversion of St. Paul, which are surely too elaborate to be typical of the genre in any case.[3] The archival and textual limits on how well we can understand hagiographic drama are especially frustrating in the context of increasing critical interest in the role of gender in communal performance.[4] Plays such as the London St. Katherine raise fundamental questions about the practice of devotion in the late medieval city: How did the performance of female sanctity intersect with the civic ideologies and social tensions explored by scholars of the Corpus Christi plays? How might we understand the public representation of feminine sanctity and its relation to the space of the late medieval town? And—most important for our purposes here—what is the relation between the mimesis of saints' legends as urban drama and the mimesis of saints' legends as ethical practice, that is, between the communal performance and the exemplarity of female saints' legends?

We do not have enough information about the performance of virgin martyr legends as community drama to answer these questions confidently. But the silences of the historical record indicate cultural expectations just as its emphases do. Indeed, some saints' pageants *are* carefully recorded: the London *Chronicle*, which offers such an abbreviated account of the 1393 play, provides an expansive one of a St. Katherine pageant presented in London some hundred years later on the occasion of Catherine of Aragon's procession into the city in anticipation of her marriage to the young Prince Arthur. How Catherine was "receyved w[ith] moost Triumphe of the Mayre and the Citezeins" and honored with an elaborate pageant is narrated in ample and specific detail in the *Chronicle*, which provides not only information about the geography, staging, audience, and participating institutions but even the script of the pageant, which began with a tableau of St. Katherine and St. Ursula, attended by "dyuers living virgins," on London Bridge.

As we will see, the speeches of these two virgin martyrs, preoccupied as they are with the relation between exemplarity, political policy, and genealogy, demonstrate how hagiographic pageantry might represent not only the spiritual meaning of sacred narrative but also the ideological meaning of the city and the marriage of the royal couple. This performance is a useful point of entry for a discussion of saints' plays that surface more cryptically in the archival record—not because it presents the full articulation of that tradition, however, but something more like its antithesis.[5] This chapter explores the possibility that the historical record fairly represents the political authority, and hence historical legibility, of both the fourteenth- and the early sixteenth-century pageants; that is, we might know so little about most saints' plays because—perhaps only implicitly, even inadvertently—they challenged political and religious institutions in ways that made their textual inscription more difficult and less likely.

Turning from textual to dramatic traditions in this chapter requires us to investigate two of the likely performance contexts for the 1393 play and others like it: the parish guilds that sponsored much of the vernacular hagiographic drama in late medieval England and the theatrical conventions, such as cross-dressing, that created and reflected tensions between the narrative represented in performance and the social space in which it was performed. The ethical demands of hagiographic narrative had significant implications for its mimesis in the public spaces of the medieval town, as did the possibility—also raised by the *Book of Margery Kempe*—that audiences might understand narratives of the early Church as commentary on the contemporary one. The dramatic mapping of sacred narrative onto urban space, which creates a topography of civic authority and social hierarchy in the cycle plays, could work very differently in performances sponsored by religious guilds. At the end of the chapter, I extend my analysis of the cultural work of the plays and pageants of virgin martyrs through an analysis of the *Second Nun's Tale*, a text that, although not dramatic from a strictly formalist perspective, may nevertheless register some of the broader cultural issues occluded in the taciturn archival records of hagiographic drama. The Second Nun's performance of the St. Cecilia legend represents, and comments on, the public performance of feminine sanctity in ways that may not only help us understand the social meaning of the 1393 London St. Katherine play but also account for the abbreviated entry recording it in the city chronicle. Roughly contemporary with Julian of Norwich's response to the same legend, the *Second Nun's Tale* also returns us to the beginning of this book, offering new perspectives on the limits and meaning of hagiographic exemplarity through its representation of a public imitation of a virgin martyr.

Playing for the Queen: Sanctity and Political Authority in a Tudor Pageant

As Catherine of Aragon approached London Bridge on a Friday afternoon in November 1501, the London *Chronicle* reports, she was greeted by the figure of St. Katherine, the first in a series of pageants celebrating the princess's arrival and imminent marriage to Prince Arthur.[6] St. Katherine's precedence in this series is implicitly related to her onomastic, and thus patronal, relationship to the Spanish princess: their close identification is emphasized from the opening lines, in which the saint announces herself as "Kateryn of the Court Celestyall" and recalls that Lady Catherine was entrusted to her when she took her baptismal name. As "shild and proteccion" for Catherine at her "first Entre / Into this world," the saint also oversees her entry into London, a kind of political baptism that will transform her from a Spanish princess into an English queen. Catherine of Aragon's devotional and political identity, moreover, authorizes that of the prince she is due to marry. In the saint's speech, Catherine is the shared spouse of Christ and Arthur, an unsettling image that vividly establishes her as the point of intersection between divine and earthly realms. St. Katherine announces:

> And as I halp you to Crist, your first make,
> So haue I purveid a Second Spowse trewe;
> But ye for hym the first shall not forsake,
> Love your first spouse chief, and after that your newe. (235)

The monologue purports to be a spiritual and ethical education for the young princess, establishing the priority of her heavenly spouse over her earthly one. But if St. Katherine's speech doubles Catherine's husbands in order to enjoin her to prefer the "glory perpetuall" promised by the first to the "honour temporall" she will gain with the second (235), it also establishes Catherine as the ground for a comparison between Christ and Prince Arthur, heaven and earth—or, more precisely, heaven and England.

The political implications of St. Katherine's appearance come to the fore at the close of her speech, as she sends the princess to the pageant of Policy, "W[ith]out whose help all they that thynk to Reign / Or long to prosper, labour all in vayn," who will lead Catherine ultimately to the court of Honor (235). The tableaux, which comprise Noblesse, Virtue, Raphael (as a patron of marriage and procreativity), Alphons (Catherine's ancestor), Job, and Boethius, are presented at once as political education—literally leading Catherine of Aragon through the exempla and abstractions that will make her a fit queen for England—and as illustration that Catherine is already a double for St. Katherine, just as by implication here and later by explicit dramatic analogy the English court will be seen as an image of the heavenly one, with Catherine and Arthur seated next to one another on the throne of Honor, "fixed upon the eternal foundation of the seven virtues and set above the cosmos," as Gordon Kipling writes.[7]

Before proceeding to the pageant of Policy, however, Catherine is addressed by St. Ursula, and the shift in speakers marks a shift in emphasis from the more general celebration of aristocratic virtue that characterizes St. Katherine's monologue to a more English—and specifically Lancastrian and Tudor—focus. Where St. Katherine offers onomastic authority for Catherine's political status and royal identity, St. Ursula offers genealogical authority, at once recalling the princess's Lancastrian roots (as the descendant of John of Gaunt's daughter) and collocating this with the saint's own legendary association with England. In fact, in the vague syntax of the speech, Ursula, too, seems to claim Lancastrian origins:

> Madame Kateryn, because that I and ye
> Be comyn of noble blood of this land,
> Of Lancastre, which is not oonly of Amyte
> The cause but also a ferme band
> Bitwene you and this Realme to stand,
> Nature shall move vs to love alwey,
> As two comyn out of one Cuntrey. (236)

St. Ursula presents herself as Catherine's genealogical twin, sharing the "noble blood" of England. This doubling points to another, between Catherine of Aragon and the Tudor prince she is about to marry, both of whom descend from the house of Lancaster. Catherine's affiliations with St. Ursula, in turn, become yet more concrete, if more convoluted, in the context of her imminent marriage: St. Ursula announces that she is of the same lineage as King Arthur, and thus as Catherine's intended spouse is the second Arthur, so Catherine will be a second Ursula. Whereas in St. Katherine's speech Catherine of Aragon is the ground of the relationship between Christ and Arthur—an association that grants his rule a divine status—here Arthur is the ground of a relationship between Catherine and the native saint—an association that grants the Spanish princess an honorary Englishness.

Conflating feminine sanctity, royal "policy," and the Lancastrian genealogy of the Tudor line, the speeches of St. Katherine and St. Ursula suggest how hagiographic performances could work to consolidate political institutions and the authority on which they rest. The tableau evinces an intimate relation between pageantry and politics—between, that is, two critical categories of "performance," the histrionic and the ideologically constitutive, to borrow James Paxson's concise formulation.[8] In rewriting London as the site of Catherine's feminine piety through the speeches of St. Katherine and St. Ursula, the pageant argues for the spiritual authority of the monarchy, the legitimacy of political policy, the value of genealogy, and the preeminence and continuous history of the Lancastrian line.

In authorizing political and social categories through religious performance, the pageants for Catherine's royal entry recall the cultural work underlying the cycle plays performed in northern towns. Mervyn James's groundbreaking reading of Corpus Christi plays as myths of civic community—myths now recognized as contested rather than celebrated in their performance[9]—paved the way for more recent work that charts the symbolic link between dramatic play and political ideologies as they map onto the geography of the late medieval town. So, for example, several scholars have drawn attention to the fact that in York the same route was used for royal processions and for the pageant representing Christ's entry into Jerusalem, in a dramatic collation of sacred narrative and sociopolitical ceremony.[10] Anne Higgins has continued this work, reading the York cycle in light of the streets of the city and their social meaning for the play's contemporary audience: the Last Judgment, for example, which was played in a space bordered on one side by the gutter issuing from the butchers' street and on the other by the homes of wealthy merchants and the churches where most of the town's mayors were buried, might well have used these material and architectural features as part of its dramatic vocabulary, in turn assigning spiritual meaning to the social and economic differences evident in the geography of the town.[11] As such evidence shows, the symbolic significance of religious drama was articulated through its enactment in social space, and that space was, in turn, configured by religious performances, which offered authority and meaning to the civic hierarchies and institutions that inhabited it.

The London pageant gains its meaning not only from its urban setting but also its address to the Spanish princess. Catherine of Aragon is not, of course, the exclusive audience—indeed, she could not have understood the English pageants[12]—but in the fiction of the performance, the virgin saints speak directly to her. She is the audience-as-participant, the addressee who makes the performance meaningful, even though she could not understand it herself. Her identity trumps that of the saints presented in the pageant: neither St. Katherine nor St. Ursula appears as the protagonist of her own legend. They are rather expressions and extensions of Catherine of Aragon's royal identity. This is most strikingly so in the speech of St. Ursula, whose own immanent marriage to an English prince is the occasion for her martyrdom and that of the eleven thousand virgins accompanying her. Given her fate, it is hardly surprising that no analogy is made between the nuptial Ursula and Lady Catherine; as we have seen, the analogy is instead founded on the genealogical connection between them, pointedly rooted in the person of Catherine's betrothed. More subtle is the potentially awkward role of St. Katherine, who adamantly refuses marriage, her devotion to her first spouse, Christ, precluding a second, earthly, husband. In advising the young bride to remain true to her heavenly spouse as she marries Prince Arthur, the St. Katherine of the pageant assumes the compatibility of these two commitments, a radical departure from the narrative expectations of virgin martyr legends, including her own.

Thus stripped of their legendary contexts, the two virgin martyrs are exemplary, but only in the most general way. They do not stand for specific devotional postures or ethical practices, as the foundation for a mimetic relationship between past sanctity and present behavior. Instead, they represent something like the apotheosis of both royal feminine goodness and, more specifically, the political authority of Catherine and the Tudor family about to welcome her in marriage. The saints can stand for that political authority, I would argue, only because their function as metonyms for Catherine's identity supplants their own legendary identities and the narratives that commemorate them, which might otherwise remind the audience—this time the citizens of London who could understand the speeches—of the incompatibility of divine and social authority demonstrated again and again in virgin martyr legends.

As a script for Catherine of Aragon's identity and the authority of the Tudor line, this pageant was readily available for commemoration in the London *Chronicle*, a record likely kept by a city alderman or other prominent citizen eager to record the spectacular welcome that the city had offered to the new queen.[13] Is there, then, a corollary relation between the silence of the 1393 entry and the performance it represents? Saints' pageants, including the 1393 play, may have had a less clear relationship to late medieval political configurations for two reasons explored in the next two sections of this chapter. First, they were often sponsored by parish guilds, voluntary and relatively independent groups of laypeople, whose populations could be markedly heterogeneous, including men and women from a broad socioeconomic range. Although not necessarily antithetical to official institutions, such as the parish church or civic or royal government, religious fraternities were independent of, and so potentially threatening to, them. My second claim is an extension of the first: the performance of virgin martyr narratives in particular may have seemed to articulate this latent, and perhaps on occasion overt, challenge. As we have seen, these legends celebrate the devout and adamant resistance of the female saint to the authorities, civic and religious, who oppose her. They are invariably concerned with the incompatibility of earthly priorities and spiritual ones, and they offer no support for the authority of institutions of any kind. The sanctity of the virgin martyr is defined precisely by her rejection of the social and political order, especially compulsory heterosexuality, filial obligations, and local political authority. As we saw, even the royal pageants for Catherine of Aragon carefully avoid reference to the legends of St. Katherine and St. Ursula in the text of their speeches in order to replace the radical incompatibility of earthly power and spiritual value demonstrated in vernacular hagiography with a confident assertion of the continuity between them, a continuity established and epitomized by the princess.

The reticence of the 1393 entry, then, may not be simply an inadvertence of the terse style of Middle English historical prose but rather a consequence of the challenge to late medieval political and religious institutions that would be implicit in any mapping of virgin martyr legends onto public space. If, as Patricia Badir has argued, historical records that include dramatic activity amid other social practices recall "urban topography as its site or place of origin,"[14] and so point to the imagined relation between the represented past and the civic present, the London *Chronicle*'s record of the 1393 Katherine play, in its stark omission of all social and institutional contexts, may well be an exercise in forgetting the play's intimate relation to civic space.

Religious Guilds: Tactics of Devotion in the Late Medieval Parish

The prevalence of parish guilds in the sponsorship of noncycle plays and pageants is a commonplace of drama scholarship.[15] The success of a Paternoster play in York prompted the foundation of a guild for the express purpose of ensuring its continuing performance.[16] More typical is the pageant sponsored by the Beverly guild of St. Helen on her feast day, in which the fairest boy was chosen to represent St. Helen and two men, one carrying a cross and the other a shovel, accompanied him in a dramatic tableau of the Invention of the Cross. Another Beverly guild, the fraternity of St. Mary, had a more elaborate and mimetic procession, with actors representing Mary holding a child in her arms, Joseph, Simeon, and two angels.[17] The Chester Assumption play, eventually incorporated into the city's Corpus Christi cycle, seems originally to have been an independent performance sponsored by a women's guild.[18] The St. Anne guild in Lincoln also sponsored plays, perhaps related to the Marian plays incorporated into the N-Town cycle. The cultural status of the parish guilds that sponsored hagiographic drama is a crucial part of the plays' social meaning, the range of interpretations available to the varied audiences of their public pageantry. As Claire Sponsler reminds us, the interpretive practice of those audiences is always "divergent," reflecting both "personal histories" and collective experiences as members of particular genders, social classes, and vocations.[19] But these divergent interpretations are framed by, if not limited to, the institutional affiliations of a performance, the relationship between the play and the social geography in which it takes place.[20] For both practical and ideological reasons, the guilds' position outside of the powerful institutions of city, state, and church may explain, in part, why some of the performances they sponsored are not well documented.[21]

In his recent study of Yorkshire guilds, David Crouch has argued that the relations between parish guilds and political institutions fluctuated widely over the course of the late Middle Ages, from official suspicion to official endorsement, with considerable regional variation in the relations between guilds and civic authority in particular. This judicious assessment is confirmed by other regional studies by Virginia Bainbridge and Katherine French that demonstrate further how difficult it is to make general claims about a social phenomenon closely dependent on local circumstances.[22] But the intense distrust of religious guilds that surfaced at moments in the late Middle Ages makes clear that they were perceived as potential arenas for activities counter to the interests of official institutions. My argument is not that guilds frequently and overtly challenged such institutions, but that cultural expectations that they *could* present such a challenge may have informed not only legislation intended to render them more visible and responsive to authority but also the social meaning of the hagiographic performances they sponsored.

Official concern about their identity and agenda was the impetus for our most complete resource for late medieval religious guilds, the collection of returns submitted to the Chancery in 1398. Burgeoning interest and participation in parish guilds in the course of the fourteenth century drew attention to them in the Cambridge Parliament of 1388, which mandated that writs be sent to sheriffs ordering them to make public proclamations that all fraternities identify their origin, customs, gatherings, property, and oaths to the Chancery.[23] As Caroline Barron argues, the official inquiry may have been motivated partly by financial interests, and in particular a concern that guilds might acquire lands in mortmain without compensating the king,[24] but it may also have been motivated by a suspicion that parish guilds were "secret societies" like those thought to have been behind the Peasants' Revolt.[25] This may be why the Lady Guild in Tideswell, Derbyshire, for example, reports that its feast has been suspended for seven years, that is, since 1381: Crouch suggests that this is evidence of local suppression of a ritual that may have been seen as conducive to social unrest.[26]

The guild returns offer no evidence of subversive political activity; some explicitly disavow it. The guild of St. Peter in Lawshall, Suffolk, for example, insists that the fraternity is organized for devotional activity "and not to the injury of our lord King or his people."[27] The St. Christopher guild in Norwich carefully specifies that its bylaws pose no threat to common law and that its purposes are strictly devotional: "Ande this is here entent, to make non ordinaunce in prejudice ne lettyng of the common lawe, but only in worshepe of god and seynt cristofore, and norisshyng of loue and charitee."[28] As Barron points out, however, such denials prove little. Indeed, the eagerness with which guilds emphasize their poverty and pious purpose may well register a certain nervousness about why the returns had been mandated and how they would be used. Even as the guild returns insist that the fraternities were apolitical, official anxiety about their very existence suggests that lay religion, however orthodox, could be threatening to political authorities, especially when it became a forum for organized collective activity. The devotional practices of the guild—whether or not they included overt political activity—are in this sense "tactical," as that term is defined by Michel de Certeau in *The Practice of Everyday Life*.[29] That is, the guilds' appropriation of "official culture," far from being merely passive consumption, is marked by independent agency and inevitable difference. The guild festivities—whether procession, pageant, or feast—made clear that the guild was, as Ben McRee writes, "an independent body with its own goals, its own rules, and its own corporate identity."[30] Such ritual thus establishes, if only temporarily and provisionally, a place outside of dominant institutions and independent of the social protocols produced by those institutions. This does not, of course, mean that it will necessarily be used or perceived as a strategy of dissent, but it makes this a structural possibility.

To be sure, if Parliament found religious guilds threatening, they did sometimes have more comfortable relationships with civic government—as, for example, the powerful Trinity guild in Lynn and the Corpus Christi guild in York did.[31] But not all, or even most, of the myriad guilds in late medieval England can have had such intimate connections to urban authority.[32] Many had a more diverse and less economically elite membership, as did the St. Michael guild at Lincoln, which announced in its return that it was founded by "common and middling folks" and confined its membership to those ranks.[33] In cities in which participation in civic government was not related to participation in powerful fraternities, even prominent guilds might embrace priorities and populations that differed from those of city institutions. French notes, for example, the tensions between town and parish officials in Bridgewater, Somerset, where civic and parish offices were divided along socioeconomic lines, with merchants serving in town government and artisans and small shop owners active in parish administration. This difference was given material expression when the parish began to sell pews in the fifteenth century, French shows: the pews quickly became the exclusive domain of civic officials and "men of substance," refiguring the space of the church to reflect the social hierarchies of the city.[34]

That parochial activity could provide an alternative domain for those excluded from civic authority seems demonstrated in more vivid terms in the history of the St. George guild in Norwich traced by Benjamin McRee. In this instance, the tensions were between two economically and politically powerful factions: one led by Thomas Wetherby, who had been mayor in 1432 and was supported by the duke of Suffolk; and an alternative political group that replaced Wetherby. The unrest provoked by these tensions led to the revocation of the city's liberties in 1437 and 1443. McRee suggests that Wetherby and his allies, all members of the St. George guild, used the guild's hagiographic pageant to imply that Norwich, like Silene, required the heroic intervention of a latter-day St. George. McRee notes that the opposition mayor and all the other city officers became guild members in an effort to diffuse the its partisan identity and that the pageant was not presented again for some fifteen years, resuming only when the last of Wetherby's opponents died. McRee suggests, that is, that the civic officials joined the guild in order to mitigate its ability to embody oppositional politics and that they recognized hagiographic pageantry as the most significant performance of the guild's political meaning.[35]

The Norwich St. George guild provides rare local and specific evidence that guilds and their public performances could serve to challenge civic authority. This is implicit, too, in state regulations that coincide roughly with the events in Norwich. While the only action taken following the returns of 1389 was the enactment of mortmain legislation in 1391, more strenuous measures were taken by Henry V in 1436. Declaring that parish guilds threatened the king's "profit and franchises" with their "unlawful and unreasonable ordinances" and caused "common damage to the people," he required guilds to register with justices of the peace and local civic authorities.[36] The statute registers, that is, the "tactical" potential of religious guilds that attends their independence from official institutions, a potential limited here by making them subordinate to civic as well as royal authorities.

That the guilds were interested in establishing a measure of independence is clear from their development of alternative social codes and legal procedures. Two common features of guild ordinances are relevant here: the guilds' requirements regarding the behavior of their members, and the frequent insistence that disputes between members be brought before guild leaders rather than legal authorities.[37] The behavioral codes designate the guild—rather than the church or civic government—as the most immediate arbiter of social behavior. They reflect, as McRee argues, a lay desire to fashion a collective identity, which in turn depended on the good behavior of all members.[38] As the requirement that members resolve disputes without recourse to legal institutions suggests, this group identity was a shield against official structures that did not serve all economic classes well. By forming a more proximate and intimate community in which disputes could be settled by one's peers, guilds obviated recourse to a judicial system that—as Richard Firth Green has taught us—increasingly favored the literate elite with access to documentary evidence.[39]

More subtly, but significantly, the comparatively open membership of the guilds created a local community not structured, or less structured, by the categories of sex and vocation that organized much of late medieval urban life. Identified with a parish, rather than with a craft or vocation, religious guilds represented a more diverse social group than did professional fraternities. As Gervase Rosser writes, "by far the greater number of these associations welcomed recruits from virtually all occupations, of both sexes, and of most social degrees."[40] The social range was not absolute: as Rosser notes, guilds required a fee to join, excluding the poorest members of society, and at least one guild, the St. Michael fraternity in Lincoln, excluded the ruling class, explicitly refusing membership to mayors and bailiffs. Even so, religious fraternities were remarkably inclusive compared to other social organizations in late medieval towns.[41] Although the archival sources on which our knowledge depends favor socioeconomic elites, the statistics show the notable degree to which artisans and peasants constituted guild membership: Crouch's sampling of Yorkshire wills (exclusive of the city of York) finds that twenty-four craftsmen and ninety-six husbandmen made bequests to religious guilds, while only nineteen merchants did so.[42] This diversity is true from the perspective of sex as well as social class: the membership of married women was sometimes linked to that of their husbands, as reduced entrance fees for them suggest, but women—single, married, and widowed—could join independently of a male sponsor. Sylvia Thrupp found in the membership list for the Holy Trinity guild at St. Botolph's Aldersgate, one of the few guilds for which such a list survives, "a marbler's wife, a huckster, and a single woman named Juliana Ful of Love" among the women who participated separately from a male sponsor.[43] We might compare parish guilds, as Carl Lindahl has, to the pilgrim company of the *Canterbury Tales*: a group of diverse persons from a variety of backgrounds, linked together for a shared devotional experience, who while certainly not ignorant of social hierarchies sometimes confuse them by their very proximity.[44]

This social diversity is reflected in the range of Londoners who left bequests to fraternities of St. Katherine, who was second only to the Virgin Mary as the most popular patron of parish fraternities.[45] Margery Broun left a bequest in 1370s to the common box of the fraternity of St. Katherine, affiliated once with the church of St. Katherine de Coleman but now with the monastery of Newchirchehawe.[46] Agnes Pikerell, widow of a saddler named William, made a bequest to a St. Katherine guild in Fridaystreet in a will proved in April 1373.[47] Juliana Fairhed left a bequest in 1442 to a fraternity of St. Katherine associated with the church of St. Andrew Huberd, near Estchepe, where she was to be buried alongside her husband, William, a butcher.[48] In a will proved in 1384, Cristina Coggere left a bequest to the guild of St. Katherine in her parish church, St. Botolph, near Billingsgate.[49] John de Wendelyngburgh, a pouch maker, made a bequest to a St. Katherine guild at St. Paul's in a will proved in 1380.[50] Another fraternity of St. Katherine, associated with the church of the Holy Trinity, is mentioned in the will of William Hynelond, clerk, proved in 1371.[51] A St. Katherine guild "near the Tower" is mentioned in the will of John Halfmark, a smith, in a 1386 will.[52] Although none of these guilds can be confidently linked to the late fourteenth-century parish play recorded in the London *Chronicle*, the prevalence of St. Katherine guilds and the enthusiastic support given to them by artisans and their widows suggest the most likely social context for the performance.

The number of St. Katherine fraternities mentioned in wills demonstrates, too, that parish guilds, however marginal in relation to dominant late medieval political institutions, were in fact a prominent feature of lay piety and devotional performance. Indeed, religious guilds may represent a tactical response to religious as well as secular authority.[53] The guilds' independence from the parish church is obliquely suggested by the fact that only incidental information about them can be found even in churchwardens' accounts—the registers kept by lay wardens responsible for the maintenance of the parish—indicating that most guilds kept separate records.[54] More significant is the degree to which religious fraternities allowed laypeople to assert some control over their religious advisers and their own spiritual health. Guilds often aspired, though they did not always manage, to hire a chantry priest for the souls of the dead brothers and sisters of the fraternity, just as aristocrats and wealthy merchants did for themselves. If the collective resources of the members were not sufficient to hire a priest, the guild brothers and sisters themselves said prayers for their deceased members, offering some of the spiritual benefit that wealthier Christians could more easily afford.[55] In either case, the guild provided for the welfare of its members' souls, supplementing—and provisionally supplanting—the exclusive control of ecclesiastical authorities. This may have been an intentional assumption of pastoral responsibility if, as Bainbridge suggests, they did so because the poorly paid parish priests were also poorly trained.[56] George Unwin calculates that religious fraternities ultimately employed more ordained priests than parish churches did,[57] a remarkable indication of the laity's enthusiasm for organizing their own religious lives.[58]

The public ceremonies of the guild also suggest a temporary appropriation of ecclesiastical prerogatives. Gervase Rosser has argued that the festive activities of parish guilds were a kind of paraliturgical ritual that allowed the laity to "recover some of the spiritual dignity and moral authority which had been officially arrogated to the priesthood."[59] Rosser's focus is the guild feast, to which the poor were often invited. The event, Rosser argues, alluded to the Mass in its symbolism and so granted the fraternities' charity the dignity of spiritual work. Guild processions, which often included dramatic tableaux, were also lay imitations of paraliturgical ritual. Often ending at the church with a ceremonial donation by each member, the procession gave guild members, dressed in their specialized livery, the opportunity to sponsor and perform a solemn religious ritual.

Barbara Hanawalt suggests that if the activities of the religious fraternities "can be seen as an implicit criticism of the established Church and an attempt on the part of the laity to take religion into their own hands and exclude the corrupt clergy," they would have been as threatening to the Church as heresy was.[60] But heresy is not the only measure of the challenge posed by the laity's enthusiasm for taking religion into their own hands. The guilds' relation to ecclesiastical authority is not a question of overt dissent, and some are quick to insist on their orthodoxy in their chancery returns, just as they insist on their obedience to the Crown and common law. So the fraternity of St. Leonard in Lynn claims to ostracize heterodox members: "what man or woman of this gilde be rebel ageyne the lawe of holy chirche, he shal lese the fraternite of this gilde tille he come to amendment."[61] The dissolution of parish fraternities in 1547 also indicates that they were understood to be traditionally orthodox. But their activities nevertheless challenged the sufficiency of the sacramental and pastoral care provided by the Church. Here again Michel de Certeau's demonstration that official culture, in the hands of the ordinary "consumer," allows for tactical interventions—interventions that may not succeed in, or even seek to, establish an oppositional voice—provides a theoretical model for how the devotional practice of parish guilds, though often literally oriented toward the church, established an arena outside of the official institutions that otherwise defined urban space and social practice. As we have seen in the *Book of Margery Kempe*, orthodox devotion that insists on an extra-institutional position could be as unsettling—perhaps more unsettling—to religious and secular authority as heresy itself.

Playing the Virgin Martyr in Late Medieval England

The unsettling quality of saints' plays may be suggested, above all, by the number of parish pageants subsumed into larger performances sponsored by civic authorities. I have already mentioned the Marian plays of the N-Town cycle, which scholars have long associated with the guild of St. Anne in Lincoln, and the Chester Assumption, which seems to be related to a play originally performed independently of the cycle by a Wives' guild and, according to Lumiansky and Mills, appropriated for the civic festival only in the sixteenth century.[62] Lumiansky and Mills remark that the women's guild that sponsored the Marian play could have been an association of free women engaged in trade but was more likely a religious fraternity, a hypothesis supported by the evidence of all-women guilds recently documented by Katherine French.[63] We can only speculate about why the independent public performance sponsored by the women eventually came under the auspices of the civic authorities—perhaps the Wives themselves wanted to participate in the larger festival. It seems probable, in any case, that the performance raised questions about institutional sponsorship and control over the social space created by the performance. The plays sponsored by parish guilds—groups that defined and inhabited a potentially threatening space outside of the institutions of church and state—were neutralized by their appropriation by larger civic enterprises.

Like the better-known Marian pageants of the N-Town and Chester plays, several virgin martyr pageants were subsumed into larger cycles as well, and thus performed under the auspices of the civic sponsor rather than those of the parish guild with which they may have originally been affiliated. A play of St. Katherine performed "in the Little Park" in Coventry in 1490/1, likely associated with the St. Katherine guild founded in 1343,[64] may be the origin of the unusual hagiographic pageant—featuring St. Katherine, St. Margaret, and several other virgins—that concludes the Coventry Corpus Christi play.[65] Perhaps this was the case, too, with the pageant of St. Katherine and "tres tormentors" that concluded the Hereford cycle. The pageant was the responsibility of the journeymen—that is, members of the artisanal class, which was often closely involved with parish fraternities—but it is under the authority of the wealthier Corpus Christi guild and the civic government when it surfaces in the Mayor's Book in 1503.[66] As few guild records survive from Hereford, it is impossible to know whether this reflects the incorporation of a separate pageant or was invented for the Corpus Christi play. Nevertheless, the cumulative evidence that individual plays associated with religious guilds were gradually folded into larger enterprises overseen by civic officials suggests that the contest for space was not only between the laity and the church but—as Sarah Beckwith has persuasively argued for the York Corpus Christi plays—also between different constituencies of laypeople.[67]

The civic officials who organized Corpus Christi cycles may have been eager to incorporate saints' pageants sponsored by parish fraternities because the very fact of their performance created, however temporarily, a social space outside of their control. This challenge may have been especially keen in the case of virgin martyr legends, given their thematic emphasis on the saint's resistance to institutional authority. Of course, plays of female saints were not the only performances that might have presented this challenge; a poem of the early fifteenth century sharply criticizes a play of St. Francis,[68] which may have represented the saint's rejection of worldly institutions and social protocols. But the legends of female saints are generally more emphatic in their rejection of social practice: as we have seen in earlier chapters, the female saint repeatedly refuses the authority of father, husband, and judge in favor of an alternative divine one to which she has privileged access.

We have evidence of a considerable number of plays based on legends of female saints, many of them virgin martyrs whose stories are structured by the holy woman's resistance to male authority.[69] There were plays of St. Margaret, St. Lucy, St. Katherine, St. Christina, St. Dorothy, St. Agnes, St. Feliciana, St. Sabina, St. Helen, St. Clare, and St. Susana.[70] We can perhaps best measure the potential threat they could pose to urban authorities by the efforts in moral literature to limit imitation of these legends to private space—as we have seen in the *Book of the Knight of the Tower* and Bokenham's legendary—a restriction apparently flouted by their public performance as community drama. The concern over ethical mimesis of virgin martyr legends that I have traced through this book points also to the challenge implicit in dramatic mimesis of these legends.[71] Considering these legends in the context of late medieval devotional practice as defined by orthodox writers, sometimes in response to heterodox ones, highlights what might have been at stake in performing feminine sanctity in the late medieval city. Conversely, understanding the concerns raised by parish guild performances clarifies the anxious efforts of moralists such as the Knight of the Tower to find allegorical models of ethical mimesis that would prevent women from direct and public imitation of female saints. The relationship between the two phenomena—ethical mimesis that demanded an inward focus and dramatic mimesis that was publicly performed—can complicate our understanding of the increasingly interior and meditative nature of late medieval devotion.[72] This is especially true when we remember women's active participation in the guilds that sponsored saints' plays, for as we have seen, women were repeatedly enjoined to imitate the public devotions of female saints through private religious and ethical practices—to be like a virgin martyr, as Nicholas Love exhorts his audience to imitate St. Cecilia in *The Mirror of the Blessed Life of Jesus Christ*, not through an outspoken proclamation of faith but through silent meditation on the life of Christ.

As I argued in Chapter 1, this sort of allegoresis of saints' legends registers not only the desire to designate their proper reception but also the cultural context that made this an urgent concern. Love's *Mirror* was undertaken as an orthodox alternative to Lollard texts, and his emphasis on meditative devotional practice may well respond to the increasing visibility of the heresy and its validation of the public performance of lay devotion, which was sometimes justified with reference to female saints. The affiliations of Love's text suggest that the emphasis on interiority, privacy, and imaginative engagement in late medieval devotional literature was part of a broader pastoral program designed to regulate and restrict more public expression that would confute social ideologies and, perhaps, challenge the authority of the institutional church.[73]

Saints' plays stand precisely opposed to official efforts to limit lay devotion to private space, and yet they were not heterodox. As self-conscious *representations*, they are markedly different, too, from Lollard arguments for a fully present mimesis of hagiographic narrative in the practice of lay preaching. The discursive structures that framed saints' plays—the ritual occasions on which they were performed, the tacit approval of the churches where the pageants often ended with a mass, and theatrical conventions that informed their presentation—mark the performances as theatrical, and so distinct from contemporary social life. Indeed, parish plays did not contradict orthodox expectations that laywomen would imitate virgin martyrs in private, not public, devotions, for it was, of course, boys or men who acted the part of the female saint in public performances.[74] As Badir argues, "The acting figure on stage, as framed, ordered, and disciplined by theatrical conventions, becomes a primary indicator of what subjects can and cannot do; its movement becomes a paradigmatic standard for the construction of boundaries and prohibitions."[75] Cross-dressing, in particular, may have reinforced cultural expectations about women's religious activities by rooting public practices, even those associated with female saints, in male bodies. Theatrical cross-dressing performs the limits of feminine devotion: it alienates women from certain kinds of religious expression by associating them with a male body.[76] We see this, for example, in the Beverly guild of St. Helen: though women were active in the guild, and immediately followed the dramatic tableau in the procession, it was a beautiful boy who played the saintly queen, in a performance not only of the saint's place in the community but also of the social expectation that laywomen would not, as St. Helen did, embark on independent interventions in the ritual and material life of the Church.

The cultural semiotics of cross-dressing in medieval drama are strikingly suggested by the annual festivities sponsored by the guild of St. John the Baptist at Baston. The maidens of the guild were required to dance in a public performance that, as H. F. Westlake notes, was "evidently directly connected with the story of the patron saint."[77] The maidens' dancing, that is, was an enactment of Salome's seductive performance, in reward for which she received St. John's head. The maidens' participation was mandatory: they could be excused only for age, illness, or "urgent business" but were otherwise fined a measure of barley if they failed to attend. It is clear from this event that the theatrical convention of cross-dressing was not a response to social decorum, certainly not to a concern about promiscuity or the display of the female body. The Salome dance is not the only exception to the general rule that boys played female roles in medieval performance: women participated, too, in some Marian plays. Best known is the Chester play of the Assumption, which was the responsibility of the Wives. The Digby Candlemas and Killing of Innocents, associated with the feast of St. Anne, was also apparently performed by women, including an unspecified number of "virgins" who are exhorted to "shewe summe sport and plesure" in the Poeta's introduction and who are later mentioned in a stage direction.[78]

The difference between women's performance in the Baston St. John play (dancing the part of Salome) and that in the Marian play (the dramatic enactment of Mary's purification after childbirth) might obscure their fundamental similarity. Both performances conform in some way to social expectations for late medieval women: the first confirms their role as objects of heterosexual desire—indeed confirms antifeminist expectations of the danger of feminine sexuality even as it celebrates it—and the second endorses women's participation in a feast that authorized the ritual of churching that they, in imitation of Mary, underwent after childbirth.[79] Virgin martyr plays, on the other hand, represent behavior that, as we have seen, was proscribed for late medieval laywomen: claiming public space as the site of feminine devotion. Dramatic mimesis here has a surprisingly intimate relation to ethical practice and social expectation, as if theatrical presentation of the public devotion of virgin martyrs would warrant nontheatrical imitation if it were performed by an actress.

This evidence highlights the paradoxical fact that it is *female* performance of feminine sanctity that is disruptive of gender ideology in late medieval drama, not—as we might expect—the convention of cross-dressing.[80] Women's performance of feminine sanctity, as represented in hagiographic narrative, is rendered not only unstable but also potentially subversive by theatrical cross-dressing, which marks certain behavior as outside of the purview of female communities. So Margery Kempe, as we have seen, seems heretical to some audiences, the form and especially the forum of her imitation of virgin martyrs marking them as dissenting, even though her beliefs are perfectly orthodox.

The convention of cross-dressing does not, however, work simply to reinforce gender expectations and restrict women's performance of hagiographic sanctity. It also forecloses the dramatic analogy between the sacred past and the social present in which the religious narrative is performed. It interrupts, through the disjunction of the actor's sex and performed gender, the mapping of sacred narrative onto urban space. As Marjorie Garber argues in *Vested Interests*, cross-dressing does not so much provoke as register category crisis, expressing the instability not just of gender but also the larger system of binary opposition of which gender is a constitutive part.[81] In saints' plays, that crisis is related to the increasing divide between the rhetoric of private devotion and the laity's enthusiasm for public religious expression. It is related, as well, to the concomitant problem of historical analogy, the possibility that a parish guild's performance of a virgin martyr legend might read the institutions of the late medieval city as oppressive as the persecuting judges and prefects of hagiographic narrative. Public drama posits a relation between narrative and space in which it is performed, what Patricia Badir, following Stanton Garner, calls the "irreducible oscillation between represented and lived space," that makes the analogy between past and present specifically relevant to the context in which it is performed.[82] Cross-dressing is a limit and control on this oscillation: it serves, that is, as a mark of historical difference. The discontinuity between the sex of the actor and that of the female saint he represents becomes a sign of another kind of discontinuity, a reminder that the play is a representation of the past, a historical other, unfamiliar and alienated from contemporary gender and social roles. It thus stands in close parallel to the moralized readings of virgin martyr legends that we have seen, for example, in the *Book of the Knight of the Tower*: both prevent female audiences from taking virgin martyr legends as immediate ethical models for their own late medieval lives. Both do so to restrict not only the possibilities of women's devotional practice but also the model of history implied by unmediated ethical imitation: the continuity of social institutions that might equate late medieval cities and churches with their pagan analogs in hagiographic narrative. It is significant that when the status of the virgin martyr as referent for contemporary social forms is restored in political pageantry, such as the virgin martyr pageant that greeted Catherine of Aragon on London Bridge, the performances *are* rooted in female bodies, confirming the historical continuity between the young princess and Sts. Katherine and Ursula through the actresses' sexual identity with the figures they represent.[83]

There is, unfortunately, no extant virgin martyr play from late medieval England, but we can explore the issues raised by saints' plays—the question of historical analogy, the role of the self-identity of performer and performed role, and the semiotics of cross-dressing—in a text that shares with them not only a marked generic affiliation but also a thematic development of these issues and the relations between them: Chaucer's tale of the Second Nun, the legend of St. Cecilia, first written in his own voice but included in the Canterbury fiction of communal performance and attributed to an anonymous religious woman in all manuscript witnesses.[84] As a late medieval representation of a public performance of a virgin martyr narrative, the Second Nun's tale of St. Cecilia engages many of the broader cultural issues raised by saints' plays. Conversely, locating the *Second Nun's Tale* in the context of the communal performance of hagiographic drama—a tradition familiar to Chaucer and his London audience[85]—points to the tale's engagement with contemporary social and political categories.

Saints' Plays and the *Second Nun's Tale*

The *Second Nun's Tale* may at first seem an unlikely vehicle for exploring saints' plays. It is, at least in the figurative sense of the term inaugurated by Kittredge, perhaps the least "dramatic" of the *Canterbury Tales*. It eludes subsequent critical categories of performance just as readily—whether a formalist interest in drama as direct discourse,[86] a Bahktinian emphasis on the performance of "popular" forms,[87] or more recent interest in political spectacle and the performance of power.[88] Given no portrait in the *General Prologue*, the Second Nun has no "body" or personal history to ground her performance, and in the absence of a clearly distinguished voice in her tale—composed independently of the *Canterbury Tales* and evidently not revised substantially for its new context—no distinct personality emerges.[89] Indeed, with its continual invocation of its Latin source and references that identify it as a written text ("Yet preye I yow that redden that I write" [78]), the tale insists on categories of authority and textuality that seem to distance it further from the category of performance.

But if the tale seems to defy the fiction of tale-telling and the embodied voicing on which the metaphors of theatricality and performance generally depend, it is—in the fiction of the *Canterbury Tales*—a public performance of hagiographic narrative, offered as devotional "busyness" and communal entertainment. In fact, the very features of the text that render it nondramatic from the perspective both of formalism and narrative realism—the insistence on textuality and the absent and ambiguous identity of the speaker—speak to the cultural parameters of representing virgin martyrs in the cities of late medieval England or on the roads between them. Rather than a simple case of recycling an earlier poem, Chaucer's assignment of a virgin martyr narrative to a female speaker points to a series of interrelated questions about the gendering of late medieval religious practice, the unstable boundaries between orthodoxy and heresy, and the danger posed by unlicensed translation of textual traditions into public performance that I have explored above. Though it may seem less unsettling to late medieval gender ideology than the Wife of Bath's tale, the Second Nun's performance of a hagiographic text responds to discursive arenas—public preaching, civic performance, and feminine devotional practice—that were as closely controlled and potentially threatening to dominant social codes as female sexuality.

The *Second Nun's Tale* is, admittedly, not affiliated with a parish guild, as many saints' plays were. The *Canterbury Tales* does represent a religious fraternity in the five guildsmen of the *General Prologue*:

> An haberdasshere and a carpenter,
> A webbe, a dyere, and a tapycer—
> And they were clothed alle in o lyveree
> Of a solempne and a greet fraternitee. (361–64)

As with the historical record for actual parish guilds, however, the poem is silent about their performance.[90] Yet if the *Second Nun's Tale* cannot comment on the social affiliations of most saints' plays, it does speak to what was at stake in performing late medieval civic space as the site of female sanctity. As Seth Lerer has argued, Chaucer's citations of late medieval drama address the "competing and potentially disruptive forms of dramatic public expression."[91] Even absent the guild context, therefore, the Second Nun's tale, as the performance of a saint's legend, should be understood with reference to the other performances that it would have recalled for Chaucer's audience.

It is an especially useful text for our purposes because it not only invokes the public performance of virgin martyr narratives, in distant but meaningful analogy to parish plays, but also relies on the idea of ethical imitation central to the reception of virgin martyr narratives in nondramatic contexts. The Second Nun presents the legend of St. Cecilia to an audience, and in doing so she imitates the saint's public preaching. Chaucer investigates, that is, the ethical and dramatic mimesis of a saint's legend at once and thus also the relationship between them. As a fictional counterpart to that other late fourteenth-century avatar of St. Cecilia, Julian of Norwich, the Second Nun returns us to the central focus of this book, ethical imitation, by way of its resonance with public performances that also helped define the cultural meaning of virgin martyr legends.

The prologue establishes the Second Nun's performance as an ethical imitation of the legend she tells:

> And for to putte us fro swich ydelnesse,
> That cause is of so greet confusioun,
> I have heer doon my feithful bisynesse
> After the legende in translacioun
> Right of thy glorious lif and passioun. (22–26)

The Second Nun here identifies her translation as devotional "bisynesse," in an explicit parallel to St. Cecilia, whom she later praises for "hire lastynge bisynesse" (98)—praise echoed by Pope Urban, who notes that Cecilia serves God "lyk a bisy bee" (195) in converting her husband to Christianity. Indeed, we may read the Second Nun's claim that her translation is "after the legende" not only as an explanation of her relationship to her source, but also as an acknowledgment of its grounding in the idea of exemplarity. "After" can mean "in imitation of, in the likeness or image of, according to the pattern of":[92] in translating the legend, the Second Nun also imitates the devotional busyness that the legend represents in the figure of Cecilia. She imitates the outspoken saint still more directly in offering the saint's life, framed by a moral lesson about idleness and its attendant dangers, to the pilgrim audience. The posture of imitation—so familiar as to seem perhaps merely formulaic—here authorizes a woman's public voice, her right to preach to the assembled company.

The audacity of the Second Nun's performance is focused by the juxtaposition of the tale's celebration of St. Cecilia's public preaching and the Second Nun's own limited authority, ironically recalled in the long *Invocacio ad Mariam* that interrupts the sermon on the dangers of idleness with which her prologue begins. Addressing the issue of feminine authority raised implicitly by her public preaching, the Second Nun points to the Virgin Mary, mother of the divine Word, as the origin of feminine verbal authority. Even this authority is sharply restricted, however, as the metaphorics of the Second Nun's prayer makes clear: the Word is made flesh, the Second Nun recalls in her prayer to Mary, "Withinne the cloistre blisful of thy sydis" (43). In the equation of Mary's womb and the monastic context of her own spiritual authority, the Second Nun's strongest argument for women's performance of sacred speech recalls the restriction of that speech to the intensely private space of the womblike cloister. It stands in stark contrast to the place of feminine spiritual authority featured in her tale: St. Cecilia's house, transformed into a public place of worship.

Cecilia's public role is given particular thematic and narrative emphases that help to define the Second Nun's imitation. In the etymological allegory that prefaces the legend, the Second Nun glosses the saint's name as "the wey to blynde" (92) because "she ensample was by good techynge" (93). Her "sapience" is emphasized twice in the etymology, first in the reading of her name as lacking blindness and therefore indicating "hir grete light / Of sapience" (100–101), and again as the bright object of the people's gaze, embodying "the cleernesse hool of sapience" (111). The tale elaborates this representation of the saint. As Sherry Reames has shown, Chaucer's use of the "Franciscan abridgement" of the legend allows for a more sustained focus on Cecilia as the roles of Tiburce and Valerian are reduced.[93] This highlights, specifically, her role as spiritual authority and guide. The conversions of her husband and brother-in-law preface the more public role she plays during and after her trial. Where Cecilia is initially represented in the feminized role of spiritual mother, as V. A. Kolve has shown,[94] she occupies the more transgressive role of preacher after the unsuccessful attempt to kill her with three blows to her neck:

> Thre dayes lyved she in this torment,
> And nevere cessed hem the feith to teche
> That she hadde fostred; hem she gan to preche. (537–39)

When Cecilia turns her house into a church, it gives her a forum for the pastoral work reserved in late medieval England to male clerics. She now "preaches" to those she had once "fostered." By contrasting the two activities, the Second Nun insists that Cecilia's work be identified with the full authority of preaching: her activity is defined against a more generalized and gender-appropriate role as spiritual teacher. The Second Nun, that is, specifically refuses to circumscribe Cecilia's authority in the way that Margery Kempe circumscribes her own when she observes that she does not speak from a pulpit and therefore does not preach.

In identifying her own devotional busyness as an imitation of St. Cecilia, the Second Nun aligns her own homiletic prologue and exemplary tale with the saint's public preaching. They are, after all, not confined to the cloister, the limited ambit of authority to which she alludes in the prologue, but presented to the pilgrim company on the road to Canterbury.[95] In this context, the Second Nun's posture of imitation does not so much establish the authority, as the provocation, of her performance: as we have seen, Lollards, too, argued that women's preaching was warranted by female saints in this period. The tale she tells is orthodox, of course, but the privilege of telling it as a moral exemplum to a public audience is reserved for others, such as the man of holy church from whom Julian of Norwich hears it. I am not claiming that the Second Nun is a Lollard, but I want to argue that—like some Lollards—her endorsement of the saint as example points to an uncomfortable historical continuity between pagan Rome and late medieval England, especially the shared restrictions, sometimes violent, against women's public religious expression.

At the same time, the Second Nun's imitation—as both ethical imitation and public performance of the Cecilia legend—invites analysis of the difference between the forms of Christianity endorsed and embodied by St. Cecilia and the forms of contemporary practice. Herein lies the dissenting potential of the tale identified by Lynn Staley Johnson, who notes the relevance of "Cecilia's opposition to paternalism, her reinterpretation of the marriage contract, her spiritual and intellectual leadership, and her confrontation with secular authority" to late medieval concerns.[96] Staley specifically identifies the contentious debates about papal and royal authority, increasing anticlericalism, and the Schism as the ultimate referents for the legend's interest in the early Church, still innocent not only of the shocking divisiveness that came to a head in 1378, but also of the ordinary vices that inevitably attend the institutionalization of religious belief. Staley's analysis demonstrates that the legend's nostalgia for a Christianity unencumbered by property and power comments pointedly on the late medieval Church.

This analogy between the legend and the configuration of late medieval political and religious institutions is, I would like to emphasize, a "dramatic" feature of the *Second Nun's Tale*—a consequence of the fiction of performance that locates the tale explicitly in the context of late medieval social life. Like late medieval drama, this fiction asks its audiences to consider the relation between the sacred narrative and the social present in which it takes place. This historical analogy—again as in drama—is grounded in the performer: the Second Nun's mimesis of St. Cecilia, which implicitly maps the narrative paradigm of the legend onto the social context of her performance. It is all the more striking, then, that the tale also seems to echo the theatrical practice of cross-dressing in the narrator's reference to herself as a "sone of Eve." The slip has long been read as evidence of the hasty inclusion of the tale in the Canterbury collection, a mark of its original (and therefore implicitly authoritative) identification with Chaucer's own voice rather than with that of the Second Nun, who may, after all, be only a scribal fiction. The startling reminder that the tale is ultimately a man's performance speaks not only to the genesis of the text, however, but also to its current location and the cultural performances it echoes there: theatrical cross-dressing, like that in the Beverly

St. Helen procession, which produced public representations of female sanctity that identified saints as *inimitable* and their legends as historically other. The audacity of the Second Nun's violation of restrictions on feminine performance of sacred narrative and women's preaching registers here through a reminder that such performances are licensed only when grounded in a male body.

The tale's nostalgia for the early Church, read as implicit criticism of contemporary religious institutions, also comments in important ways on the status of women within late medieval religious practice. The concerns about the practice and authority of late medieval Christianity raised by the tale are inextricably bound up with issues of gender, specifically with the difference between the role of women in the early Church and their role in the late medieval one. Cecilia's preaching is intimately associated with lay access to theology: Pope Urban merely shows Valerian a book with a cryptic assertion of monotheism ("O Lord, o feith, o God, withouten mo, / O Cristendom, and Fader of alle also, / Aboven alle and over alle everywhere" [207–9]), and the angel who bears crowns of roses and lilies addresses only broad moral categories, enjoining Valerian to "be chaast and hate vileynye" (231). But Cecilia carefully preaches to Tiburce about a range of theological issues, including the materiality of pagan idols (284–87), the existence of an afterlife (320–25), the creation and ensoulment of the body (326–29), the nature of the Trinity (337–41), and the role of Christ in salvation history (342–47). The legend insists on the close relation between women's sanctioned preaching and the theological substance and seriousness of lay devotion. If theatrical cross-dressing usually registers the discontinuity between the forms of female sanctity represented in hagiographic drama and contemporary religious practice, the *Second Nun's Tale* offers an implicit corollary: preventing women from performing the active role embraced by virgin martyrs of the early Church necessarily vitiates the practice of Christianity.

Jennifer Summit has demonstrated that the tale's representation of Rome constitutes "an exploration of historical change" through its development of a "material typology" that traces the city's conversion from pagan to Christian.[97] The presentation of the tale as a story offered on the road to Canterbury adds another layer to its complex investigation of history and change. If the tale itself exhibits an understanding of "the past as temporal other," its performance by the Second Nun evinces a more ambivalent conception of historical continuities and discontinuities, marked by nostalgia for the early Church and the place of women in it.[98] In this, it provides a striking counterpoint to Julian of Norwich, with whom this study began. As we saw, Julian's imitation of St. Cecilia insists on historical distance: where devotional identity in the hagiographic past is structure by the violent differentiation of self and other in martyrdom, in late medieval England—for Julian at least—it is structured by desire. The flexible use of exemplarity to mark historical continuity and change that we have traced throughout this study is neatly demonstrated by these two late fourteenth-century religious women, one fictional and one real, who each provide striking perspectives on the resources and limitations of late medieval Christianity.

* * *

Recent work, most notably by David Aers in *The Powers of the Holy*, has challenged the assumption that the "feminization" of late medieval religion was progressive with important analyses of the ways in which it supported conservative religious and political ideologies. The sponsorship of such practices by religious women or lay people, however, could be a tactical intervention in the production of ecclesiastical and civic authority. As a response to the Church's control over lay devotion, saints' plays may have offered a trenchant commentary on the structures of power and the forms of social life in late medieval England. As we have seen, the *Book of Margery Kempe*—which like the *Second Nun's Tale* explores the implications of the public performance of virginal sanctity—demonstrates the oppositional potential inherent in the performance of orthodox forms by those excluded from social authority by sex or vocation. The surprising proximity of orthodox and oppositional meaning might, in fact, be the most salient and unsettling feature of civic drama, insofar as it destabilizes the fiction of a narrateable, coherent urban space—the fiction of the legibility of social life on which political institutions depend.

I have argued that the oppositional potential of female saints' plays seems to have been recognized by some civic authorities, who appropriated them for official performances that would have been much more difficult to read as subversive narratives about the saintly rejection of social institutions. An eagerness to mitigate the oppositional potential of saints' plays may explain not only the virgin martyr pageants that ended some cycle plays but also those performed in honor of English queens. The pageant for Catherine of Aragon in 1501 is part of a long tradition: there were two St. Margaret pageants performed for Margaret of Anjou, one to celebrate her entry into London in 1445 and a second, which represented the saint slaying a "grete dragon," at Coventry some ten years later.[99] In 1469 Elizabeth Woodville, wife of Edward IV, was honored in Norwich with performances representing unspecified, but no doubt saintly, "virgins."[100] Anne of Denmark, James I's queen, was similarly honored with a pageant of St. Ursula on the occasion of her visit to Somerset in 1613.[101] The long history of such hagiographic pageantry suggests the continuing contestation over both the powerful symbols that configured social space in late medieval cities and the affiliation of those symbols with different sponsors. The spectacle marking Catherine of Aragon's entry into London may have opened with a virgin martyr pageant not only for the powerful argument it makes for Catherine's and Arthur's divinely sanctioned authority but also as a way of transforming a parochial tradition—at times in tension with royal or civic prerogatives—into Tudor spectacle.

Afterword

THE STORY OF MIDDLE ENGLISH SAINTS' LIVES does not end with the 1501 pageant. The early sixteenth century witnessed a marked increase in the hagiographic texts available to English readers. Many large collections, including John Mirk's *Festial* and Caxton's *Golden Legend*, circulated in print, as did some of the native saints' lives discussed in Chapter 4.[1] There was, of course, a sudden change in the status of saints in the 1530s, as reformers began to challenge and dismantle material and collective forms of devotion to the saints—relics, pilgrimage, guilds, shrines, feast days—but this does not herald the end of the narrative tradition. Indeed, some of the changes already taking place in the Middle English hagiography take on new significance and impetus after the Reformation: the sudden fascination with native saints in the fifteenth century, for example, provides an important resource to early modern antiquarians, martyrologists, and historiographers. The early modern "afterlives of the saints," to borrow Julia Reinhard Lupton's resonant phrase, are complex, and I close my story before the Reformation because accounting fully for them would be a project in itself.[2] This is so not only because of the complicated history of religious change in this period,[3] but also because of the period's equally complicated continuities with and debts to the one that precedes it.

Insisting on such continuities requires some comment. The change in the status of saints and saints' lives in England is part of what has long and generally been held to be one of the defining historical boundaries organizing English cultural and intellectual history. The boundary between the Middle Ages and the Renaissance is frequently understood as the boundary between the premodern and the "early modern," a division structured by the absence and invention of the phenomena that define modernity, especially historical consciousness and the idea of the individual.[4] Scholars of medieval England—notably Lee Patterson, David Aers, David Wallace, and Jennifer Summit—have offered important critiques of this historical narrative, showing that it is grounded in the Renaissance's own myths of self-invention and demonstrating the range and seriousness of medieval understandings of the self and its historical location.[5] This book contributes to this argument by showing how the reception of saints' lives as exemplary encouraged, even required, a complicated negotiation of the relationship between the sacred past and the social present. Female saints' lives, as we have seen, provided medieval writers and readers with an occasion for nuanced explorations of the historicity of their devotional and social lives and of the communities they inhabited.

Reading saints' lives as a forum for historical reflection challenges one of the central assumptions of the Renaissance claim to discover the difference of the past: that the Middle Ages knew only one "homogeneous" or undifferentiated "temporality," structured by typological correspondences between events or by eschatology, in which the temporal order of the secular world is dissolved.[6] In opening religious doctrine to new ways of thinking and in facilitating the secularization of some intellectual domains formerly under clerical control, the Reformation splinters the undifferentiated temporality of medieval Christianity and makes possible historical thought, an understanding of the past as past. But the premise of this argument is easily disproved with some attention to medieval literary, religious, and historiographical traditions, which exhibit a wide-ranging analysis of the relationship between past and present, not always dissolved by typological repetition or collapse.[7] Typology and eschatology were important to some models of time, but they were far from the only ones available in the Middle Ages.

This is not to say that medieval and early modern forms of history are identical. The narrative and hermeneutic structures that represent the past as past are related to other cultural forms and discourses:[8] in the premodern period, to religious theory and practice, to ideas of cultural inheritance, to structures of monarchical and institutional legitimation, and to emerging definitions of the nation.[9] As those were altered dramatically during and after the Henrician reforms, the modes of historical thinking changed too, but we should not let this change obscure the ways in which medieval writers and readers thought about their own historical location. The new Renaissance forms of historical consciousness respond to the loss—not the lack—of medieval ones.

Hagiographic exemplarity, I have argued, was one form of historical thinking in the Middle Ages. This is a significant revision of how exemplarity in the moral and religious literature of the Middle Ages has been understood. Medieval exemplarity is generally assumed to be a form of prescription, one that ignores the historical difference separating the subject of the story from its audience. That is, it follows and ostensibly confirms the expectation that the Middle Ages (read, medieval Christianity) failed to recognize the alterity of the past. In sharp contrast, early modern exemplarity is widely recognized as an important form of historical thinking: so in Thomas Greene's *The Light in Troy: Imitation and Discovery in Renaissance Poetry*—whose claims for the Renaissance invention of historical consciousness have received spirited analysis by Patterson and Summit—poets who imitate the classical past discover and investigate their historical location.[10] More recently Timothy Hampton has offered a subtle account of the place of exemplarity in Renaissance understanding of the historical location of identity and political forms that insists that such an understanding was wholly unavailable to medieval thinkers.

Greene and Hampton are concerned primarily with the classical past as an impetus to Renaissance thinking about history, and we might expect the difference between medieval and early modern exemplarity to reside in a shift from sacred to secular example. But the evidence cannot sustain this expectation either. Exemplarity remains an organizing structure for religious identity and practice in the course of the Reformation.[11] Indeed, Henrician reforms were not aimed at saints' lives as exemplary literature. Reformers took particular target at images and relics, material objects that they believed were themselves worshipped in idolatrous ways or used to dupe ignorant laity with promises of protection or cures, spiritual and physical. Feast days and pilgrimage, as occasions for revelry and diversions from work, also came under attack. Defining aspects of the medieval cult of the saints—in particular their intercessory role and the special favors that individual saints were thought to bestow for specific needs or to specific kinds of suppliants—were challenged and rejected by reformers. Particular saints, most famously Thomas Becket, also came under attack, as did saints whose historicity was challenged as humanist modes of inquiry and canons of evidence were applied to religious history. But holy women and men remained models of sacrifice and devout living, and reformers did not generally speak against their exemplarity: as late as 1563 the *Second Book of Homilies* enjoined "the folowyng of the vertues of the sainctes, as contempt of this world, povertie, sobernesse, chastitie, and such like vertues, which undoubtedly were in the saints" (166).[12] To be sure, some

Protestant writers vehemently opposed the virtues they exemplify: John Bale rails against medieval saints as perverse and frequently false examples of sexual abstinence in *The First Two Partes of the Actes, or Vnchast Examples of the Englysh Votaryes*.[13] Even Bale retains the idea of exemplarity, however, as his title reveals, at least in its negative form: he argues that saints are examples not of chastity but of unchastity. More telling, exemplarity—in its positive articulation—informs the rhetoric and rationale for Protestant martyrologies, notably John Foxe's *Actes and Monuments*. Foxe's "Declaration concerning the utilitie and profite of thys history" defines the value of the book primarily in terms of exemplarity: he offers the stories of "most mylde and constant martyrs, which may serve, not so much to delight the eare, as to garnish the lyfe, to frame it with examples of great profite, and to enstruct the minde in all kinde of Christian godlynes" (xxiii).[14]

Indeed, exemplarity posed problems for Foxe similar to those faced by medieval hagiographers and moralists. Under the reign of Elizabeth I, the examples of godly men and women who die for their faith should be less relevant, less immediately imitable than they were in Marian England. Foxe thus modifies and generalizes the model they provide in a way that is familiar from medieval attempts to define the exemplarity of saints, as we can trace in this passage:

In these men we have an assured and plaine witnes of God, in whose lyfe appeared a certaine force of divine nature, and in their death a farre greater signification, whiles in such sharpenes of tormentes wee beholde in them a strength so constant above mans reache, a redynes to answer, patience in prison, godlynes in forgiving, cherefulnes in suffering, beside the manifold sense and feling of the holy ghost, which they learned in many of their comfortes, and we by them. Over and besides this, the mylde deathes of the saintes do much prevayle for the attaining of a good conscience, and the contempt of the world, and to come to the feare of God. (xxiii)

Foxe's reader, addressed in the collective "we" of the first sentence, learns from the martyrs the virtues of Christian fortitude, not more specific lessons in resistance to state or ecclesiastical authority nor the opposition between true belief and institutional power that defines godliness through much of *Actes and Monuments*. Finally—"over and beside this," Foxe asserts—the martyrs provide a broad example that will inspire readers to seek a good conscience, to reject the world, and to fear God. The martyrs, that is, have become rather generic examples of Christian virtue, more suitable to contemporary conditions than they might be as more particular, and more volatile, examples of principled resistance to the protocols of religious conformity. Foxe reserves more immediate imitation of the martyrs as a possibility for the future—"if by Gods permission they [that is, "lyke conflictes"] shal happen hereafter" (xxiii)—and so, implicitly, identifies it as *inappropriate* to the present.

For the present, Foxe's readers are to "imitate their death (as much as we may) with the like constancy, or their lives at the least with the like innocency" (xxiv), the parenthetical qualification highlighting the important limits of the martyrs' exemplarity. These limits are given more careful articulation as Foxe specifies how readers should follow their example:

They offered their bodies willinglye to the rough handling of the Tormentours. Is it so great a matter then for our part, to mortifie our flesh, with all the members therof? They neglected not onelye the riches and glorye of the worlde for the love of Christe, but also their lives. And shall we then keepe so great a stirre one with an other for the vaine and transitorye trifles of this world? They continued in patient suffering, when they had most wrong done unto them, and when their very hart bloudes did gush out of their bodies. And yet wyll not wee forgeve our poore brother then smallest wrong that may be, but are ready for every trifling offense to seke his destruction and cut his throte. They wishing well to all men, did of their own accord forgeve their Persecutors, and therefore ought we, which after a sort are the posterity and children of martirs, not to degenerate from their former steppes, but being admonished by their examples, if we cannot express the same charity to all men, to imitate it at leaste wayes to our power and strength. (xxiv)

Foxe makes the martyrs exemplary by transforming their public trials into personal ones: the violence of state-sponsored persecution is replaced by the petty annoyances of social life (imagined as occasions for murderous violence), which Foxe's readers are taught to endure by comparing the patience required of them to that shown by those who died for their faith. This is, in some respects, notably different from medieval exemplarity. The audience of this text has a much more recent and real memory of martyrdom than did the audiences of Middle English hagiography. The rhetorical flair of the passage registers how energetically Foxe must work to represent the (Marian) past as past. But if the exemplary structure linking past and present is more anxious in Foxe than in many medieval analogs, it serves similarly to articulate a period boundary. Foxe, that is, makes the same argument with his account of the martyrs' exemplarity that he makes with his representation of Elizabeth as a second Constantine:

both insist on a defining rupture that separates the present from what precedes it. We are a good distance from Julian of Norwich here, but we are, I think, on the same map. Both Julian and Foxe mitigate the oppositional force of martyr narratives by transforming public torment into private trial, though Julian's turn inward is more absolute than Foxe's, which is still firmly rooted in social life. Both do so in order to define contemporary religious culture in relation to a past they find, or want their readers to find, categorically different. With regard to exemplarity, the relationship between medieval and Reformation discourses follows the paradox of the mode: an active tension between past and present, not a firm boundary.

From this perspective, exemplarity may have lessons for medievalists too, for whom long-standing debates about the "alterity" of the Middle Ages or the period's continuity with contemporary cultural forms still divide the field.[15] This is the methodological version of the historiographical question addressed above, between a commitment to the past as past and one to the past as a projection of our own desire. The apparent divide between these two ways of approaching the Middle Ages might be usefully reconsidered through the model of exemplarity, which reminds us that we know the difference of the past only in trying to understand its relation to the present. Of course, in suggesting exemplarity as a model for our historical understanding I do not propose we should or could imitate the Middle Ages. Modern readers, and especially modern women, have a much broader arena for understanding their historical location than medieval ones did. But the challenge that medieval narrative might present to our expectations for how that arena is defined can still be salutary. In acknowledging that we study the past to learn more about ourselves, we see more readily that it is exemplary, even if—and especially when—we do not imitate it.

Notes

Preface

1. By the fifteenth century, "historial" could mean "belonging to history," "of historical importance," "dealing with history," or "factual." See *Middle English Dictionary*.

2. See especially Lee Patterson, *Chaucer and the Subject of History* and *Negotiating the Past: The Historical Understanding of Medieval Literature*. See also Christopher Baswell, *Virgil in Medieval England: Figuring the Aeneid from the Twelfth Century to Chaucer*.

3. Such is suggested, for example, by women's ownership of Lydgate's *Siege of Thebes*: see Catherine Sanok, "Criseyde, Cassandre, and the *Thebaid*: Women and the Theban Subtext of Chaucer's *Troilus and Criseyde*," 49 n. 22.

4. This is true even in recent reference works: e.g., Carolyn Dinshaw and David Wallace, eds., *Cambridge Companion to Medieval Women's Writing*.

5. Michel de Certeau, *The Practice of Everyday Life*, xix–xx and passim.

6. Judith Butler, *Gender Trouble: Feminism and the Subversion of Identity*, 25–34 and passim. See also Butler, *Bodies That Matter: On the Discursive Limits of "Sex."*

7. This understanding of normative or prescriptive genres informs some important recent work on late medieval culture: e.g., Kathleen Ashley and Robert Clark, eds., *Medieval Conduct*; Claire Sponsler, *Drama and Resistance: Bodies, Goods and Theatricality in Late Medieval England*; Sarah Salih, *Versions of Virginity in Late Medieval England*.

8. E.g., Karen Winstead, *Virgin Martyrs: Legends of Sainthood in Late Medieval England*, and Jocelyn Wogan-Browne, *Saints' Lives and Women's Literary Culture, c. 1150–1300*. Winstead shows that virgin martyr legends change across the late Middle Ages in response to the assumed interests and needs of their audiences. She articulates three periods: an early period, in which legends were written for a monastic audience (1100–1250); a middle one, in which clerical authors insisted on their special authority to new lay audiences (1250–1400); and a late period, defined by the interests of aristocratic patrons (1400–1450). This study is indebted to Winstead's important work, but where Winstead traces how the genre changed in response to historical audiences and the social context in which legends were produced, I investigate the social fictions that saints' lives construct through their imagined audiences. Wogan-Browne's essential history of the place

of saints' lives in women's literary culture in the twelfth and thirteenth centuries has done much to challenge and change assumptions about the genre as monolithic and simply misogynist. I hope to show in this book that her argument that "the pervasiveness of a representational code is a different matter from the politics and possibilities of its particular instantiations" (5) holds for a later period as well.

9. Other scholars have recently shown that women's spirituality could serve as an allegory of—or provide cultural capital for—masculine political culture. See Sheila Delany, *Impolitic Bodies: Poetry, Saints, and Society in Fifteenth-Century England*; Mary-Ann Stouck, "Saints and Rebels: Hagiography and Opposition to the King in Fourteenth-Century England"; Nancy Warren, *Spiritual Economies: Female Monasticism in Later Medieval England*, chaps. 5 and 6; and Karen Winstead, "Capgrave's Saint Katherine and the Perils of Gynecocracy." Of course, saints' lives present feminine spirituality not only as a figure for some more consequential masculine concern but also as a focus of interest in its own right, one that can comment on political and social concerns precisely because it is not fully segregated from them and so is not able to be fully objectified or allegorized.

Chapter 1

1. There are seven extant Middle English versions of the St. Cecilia legend, including legends found in the *South English Legendary*, Osbern Bokenham's *Legendys of Hooly Wummen*, the *Gilte Legende*, and the *Canterbury Tales* (the *Second Nun's Tale*). See Charlotte D'Evelyn and Frances Foster, "Saints' Legends," 574–75. The versions vary in small details, but the basic narrative is shared by all.

2. I provide evidence for this in the course of this chapter and the next. On the exemplarity of saints' lives for female readers, see also Katherine Lewis, "Model Girls? Virgin-Martyrs and the Training of Young Women in Late Medieval England"; Winstead, *Virgin Martyrs*, 112–41; and Jocelyn Wogan-Browne, "Saints' Lives and the Female Reader." Explicit encouragement to imitate saints is especially prevalent in fifteenth-century traditions, on which this study focuses. Karen Winstead has recently suggested that fourteenth-century hagiographers were, in contrast, more concerned to prevent than to encourage imitation of saints: see her "Fear in Late-Medieval English Martyr Legends." Her evidence for the careful management of readers' identification with and imitation of the saint, however, seems to me to confirm the availability, even prevalence, of exemplarity as a mode of response even in the earlier period.

3. The Sarum breviary and missal indicate that readings about St. Cecilia were given on this day. See the *Breviarium ad usum insignis ecclesiae Sarum*, calendar for November (unpag.); and *Missale ad usum insignis et praeclarae ecclesiae Sarum*, 27.

4. See the works cited in note 2 and Karen Winstead, "Piety, Politics, and Social Commitment in Capgrave's *Life of St. Katherine*."

5. Winstead, *Virgin Martyrs*, 113, passim.

6. Ibid., 122.

7. Katherine's first confrontation with the emperor is at 5.555–602. All citations are to John Capgrave, *Life of Saint Katherine*, ed. Karen Winstead.

8. All references are to Bokenham, *Legendys of Hooly Wummen*.

9. I follow Nicholas Watson in referring to the text by its manuscript title; see Watson, "Julian of Norwich," 210.

10. All citations are to Julian of Norwich, *A Book of Showings to the Anchoress Julian of Norwich*, ed. Edmund Colledge and James Walsh.

11. There has been a great deal of important work on the crises of the fifteenth century and its effect on representational practices and narrative forms. Important recent contributions include James Simpson, *Reform and Cultural Revolution, 1350–1547*; and Paul Strohm, *England's Empty Throne: Usurpation and the Language of Legitimation, 1399–1422*.

12. David Bell, *What Nuns Read: Books and Libraries in Medieval English Nunneries*; Susan Cavanaugh, "A Study of Books Privately Owned in England: 1300–1450"; Anne Dutton, "Passing the Book: Testamentary Transmission of Religious Literature to and by Women in England, 1350–1500"; Mary Erler, *Women, Reading, and Piety in Late Medieval England*; Carol Meale, ". . . All the Bokes that I Haue of Latyn, Englisch, and Frensch': Lay Women and their Books in Late Medieval England."

13. All references are to Caxton's text; see M. Y. Offord, ed., *The Book of the Knight of the Tower, Translated by William Caxton*. The other version is found in Thomas Wright, ed., *The Book of the Knight of La Tour-Landry*.

14. The Knight explains in the prologue that he has made the book "for my doughters to lerne. to rede and vnderstonde / how they ought to gouerne them self / and to kepe them from euylle" (13). The Middle English translation is also addressed explicitly to a female audience: Caxton's prologue insists that "this book is a special doctryne & techyng by which al yong gentyl wymen specially may lerne to bihaue them self vertuously / as wel in their vyrgynyte as in their wedlok & wedowhede," and he claims to translate it at the request of "a noble lady which hath brought forth many noble & fayr doughters" (3).

15. A similar strategy obtains in the Knight's identification of St. Katherine and St. Agatha as examples of charity in chap. 52. As Katherine Lewis notes, he cites them as examples of giving their gowns to poor people, but their legends include no such detail; see Lewis, "Model Girls?," 29. Katherine and Agatha, like Cecilia, have strong associations with public speech: Katherine not only challenges the Emperor Maxentius but also faces fifty philosophers in a theological debate, and Agatha's name is traditionally etymologized to mean "perfect speech" (see Chapter 3). Identifying them, like Cecilia, as models of humility and charity mitigates the example of public devotion that they present.

16. On exemplarity in the *Book of the Knight of the Tower*, see Elizabeth Allen, *False Fables and Exemplary Truth in Later Middle English Literature*, 27–52. Allen argues that the *Book* evinces anxiety about the unpredictability of its audience, as a range of readerly contingencies challenge its presentation of transparent moral authority.

17. St. Agnes, for example, chooses to be sent to a brothel rather than to worship pagan gods. Stories such as this highlight the importance of consent: the virgin saint refuses to marry, which would demand her consent to a sexual relationship, but she is usually sanguine in the face of threatened rape, which does not compromise her vow of virginity precisely because it is not consensual. The saint's steadfast rejection of active sexuality, however, seems to protect her from rape: she is always miraculously saved from sexual attack. On medieval theories of virginity as a practice involving issues of intention and consent, rather than a physical state, see Salih, *Versions of Virginity*.

18. Significantly, Cecilia is left out of the list of virgin saints who exemplify wifely chastity, even though she is the only married virgin martyr widely venerated in late medieval England. She would surely provide a more confusing example because of the closer proximity of her situation to that of the *Book*'s audience, who might assume that she provides authority for refusing marital sex. St. Ursula, who agrees to marry on the condition that her fiancé convert to Christianity, is included as a model in this chapter: since she is martyred before her wedding, she does not present as awkward an example as the married, and militantly virginal, Cecilia does.

19. As Winstead notes, however, the Knight must still mute aspects of the story to make it exemplary for laywomen: Anastasia is imprisoned for disobeying her husband and is released only on his death. See Winstead, *Virgin Martyrs*, 117.

20. In contrast, the *Book* is ambivalent about the merit of teaching women to write: "as for wrytyng it is no force / yf a woman can nought of hit" (122).

21. The Katherine-Group legends, *Ancrene Wisse*, *Hali Meidenhad*, and *Sawles Ward* constitute the so-called AB Group, first identified by J. R. R. Tolkien, "Ancrene Wisse and Hali Meidenhad." See also E. J. Dobson, *The Origins of the Ancrene Wisse*. Both copies of the early Middle English legend of St. Margaret are found in manuscripts with *Ancrene Wisse*. References to *Ancrene Wisse* are to J. R. R. Tolkien, ed., *The English Text of the Ancrene Riwle: The Ancrene Wisse*; and to the translation in Anne Savage and Nicholas Watson, *Anchoritic Spirituality: Ancrene Wisse and Associated Works*.

22. Frances Mack, ed., *Seinte Marherete the Meiden ant Martyr*, 4.

23. Tolkien, ed., *The English Text of the Ancrene Riwle*, 125.

24. Sexual purity works in the same way in the early Middle English legends of St. Katherine and St. Juliana associated with *Ancrene Wisse*. The theme is especially prominent in the legend of the virgin princess Katherine, who confronts and triumphs over male authority represented first by the emperor Maxentius and then by an assembly of philosophers. For texts of these two legends, see Eugen Einenkel, ed., *The Life of Saint Katherine*; and S. R. T. O. d'Ardenne, ed., *The Liflade ant te Passiun of Seinte Iuliene*.

25. Tolkien, ed., *The English Text of the Ancrene Riwle*, 38–89.

26. I have slightly modified the translation of Savage and Watson, 75.

27. Henry Hucks Gibbs, ed., *The Life and Martyrdom of Saint Katherine of Alexandria, Virgin and Martyr*, 65.

28. Bella Millet offers a careful analysis of the audiences, both lay and religious, addressed by the saints' lives which understands them broadly in the way I do here; see Millet, "The Audience of the Saints' Lives of the Katherine Group."

29. Claire Sponsler provides a nuanced discussion of this point in "The Culture of the Spectator: Conformity and Resistance to Medieval Performances."

30. It shares this with other exemplary genres: as Allen argues, "the awareness of historical contingency . . . is always the flip side of the example's authoritative claims" (9).

31. Lollard opposition to the cult of the saints may be overstated or at least overgeneralized. As Anne Hudson has shown, there is some evidence—admittedly in hostile sources—that Lollards sometimes identified as martyrs and saints those who had been executed for Wycliffite beliefs and sometimes followed the protocols of veneration familiar from orthodox cults. So the *Great Chronicle of London* records that the ashes of Joan Boughton were gathered as relics after her burning, and Margery Baxter is said to have confessed to praying to William White as a saint. See Anne Hudson, *Premature Reformation: Wycliffite Texts and Lollard History*, 171–72. Lollards questioned the validity of post-biblical saints and especially accounts of their miracles, but they were less concerned to prove that they were fictions than to argue that they should not be used as intercessors—and especially that their images should not be venerated—since worship and prayer could more profitably be directed to Christ. Saints, that is, were not necessarily spurious but simply unnecessary.

32. *Mulieres, sancte virgines, constanter predicarunt verbum Dei et multos ad fidem converterunt sacerdotibus tunc non audentibus loqui verbum.* The quotation is from William W. Capes, ed., *Registrum Johannis Trefnant, episcopi herefordensis, A. D. 1389–1404* (London: Canterbury and York Society, 1916), 345; the translation is from Alcuin Blamires, K. Pratt, and C. W. Marx, eds., *Woman Defamed and Woman Defended*, 257–60. Both are cited by Blamires, "Women and Preaching in Medieval Orthodoxy, Heresy, and Saints' Lives," 136–37.

33. Blamires, "Women and Preaching," 151.

34. I have found little work on Lollard views of history, with the exception of studies of apocalyptic thought and Wyclif's discussion of divine and earthly modes of time. For the first, see Ruth Nissé, "Prophetic Nations"; and Michael Wilks, "Wyclif and the Great Persecution." For the second, see J. A. Robson, *Wyclif and the Oxford Schools*, 155–61; and Wilks, "Wyclif and the Wheel of Time." See also Allen Breck, "John Wyclyf on Time."

35. Wilks, "Wyclif and the Great Persecution," 40–41.

36. Norman Tanner, ed., *Heresy Trials in the Diocese of Norwich, 1428–1431*, 47, cited by Rita Copeland, "Why Women Can't Read: Medieval Hermeneutics, Statutory Law, and the Lollard Heresy Trials," 275. Baxter is said to have prayed to White as a saint to intercede for her: *omni die ipsa oravit ad eundem sanctum Willelmum Whyte, et omni die vite sue orabit at eum ut ipse dignetur intercedere pro ipsa ad Deum celi* (Tanner, 47). The "Testimony of William Thorpe," which I discuss in Chapter 5, similarly presents a heresy trial as a reiteration of the saint's

ordeal; see Anne Hudson, ed., *Two Wycliffite Texts: The Sermon of William Taylor 1406, the Testimony of William Thorpe 1407*, 24–93.

37. It would be interesting to compare Lollard imitation of hagiographic narrative with the concern that dramatic imitation of biblical narrative reverses salvation history expressed in the Wycliffite *Tretis of Miracles Pleying*. See Ruth Nissé, "Reversing the Discipline: The *Tretise of Miraclis Pleyinge*, Lollard Exegesis, and the Failure of Representation."

38. The use of similar hagiographic paradigms by both orthodox and heterodox writers bears out Paul Strohm's claim that "interpretative schemes are likely to be the property not just of a single social segment but of a society as a whole." As he explains, this means that a narrative paradigm or interpretive structure "might make a dual appearance, wielded by a chronicler to condemn a rebel action and (rotated on its axis) wielded by the rebels to produce that action in the first place." See "'A, Revelle!': Chronicle Evidence and the Rebel Voice," in Strohm, *Hochon's Arrow: The Social Imagination of Fourteenth-Century Texts*, 34. Of course, the rotation can go in the other direction as well, with marginal groups borrowing discourses from dominant ones; see, for example, Ruth Nissé's analysis of the Norwich heresy trials in "Grace under Pressure: Conduct and Representation in the Norwich Heresy Trials."

39. Hudson, *Premature Reformation*, 303. The story may have circulated in other forms as well: Knighton gives Latin verses on the topic by "quidam metricus" and records that Smith was required to carry an image of St. Katherine in the marketplace as penance. See Henry Knighton, *Knighton's Chronicle, 1337–1396*, ed. and trans. G. H. Martin, 296–98, 534. Martin proposes that the verses are by Knighton himself but does not elaborate (297 n. 2).

40. *Hec sancta ymago certe iam erit nobis focale sanctum. Et sic per securim et ignem nouum pacietur martirium, si forte per inmanitatem nouorum tormentorum, uenire aliquando poterit ad regnum celorum.* Knighton, 296. The translation is Martin's, 297.

41. Sarah Stanbury, "The Vivacity of Images: St. Katherine, Knighton's Lollards, and the Breaking of Idols," 132.

42. We find the corollary of this in John Mirk's sermon for Trinity Sunday, which equates Lollards with pagan persecutors: "Wherfor ryght as heritykes yn the begynnyng of the holy chirch pursuet holy popes, martyres, and confessores to the deth, ryght so now thes Lollardes pursuen men of holy chirche, and ben about forto vndo hom all that thay mow, yf that myghten haue hor purpos forth," cited in Hudson, *Premature Reformation*, 432–33. Hudson quotes from Erbe's edition but emends "Lombardes" to "Lollards" on the basis of manuscript evidence (433 n. 184).

43. On Love's *Mirror* as a response to Lollardy, see Nicholas Watson, "Censorship and Cultural Change in Late-Medieval England: Vernacular Theology, the Oxford Translation Debate, and Arundel's Constitution of 1409."

44. Nicholas Love, *The Mirror of the Blessed Life of Jesus Christ*, ed. Michael Sargent, 11.

45. Love follows his source closely in the passage cited. For an English translation of the Latin text, see Isa Ragusa and Rosalie Green, trans., *Meditations on*

the *Life of Christ: An Illustrated Manuscript of the Fourteenth Century*, 1–2. The editors note that the *Meditations* borrows the image of the gospel born in Cecilia's breast from the *Legenda Aurea*.

46. Margery Kempe, *The Book of Margery Kempe*, ed. Sanford Brown Meech, III. All references are to this edition.

47. Simpson, *Reform and Cultural Revolution*, chap. 8, "Moving Images," esp. 406–29.

48. On this, see Allen, *False Fictions*; and Larry Scanlon, *Narrative, Authority, and Power: The Medieval Exemplum and the Chaucerian Tradition*. Scanlon approaches the exemplum from the perspective of literary production and so "a narrative enactment of cultural authority" (34). My interest in exemplarity as a mode of reception leads to different, but compatible, conclusions about the complications or limits of the authority granted to the present by stories of the past.

49. Timothy Hampton, *Writing from History: The Rhetoric of Exemplarity in Renaissance Literature*, x. Hampton's otherwise excellent book identifies this sharp awareness of history as properly humanist/Renaissance by reducing medieval understandings of modes of time to "the linear pulse of Christian eschatology" and medieval responses to the difference between past and present to the "typological resolution" of alterity (13–14).

50. Hampton, 3.

51. I cannot account fully for the many modes of historical thinking in the Middle Ages. I have found the following to be especially useful: Antonia Gransden, *Historical Writing in England*; and Hans Ulrich Gumbrecht, Ursula Link-Heer, and Peter-Michael Spangenberg, eds., *La Littérature Historiographique des Origines à 1500*. On *translatio* and Christian teleology as structures of medieval history, see Patterson, *Chaucer and the Subject of History*, 84–99.

52. Instead, there is a narrow exemplary relationship between, say, a saintly king and a contemporary one: e.g., Lydgate's *Life of St. Edmund* and Henry VI. This relationship could speak to questions of historical continuity or change, but its singularity militates against this; instead, the exemplary relationship between saint and king reads as a moral and/or political commentary on an individual, as evidence of the current monarch's virtue or a measure of his kingship. While there are few lay male saints (aside from holy kings like Edmund), virgin martyrs occupy a nicely ambiguous status between religious and lay: they make a vow of chastity—a crucial aspect of late medieval women's religious vocations—but are never formally professed.

53. Michel de Certeau, *Practice of Everyday Life*, especially chap. 3, "'Making Do': Uses and Tactics," 29–42.

54. "The ability to mime, and mime well," Taussig writes, "is the capacity to Other" (Michael Taussig, *Mimesis and Alterity*, 19).

55. Cf. Pierre Bourdieu on *habitus; Outline of a Theory of Practice*, 16–22 and passim.

56. Alain Boureau makes the claim for the *Legenda Aurea*, the legendary with the greatest influence on the English vernacular tradition: "Il ne s'agit ne d'émerveiller, ne d'innover, ni de surprendre, mais d'occuper la plus grande surface

possible dans le champ culturel" (*La Légende dorée: le systéme narratif de Jacques de Voragine*, 56).

Chapter 2

1. The early Middle English Margaret is discussed above in Chapter 1. The Auchinleck Margaret is edited by Carl Horstmann in *Altenglische Legenden, Neue Folge*, 225–35; the reference to a female audience is at line 408.

2. Important treatments of this phenomenon include Carolyn Walker Bynum, *Holy Feast, Holy Fast*; and, in response to Bynum and others who follow her, David Aers, "The Humanity of Christ: Reflections on Orthodox Late Medieval Representations," 28–42, in Aers and Lynn Staley, *Powers of the Holy: Religion, Politics, and Gender in Late Medieval English Culture*.

3. Anglo-Norman hagiography, however, boasts several women writers: Clemence of Barking is the best-known, but far from unique, example. See William MacBain, "Anglo-Norman Women Hagiographers"; Jocelyn Wogan-Browne, "'Clerc u lai, muïne u dame': Women and Anglo-Norman Hagiography in the Twelfth and Thirteenth Centuries"; Wogan-Browne, "Wreaths of Thyme: The Female Translator in Anglo-Norman Hagiography."

4. An important exception and corrective is provided by Jocelyn Wogan-Browne, *Saints' Lives and Women's Literary Culture, c. 1150–1300: Virginity and Its Authorizations*.

5. The Douce legends are edited by Carl Horstmann, "Prosalegenden: Die legenden des ms. Douce 114."

6. Saints' lives enter vernacular literary culture by way of pastoral legendaries, such as the *Legenda Aurea*, many of which were compiled by Dominican clerics. The most prominent hagiographers of the Middle English tradition were monks or friars: for example, the Benedictine John Lydgate and the Augustinians Osbern Bokenham and John Capgrave.

7. But see Jocelyn Wogan-Browne's important critique in *Saints' Lives and Women's Literary Culture*, 57–90, where she offers a revisionary reading of the tropes of sacrifice and bodily fragmentation in terms of the "gift." See also Wogan-Browne, "The Virgin's Tale," on how saints' lives might have taught women strategies for "resistant readings" of romance.

8. Especially Kathleen Ashley and Pamela Sheingorn, *Interpreting Cultural Symbols: Saint Anne in Late Medieval Society*; Katherine Lewis, *The Cult of St. Katherine of Alexandria in Late Medieval England*; Karen Winstead, *Virgin Martyrs*; and Wogan-Browne, *Saints' Lives and Women's Literary Culture*.

9 For example, Catherine Innes-Parker, "Sexual Violence and the Female Reader: Symbolic 'Rape' in the Saints' Lives of the Katherine Group."

10. Christine de Pizan, *The Treasure of the City of Ladies*, trans. Sarah Lawson, 161.

11. Of course, this does not deny the potential usefulness of comparing the representations of girls subject to sexualized violence in medieval and modern dis-

courses, but it is important not to overstate the similarities. It is, I think, significant that virgin martyr narratives are more often boring than titillating to modern readers. This does not prove that medieval audiences did not find them exciting, but it is at least as sound an argument (relying likewise on a transhistorical paradigm of desire) as that which says they did. The genre might reproduce its central message about the saint's miraculous resistance to sexualization in the experience of reading itself: a story of a beautiful girl stripped naked that conspicuously fails to arouse. Interestingly, vernacular legends are rarely illustrated; the only illuminated vernacular legendaries I know are French. There are illustrated copies of Jean de Vignay's *Légende Dorée* (see Hilary Maddocks, "Illumination in Jean de Vignay's *Légende dorée*"), but this is an anomaly. Most of the sexualized images that often supplement the argument that female saints' lives are pornographic come from other contexts, primarily Books of Hours.

12. See also the "Banna Sanctorum" in Charlotte D'Evelyn and A. J. Mill, eds., *South English Legendary*, which offers to satisfy a desire for the stories of hardy knights and hard-fought battles with the true stories of apostles and martyrs (59–65). All references are to this edition.

13. Michael Goodich, *Vita Perfecta: The Ideal of Sainthood in the Thirteenth Century*, 55.

14. See Watson, "Censorship and Cultural Change in Late-Medieval England," 833. Watson notes that Margery Kempe is another rare example, which we might understand, in part, in terms of her *Book*'s affiliation with hagiography.

15. John Capgrave, *Lives of St. Augustine and St. Gilbert of Sempringham*, 1. Further citations are given parenthetically.

16. The *Middle English Dictionary* gives "biographical, historical" as the definition, but I find no warrant for this in either its etymons, Latin *narrativus* and French *narratif*, or in Capgrave's use, all of which point to a broader definition of "that which tells a story." Interestingly, the Latin and French terms also date to the first part of the fifteenth century. See R. E. Latham, *Revised Medieval Latin Word-List*; and *Le grand Robert de la langue française*.

17. Elsewhere, however, Capgrave uses saints' lives as a vehicle for discussion of theological concerns: his dilation of the legend of St. Katherine to include substantive religious debate is especially notable. See Karen Winstead's forthcoming book, *John Capgrave's Fifteenth Century*, chap. 3, which she was kind enough to share with me in manuscript.

18. Carl Horstmann, ed., "The Lyf of Saint Katherine of Senis." Horstmann notes that the translator has changed the address of the Latin text, from "lector" to "maydens" (33 n).

19. The poem is attributed to Bradshaw on the basis of parallels in narrative structure, meter, and vocabulary. See F. Brittain, ed, *The Lyfe of Saynt Radegunde*, vii–viii. All citations are to this edition, which is based on Pynson's undated edition.

20. The category of sex is importantly circumscribed by class here; I address the complication that class presents to the fantasy of gendered exemplarity in Chapter 4.

21. J. G. Sikes and Freda Jones, "Jesus College," 421.

22. Brittain, xiv. Bradshaw otherwise closely follows his source, Antoninus of Florence's chronicle.

23. See Gail McMurray Gibson, "Saint Anne and the Religion of Childbed: Some East Anglian Texts and Talismans"; Sylvie Laurent, *Naître au Moyen Age*, 194–95; and Jocelyn Wogan-Browne, "The Apple's Message: Some Post-Conquest Hagiographic Accounts of Textual Transmission."

24. John Lydgate, "The Legend of Seynt Margarete," in *The Minor Poems of John Lydgate*, ed. Henry MacCracken, 173–92. Citations to this poem are given parenthetically by line number.

25. The intercessory value of the legend is also suggested by a medical miscellany, British Library MS Sloane 1611, which contains an Anglo-Norman version of the legend of St. Margaret, presumably for reading to a woman in difficult labor. See P. Meyer, "Notice du MS Sloane 1611 du Musée Britannique."

26. The invention of a feminine audience may complement the construction of the "lost woman writer" that Jennifer Summit has brilliantly shown was essential to the emerging definition of an English literary tradition. See Summit, *Lost Property: The Woman Writer and English Literary History, 1380–1589*. Summit's attention to the relationship between the representation of the woman writer and its material and historical consequences has provided a very helpful model for some of my thinking in this chapter.

27. Samuel Moore, "Patrons of Letters in Norfolk and Suffolk, c. 1450," especially 79–93; Karl Julius Holzknecht, *Literary Patronage in the Middle Ages*; A. I. Doyle, "Books Connected with the Vere Family and Barking Abbey."

28. Karen Jambeck, "Patterns of Women's Literary Patronage: England, 1200-ca. 1475," 246–48. As Jambeck (230) notes, the other legends include prominent women as examples: Monica in Capgrave's *Life of St. Augustine*; Mabel Rich in the *Life of Edmund of Abingdon*; and Paula and Eustochium in the *Life of St. Jerome*.

29. John Lydgate, *The Minor Poems of John Lydgate*, ed. Henry MacCracken, 130–33. In Bodley MS Ashmole 59, the poem's title records that Lydgate made the poem "at the commaundement of my Ladie Anne Countasse of Stafford" (130 n). A. S. G. Edwards notes that Lydgate, unlike Bokenham, usually wrote for male or institutional patrons; his hagiography, often written for women, is an important exception to this rule. See Edwards, "The Transmission and Audience of Osbern Bokenham's *Legendys of Hooly Wummen*," 167.

30. Capgrave, *The Life of St. Norbert by John Capgrave, O.E.S.A.*, ed. Cyril Lawrence Smetana, 154–55, lines 4096–103.

31. Capgrave, *John Capgrave's Lives of St. Augustine and St. Gilbert of Sempringham*, ed. J. J. Munro, 61. The holograph manuscript of the Life of St. Gilbert is British Library MS Additional 36704; I have not consulted the manuscript and rely on the apparatus provided by Munro. As Munro identifies marginal notations in later hands, I assume that this one not so identified is in the author's hand. On Capgrave's holograph manuscripts, see Peter Lucas, *From Author to Audience: John*

Capgrave and Medieval Publication, chap. 4, "Capgrave as Copyist of His Own Work."

32. Lydgate, *Minor Poems*, ed. MacCracken, 145–54.

33. The legend of St. Anne is the second text in Roscoe Parker, ed., *Middle English Stanzaic Versions of the Life of St. Anne*.

34. Cited by Christopher Cannon, "Monastic Productions," 345. John Denston and John Hunt, both mentioned in Bokenham's collection, are sometimes identified as patrons, but they are named only as beneficiaries of saintly intercession; see Chapter 3. Karen Winstead suggests that Chaucer and William Paris wrote their virgin martyr legends "most probably for other men" (Winstead, *Virgin Martyrs*, 17). If so, it is nevertheless significant that they do not explicitly address their male audiences.

35. Bodleian Library MS Douce 872, f. 163. See Horstmann, *Altenglische Legenden, Neue Folge*, cxxxii.

36. Edwards, "Transmission and Audience," 164.

37. On Anne Harling and her manuscript, see Anne Dutton, "Piety, Politics and Persona: MS Harley 4012 and Anne Harling."

38. Deanesly, 357 n 8.

39. See Chapter 3.

40. See Susan Groag Bell, "Medieval Women Book Owners: Arbiters of Lay Piety and Ambassadors of Culture," 157; Carole Meale, "... Alle the Bokes that I Haue of Latyn, Englisch, and Frensch,'" 130–32; and Joel Rosenthal, "Aristocratic Cultural Patronage and Book Bequests, 1350–1500," 535.

41. Susan Cavanaugh, "A Study of Books Privately Owned in England: 1300–1450," 222–23.

42. Ibid., 151.

43. Ibid., 459, 467.

44. In addition to Cavanaugh, I rely especially on Margaret Deanesly, "Vernacular Books in England in the Fourteenth and Fifteenth Centuries."

45. Cavanaugh, 477.

46. Ibid., 211.

47. Ibid., 334.

48. Ibid., 816.

49. Deanesly, 357.

50. Ibid., 357.

51. Ibid., 357.

52. Rosenthal, 545–46.

53. Cavanaugh, 452. See also Meale, "... Alle the Bokes," 128.

54. Deanesly, 357.

55. Jambeck, 241.

56. C. A. J. Armstrong, "The Piety of Cecily, Duchess of York," 68–91; Jambeck, 240.

57. Felicity Riddy, "Women Talking about the Things of God: A Late Medieval Sub-Culture," 108.

58. Carol Meale, "Patrons, Buyers, and Owners: Book Production and Social State," 222.

59. Cavanaugh, 110.

60. Ibid., 90.

61. Ibid., 747–48.

62. Ibid., 748.

63. Ibid., 651.

64. Deanesly, 357.

65. Dutton, "Passing the Book: Testamentary Transmission of Religious Literature to and by Women in England, 1350–1500," 48. Dutton explains her database on 42–43.

66. Kate Harris, "Patrons, Buyers and Owners: The Evidence for Ownership and the Role of Book Owners in Book Production and the Book Trade," 163, 167.

67. Gordon Hall Gerould, *Saints' Legends*, 136.

68. Jambeck, 242, citing A. Baker, "Saints' Lives Written in Anglo-French: Their Historical, Social and Literary Importance," *Transactions of the Royal Society of the United Kingdom*, new series, 4 (1924): 145.

69. John Carmi Parsons, "Of Queens, Courts, and Books: Reflections on the Literary Patronage of Thirteenth-Century Plantagenet Queens," 176. The text is edited by Kathryn Young Wallace, *La Estoire de seint Aedward le Rei*; the reference to "alianor, riche reïne" is at line 52.

70. Cavanaugh, 636.

71. Osten Södergård, *La Vie d'Edouard le Confesseur*, lines 5296–311, cited by Dominica Legge, *Anglo-Norman Literature and Its Background*, 60–65.

72. See Legge, 261. Alice's son had commissioned the Latin text. See Wogan-Browne, "Saints' Lives and the Female Reader," 331 n.

73. Women's patronage of Anglo-Norman legends has recently been discussed by Wogan-Browne, *Saints' Lives and Women's Literary Culture*, 160–63, 249–55.

74. Wogan-Browne, "Saints' Lives and the Female Reader," 314. For a similar caution, see Julia Boffey, "Middle English Lives," 623.

75. The Life of St. Jerome is addressed to a "Right nobill and worthy lady" in London, Lambeth Palace MS 432; she is identified as "the high pryncesse Margarete duchesse of Clarence" in a colophon of Yale, Beinecke MS 317 (fol. 5r). See George Keiser, "Patronage and Piety in Fifteenth-Century England: Margaret, Duchess of Clarence, Symon Wynter and Beinecke MS 317." See also Jambeck, 247.

76. Gibbs, 65.

77. Pierre Bourdieu, *Distinction*; and Bourdieu, *The Field of Cultural Production*.

78. This is based on the edition of D'Evelyn and Mill. The textual tradition of the *SEL* is extremely complicated, but the EETS edition is representative of the percentage of female saints' lives for its various versions.

79. The *Gilte Legende* has not yet been edited in its entirety, and the manuscripts exhibit some variation. I base my remarks on British Library MS Additional 35298, one of the most complete. The so-called "Additional Lives" common to

this manuscript and two others have been edited by Richard Hamer and Vida Russell as *Supplementary Lives in Some Manuscripts of the* Gilte Legende.

80. About 17 percent of the *vitae* in the *Legenda Aurea* are of female saints. The figure is based on Th. Graesse, ed., *Jacobi a Voragine Legenda Aurea*. See also William Granger Ryan's translation of Graesse's edition: *The Golden Legend*. For an account of the origin and reception of the *Golden Legend*, see Sherry Reames, *The Legenda Aurea: A Reexamination of Its Paradoxical History*.

81. Donald Weinstein and Rudolph Bell's influential argument that hagiography provides counterevidence to the thesis that the late Middle Ages witnessed a "feminization" of religion refers to saints, not saints' lives. See Weinstein and Bell, *Saints and Society: The Two Worlds of Western Christendom, 1000–1700*. They thus prefer the earliest available *vita* for the evidence it provides of the sociology of sainthood. The same is true of Jane Tibbetts Schulenburg, *Forgetful of Their Sex: Female Sanctity and Society, ca. 500–1100*; and her "Sexism and the Celestial Gynaeceum from 500 to 1200." Saints' lives provide a different kind of evidence for those interested in narrative culture as a social institution.

82. Gibbs, 1.

83. Edwards suggests that individual legends might have circulated as "pious booklets," which only rarely survive due to their fragile state. See Edwards, "Transmission and Audience," 162.

84. I do not mean here to imply a chronology in which devotional legends supplant pastoral legendaries. Indeed, the earliest Middle English legends extant are the Katherine Group legends, which were most likely produced for a small community of women. The traditions of pastoral legendaries and devotional legends are contemporaneous.

85. Based on Charlotte D'Evelyn's bibliography of legend of individual saints in D'Evelyn and Foster, "Saints' Legends," 2.561–635. Texts found in the *South English Legendary*, the *1438 Gilte Legende*, Mirk's *Festial*, the *Speculum Sacerdotale*, the *Northern Homily Cycle*, and the *Scottish Legendary* have been excluded. In a paper surveying recent work in Middle English hagiography presented at the 34th International Congress on Medieval Studies (Kalamazoo, Mich., 1999), Winstead observed the relative parity in the number of female and male saints whose legends exist outside the large legendaries.

86. Mary handed this book down to her daughter Phillipa. See the on-line facsimile with introduction at www.kb.dk/elib/mss/mdr/th517/index-en.htm.

87. The exception is the *SEL* life of St. Margaret.

88. Carol Meale, "'Gode Men / Wiues Maydnes and Alle Men': Romance and Its Audiences." Meale takes the title of her essay from *Havelock the Dane*, noting that the gendered address and especially the identification of a female audience found there is "especially rare in English romances." She provides evidence that Middle English romance tended to address men, often by social class or age, until the age of printing, when women were more frequently included as well (209–10 n. 3).

89. Tauno Mustanoja, ed., *The Good Wife Taught Her Daughter, The Good Wyfe Wold a Pylgremage, The Thewis of Gud Women*. In "The *Miroir des bonnes femmes*: Not for Women Only?," Kathleen Ashley emphasizes the disjunction be-

tween the feminine address of some conduct books and evidence of male ownership, arguing that this tradition contributed to emerging ideologies of the family.

90. We might expect the representation of women to be categorically different across these two discourses, but—with the crucial exception of sexuality—they are surprisingly similar. Women in both are outspoken, disobedient, and dangerous to men. Also relevant is literature written in response to antifeminism, literature that makes a "case for women," which also makes a feminine audience visible by identifying with women as victims of gross generalization and double standards: see Alcuin Blamires, *The Case for Women in Medieval Culture*; and Blamires et al., *Women Defamed, Women Defended*.

91. See Sponsler, *Drama and Resistance*.

92. For a more fully elaborated version of the reading of the *Legend of Good Women* I offer here, to a somewhat different end, see Catherine Sanok, "Reading Hagiographically: Chaucer's *Legend of Good Women* and its Feminine Audience."

93. Cf. Paul Strohm's argument for Chaucer's "early recognition that alternative situations of address can open alternative narrative and stylistic possibilities" in *Social Chaucer*, 55.

94. All citations to Chaucer's works are to the *Riverside Chaucer*, ed. Larry Benson. As Paul Strohm has shown, "legend" was a generically specific term: its primary meaning in the late fourteenth century was a collection of hagiographic narratives, especially the best known of such collections, the *Legenda Aurea*. See Strohm, "Passion, Lyf, Miracle, Legende: Some Generic Terms in Middle English Hagiographical Narrative."

95. On the *Physician's Tale* and its relation to the *Legend of Good Women*, see especially Anne Middleton, "The *Physician's Tale* and Love's Martyrs."

96. "It satte me wel bet ay in a cave / To bidde and rede on holy seyntes lyves" (Chaucer, *Troilus and Criseyde*, 2.117–18).

97. See especially John Fyler, *Chaucer and Ovid*, chap. 4, "The *Legend of Good Women*: Palinode and Procrustean Bed"; Lisa Kiser, *Telling Classical Tales: Chaucer and the* Legend of Good Women; and, for the feminist reconsideration of the poem's hagiographic form, Carolyn Dinshaw, *Chaucer's Sexual Poetics*, 72–74. Although my emphasis is different, my understanding of the *Legend* is influenced by these important studies.

98. We see this paradox at work, for example, in the *Pardoner's Tale*, in the old man, an allegorical figure for Death, who himself cannot die. Although source study of the *Legend of Good Women* has long pointed to the *Roman de la Rose*, Love's derivation from that poem has sometimes been obscured, perhaps largely because of his self-contradictory criticism but also because he is referred to as Cupid in much modern scholarship. As in the *Roman de la Rose*, Chaucer's God of Love is named after the emotion or condition he represents, not after the classical god. In fact, when Cupid appears as a character in the legend of Dido, his name is glossed as if he might be unfamiliar to the audience—"Cupido, that is the god of love" (1140)—with no acknowledgment of any relation to the God of the prologue. See also Kiser, who notes the important iconographic details that distinguish Love from Cupid (63–64).

99. These lines are from the B fragment of the Middle English translation of the *Roman de la Rose*, the fragment most confidently excluded from the Chaucer canon on linguistic grounds. Though no completed translation can be ascribed to Chaucer, however, the poem as a whole was known in England, and the God of Love's reference to Chaucer's translation is not qualified in any way. The assumption is that the poet in the prologue translated the entire work, whether or not Chaucer himself had in fact finished one. For a modern English translation of these lines, see Jean de Meun and Guillaume de Lorris, *The Romance of the Rose*, trans. Charles Dahlberg, 2115–24.

100. Cf. Janet Cowen, "Woman as Exempla in Fifteenth-Century Verse of the Chaucerian Tradition," 61; and Ruth Ames, "The Feminist Connections of Chaucer's *Legend of Good Women*," 59. But see also Kiser, 89, 97.

101. The narrator, in contrast, distances himself from this position in explaining his "entente" in writing the *Troilus*: "Ne a trewe lover oght me not to blame / Thogh that I speke a fals lovere som shame," he argues, for his purpose was "To forthren trouthe in love and yt cheryce, / And to ben war from falsnesse and fro vice / By swich ensample" (F 466–67, 472–74).

102. The temptation to identify Queen Anne with Alceste and Alceste with the God of Love has led some critics to assume that the criticism of *Troilus and Criseyde* and the translation of the *Roman de la Rose* voiced in the prologue reflects the response of Chaucer's female audience, but this angry response is clearly identified with a male figure. Interestingly, the evidence that Carolyn Dinshaw provides that medieval readers were unnerved by *Troilus and Criseyde* all suggests the discomfort of male readers (*Chaucer's Sexual Poetics*, 67).

103. Readings of this apparent contradiction as "paradoxical" or ironically flawed begin with Paull Baum, "Chaucer's 'Glorious Legende.'"

104. See F 470–77. On the relation between Love's tyranny and his reading practice, see James Simpson, "Ethics and Interpretation: Reading Wills in Chaucer's *Legend of Good Women*," 77–80, which locates the disregard for authorial intention in Augustinian paradigms.

105. Such a pairing of diametrically opposed views of women reaches its most elaborate expression in the literary diptychs that present an antifeminist poem alongside a defense of women. Jean le Fevre's translation of Matheolus and the palinode purportedly written to atone for it, the *Livre de Leesce*, are the best known example of such a pairing. This phenomenon is, of course, an important context for the *Legend of Good Women*, itself presented as a palinode for the *Troilus*. I confine my discussion of antiphrasis to its use in literary antifeminism, leaving aside its articulation in the rhetorical tradition, because I am interested in this specific (though not exclusive) discursive location of the trope. For the relation between the *Legend* and the rhetorical tradition, see Rita Copeland, *Rhetoric, Hermeneutics, and Translation in the Middle Ages*, 186–202.

106. Rossell Hope Robbins, ed., *Secular Lyrics of the XIVth and XVth Centuries*, 35–36 (no. 38).

107. It should be noted that laymen may have been the butt of this clerical joke as well. Misogyny and misogamy were closely related in the Middle Ages.

108. This is not to claim that hagiography was sacrosanct, impervious to comic treatment. The mock *vita* of St. Nemo is evidence that the genre could be parodied. See Martha Bayless, *Parody in the Middle Ages: The Latin Tradition*. Burlesques of the genre are different from satiric readings of its texts, however, and I know of no antiphrastic assessments of female saints' lives.

109. Cf. Janet Cowen, "Chaucer's *Legend of Good Women*: Structure and Tone," 420. For a different interpretation of the congruence between hagiography and Chaucer's "legends," see Dinshaw, *Chaucer's Sexual Poetics*, 72–74.

110. Cf. Jill Mann, *Geoffrey Chaucer*, 43–44, which notes that the few legends not borrowed from the *Heroides* are, without exception, concerned with rape or suicide, an indication, she argues, that the poem's concerns are serious.

111. Cf. Alastair Minnis, "Repainting the Lion: Chaucer's Profeminist Narratives," 157–58, which argues that the poem is meant to encourage debate, in the tradition of *question d'amour* poems such as the *Parliament of Fowls*; and Florence Percival, *Chaucer's Legendary Good Women*, 299–323, which argues that the poem fosters debate through its affiliation with both the tradition of *louange des dames* and clerical antifeminism. On the poem's lack of closure, see Rosemarie McGerr, *Chaucer's Open Books*, chap. 6. Minnis, however, argues for the possibility that the poem was once complete, or at least comprised twenty-five legends, based on references in the Retraction and the *Man of Law's Tale*, as well as one in Edward, second duke of York's early fifteenth-century *Master of the Game* (Minnis, *Oxford Guide to Chaucer: The Shorter Poems*, 326–27).

112. Anne Clark Bartlett, *Male Authors, Female Readers: Representation and Subjectivity in Middle English Devotional Literature*; and Roberta Krueger, *Women Readers and the Ideology of Genre in Old French Verse Romance*. Perhaps the most influential theoretical discussion of the sort of agency described by Bartlett and Krueger is Michel de Certeau's *Practice of Everyday Life*, which argues that consumption is an active process that allows for the transformation of cultural products, a process related, but not wholly subject, to discursive structures that seek to determine proper use of those products.

Chapter 3

1. On the political role of late medieval queens as it shapes Chaucer's representational strategies, see Paul Strohm's chapter, "Queens as Intercessors," in his *Hochon's Arrow*. See also David Wallace, *Chaucerian Polity: Absolutist Lineages and Associational Forms in England and Italy*, chap. 12, especially 362–78, which argues that Anne's mediating role in Richard's court, refracted in the representation of Alceste, was crucial to the model of political community that Chaucer figured throughout his poetry. Most political readings of the poem focus on the prologue; an important exception is Andrew Galloway, "Chaucer's Legend of Lucrece and the Critique of Ideology in Fourteenth-Century England."

2. In this regard it is worth remarking again that Love designates "women" as a class, in keeping with the totalizing logic of antifeminism, and identifies Al-

ceste with them. She does not present herself as part of a larger collectivity of women. On women's collective action in the context of their religious, economic, and social obligations, see R. A. Houlbrooke, "Women's Social Life and Common Action in England from the Fifteenth Century to the Eve of the Civil War."

3. There is no reason to doubt the historicity of this event, but we must, of course, remember that Bokenham's account is part of a narrative governed also by formal and social concerns. My interest is in his representation of the commission as a "historical" event, with actual persons and a precise and realistic setting and date.

4. Although this is the most significant and conspicuous aspect of its form, it is also unusual in being a single-author collection. See A. S. G. Edwards, "Fifteenth-Century Middle English Verse Author Collections."

5. Bokenham, *Legendys of Hooly Wummen*, ed. Mary Serjeantson. All citations are to this edition.

6. Edwards argues that the legends originally circulated singly in pamphlets and that Thomas Burgh, Bokenham's friend and fellow Augustinian, was responsible for collecting them in British Library MS Arundel 327. See Edwards, "Transmission and Audience," 157–67.

7. Bokenham, *Legendys of Hooly Wummen*, ed. Serjeantson, xix. The two earlier editions use more generic titles: Bokenham, *Lives of Saints*, and *Osbern Bokenam's Legenden*, ed. Carl Horstmann.

8. In the introduction to the *Mappula Angliae*, Bokenham mentions that he has translated the lives of Sts. Cedd, Felix, Edward, and Oswald; see text below for a fuller discussion of this reference.

9. See Carroll Hilles, "Gender and Politics in Osbern Bokenham's Legendary," which argues that Bokenham's self-representation as a translator of saints' lives for women readers is "a means of conflating the historical and textual communities of women" (196). As will become clear, I have a different sense of the political ends for which Bokenham creates this textual community, but I agree with Hilles that "the legendary's focus on the world of women's domestic piety" is part of a "strategy of dissent" (195–96).

10. It says that the book "was doon wrytyn in Canebryge by [Bokenham's] soun Frere Thomas Burgh. The yere of our lord a thousand foure hundryth seuyn & fourty Whose expence dreu thretty schyligys & yafe yt onto this holy place of nunnys that thei shulde haue mynd on hym & of hys systyr Dame Betrice Burgh" (Bokenham, *Legendys of Hooly Wummen*, ed. Serjeantson, 289).

11. Delany, *Impolitic Bodies*, 21–22, 129–44. I follow Delany in understanding Bokenham's legendary in terms of the urgent dynastic issues that surfaced in the 1440s and am much indebted to the useful work she has done to provide a historical context for Bokenham's work, but I do not find, as she does, a clear opposition between Lancastrian and Yorkist positions during the period in which the legendary was produced (that is, between 1443 and 1447). Hilles also argues for the legendary as Yorkist propaganda.

12. Warren also notes that these two women "were on opposite sides of the fence," suggesting that the passage points to "political competition for the symbolic capital of female sanctity" (136).

13. Gibson focuses on a single legend, the life of St. Anne, and its patron, Katherine Denston, but the interest in themes of procreation and maternity she identifies there can be found throughout the book. See Gibson, "Saint Anne and the Religion of Childbed."

14. Cf. Summit's argument in *Lost Property* that the idea of English literature was formed through the representation of a lost tradition of women's writing.

15. Doyle; Holzknecht; Jambeck; and Moore. Moore's discussion of Bokenham's patrons is found in the second part of the essay, 79–93.

16. Where early work on Bokenham's collection generally followed the studies of patronage in attributing considerable influence to Bokenham's patrons, others have begun to challenge this by emphasizing his debt to a masculine literary tradition. For the first, see Gibson, "St. Anne and the Religion of Childbed," 101–7; and Winstead, *Virgin* Martyrs, 141–46. For the second, see Delany, *Impolitic Bodies*, chap. 2; and Ian Johnson, "Tales of a True Translator: Medieval Literary Theory, Anecdote and Autobiography in Osbern Bokenham's *Legendys of Hooly Wummen*."

17. Seth Lerer, *Chaucer and His Readers: Imagining the Author in Late-Medieval England*, 16.

18. Hilles, also citing Lerer, announces a similar approach (195), though our conclusions differ.

19. Citations are to Bokenham, "Mappula Angliae," ed. Horstmann. The manuscript that contains the unique copy of Bokenham's *Mappula*, British Library MS Harley 4011, reflects the imbrication of national concerns and devotional ones characteristic of fifteenth-century textual traditions. It contains texts such as the *Libelle of English Policy*, "exhorting all Englonde to keepe the See envyron, and mainly the narrow See. Shewyng what profite cometh thereof, and also what worship and salvation to Englond"; "Lenvoye to Humfray late Duke of Glowceter"; and the Domestic Precepts for King Edward III; as well as devotional works including Lydgate's *Life of Our Lady*. It is interesting that Bokenham's work finds a place in this collection, which has clear Lancastrian affiliations. The *Life of Our Lady*, for example, was written for "oure worshipfull prince kinge harry the fifth" (f. 21r), as the rubric recalls.

20. It has long been assumed that the book to which Bokenham refers contained a complete translation of the *Legenda Aurea*, and attention to this reference has been confined to a long debate about whether it is the so-called 1438 *Gilte Legend* (henceforth *GL*). But Bokenham makes the more modest claim that the English book was "compiled of legenda aurea and of other famous legendes"; that is, it is a collection taken from various sources. We cannot even be certain that the text we know as the *Legenda Aurea* is one of them: Manfred Görlach, *Studies in Middle English Saints' Legends*, identifies a manuscript of the *South English Legendary*, MS Lambeth Palace 223, that is referred to as the *Legenda Aurea* in its colophon (55). Although it is beyond the scope of my argument to address the question of Bokenham's authorship of the *GL* in detail, a quick comparison of the legends common to the *GL* (as presented in the most complete manuscript, British Library MS Additional 35298) and the *Legends of Holy Women* (*LHW*) ar-

gues against Bokenham's authorship of the *GL*. There are significant difference between these two texts for the legends of Anne, Lucy, Agnes, Margaret, Dorothy, and Elizabeth of Hungary. The *LHW*, for instance, provides an etymology of Lucy's name and an elaborate medical description of her mother's illness, neither of which is found in the *GL* legend. Moreover, Lucy's persecutor is called Haspasien in the *GL* and Paschasye in the *LHW*. In the *LHW*, Agnes is asked to choose between serving Vesta or being sent to a brothel; in the *GL*, the brothel is her only option. A more conspicuous difference is that Bokenham includes the account of the vision of the lamb and the salutation to virgins from Ambrose's *vita* of St. Agnes, while both are absent from the *GL* legend. The *GL* St. Margaret follows the *Legenda Aurea*, in which the narrator doubts the story of the dragon swallowing the saint, an anecdote found in the *LHW* version. Theodora is (mistakenly) identified as St. Dorothy's father in the *GL*, rather than her mother, as in the *LHW*. Although Bokenham probably relied on the *Legenda Aurea*'s legend of St. Elizabeth of Hungary, as did the translator of the *GL*, here too the narratives differ. In the *GL*, a Candlemas miracle illustrates Elizabeth's humility; Bokenham changes the holiday to St. Valentine's Day, and Elizabeth chooses a candle engraved with the name of John the Evangelist, to whom she had a particular devotion. St. Anne figures in the *GL* under the rubric of the Nativity of the Virgin, not separately in her own right, as in Bokenham's legendary. It seems likely that Bokenham would have acknowledged earlier translations of the legends of female saints if he had made them, as he mentions a Latin poem he had previously written about St. Anne (2080–82).

D'Evelyn provides a summary of the question of Bokenham's authorship of the *GL* and relevant bibliography in her discussion of English translation of the *Legenda Aurea* in D'Evelyn and Foster, 434–35. Görlach, *Studies in Middle English Saints' Legends*, 133–35, argues against Bokenham's authorship on the basis of his vocabulary. For Horstmann's original speculations, see his introduction to his edition of Bokenham's "Mappula Angliae," 2–3. As I was completing this book, another manuscript of saints' lives was identified as Bokenham's lost legendary; see Simon Horobin, "The Angle of Oblivion: A Lost Medieval Manuscript Discovered in Walter Scott's Collection." According to Horobin, the collection includes slightly revised versions of the lives from the *Legends of Holy Women*. Horobin's anticipated EETS edition of the manuscript will make possible detailed analysis of the evidence for the authorship of the other legends.

21. It does so perhaps most clearly in Bokenham's claim that once Higden's geographical description is available to readers, "hit shalle byne easy ynoughe to vnderstande alle that is towched ther-of in the seyd legende" (6), implying that the only geographical references in the legendary are to English territories.

22. I borrow the term "imagined community" from Benedict Anderson, *Imagined Communities: Reflections on the Origin and Spread of Nationalism*, whose analysis of nationalism has been extremely influential. The teleology that structures his analysis depends on a paradigm, one familiar to medievalists, that posits the Middle Ages as radically different from modernity. This is accomplished by totalizing medieval ideas of kingship, language, and temporality: thus, medievals

believed in "an idea largely foreign to the contemporary Western mind: the nonarbitrariness of the sign" (14), and their single concept of time was of typological simultaneity. Despite such reductive representations of medieval cultural formations, Anderson's book remains useful for its insistence on the status of the "nation" as an imaginary construct, a fantasy of community larger than any one person's acquaintance, which depends on a historical or "genealogical" sense—that is, nationalism understood "as the expression of an historical tradition of serial continuity" (195).

23. Aubrey was interred at a church of Augustinian friars in London, showing the close connections the family maintained with Bokenham's order. See *Complete Peerage of England, Scotland, Ireland, Great Britain, and the United Kingdom*, 10: 239.

24. Gibson, "St. Anne and the Religion of Childbed," 100.

25. Delany, *Impolitic Bodies*, also remarks an interest in "female collectivity and solidarity" here; she mentions St. Christine as well (181–2).

26. In September 1445, a few months before Bokenham translated the Magdalene legend for Richard's sister, the king had made his young sons, Edward and Edmund, the earls of March and Rutland. T. B. Pugh, "Richard Plantagenet (1411–60), Duke of York, as the King's Lieutenant in France and Ireland," notes that the two-year old Edmund was hardly in need of landed endowment and that giving titles to such young children was unprecedented (123). After the death of Gloucester, Richard was granted the Isle of Wight and other important territories. Pugh remarks that he "was one of the very few English magnates who were fortunate enough to receive grants of valuable estates on both sides of the Channel" during this period (127), and he notes that Richard in turn supported the controversial negotiations Henry VI had pursued with Charles VII.

27. Ralph A. Griffiths, *Reign of King Henry VI*, 586–87.

28. Rotuli Parliamentorum (1767), 5:200, cited by Griffiths, *Reign of King Henry VI: The Exercise of Royal Authority, 1422–1461*, 594.

29. *An English Chronicle of the Reigns of Richard II, Henry IV, Henry V, and Henry VI*, ed. John Silvester Davies, 64–65. The chronicler later represents Cade and his followers as criminals intent on "tiranny and robory" (67), but the political protest is qualified only by the comment that Cade was a "sotill man" (65).

30. Delany, *Impolitic Bodies*, 127.

31. R. A. Griffiths, "The Sense of Dynasty in the Reign of Henry VI," 17–18.

32. On the implications of the trial, see Griffiths, "Sense of Dynasty"; for the trial itself, see Griffiths, "The Trial of Eleanor Cobham: An Episode in the Fall of Duke Humphrey of Gloucester."

33. Griffiths, "Trial of Eleanor Cobham," 397, 381 n. 5.

34. *English Chronicle*, 60.

35. Ibid., 64.

36. On Lydgate, see lines 2005–7; on Capgrave, see lines 6354–60.

37. Griffiths, *Reign of King Henry VI*, 447. Griffiths remarks that Henry Bourchier was named viscount "as a means of providing compensation for those who, after the congress of Arras, found that their French estates were gradually re-

duced in value and size by the resurgent French" (355). Griffiths identifies a writ of summons, dated December 14, 1446, as the earliest evidence of Bourchier's new title (372 n. 110). It is preceded, however, by Bokenham's reference to Isabel as countess of Eu in the prolocutory, internally dated to 1445; the record of her patronage, that is, may be the first evidence of the family's changing fortunes and of the circumstances that would have linked Bourchier and Gloucester in a common cause.

38. On York's affiliation with Gloucester, see K. H. Vickers, *Humphrey, Duke of Gloucester*, 288; and P. A. Johnson, *Duke Richard of York, 1411–1460*, 41.

39. Following a suggestion originally made by Horstmann, I emend the manuscript reading "relygyoun" to "regyoun" in line 3137.

40. The *Middle English Dictionary* identifies the figurative use in its second definition of the word, but Bokenham's legendary is the only source of the citations it gives with this metaphorical sense.

41. Philippa Maddern, *Violence and Social Order: East Anglia 1422–1442*, details the procedure: outlawry followed attempts to "attach" the defendant (hold goods in surety), to arrest him (capias), and to summon him at five county courts (exigent) (31).

42. The legend runs from line 337 to line 868; the account of the translations, from 921 to 1393. Bokenham's elaborate description of his fatigue and specifics about the dates of his holiday separate the two sections.

43. David Lawton, "Dullness in the Fifteenth Century."

44. On the academic degrees pursued by Augustinian friars, see Francis Roth, O.S.A., *The English Austin Friars, 1249–1538*, 1.136–77. Bokenham had received the title of master at least by 1438, when "all graces" to him were reconfirmed at a chapter meeting; see Roth, 2.322–23 (item 789). Bokenham's education may have been especially conspicuous in the 1440s, when his order was rebuked on several occasions for its failure to send the required number of members to Oxford or Cambridge. Complaints were made at chapter meetings in 1443 and again in 1446; after the latter, Henry VI agreed to tax houses that failed to comply, with the proceeds to go to the foundation of a college in honor of the Virgin. Failure to provide university training was still a concern in 1449. See White Kennett, *Parochial Antiquities Attempted in the History of Ambrosden, Burcester and other Adjacent Parts in the Counties of Oxford and Bucks*, 214–15. See also Charles Henry Cooper, *Annals of Cambridge*, 1: 190, 197, 204.

45. That is, December 17, 1443 (187–91). The date is underlined in black in the manuscript.

46. On Bokenham's Yorkist affiliations, see Delany, *Impolitic Bodies*, 21–22, 129–44, and A. S. G. Edwards, "The Middle English Translation of Claudian's *De Consulatu Stilichonis*."

47. *Annals of Cambridge*, 173–74.

48. There is not, however, strong enough support for Delany's claim that the Augustinian friars as an order were affiliated with the house of York. John Capgrave, the order's most prominent member, was an eager supporter of the Lancastrians, as is witnessed by his *Liber De Illustribus Henricis* (*Impolitic Bodies*, 130).

49. Griffiths, "Trial of Eleanor Cobham," 391, 393. The *English Chronicle* records that Jourdemain confessed to making "medicinez and drynkis" for Eleanor that would cause Gloucester "to loue her and to wedde her" (58–59).

50. See Griffiths, "Trial of Eleanor Cobham," 393. The trial of Eleanor Cobham and her companions prompted the formation of a commission to investigate the use of necromancy and sorcery against the king (*English Chronicle*, 58).

51. For the *Gilte Legende*, I use British Library MS Additional 35298. The St. Margaret Legend in Bodleian Library MS 6922 (Ashmole 61) has Margaret's persecutor, not the saint herself, accused of witchcraft: the demon who torments her in prison explains that Olibrius has sent him and his brother devil in a terrifying guise "Forto strey thi fare body, / With hys craft & nygramansy" (364–65). See Horstmann, *Altenglische Legenden, Neue Folge*, 239.

52. The St. Margaret pageant performed in honor of Margaret of Anjou's entry into London in 1445 shows that the queen became a reference point for the saint during the years Bokenham composed the legendary. On the pageant, see Carleton Brown, "Lydgate's Verses on Queen Margaret's Entry into London"; and Gordon Kipling, "The London Pageants for Margaret of Anjou: A Medieval Script Restored." Another St. Margaret pageant in her honor was performed ten years later in Coventry. See *Records of Early English Drama: Coventry*, ed. R. W. Ingram, 34.

53. As discussed in the last chapter, it has been identified as the only genre of vernacular theology that did not open the author to suspicion of dissent and violation of Arundel's Constitutions. See Nicholas Watson, "Censorship and Cultural Change in Late-Medieval England," 833.

54. Bokenham, *Legendys of Hooly Wummen*, ed. Serjeantson, 291 n. 216, citing personal communication from F. M. Stenton. Stenton notes that the name is attested on the Gough map, but that it is "very rarely mentioned in records." This is borne out by its absence in place-name research: there is no mention of Ageland in the five volumes devoted to Lincolnshire in the English Place-Name Society series. See Kenneth Cameron, *The Place-Names of Lincolnshire*.

55. St. Anne was a relatively "new" saint in the fifteenth century; her feast was granted papal authorization only in 1381, perhaps at the request of Richard II as a compliment to his fiancée, Anne of Bohemia. See H. A. Kelly, "St. Anne." By the mid-fifteenth century, however, there were already several extant versions of her legend, testimony to the saint's popularity and the promotion of her cult. See the three stanzaic versions in Parker; the 1438 *Gilte Legende* contains an additional version. Excellent readings of the texts and cultural traditions associated with the cult can be found in Ashley and Sheingorn. Gibson's essay in this collection, "St. Anne And the Religion of Childbed," places Bokenham's St. Anne in the context of East Anglian devotion, the social history of childbearing, and the personal life of Katherine Denston, the legend's patron. My reading of the legend owes much to it.

56. I quote this passage below in a discussion of Bokenham's trope of the saint as muse. It should be noted that the strategies Bokenham uses to grant women agency and authority also articulate their limits: where Anne prays alone, in unmediated communication with her God, Katherine Denston commissions an

Augustinian friar. Bokenham, however, obscures his own mediating role by identifying his patron as a necessary mediator between himself and the successful production of the text.

57. Anthony Goodman and David Morgan, "The Yorkist Claim to the Throne of Castile," 63.

58. John Hardyng makes the claim explicit in a chronicle he presented to Richard a decade later, which insists, "The first heire male whiche of the sisters came / The kyng should been, and haue the regiment." See *The Chronicle of Iohn Hardyng*, ed. H. Ellis (London, 1812), cited by Goodman and Morgan, who suggest that Bokenham's mistake is "so gross an error that it should be attributed to ignorance rather than malice" (64).

59. Goodman and Morgan, 63–64; Pugh, 123–24; Delany, *Impolitic Bodies*, 132.

60. It is significant in this regard that Bokenham's rejection of classical rhetoric is at certain moments phrased not in terms of religious rectitude or literary inheritance, as is conventional, but in terms of its reception by a female audience. Bokenham criticizes "swych eloquence /As sum curyals han," who make "baladys or amalettys" for their ladies, "In wych to sorwyn & wepyn thei feyn / As thow the prongys of deth dede streyn / Here hert-root, al-be thei fer thens" (5225–33). Bokenham's criticism of court poetry as literature of seduction reads the secular tradition from the perspective of a feminine audience, who might be misled by the claims of erotic poetry. In lieu of court poetry about the "prongs of death" a courtier suffers for his lady, Bokenham offers his female readers legends about the pains a girl suffers for her Lord.

61. For a different reading of Bokenham's representation of procreativity and poetic production, see Warren, 147–62. See also Theresa Coletti, *Mary Magdalene and the Drama of Saints*, which argues that the parallel descriptions of courtly rhetoric and the children's clothing work to criticize "the dangerous ambiguities of courtly representation," in contrast to Bokenham's own "pleyne" religious narrative (75–76).

62. They stand in for their classical forebears, whom Bokenham explicitly renounces; see lines 5214–24, where Bokenham rejects Clio, Melpomene, and the rest of the "musys nyne" in favor of Christ. Bokenham's saintly muses have some precedent in Middle English hagiography. Chaucer's *Second Nun's Tale* represents Mary as a kind of muse in the prologue: the Second Nun asks that she "do me endite / Thy maydens deeth" (32–33). See Eileen Jankowski, "Reception of Chaucer's *Second Nun's Tale*: Osbern Bokenham's *Lyf of S. Cycle*," for an argument that Bokenham knew Chaucer's legend. Lydgate borrows the trope in the *Life of Our Lady* (50–60), and Capgrave uses it in the *Life of Saint Katherine*, invoking the saint rather than Mary (64–70). But the conjunction of the saintly muse and the female patron is unique to Bokenham.

63. Ian Johnson discusses Bokenham's saints as sources of literary authority in "*Auctricitas*? Holy Women and Their Middle English Texts." See also Johnson, "Tales of a True Translator," 117–22. The classic discussion of Christian responses to the classical muses is E. R. Curtius, *European Literature and the Latin Middle Ages*, 228–46.

64. The manuscript reads "sowde" in line 8333. D'Evelyn notes that Horstmann proposes "sowe" or "sownde"; she follows the latter suggestion (227 n).

65. Winstead, "Capgrave's Saint Katherine and the Perils of Gynecocracy."

Chapter 4

1. All references to the legend and its Latin source are to Henry Bradshaw, *The Life of St. Werburge of Chester*, ed. C. Horstmann. The text was printed by Pynson in 1521, but it was written earlier, perhaps in 1513, as scholars have long assumed because of a short poem that follows the legend in Pynson's edition which cryptically mentions 1513 as the date of the translation. This is uncertain authority, however, as the writer does not seem to know who wrote the poem. The end of the legend, with its extended request that its lay audience respect the rights of the abbey devoted to St. Werburge in Chester, may suggest composition at the end of the fifteenth century, during a brief period when the often violent encounters between the monastery and the city had ceased and before the city acquired several significant privileges that the abbey had long enjoyed. The third poem appended to the legend in Pynson's edition has an acrostic signature, B V L K L E Y, which may also suggest composition in the fifteenth century, when the Bulkeley family was particularly active in the affairs of the monastery. Thomas Bulkeley of Ayton posted bail for the abbot Richard Oldham in 1466; and George Bulkeley, as mayor, agreed with Abbot Simon Ripley to commit the parishioners of St. Oswald to pay for certain repairs to the abbey church. It seems most likely that Bradshaw's poem was composed under the abbacy of Ripley (1485–93), the only abbot whose relationship with the city and local gentry was positive. Under Oldham, the relations were especially bad, even violent: some monks received injunctions from the mayor's court to keep the peace, charges of murder and rape were brought against others, and the abbot was discovered to have embezzled money bequeathed to the monastery for masses. Although the abbacy of John Birchenshawe, from 1493 until he was dismissed by Cardinal Wolsey in 1524 (to be reinstated five years later), was not marred by criminal monks, his strong-willed efforts to preserve ancient rights of the monastery led to extremely tense relations with Chester, especially after 1506, when many of those rights were given to the city by Henry VII. Bradshaw's plea for the preservation of the abbey's rights, especially concerning the fair (2.1786–93), would be hopelessly belated after 1509, when the 1506 changes were confirmed by the king. For the history of the abbey, I rely on R. V. H. Burne, *The Monks of Chester: The History of St. Werburgh's Abbey*, 128–53; J. T. Driver, *Cheshire in the Later Middle Ages, 1399–1540*, 153–60; and Ann Kettle and A. P. Baggs, "Religious Houses," 132–44.

2. David Mills discusses Bradshaw's legend as part of a Chester tradition in *Recycling the Cycle: The City of Chester and Its Whitsun Plays*.

3. Richard Helgerson remarks a similar phenomenon in early modern chorographic discourses in *Forms of Nationhood: The Elizabethan Writing of England*, 131–39. "The dialectic of general and particular that is built into the struc-

ture of a chorography," Helgerson argues, "in the end constitutes the nation it represents" (138).

4. E.g., E. J. Hobsbawm's argument in *Nations and Nationalism Since 1780: Programme, Myth, Reality* (Cambridge: Cambridge University Press, 1992) that states necessarily precede "nations" (9–10); discussed by Helgerson, 296, 350 n. 2.

5. See, for example, the essays in Kathy Lavezzo, ed. *Imagining a Medieval English Nation*.

6. This, in particular, may have complemented other Tudor efforts to represent England and Englishness.

7. For Anderson, the nation is the antithesis (if also the analog) of religious community. Especially suggestive for my reading of Bradshaw's legend is Anderson's argument, discussed further below, that the "homogenous" time of Christian eschatology is replaced by the homogeneous time of national identification produced by modern technology (especially the daily newspaper). Not all modern theorists agree that modern nationalism is a fully secular phenomenon: e.g., Etienne Balibar, "The Nation Form."

8. Homi Bhabha, "Dissemination: Time, Narrative and the Margins of the Modern Nation," in *The Location of Culture*, 145 (emphasis in the original).

9. The textual tradition of the *South English Legendary* is notoriously complex. I base this figure on the analysis of the major manuscripts in Manfred Görlach, *The Textual Tradition of the South English Legendary*, 306–9.

10. Cf. also British Library MS 949, which adds three rare legends: it is the only *SEL* manuscript to include the legend of St. Fremund; it is one of only three that contain the legend of St. Edmund the Confessor; and it offers a different legend of St. Frideswide from those found in other *SEL* collections. British Library MS Egerton 1993 adds the legends of St. Tolotou (unique to *SEL* tradition), King Ethelbert of East Anglia, St. Edburga of Winchester, St. Botolph, St. Audry, St. Mildred, and St. Egwine. I rely on the British Library manuscript index for this information, not having examined these books myself. The Egerton manuscript is part of Görlach's "E" branch of the tradition (comprising four manuscripts and a fragment), a group that includes legends affiliated with the Worcester and the Hereford liturgy, 55. Görlach considers the possibility that these were part of the original collection, which is associated with Worcester on linguistic grounds, and suggests that they were gradually omitted as the collection was reconciled with the Sarum liturgy, 36–37. If they were original, however, we might expect to find some of them in the earliest manuscripts, such as Bodleian Library MS Laud 108 (c. 1300). Given that many of these saints are confined to the E tradition, it seems more probable that the original collection contained only two Worcester saints, Wulfstan and Oswald, represented in most manuscripts, and that the others were added later. Another indication that this tradition is later is the shortening of the poetic line to six stresses; see Görlach, *Textual Tradition*, 81.

11. They are British Library MS Additional 11565 and 35298 and Lambeth MS 72. The additions are substantial: British Library MS Additional 35298 contains the lives of Edmund of Canterbury, Bridget, Edmund King and Martyr, Frideswide,

Edward King and Martyr, Alphege, Augustine of Canterbury, Oswald of Worcester, Dunstan, Aldhelm, Swithun, Kenelm, Chad, Cuthburt, Brendan. These so-called "Additional Lives" are edited by Richard Hamer and Vida Russell, *Supplementary Lives in Some Manuscripts of the* Gilte Legende.

12. See Görlach, *Textual Tradition*, 23.

13. Southwell Minster MS 7. In addition to the prose Katherine, it includes the lives of St. Ursula, St. Oswald, St. Dunstan, St. Edmund the Confessor, St. Edmund King and Martyr, St. Edward King and Martyr, and St. Faith. St. Faith is not an Anglo-Saxon saint; she represents a different definition of English identity in terms of Continental territory and claims to the French throne. She comes from Aquitaine, long held by the English and a central theater of the Hundred Years' War. The legend, the only other from this collection to be published, is edited by Päivi Pahta in "The Middle English Prose Legend of St. Faith in MS Southwell Minster 7," which identifies the *SEL* as the legend's source. On St. Faith and English Gascony, see Delany, *Impolitic Bodies*, 165–68.

14. The colophon to the manuscript specifies that it once belonged to the church of St. Mary and St. Ethelfride in Romsey. I have not seen the manuscript and rely on the British Library manuscript description. On the relation between this manuscript and the *South English Legendary* and later collections of English saints, see Görlach, *Textual Tradition*, 8 n. 3.

15. Like the Romsey collection, Tynemouth's legendary has only one manuscript witness, Cotton MS Tiberius E1; see Görlach, *Textual Tradition*, 7–9. This suggests the very local character of such collections at this period.

16. These two collections have long been associated with Capgrave. Together with his monumental *Life of St. Katherine*, they suggest a parallel to Bokenham's dual interest in women and England. The attribution, however, is late and unreliable. See Peter Lucas, "John Capgrave and the *Nova Legenda Anglie*."

17. The English text has recently been edited by Manfred Görlach as *The Kalendre of the Newe Legende of Englande*. All citations are to this edition. The *Kalendre* is surpassed in number of native saints by Nicholas Roscarrock's *Lives of the Saints*, a recusant legendary that uses the national affiliation of the saints as an argument for Catholicism: Cambridge University Library MS Add. 3041.

18. Both legends are edited by Carl Horstmann. See Horstmann, ed., *S. Editha sive Chronicon Vilodunense* and "Vita S. Etheldredae Eliensis," in Horstmann, ed., *Altenglische Legenden, Neue Folge*, 282–307.

19. G. N. Garmonsway and R. R. Raymo, eds., "A Middle English Prose Life of St. Ursula."

20. There is a printed legend of St. Margaret (Pynson, 1493) and one of St. Katherine of Alexandria (1550?), but they are in a distinct minority. See H. S. Bennett, *English Books and Readers, 1475–1557*, 75, 290.

21. Her legend had appeared only once before in English, in abbreviated form, in the *Kalendre of the New Legende of Englande*, which was printed only five years before the longer legend was printed.

22. Bennett, 75.

23. Costus is, in this version of the legend, an Armenian rather than Alexandrian king. The change may reflect late medieval English awareness of Armenia as an early Christian kingdom, on which see Carolyn Collette and Vincent DiMarco, "The Matter of Armenia in the Age of Chaucer."

24. Saara Nevanlinna and Irma Taavitsainen, eds., *St. Katherine of Alexandria: The Late Middle English Prose Legend in Southwell Minster MS 7*, 68–69.

25. See the manuscript list provided by Nevanlinna and Taavitsainen, xi–xii, as well as their summary of the different versions of the legend, 11–14.

26. These, along with Alfred and Gerald of Wales and "mo in deed," are cited as Bradshaw's authorities at the end of the prologue (1.127–30).

27. On genealogy as a mode of medieval historiography, see Gabrielle Spiegel, "Genealogy: Form and Function in Medieval Historiography," in Spiegel, *The Past as Text*, 99–110.

28. Bradshaw here considerably expands the single genealogical chapter in his source, a Latin *vita* attributed to Goscelin. Although the Latin *vita* identifies Werburge's lineage with four kingdoms, he details only the Kentish and Mercian lines, mentioning Werburge's French and East Anglian forebears only briefly. Bradshaw adds the Northumbrian genealogy and greatly expands the East Anglian one, increasing the significance of Werburge's maternal line. His increased attention to Werburge's descent from the royalty of France through the maternal line—Berta, her great great-grandmother, and her great-grandmother Emma—reflects English claims to the French throne. Citing gaps in our knowledge of his career, Rosalind Love does not endorse the traditional attribution of the Anglo-Latin life of Werburge to Goscelin, although she notes its similarity to other lives of female saints associated with Ely that are confidently ascribed to him: See Love, *Three Eleventh-Century Anglo-Latin Saints' Lives*, xliv.

29. These legends are both integral to and separate from the legend of St. Werburge, as the chapter rubric to the life of St. Audry makes clear, labelling it "A lytell treatyse of the lyfe of saynt Audry, abbesse of Ely" (Book 1, chap. 18). It is misleading, however, to list them as independent legends, as they are in D'Evelyn and Foster, 584.

30. On the importance of the latter to nationalism, and thus the importance of women in "reproducing" the nation, see Nira Yuval-Davis, *Gender and Nation*, 26–38.

31. See also a similar comment made in the account of St. Sexburga's genealogy: 2.2003–9.

32. On the cloistered virgin's separation from history, see Wogan-Browne, *Saint's Lives and Women's Literary Culture*, 19–24.

33. Thomas Warton, who declared Bradshaw's poem "infinitely inferior to Lydgate's worst manner," identified the marriage scene and especially the description of the tapestries and minstrel's song as "the most splendid passage of this poem," as cited in Henry Bradshaw, *The Holy Lyfe and History of Saynt Werburge*, ed. Edward Hawkins, xi, xiii.

34. See Chapter 5.

35. See also Werburge's words to her father, 2. 1464ff.

36. Unlike Bradshaw's legend, however, the tapestries represent international histories, rather than national ones.

37. The miracle borrows from the legend of St. Chad, whose holiness is revealed to Wulfhere when he hangs his vestments on a sunbeam.

38. The second miracle is a striking reformulation of Ovidian narrative: Daphne, fleeing Apollo, is granted a similar divine intervention, but it is, of course, a permanent metamorphosis, not a temporary asylum. In the *Life of St. Werburge*, the tree miraculously remains fresh and living "to this day" (1.2807) and it continues to respond to human virtue, allowing only those of "clene perfyte lyfe" to enter its hollow (1.2812).

39. Bede, *History of the English Church and People*, trans. Leo Sherley-Price.

40. On this as a defining feature of early saint cults, see Peter Brown, *The Cult of Saints*.

41. The metaphor is repeated when Werburge's incorrupt body is translated to a new sepulcher nine years after her death (1.3376–77).

42. On the holy theft of saints' bodies and relics, see Patrick Geary, *Furta Sacra: Thefts of Relics in the Central Middle Ages*.

43. The claim is repeated at greater length at the beginning of the second book; see 2.148–68.

44. Anderson notes that both nationalism and eschatology depend on "homogenous" temporality (24). Because he characterizes all of medieval culture by the eschatological mode, and because he assumes that one "homogenous" ideology would prevent the other, the Middle Ages are for him necessarily pre-national. Anderson's assumption about the incompatibility of a nationalist and religious worldview can be refuted with modern examples as readily as with medieval ones.

45. In this, the legend offers an interesting departure from William of Malmesbury, who, as Robert Stein argues, identifies the uncorrupted bodies of Anglo-Saxon saints, including Werburge, as evidence of national identity. See Stein, "Making History English: Cultural Identity and Historical Explanation in William of Malmesbury and Layamon's *Brut*," 97–115.

46. This narrative, however, rather than demonstrating the variability of history, demonstrates the variability of historiography, through the competing versions of the city's origins that Bradshaw offers: the legendary foundation as Caerleon by the giant Lleon Gaver or, alternatively, the Briton King Leil or perhaps King Marius, or by the Roman legions sent by Emperor Julius Caesar to subdue Ireland. Bradshaw declares with some resignation that "eche auctour holdeth a singular opinion" (2.397), a claim that is undone by the fact that he attributes only two of these possibilities: the giant is attested by the *Polychronicon* and the Roman foundation by Ranulf Higden. Bradshaw apparently does not expect his audience to know that these are the same source, that the problem is not multiple historians but multiple histories. The effect, however, is the same as in the first book: a history of fits and starts, of the many points of origin that can be adduced, and the discontinuous history of places.

47. The refrain "Wherfore to the monasterye be neuer vnkynde" ends each paragraph in this chapter.

48. A central issue was the struggle over the sponsorship of a fair on St. Werburge's day, June 21 (the date commemorates her translation from Hanbury to Chester; see M. R. Newbolt, *St. Werburgh and Her Shrine*). Tensions were particularly high at the end of the fifteenth century, and the right to host the fair was given to the city in 1506. See Burne, 144–47; J. T. Driver, 154. See also note 1 above.

49. After a series of chapters tracing the privileges of Chester abbey, Bradshaw returns to the national perspective that characterizes the first book. A long chapter offers a litany of good kings—from King Edward "senior," to Ethelstan his son, his brother Edmund, the princes Elred and Edwin, and "meke Edgare" (2.1133)—and it recounts the victory over invaders and the increase of religion and virtue that accompany their beneficent rule. The encomium to Edgar, for example, praises him as "The floure of Englande regynyg as emperour" (2.1200), and his relationship to his nation is compared to Romulus and Rome, Cyrus and Persia, Alexander (identified only as "conquerour") and the Greeks, Charlemagne and France, and Hector and the Trojans (2.1201–3). The focus of the legend has widened again, not only to address English history and identity, but also to place it in a universal history.

50. Cf. Lydgate's *Troy Book* for Henry V.

51. Cf. Peter Womack's discussion of the Digby play of Mary Magdalene in "Shakespeare and the Sea of Stories."

52. Anderson identifies this as a key feature of modern nationalism, 7.

53. For English sumptuary law, see Frances Baldwin, *Sumptuary Legislation and Personal Regulation in England*. Sponsler, *Drama and Resistance*, offers an insightful analysis of these codes and the "regulation of difference" (1–23).

54. The life of Bridget of Sweden is presented as part of the *Kalendre*; it is listed in the index for that work, despite the difference in its subject and length (it is much longer than the entries for native saints). The volume also includes a second text, Hilton's treatise on the mixed life, not listed in the index for the *Kalendre* and identifies it as a separate text in Pynson's introduction. Pynson explains there that he has already printed the Hilton before but believes that it deserves a wider distribution.

55. Other evidence that vernacular hagiography was so influenced is found, for example, in Capgrave's *Life of St. Katherine*, which is represented as a translation from a legend found by a crusader in the time of the siege of Alexandria.

56. Indeed, the prologue here inverts an argument made by Peter the Venerable, who argued for the possibility of converting Muslims based on the conversion of the English, his account of which draws largely from Bede and highlights the role of St. Augustine and Pope Gregory. Peter concludes from this history that Muslims should be treated in the same way: "Decet vos hoc idem facere." See Peter the Venerable's prologue to the *Liber contra sectam sive haeresim Saracenorum*, also known as *Adversus nefandam sectam saracenorum*, cols. 684b–685c.

57. By addressing the life of St. Bridget separately, Pynson does acknowledge its difference from the English legends, but it is not identified as a wholly distinct text in his edition. As noted above, it is included in the table of the saints that pref-

aces the volume, which does exclude the final text, Walter Hilton's *Epistle on the Mixed Life*.

58. Bhabha, 145.

59. The text of the legend, not included in Görlach's edition of the *Kalendre*, is available in J. H. Blunt's edition of *The Myroure of Oure Ladye*, xlvii–lix; see ix for the ascription of the legend to Gascoigne. Görlach suggests more concrete evidence of the affiliation between the legend and Syon: he cites S. H. Johnston, "A Study of the Career and the Literary Publications of Richard Pynson" (Ph.D. diss., University of Western Ontario, 1977), 101, which claims that the woodcut includes the initials E. G., for Elizabeth Gibbs, a Syon abbess. See Görlach, *Kalendre*, 12. I cannot find these initials in the woodcut; it may have been confused with a woodcut depicting St. Bridget in the 1530 edition of the *Myrour of Our Lady*, which does include them. Another of the *Myrour*'s three images of the saint seems to have been the model for the woodcut in the *Kalendre* and, as we will see, for the one illustrating Pynson's edition of Bradshaw's *Werburge*.

60. This institutional context may be relevant to the legendary as whole, for a manuscript in the Syon library (MS Karlsruhe St. Georgen 12) included the first part of the revised *Sanctilogium Angliae, Walliae, Scotiae et Hibernia* of John of Tynemouth, perhaps made for the nuns by Simon Wynter. See Görlach, *Kalendre*, 9 n. 6.

61. See Edward Hodnett, *English Woodcuts, 1480–1535*, no. 1349. In addition to the few extant copies of the 1521 edition (Horstmann reports two at the Bodleian, one at the British Library, one in the York minster library, and one in a private collection, v), Hawkin's 1848 edition of Bradshaw's *The Holy Lyfe and History of Saynt Werburge* for the Chetham society reproduces the image. The relationship between the two texts may be one of institutional affiliation. Martha Driver has recently suggested that woodcuts of St. Bridget point to the role of Syon abbey in sponsoring printed editions of devotional works; see Driver, "Nuns as Patrons, Artists, Readers: Bridgettine Woodcuts in Printed Books Produced for the English Market." Her argument centers on the woodcut used by Wynkyn de Worde, but it seems possible that it could be extended to Pynson's woodcut too. Although Bradshaw's legend has no other known connection to Syon, the two other books with this woodcut, the *Life of St. Bridget* and the *Pylgrimage of Perfection*, do (Driver, 251). If so, Syon abbey contributed in significant ways to the development of a printed canon of national hagiography. On Syon's importance to the printing of devotional literature in the sixteenth century, see also J. T. Rhodes, "Syon Abbey and Its Religious Publications in the Sixteenth Century."

Chapter 5

1. "Rannulphus episcopus Dunelmi ante episcopatum dum esset tocius Anglie iudex. secundus post regem" (text and translation from *The Life of Christina of Markyate*, ed. and trans. C. H. Talbot, 40–41). All references are to this edition.

2. On emerging and competing definitions of marriage in the period, see Thomas Head, "The Marriages of Christina of Markyate."

3. "Et apud lectum suum cum ipso residens. multum ad caste vivendum exhortans. exempla quoque sanctorum ei proposuit. Historiam ordine retexuit illi beate Cecilie et sponsi sui Valeriani. qualiter illibate pu[dici]cie coronas eciam morituri meru[erunt] accipere de manu angeli. Nec solum [hoc] set et illi et per illos alii postmodum [ad] viam martirii pervenerunt. sicque a Domino duppliciter coronati: in celo et [in ter]ra honorati sunt. Et nos inquid [quan]tum possumus sequamur illorum exempla. ut consortes efficiamur in eorum [per]henni gloria. Quia si compatimur: et con[reg]nabimus" (50–51).

4. "Et tu ergo cave sponsam Christi velle tibi tollere. ne in ira sua interficiet te" (72–73).

5. She is doubted, briefly, by Sueno, her first mentor, who accuses Christina of the inconstancy of a woman (*muliebris inconstancie*) when he learns of her betrothal (54). The hagiographer plays slyly with the irony of this accusation from a man who so readily abandons the saint: while the girl had persevered, he notes, the man had faltered: *Et ecce iam puella perseverante vir defecit.*

6. *Life of Christina of Markyate*, ed. Talbot, 12. Christina comes from an Anglo-Saxon family (10). Talbot remarks that hermits in this period tend to have Anglo-Saxon names and that the records about their lives exhibit "an undercurrent of national feeling, an indirect allusion to the differences in tongue and custom between those who led the hermit life and their spiritual superiors" (12).

7. Talbot remarks this evidence of Roger's Englishness (13). The passage reads: "Et ad virginem. letare mecum. ait anglico sermone. [my]n sunendaege dohter. quod latine dicitur. mea dominice diei filia" (And he said to the virgin, "Rejoice with me." In English he said, "myn sunendaege dohter," which is to say in Latin, my Sunday daughter) (106–7). I have slightly modified Talbot's translation, which presents "letare mecum" as part of Roger's English utterance.

8. From this perspective, the inclusion of the life of St. Alexis in the psalter made for Christina may be seen as a careful response to her *vita*. Thomas Head notes that the legend of St. Alexis, another saint who resists parental pressure to marry, was "imported to England by Norman clerics," whereas Cecilia was venerated in Anglo-Saxon England. He suggests that Christina framed her experience in terms of a saint "familiar to her from preaching she had heard as a child," and the Norman monks of St. Alban's later reframed it in terms of a saint familiar to them (Head, 84). Perhaps they did so strategically, to redefine Christina's holiness as part of Norman culture, rather than as a challenge to it.

9. Thomas Renna, "Virginity in the *Life* of Christina of Markyate and Aelred of Rievaulx's *Rule*," notes the *vita*'s emphasis on the moral and spiritual value of a retreat from the world, which he understands in terms of twelfth-century monastic reform. Renna's argument that the *vita*'s depiction of the social world is not damning (most of Christina's "detractors," he claims, "are not evil" [88]) and his assumption that the text means only to warn monks of too great an engagement with secular and ecclesiastical communities ignore the *vita*'s representation of the corruption in and collusion between them.

10. The text of Roscarrock's version of the legend is found in C. Horstmann, ed., *Nova Legenda Anglie*, 2:532–37.

11. Lynn Staley offers Christina of Markyate as a comparandum for Margery Kempe in *Margery Kempe's Dissenting Fictions*, 41–45.

12. Staley demonstrates the *Book*'s debt to hagiography (which, following Thomas Heffernan, she calls sacred biography) in its use of the figure of the holy woman to criticize contemporary social practices and institutions. My argument is indebted to her reading of the *Book of Margery Kempe* as a work of social criticism and to her identification of saints' lives as the narrative structure through which Kempe formulates her critique. I also follow Staley's lead in distinguishing between Margery, the protagonist of the *Book*, and Kempe, its authorial voice.

13. Margery is certainly familiar with this tradition: her priest has read her "many a good boke of hy contemplacyon & other bokys" which include "Seynt Brydys boke, Hyltons boke, Bone-ventur, Stimulus Amoris, Incendium Amoris, & swech other" (143). On devotional literature for women, see Bartlett, *Male Authors, Female Readers*. I am especially indebted to Jennifer Bryan, "Myself in a Mirror: Envisioning Interiority in Late Medieval England" on the inward models of spirituality that this tradition develops.

14. Winstead, *Virgin Martyrs*, 74. Winstead notes that some fifteenth-century hagiographers, such as Lydgate and Bokenham, restored the prayers and meditations from Latin *passiones*, perhaps in order to satisfy the increasingly inward focus of late medieval spirituality (124, 129).

15. Early in her vocation, Margery is depicted in the posture of an ordinary laywoman, praying devoutly during mass with her prayer book in hand, when a beam and stone from the roof fall and strike her. The episode, Margery's first public miracle, is considered in more detail below. Staley discusses the variety of books—the *Lay Folks Mass Book*, missals, and books of hours—that were designed to "provide focus or direction for the experience of private prayer" during mass (181).

16. E.g., Alexandra Barratt, "Margery Kempe and the King's Daughter of Hungary"; Susan Dickman, "Margery Kempe and the Continental Tradition of the Pious Woman"; Sarah Reese Jones, "'A Peler of Holy Cherch': Margery Kempe and the Bishops"; Valerie Lagorio, "*Defensorium Contra Oblectratores*: A 'Discerning' Assessment of Margery Kempe"; David Wallace, "Mystics and Followers in Siena and East Anglia: A Study in Taxonomy, Class and Cultural Mediation." See also Karma Lochrie, *Margery Kempe and Translations of the Flesh*, which argues that the *Book* is properly understood as a mystical, not a hagiographic, text.

17. Gail McMurray Gibson, *Theater of Devotion: East Anglian Drama and Society in the Late Middle Ages*, chap. 3, "St. Margery: The *Book of Margery Kempe*."

18. Gayle Margherita, *Romance of Origins*, 34–35; Winstead, *Virgin Martyrs*, 103.

19. David Aers, *Community, Gender, and Individual Identity: English Writing, 1360–1430*, 93–95.

20. Susan Eberly, "Margery Kempe, St. Mary Magdalene, and Patterns of Contemplation"; Coletti, *Mary Magdalene and the Drama of Saints*, 80–83.

21. Recent work notes the multiple or general affiliation with virgin martyrs: Naoë Kukita Yoshikawa, "Veneration of Virgin Martyrs in Margery Kempe's Meditation: Influence of the Sarum Liturgy and Hagiography"; Salih, 166–69.

22. Horstmann, ed., "Prosalegenden."

23. Horstmann, ed., "Lyf of Saint Katherine of Senis."

24. British Library MS Claudius B. I. Another manuscript of the *Revelations*, British Library MS Julius F. II, includes a brief (less than one folio) mention of Bridget's death, writings, and canonization; it is described by William Patterson Cumming, ed., *The Revelations of St. Birgitta*, xvi–xvii. The Pynson life, discussed above in Chapter 4, is printed by Blunt, xlvii–lix. Margery is well acquainted with the life of St. Bridget, of course; perhaps there was some biographic account in the copy of "Bride's Book" (which may have been in Latin) read to her by her priest. On verbal parallels between the *Book of Margery Kempe* and the Latin text of Bridget's *Liber Celestis*, see David Lawton, "Voice, Authority, and Blasphemy in the *Book of Margery Kempe*."

25. D'Evelyn and Foster, 582.

26. Another exception is Mary of Egypt, who is also mentioned in the *Book* (49); she is, like the legendary Magdalene, a penitent prostitute (in both cases a promiscuous woman, not one paid for sex), and their legends are very similar.

27. On the relationship between Margery and Mary Magdalene, see Eberly and Coletti, *Mary Magdalene and the Drama of Saints*, 80–84.

28. See Kempe, 262 n. 16.34–35.

29. On this association, see Helen Meredith Garth, *Saint Mary Magdalene in Mediaeval Literature*, 32.

30. The Magdalene washes Christ's feet with her tears and is often shown kissing them in the iconography of the Deposition from the Cross, both events understood to represent her devotion to the humanity of Christ.

31. Eberly, 209; Lawton, "Voice, Authority, and Blasphemy in the *Book of Margery Kempe*," 99–100. Lawton notes that Margery's Passion visions, which elsewhere closely follow the *Meditationes Vitae Christi*, depart from it in the attention given to the Deposition, in which Mary Magdalene plays a prominent role.

32. God warns Margery not to travel in the ship that the pilgrim company had purveyed to sail to the Holy Land and assigns her another one (66). A storm comes up during her return voyage, but prayers quell the tempest (102). Returning from Santiago, Margery is threatened with being thrown overboard in the event of a storm, but God sends good weather in response to her prayer (110). Like Mary Magdalene in her rudderless boat, Margery and her company resign their boat to the "gouernawns of owr Lord" on their voyage to Germany (229). Her childbirth miracle, in which she restores to her right mind a woman recently delivered of a child, is discussed by Gibson, *Theater of Devotion*.

33. Margery's intimate identification with Mary Magdalene causes her sharp anxiety about the *Noli me tangere*: it is a "gret merueyl" that causes her "gret swem & heuynes" (197). Carolyn Dinshaw reads this anxiety as marking "the distance between the corporeal refashioning she attempts in her *imitatio* and her

body as it exists in the world" (Dinshaw, *Getting Medieval: Sexualities and Communities, Pre- and Postmodern*, 164).

34. God explains to Margery that tears of compunction, devotion, and compassion are the "heyest & sekerest gyftys" that he gives (31). See also 61. Kempe, 335 n. 194, cites the *Privity of the Passion*: "the fete that scho [Magdalene] weschede be-fore with teres of compuncione, aftyrwardez scho weschede theme wele better with teres of deuocyone & bitter compassione."

35. Lady Bourchier claims a "synguler deuocyoun / To that holy wumman, wych, as I gesse, / Is clepyd of apostyls the apostyllesse" (5066–68).

36. In rewriting Magdalene's public sanctity as private devotion, however, Bokenham's legend comes remarkably close to Lollard representations of the saint, which identified her washing of Christ's feet as authority for private shrift in unmediated communication with God. For the Wycliffite argument, see Staley, 90 n. 18. The figure of Mary Magdalene, like Margery, offers a clear demonstration that the categories of orthodoxy and heterodoxy were sometimes harder to distinguish than some scholarly formulations admit.

37. On intersections between the feminine, the literal, and the heretical in late medieval discourse, see Copeland, "Why Women Can't Read." See also Ralph Hanna, "The Difficulty of Ricardian Prose Translation: The Case of the Lollards."

38. On which, see Margaret Aston, "Lollard Women Priests?," in her *Lollards and Reformers: Images and Literacy in Late Medieval Religion*, 55–56; Blamires, "Women and Preaching," 137; and Staley, 126.

39. The late Middle Ages saw an extension of the idea of conjugal debt as legal theorists argued that physical danger and traditional periods of abstinence did not nullify a spouse's obligation to be sexually available. See Dyan Elliott, *Spiritual Marriage: Sexual Abstinence in Medieval Wedlock*, 148–55.

40. Carolyn Dinshaw, "Margery Kempe," 226.

41. Salih provides an excellent account of virginity as discursive rather than physiological in the Middle Ages, a category whose insistent association with physical integrity obscures the way that it is also defined by agency, intention, and spiritual disposition. On white clothing as a sign of Margery's virginity, see Gunnel Cleve, "Semantic Dimensions in Margery Kempe's 'Whyght Clothys' "; and Mary Erler, "Margery Kempe's White Clothes."

42. By chastity, Margery means complete sexual abstinence. The term could also mean proper observance of marriage vows. See Elliott, 3–4.

43. See the textual notes in Kempe, 21 n. 2, as well as the endnote, 267.

44. In her discussion of Margery's "saintly *imitatio*" (by which she refers to imitation of Christ and contemporary saints as well as traditional ones), Dinshaw reads the "disjunctivness" between Margery's life and the models she seeks to emulate as a kind of queerness (*Getting Medieval*, 158–59). She does not specify Margery's queerness here as a form of historical thinking, but the structure of her argument puts it in important relationship to the politics of historical inquiry.

45. Cf. Salih's reading of this scene, 200.

46. Gibson's *Theater of Devotion* remains the best introduction to East Anglian bourgeois and aristocratic culture and the production of devotional literature, drama,

and art. On the accommodation of secular and spiritual ideologies in these traditions, see especially Theresa Coletti, "*Paupertas est donum Dei*: Hagiography, Lay Religion, and the Economics of Salvation in the Digby *Mary Magdalene*."

47. Kathleen Ashley, "Historicizing Margery: *The Book of Margery Kempe* as Social Text."

48. Important early discussions of the economic language in the *Book of Margery Kempe*, with readings of Margery's marriage negotiations, are found in Sheila Delany, "Sexual Economics, Chaucer's Wife of Bath, and the *Book of Margery Kempe*"; and Aers, *Community, Gender, and Individual Identity*, 73–83. See also Sarah Beckwith, "A Very Material Mysticism: The Medieval Mysticism of Margery Kempe."

49. Ashley, "Historicizing Margery," 374.

50. Delany, "Sexual Economics," 80.

51. Cf. Aers: "Her heresy lies in confounding the categories virgin (white clothes) and wife" (*Community, Gender, and Individual Identity*, 110).

52. Other trials and examinations highlight Margery's sexuality as well: her appearance before an abbot and dean in All Hallows Church in Leicester offers perhaps the most extended treatment of the issue (114–17).

53. At the beginning of her examination before the abbot in Leicester, Margery prays "that sche myth han grace, wytte, & wysdam so to answeryn that day as myth ben most plesawns & worschep to hym, most profyth to hir sowle, & best exampyl to the pepyl" (114–15).

54. Ruth Sklar, "Cobham's Daughter: The *Book of Margery Kempe* and the Power of Heterodox Thinking."

55. Hudson, *Two Wycliffite Texts*, lvi–lvii. All citations to Thorpe's Testimony are to this edition. See also Ritchie Kendall, *The Drama of Dissent: The Radical Poetics of Nonconformity, 1380–1590*, 58–61.

56. As in vernacular legends, this conflict sometimes leads to conversion.

57. On Lancastrian fictions of orthodoxy and community, see Strohm, *England's Empty Throne*.

58. Salih notes that virgin martyrs arouse similarly mixed reactions; she cites Bokenham's legend of St. Agnes: "summe clepyd hyr wycche, & summe innocent" (169).

59. E.g., "Than thys creatur thowt it was ful mery to be reprevyd for Goddys lofe; it was to hir gret solas & cowmfort whan she was chedyn & fletyn for the lofe of Ihesu for repreuyng of synne, for spekyng of vertu, for comownyng in Scriptur whech sche lernyd in sermownys & be comownyng wyth clerkys. Sche ymagyned in hir-self what deth sche myght deyn for Crystys sake. Hyr thowt sche wold a be slayn for Goddys lofe, but dred for the poynt of deth, & therfor sche ymagyned hyr-self the most soft deth, as hir thowt, for dred of inpacyens, that was to be bowndyn hyr hed & hir fet to a stokke & hir hed to be smet of wyth a scharp ex for Goddys lofe" (29–30).

60. These include an English priest (96), Thomas Marschall (108), Patrick (118), and an anonymous man who hears her weeping in church (246).

61. Cf. Timea Szell, "From Woe to Weal and Weal to Woe: Notes on the Structure of the *Book of Margery Kempe*," 81.

Chapter 6

1. *Chronicle of London*, 80.

2. On saints plays, see especially Clifford Davidson, "The Middle English Saint Play and Its Iconography"; and his catalog of saints' plays in "Saint Plays and Pageants of Medieval Britain." Also useful are Davidson, "Saints in Play: English Theater and Saints' Lives"; Glynne Wickham, "The Staging of Saint Plays in England"; and M. D. Anderson's chapter on saints' plays in *Drama and Imagery in English Medieval Churches*, 193–208.

3. Lawrence Clopper has recently argued that few saints' plays were fully scripted dramatic enactments of a hagiographic story, like the Digby plays. He notes that the terms "pley" and "ludus" had a wide range of meaning and that some saints' "plays" may have been games or pageants, perhaps even mechanical devices or banners. See Clopper, "*Communitas*: The Play of Saints in Late Medieval and Tudor England." The issue has been debated further by Davidson, Clopper, and Elizabeth Baldwin in "Issues in Review: Saint Plays," *Early Theatre* 1 (1998): 97–116. In this essay I use the term "play" with the understanding that it may not always refer to a scripted dramatic enactment of hagiographic narrative. There is, as Davidson shows, strong evidence for narrative, and sometimes scripted, performances of saints' legends, including female saints' plays.

4. E.g., Kathleen Ashley, "Image and Ideology: Saint Anne in Late Medieval Drama and Narrative"; Theresa Coletti, "Genealogy, Sexuality, and Sacred Power: The Saint Anne Dedication of the Digby *Candlemas Day and the Killing of the Children of Israel*"; and Ruth Evans, "Body Politics: Engendering Medieval Cycle Drama."

5. I should emphasize that these two examples do not delineate a teleological development in which saints' plays gradually gain historical legibility. The guild play of 1393 and the royal pageant of 1501 represent different kinds of performance with very different relationships to civic institutions, not the evolution of a dramatic form.

6. Two versions of the chronicle contain an account of the pageants: I quote from the text in British Library MS Cotton Vitellius A. xvi, fol. 183b–201b, which also records the 1393 Catherine play. All citations are to Charles Kingsford, ed., *Chronicles of London (Vitellius A XVI)*. The other version is found in Guildhall MS 3313, fols. 275a–292b (A. H. Thomas and I. D. Thornley, eds., *The Great Chronicle of London*). The pageant is described in even more detail in Gordon Kipling, ed., *The Receyt of the Ladie Kateryne*. For a detailed analysis of the pageant, and especially its debt to Burgundian literature and performance, see Kipling's *Triumph of Honor*. Kipling remarks that the pageant was presented by London guilds, 73. See also Sydney Anglo, *Spectacle, Pageantry and Early Tudor Policy*, 56–97.

7. Kipling, *Triumph of Honor*, 77.

8. See his introduction to James Paxson, Lawrence Clopper, and Sylvia Tomasch, eds., *The Performance of Middle English Culture: Essays on Chaucer and the Drama in Honor of Martin Stevens*, 3.

9. E.g., Sarah Beckwith, "Making the World in York and the York Cycle."

10. See Pamela Tudor-Craig, "Richard III's Triumphant Entry into York, August 29th, 1483," 108–16. See also Martin Stevens' extensive analysis of the relation between the city and the play cycle in York in *Four Middle English Mystery Cycles: Textual, Contextual and Critical Interpretations*, 17–87.

11. Anne Higgins, "Streets and Markets," 90. For a careful theorization of the relation of drama to civic space, one that relies on Bourdieu's argument that ritual is concerned with relations rather than objects, see Sarah Beckwith, "Ritual, Theater, and Social Space in the York Corpus Christi Cycle." See also Kathleen Ashley, "Sponsorship, Reflexivity, and Resistance: Cultural Readings of the York Cycle Plays," which argues for attention to the differences in sponsorship—and therefore social meaning—between drama and political events such as royal entries.

12. Kipling, *The Receyt of the Ladie Kateryne*, xix. Kipling suggests that the Latin text inscribed on the pageant tabernacles was for the benefit of Catherine and other Spaniards who could not understand the English speeches (lxv). In this context, it is worth remarking that the Latin distiches are rather different from the English verses, omitting the genealogical and dynastic concerns for more generalized claims: The one associated with the figure of St. Catherine reads: "Ne grave sit patrias, Katharina relinquere sedes / Plus tibi splendoris, Regna aliena dabunt" (Let it not be painful to leave your native dwellings, Katharine; / foreign kingships will give more splendour to you) (13; 120 n.). The lines associated with St. Ursula read: "Sis ffelix Katherina meis, ffaustum que Britannis / Sidus nam tute, hiis Hysperus alter eris" (May you be happy and auspicious for my Britons, Katharine, for you will be another evening star to them) (14; 120). Translations are Kipling's.

13. For the authorship and textual history of the *Chronicles of London*, see Kingsford's introduction. That the *Chronicles* reflect the interest of aldermen and well-placed citizens is suggested by the careful recording of mayors and other city officers for each year, a spare record gradually supplemented with more elaborate entries.

14. Patricia Badir, "Playing Space: History, the Body, and Records of Early English Drama," 278.

15. Although widely acknowledged, the relationship between parish guilds and non-cycle drama has not received the kind of cultural analysis that has illuminated the cycle plays. Exceptions include Coletti, "Genealogy, Sexuality, and Sacred Power"; and Sheila Lindenbaum, "Rituals of Exclusion: Feasts and Plays of the English Religious Fraternities," which concentrates on the morality plays as an extension of the guilds' interest in a "productive ethic." As the title suggests, Lindenbaum's essay draws attention to the way that religious guilds sometimes excluded certain classes of people and often attended to their own social status and spiritual health before—or instead of—those less fortunate. I emphasize the relative inclusiveness of religious guilds and their challenge to some late medieval social categories, but Lindenbaum's article is an important reminder of the limits of this challenge.

16. See *Records of Early English Drama: York*, ed. Alexandra Johnston and Margaret Rogerson, 863.

17. For the Beverly guilds, see the returns edited and translated by Lucy Toulmin Smith, *English Gilds*, 148–50.

18. R. M. Lumiansky and David Mills, *The Chester Mystery Cycle: Essays and Documents*, 171.

19. Sponsler, "Culture of the Spectator."

20. Cf. Ashley on the significance of sponsorship in York plays in "Sponsorship, Reflexivity, and Resistance."

21. One practical reason, suggested above, is the fact that guild activity is rarely recorded in churchwardens' accounts. For a parish, rather than guild, play of Longinus documented in churchwardens' records, see Mary Erler, "Spectacle and Sacrament: A London Parish Play in the 1530's." Erler argues that this play confirms the sacramental role of the Church, as we might expect a play sponsored by the parish church to do.

22. Our understanding of parish guilds has been richly increased by these studies. See Virginia Bainbridge, *Gilds in the Medieval Countryside: Social and Religious Change in Cambridgeshire, c. 1350–1558*; David Crouch, *Piety, Fraternity and Power: Religious Gilds in Late Medieval Yorkshire, 1389–1547*; and Katherine French, *People of the Parish*, which focuses on Bath and Wells.

23. For the text of the mandate and examples of the sheriffs' returns, see Smith, 127–29. See also Barbara Hanawalt, "Keepers of the Lights: Late Medieval English Parish Gilds," 22.

24. The writ specifies that guilds are to identify "all lands, tenements, rents, and processions, whether held in mortmain or not" (Smith, 128). Crouch notes that guild properties were made subject to mortmain legislation in 1391 (14).

25. Caroline Barron, "The Parish Fraternities of Medieval London," 20. See also Hanawalt, 22; and William Jones, "English Religious Brotherhoods and Medieval Lay Piety: The Inquiry of 1388–89." Jones remarks that in France such suspicions were well founded, but he argues that the English inquiry was primarily about lands in mortmain.

26. Crouch, 34.

27. "Et non ad preiudicium domini nostri Regis nec populi sui," cited in William Jones, 650. The translation is mine.

28. Smith, 23. See also the return for the Lancaster guild of the Holy Trinity and St. Leonard, which claims that the guild members always observe the laws and customs of the town (Smith, 163).

29. Michel de Certeau, *The Practice of Everyday Life*.

30. Benjamin McRee, "Unity or Division? The Social Meaning of Guild Ceremony in Urban Communities," 195.

31. Bainbridge remarks that in Cambridgeshire, Trinity guilds often double local civic organizations, acting as "unofficial local councils." She specifically mentions the Trinity guilds in Bassingbourne, Oxford, and Cambridge and notes that the dedication is a favorite of merchant guilds (126–27).

32. George Unwin, *The Gilds and Companies of London*, estimates, for example, that half of the churches in London had affiliated guilds by the end of the fourteenth century (110–11); and Barron has identified references to 176 fraternities in London and its immediate suburbs between 1350 and 1550 (13).

33. Smith, 178. On the artisanal population of parish guilds in London, where there were alternative associations for mercantile classes and where guilds had no structural relationship to local government, see Barron, 30. Sylvia Thrupp, *The Merchant Class of Medieval London, 1300–1500*, remarks the low level of merchant participation in parish guilds: "only 7 of the 218 merchants' wills of the first decade of the fifteenth century contain bequests to a fraternity not connected with a company, whereas the 208 wills of other citizens, of the same date, contain 26 bequests to 19 different parish guilds" (37).

34. French, *People of the Parish*, 86, 168–70. French finds that Bridgewater is representative of the region in the evidence it provides of artisanal, rather than mercantile, activity on the parish level. Churchwardens generally "come from the lower end of the economic spectrum; they were not the largest contributors [to the parish], they did not have servants, and they did not live in the best parts of town" (86).

35. McRee, "Unity or Division?," 198–200.

36. *Statutes of the Realm* (London, 1810–24), 2.298–99, cited by Crouch, 44. Crouch interprets this as beneficial to the guilds as it gave them "formal legal status," and he understands the subsequent increase in the documentary evidence of guilds as a measure of this benefit. It is possible to read such an increase as an inevitable effect of the subordination of guilds to civic authority, however.

37. Typical is the guild return for the St. Katherine fraternity in Norwich, which includes this clause: "Ande also it is ordeynede, by comoun assent, that if eny discorde be bytwen bretheren and sisteren, first that discorde shal be shewede to other bretheren and sisteren of the gilde, and by hem acorde shal be makde, if it may be skilfully." If recourse to the fraternity does not work, members are permitted to turn to common law, but those who circumvent the guild's role are to be fined two pounds of wax. See Smith, 21. See also the return from the Lynn guilds of St. George, Holy Cross, and Purification (Smith, 76, 84, 89).

38. Ben R. McRee, "Religious Guilds and Regulation of Behavior in Late Medieval Towns."

39. Richard Firth Green, *The Crisis of Truth*.

40. Gervase Rosser, "Communities of Parish and Guild in the Late Middle Ages," 36. See also Ben McRee's analysis of the membership of the Norwich St. George guild in "Religious Guilds and Civic Order: The Case of Norwich in the Late Middle Ages," 79.

41. Rosser, "Communities of Parish and Guild," especially 36. Thrupp's catalog of the vocations represented in the Holy Trinity guild lists offers additional evidence of the social diversity of guilds (36–37). But see also Lindenbaum on the exclusivity of some guilds.

42. Crouch's sample covers the period from 1320 to 1548 (87). Literary evidence for this is provided by the guildsmen in the *General Prologue* to the *Canterbury Tales*—a haberdasher, carpenter, webber, dyer, and tapister; the quotation

is given below. Bainbridge argues that membership in rural guilds was limited to the upper financial stratum of the peasantry, though with an increasing accessibility to the "middle ranks" in the fifteenth and sixteenth centuries (45–46).

43. Thrupp, 36. Thrupp finds 530 men and 275 women among the members affiliated with the guild between 1374–1415 and 1443–45. The independent participation of women is also recorded for the Coventry Trinity guild; see *The Register of the Gild of the Holy Trinity*, ed. Mary Dormer Harris. There are, for example, some twenty members named Alicia who participate independently of a spouse; see *Register of the Gild*, 1–6. See also Barron, 30–32, and Hanawalt, 25.

44. Carl Lindahl, *Earnest Games: Folkloric Patterns in the Canterbury Tales*, 25–31.

45. Barron, 32. See also Unwin, Appendix A, 367–70, which lists London parish fraternities. Testamentary evidence, by its very nature, shows only the participation of widows, but as discussed above, single and married women also participated in parish guilds. On St. Katherine guilds, see also Lewis, *Cult of St. Katherine of Alexandria*, 161–74.

46. *Calendar of Wills Proved and Enrolled in the Court of Husting, London, 1258–1688*, ed. Reginald Sharpe, 2.220.

47. Ibid., 2.154.

48. Ibid., 2.563.

49. Ibid., 2.247.

50. Ibid., 2.223.

51. Ibid., 2.152.

52. Ibid., 2.268.

53. For a sustained demonstration of this point, see Coletti, "Genealogy, Sexuality, and Sacred Power," which argues that the Digby Candlemas play may have been associated with the influential Candlemas guild of Bury St. Edmunds and may represent the town's resistance to the authority and control of the Benedictine monastery by celebrating the alternative devotion and social protocols of the urban elite.

54. Barron, 19. This is not to say, however, that they were anticlerical: few guilds specifically excluded clerics, though they were often prevented from becoming guild officers. See Hanawalt, 24.

55. Barron argues that guild members were imitating aristocratic and mercantile forms, and that the rise of the parish fraternities follows the popularity of private chantries among the wealthy.

56. Bainbridge, 71.

57. Unwin, 111; also cited by Lindenbaum, 55.

58. They organized liturgical ritual in the process: French notes how the establishment of a guild altar or chapel could transform the liturgical processions, which would subsequently need to be rerouted in order that the additional chapel be blessed (172–73). While religious guilds allowed greater opportunity for such interventions in liturgical practice and the space of the parish, it is important to remember, as both French and Gervase Rosser argue, that the parish system as a

whole was responsive to the parishioners. See Gervase Rosser, "Parochial Conformity and Voluntary Religion in Late Medieval England."

59. Gervase Rosser, "Going to the Fraternity Feast: Commensality and Social Relations in Late Medieval England," 437.

60. Hanawalt, 21.

61. Smith, 50, noted by William Jones, 650.

62. The List of Mayors and Sheriffs records performances in 1487–88 and 1498–99; the guild is listed in the Harley list of guilds, where its association with the Assumption play is noted. See Lumiansky and Mills, 171. The Chester Assumption, according to the early banns, was presented by townswomen:

> The wurshipffull wyffys of this towne
> ffynd of our lady thassumcion
> It to bryng forth they be bowne
> And meytene with all theyre might.

See the text in *Records of Early English Drama: Chester* (hereafter *REED: Chester*), ed. Lawrence Clopper, 37–38.

63. Katherine French, "Maidens' Lights and Wives' Stores: Women's Parish Guilds in Late Medieval England." French's evidence points to the influence of women's guilds on the increasingly dramatic nature of parish processions: the new prominence of a maidens' guild at St. Margaret's, Westminster—as they adopt a livery and are accompanied by professional "syngyngmen" as they process—coincides with the inclusion of a dragon in the pageant, representing the saint's triumph over the devilish beast.

64. Recorded in the City Annals. See *Records of Early English Drama: Coventry* (hereafter *REED: Coventry*), 74. Ingram links the play to the existence of a Katherine guild (xx).

65. There are records for seven performances between 1539 and 1546; the number of anonymous virgins varies from eight to four. See *REED: Coventry*, 152, 155, 157, 162, 170, 173, 174.

66. For the record of the St. Katherine pageant, see *Records of Early English Drama: Herefordshire, Worcestershire*, ed. David Klausner, 116.

67. Beckwith, "Making the World in York and the York Cycle."

68. Davidson, "Saint Plays and Pageants." The text of the poem, found in British Library MS Cotton Cleopatra B.ii, fol. 65v, is edited by Rossell Hope Robbins as "On the Minorites" in *Historical Poems of the XIVth and XVth Centuries*, 163–64. The poem is especially critical of the play's subordination of papal authority to the figure of St. Francis.

69. As noted above (note 3), the nature of these plays has recently been the subject of debate.

70. Most of these references, many of which were identified by Chambers in 1903, are familiar to scholars of drama. See now Davidson, "Saint Plays and Pageants," for a recent list. There were plays of St. Katherine in Coventry in 1490, in addition to the 1393 London play. London also saw plays of St. Lucy and St.

Margaret in the fifteenth century. A play of St. Christina was performed in the early sixteenth century in Bethersden, Kent. The play of St. Agnes is mentioned in the records of Wincester, Hamshire, for 1409. St. Feliciana and St. Sabina were presented in Shrewsbury, Shropshire, in 1516 and St. Katherine in 1526. The plays of St. Clare and St. Susana took place in Lincoln in the mid-fifteenth century. Candlemas pageants in mid-fifteenth-century Aberdeen included St. Bride and St. Helen. The Digby Magdalene, too elaborate to have been sponsored by a parish guild, represents a female saint who assists political authorities, the king and queen of France, demonstrating a far more comfortable relationship between feminine sanctity and social hierarchies than virgin martyr plays can have presented. The same may have been true of the Mary Magdalene play in Taunton, Somerset, for which Agnes Burton bequeathed her silk mantle in 1504; see *Records of Early English Drama: Somerset*, ed. James Stokes, 495. Stokes identifies "ladie ussile" in the Wells Cordwainer's play of Crispin and Crispianus as St. Ursula, but this seems unlikely to me as the lady is accompanied by a nurse for her child (377).

71. Lawrence Clopper addresses the relationship between ethical and dramatic imitation of saints' legends, with very different assumptions and conclusions about how they might inform one another; see Clopper, "Why Are There So Few English Saint Plays?" 109–10. Indeed, the relationship is the answer offered to the question posed by his title: "there is little pressure to enact the story of the saint," Clopper argues, since she is not to be imitated.

72. On devotional literature for women, see, e.g., Bartlett; Bryan; and Sponsler, *Drama and Resistance*, chap. 5.

73. The rhetoric of private devotion that pervades fifteenth-century religious texts is often implicitly, and sometimes explicitly, offered as an alternative to Lollard practice. See text below.

74. The tradition of theatrical cross-dressing in medieval theater has been well established, especially in the work of Meg Twycross, "'Transvestism' in the Mystery Plays." Twycross discusses the St. Helen procession on p. 129. See also Twycross, "'Apparell Comlye.'" Attention to the cultural work of theatrical cross-dressing has recently been opened up by Robert L. A. Clark and Claire Sponsler's important essay "Queer Play: The Cultural Work of Crossdressing in Medieval Drama."

75. Badir's larger point, however, is that the body onstage is never fully integrated into the ideological system it represents (260).

76. Cf. Judith Butler, *Bodies That Matter*, on how cross-dressing (specifically modern drag) can reinforce as well as unsettle gender norms (231).

77. H. F. Westlake, *The Parish Guilds of Mediaeval England*, 34. My account of the guild relies on this source.

78. "Her virgynes, as many as a man wylle, shalle holde tapers in ther handes." I quote from John Coldeway's edition in *Early English Drama*, line 54. See also the note preceding line 465. On the gender politics and cultural contexts of the play, see Ashley, "Image and Ideology"; and Coletti, "Genealogy, Sexuality, and Sacred Power."

79. On the relationship between the ritual of churching and dramatic presentation of Mary's purification, see Gail McMurray Gibson, "Blessing from Sun and Moon: Churching as Women's Theater."

80. Cf. Clark and Sponsler, who note more generally that it was women's performances that required comment in medieval drama (324).

81. Marjorie Garber, *Vested Interests*.

82. Badir, 262, citing Stanton Garner, *Bodied Spaces: Phenomenology and Performance in Contemporary Drama* (Ithaca: Cornell University Press, 1994), 42. See also Beckwith's discussion of the "tension between fictive locality and public space" in "Ritual, Theater, and Social Space," 70, citing Robert Weiman, *Shakespeare and the Popular Tradition in the Theater* (Baltimore: Johns Hopkins University Press, 1978), 80.

83. Kipling, ed., *The Receyt of the Ladie Kateryne*, book 2, chap. 2. The pageant presents "a faire yonge lady with a wheel in hir hand in liknes of Seint Kateryne, with right many virgyns in every side of her" and "another lady in liknes of Seint Ursula with her great multitude of virgyns right goodly dressid and arayed" (13).

84. Aage Brusendorf, *The Chaucer Tradition*, 131. As the tale's attribution to the Second Nun (or a Nun) is only in the rubrics, however, the authorial status of the teller is not clear, and some have argued that the attribution may be only scribal. See F. N. Blake, *The Textual Tradition of the* Canterbury Tales, 33, 97. If so, the assignment of the tale to a woman, which must have happened early in the textual tradition, is all the more revealing given the internal evidence that it is in a man's voice, as I discuss in the text below.

85. Early evidence for London saints' plays is found in Fitz Stephens's *Life of St. Thomas Becket*: "Londonia pro spectaculis theatralibus, pro ludi scenicis, ludos habet sanctiores, representationes miracularum quae sancti confessores operati sunt, seu repraesentationes passionum quibus claruit constantia martyrum" (cited in Clopper, "*Communitas*," 92). St. Margaret's Southwark, just outside the city, held plays on the feasts of St. Lucy and St. Margaret frequently from 1444 until 1459; see E. K. Chambers, *The Medieval Stage*, 2:381.

86. This is suggested by Peter Beidler, "Teaching Chaucer as Drama: The Garden Scene in the Shipman's Tale," 492–93, and is developed more fully in the paper that Beidler presented on the *Shipman's Tale* in the session on "Chaucerian Performance," at the New Chaucer Society, London, 2000.

87. See, e.g., Laura Kendrick, *Chaucerian Play*, and Lindahl.

88. E.g., John Ganim, *Chaucerian Theatricality*, and Seth Lerer, "The Chaucerian Critique of Medieval Theatricality."

89. The reference to his 'lyf . . . of Seynt Cecile" in the prologue to the *Legend of Good Women* (F 426/G 416) puts the terminus ad quem around 1386/7.

90. David Wallace, like Carl Lindahl, has argued that the company of Canterbury pilgrims recalls (though does not fully reproduce) the "associational form" of English guilds. Wallace notes the close similarity between the *Second Nun's Tale* and "guild-generated narratives" (Wallace, *Chaucerian Polity*, 97).

91. Lerer, "Chaucerian Critique of Medieval Theatricality," 59–60.

92. *Middle English Dictionary* (on-line), definition 10.

93. Reames, "Recent Discovery Concerning the Sources of Chaucer's *Second Nun's Tale*."

94. V. A. Kolve, "Chaucer's *Second Nun's Tale* and the Iconography of Saint Cecilia," 151–54. The representation of Cecilia's spiritual procreativity recalls the Second Nun's equation of dedicated virginity and sacred fecundity in the metaphor of the "cloister" of the Virgin's womb, discussed above.

95. The place of the Second Nun's performance resonates with John Scattergood's argument that the tale represents activity in the space outside the city as a challenge to "stable urban organizations and their representatives" (Scattergood, "Chaucer in the Suburbs," 159).

96. Lynn Staley Johnson, "Chaucer's Tale of the Second Nun and the Strategies of Dissent," 315. See also Staley's chapter, "Chaucer and the Postures of Sanctity," in Aers and Staley, 179–259.

97. Jennifer Summit, "Topography as Historiography: Petrarch, Chaucer, and the Making of Medieval Rome."

98. Ibid., 239. The tale's interest in history and time is also, though very differently, suggested by Eileen Jankowski's reading of it as "apocalyptic"; see Jankowski, "Chaucer's *Second Nun's Tale* and the Apocalyptic Imagination."

99. For the London pageant, see Carleton Brown; and Kipling, "London Pageants for Margaret of Anjou." The text of the Coventry pageant is found in *REED: Coventry*, 34.

100. Alan Nelson, *The Medieval English Stage*, 123.

101. *REED: Somerset*, 495.

Afterword

1. The Early English Books On-line database includes editions of the *Festial* from 1502, 1508, 1519, 1528, and 1532, along with five late fifteenth-century editions: 1486, 1491, 1495, 1496, and 1499. Caxton's translation of the *Legenda Aurea*, which had been printed three times in the fifteenth century, was printed again in 1527.

2. Julia Reinhard Lupton, *Afterlives of the Saints: Hagiography, Typology, and Renaissance Literature*. Lupton's book provides an original and compelling contribution to this story with her account of how the narrative form of saints' lives informs some early modern narrative structures.

3. Recent work on the Reformation has significantly enriched our understanding of this history. See Eamon Duffy, *Stripping of the Altars: Traditional Religion in England, 1400–1580*; and Duffy, *Voices of Morebath: Reformation and Rebellion in an English Village*; Christopher Haigh, *English Reformations: Religion, Politics, and Society under the Tudors*, Peter Marshall, *Reformation England, 1480–1642*; and Richard Rex, *Henry VIII and the English Reformation*.

4. See Lee Patterson, "On the Margin: Postmodernism, Ironic History, and Medieval Studies," which provides a more comprehensive list: "humanism, na-

tionalism, the proliferation of competing value systems, the secure grasp of a historical consciousness, aesthetic production as an end in itself, the conception of the natural world as a site of scientific investigation and colonial exploitation, the secularization of politics, the idea of the state, and perhaps above all, the emergence of the idea of the individual" (92).

5. David Aers, "Whisper in the Ear of Early Modernists, or, Reflections on Literary Critics Writing the 'History of the Subject'"; Patterson *Chaucer and the Subject of History*; Patterson, *Negotiating the Past*; Patterson, "On the Margin," Summit, "Topography as Historiography"; and David, *Chaucerian Polity*. Patterson shows how this myth, given especially influential articulation by Burckhardt, received renewed vigor with New Historicist approaches that privilege a synchronic approach that assumes, but cannot investigate, the radical difference of the preceding era (Patterson, "On the Margin," 99–100).

6. This is a widespread claim. Some contexts in which it appears, which are relevant to the subjects addressed in this book, include Benedict Anderson, discussed in Chapter 4, and Hampton, discussed in chapter 1 and in the text below. A recent example can be found in Andrew Escobedo, *Nationalism and Historical Loss in Renaissance England*, 5, 24.

7. See Chapter 1, note 51.

8. For an extended meditation on different "regimes of historicity," see François Hartog, *Régimes d'Historicité: Présentisme et Expériences du Temps*.

9. This is not a comprehensive list: it leaves out, for example, genealogy and other discursive frameworks for thinking of identity in historical terms that changed little in the period under discussion.

10. So Greene distinguishes between medieval and early modern representations of the past as metonymic—marked by an imagined contiguity with the past—and metaphoric—marked by an awareness of the gap that separates them (Greene, *The Light in Troy: Imitation and Discovery in Renaissance Poetry*, 86).

11. Of course, it is also the case that the classical past had long served as an impetus to historical thinking before the Renaissance: see Baswell, Patterson, *Negotiating the Past*; Patterson, *Chaucer and the Subject of History*; and Sanok, "Criseyde, Cassandre, and the *Thebaid*."

12. Cited by Christine Peters, *Patterns of Piety: Women, Gender and Religion in Late Medieval and Reformation England*, 207. Peters also discusses the continuing invocation of saints as models.

13. See Bale's preface, especially fols. 2r–5r, where Bale criticizes those who commend saints for chastity rather than for preaching. The first part of this work was originally published in Antwerp in 1546; the second was printed in London in 1551.

14. All citations are to the 1563 edition of John Foxe, *Actes and Monuments*. In this passage Foxe contrasts martyrology to secular history and the "rough warriours" it celebrates, a contrast also inherited from medieval hagiography: viz. the prologue to the *South English Legendary*.

15. The debate has been engaged most vigorously around the relationship of historicist and psychoanalytical approaches. See Louise Fradenburg, "We are Not

Alone: Psychoanalytic Medievalism"; and Lee Patterson, "Chaucer's Pardoner on the Couch: Psyche and Clio in Medieval Literary Studies." A different perspective on the question is provided by Gabrielle Spiegel, "In the Mirror's Eye: The Writing of Medieval History in North America," in her *Past as Text*, 57–80. Influential early discussions include Hans Robert Jauss, "The Alterity and Modernity of Medieval Literature"; and Paul Zumthor, *Essai de Poétique Médiévale*.

Works Cited

MANUSCRIPTS

British Library MS Additional 35298.
British Library MS Arundel 327.
British Library MS Harley 4011.
British Library MS Harley 4012.
Cambridge University Library Add MS 3041.
Copenhagen, Royal Library MS Thott 517, www.kb.dk/elib/mss/mdr/th517/index-en.htm.
Huntington Library MS 140.

PRIMARY TEXTS

Bale, John. *The First Two Partes of the Actes, or Vnchast Examples of the Englysh Votaryes.* London, 1560 [Early English Books Online database].
Bede. *History of the English Church and People.* Trans. Leo Sherley-Price. Baltimore: Penguin, 1962.
Blamires, Alcuin, K. Pratt, and C. W. Marx, eds. *Woman Defamed and Woman Defended.* New York: Oxford University Press, 1992.
Blunt, John Henry, ed. *The Myroure of Oure Ladye.* EETS e.s. 19. London: Oxford University Press, 1873.
Bokenham, Osbern. *Legendys of Hooly Wummen.* Ed. Mary Serjeantson. EETS 206. London: Oxford University Press, 1938.
———. *The Lyvys of Seyntys.* London: Roxburghe Club, 1835.
———. "Mappula Angliae." Ed. Carl Horstmann. *Englische Studien* 10 (1887): 1–34.
———. *Osbern Bokenam's Legenden.* Ed. Carl Horstmann. Heilbronn: Gebr. Henninger, 1883.
Bradshaw, Henry. *The Holy Lyfe and History of Saynt Werburge.* Ed. Edward Hawkins. London: Chetham Society, 1848.
———. *The Life of St. Werburge of Chester.* Ed. Carl Horstmann. EETS o.s. 88. London: Oxford University Press, 1887.
Breviarium ad usum insignis ecclesiae Sarum. Ed. Francis Procter and Christopher Wordsworth. Cambridge: Cambridge University Press, 1882.

Brittain, F., ed. *The Lyfe of Saynt Radegunde.* Cambridge: Cambridge University Press, 1926.
Calendar of Wills Proved and Enrolled in the Court of Husting, London, 1258–1688. 2 vols. Ed. Reginald Sharpe. London: Corporation of the City of London, 1889.
Capgrave, John. *Life of Saint Katherine.* Ed. Karen Winstead. Kalamazoo, Mich.: Medieval Institute Publications, 1999.
———. *The Life of St. Norbert by John Capgrave,* O.E.S.A. Ed. Cyril Lawrence Smetana. Toronto: Pontifical Institute, 1977.
———. *John Capgrave's Lives of St. Augustine and St. Gilbert of Sempringham.* Ed. J. J. Munro. EETS o.s. 140. London: Oxford University Press, 1910.
Chaucer, Geoffrey. *Riverside Chaucer.* Ed. Larry Benson. 3d ed. Boston: Houghton Mifflin, 1987.
Christine de Pizan. *The Treasure of the City of Ladies.* Trans. Sarah Lawson. New York: Penguin, 1985.
A Chronicle of London from 1089 to 1483. Ed. Nicholas Nicolas and E. Tyrrell. London, 1827. Reprint, Felinfach: Llanerch, 1995.
Clemence of Barking. *The Life of St. Catherine.* Ed. William MacBain. Oxford: Anglo-Norman Text Society, 1964.
Coldeway, John, ed. *Early English Drama.* New York: Garland, 1993.
Cumming, William Patterson, ed. *The Revelations of St. Birgitta.* EETS o.s. 178. London: Oxford University Press, 1929.
D'Ardenne, S. R. T. O., ed. *The Liflade ant te Passiun of Seinte Iuliene.* EETS 248. London: Oxford University Press, 1961.
D'Evelyn, Charlotte, and A. J. Mill, eds. *South English Legendary.* EETS o.s. 235, 236, and 244. London: Oxford University Press, 1956.
Einenkel, Eugen, ed. *The Life of Saint Katherine.* EETS 80. London: Trübner, 1884.
An English Chronicle of the Reigns of Richard II, Henry IV, Henry V, and Henry VI. Ed. John Silvester Davies. London: Camden Society, 1856. Reprint, New York: AMS Press, 1968.
Foxe, John. *Actes and Monuments.* London: John Day, 1563 [Early English Books Online database].
Garmonsway, G. N., and R. R. Raymo, eds. "A Middle English Prose Life of St. Ursula." *Review of English Studies,* new series 9 (1958): 355–61.
Gibbs, Henry Hucks, ed. *The Life and Martyrdom of Saint Katherine of Alexandria, Virgin and Martyr.* London: Nichols and Sons, 1884.
Görlach, Manfred, ed. *The Kalendre of the Newe Legende of Englande.* Heidelberg: Universitätsverlag C. Winter, 1994.
Hamer, Richard, and Vida Russell. *Supplementary Lives in Some Manuscripts of the Gilte Legende.* EETS 315. Oxford: Oxford University Press, 2000.
Horstmann, Carl, ed. *Altenglische Legenden.* Paderborn: Ferdinand Schöningh, 1875.
———, ed. *Altenglische Legenden, Neue Folge.* Heilbronn: Gebr. Henninger, 1881.
———, ed. "The Lyf of Saint Katherine of Senis." *Archiv für neue Sprachen* 76 (1886): 33–112, 265–314, 353–91.

———, ed. *Nova Legenda Anglie*. 2 vols. Oxford: Clarendon, 1901.
———, ed. "Prosalegenden: Die legenden des ms. Douce 114." *Anglia* 8 (1995): 102–96.
———, ed. *Sammlung Altenglischer Legenden*. Heilbronn: Gebr. Henninger, 1878.
———, ed. *S. Editha sive Chronicon Vilodunense*. Heilbronn: Gebr. Henninger, 1883.
Hudson, Anne, ed. *Two Wycliffite Texts: The Sermon of William Taylor 1406, the Testimony of William Thorpe 1407*. EETS o.s. 301. Oxford: Oxford University Press, 1993.
Jacopus de Voragine. *The Golden Legend*. Trans. William Granger Ryan. 2 vols. Princeton, N.J.: Princeton University Press, 1993.
———. *Legenda Aurea*. Ed. Th. Graesse. 3d ed. Dresden, 1846. Reprint, Vratislavia: G. Koebner, 1890.
Jean de Meun and Guillaume de Lorris. *The Romance of the Rose*. Trans. Charles Dahlberg. Hanover and London: University Press of New England, 1983.
Julian of Norwich. *A Book of Showings to the Anchoress Julian of Norwich*. Ed. Edmund Colledge and James Walsh. 2 vols. Toronto: Pontifical Institute, 1978.
Kempe, Margery. *The Book of Margery Kempe*. Ed. Sanford Brown Meech. EETS 212. London: Oxford University Press, 1940.
Kingsford, Charles, ed. *Chronicles of London (Vitellius A XVI)*. Oxford: Clarendon, 1905.
Kipling, Gordon, ed. *The Receyt of the Ladie Kateryne*. EETS 296. Oxford: Oxford University Press, 1990.
Knighton, Henry. *Knighton's Chronicle, 1337–1396*. Ed. and trans. G. H. Martin. New York: Oxford University Press, 1995.
The Life of Christina of Markyate. Ed. and trans. C. H. Talbot. Oxford: Clarendon, 1959.
Love, Nicholas. *The Mirror of the Blessed Life of Jesus Christ*. Ed. Michael Sargent. Exeter: University of Exeter Press, 2004.
Lydgate, John. *The Minor Poems of John Lydgate*. Ed. Henry MacCracken. EETS e.s. 107. London: Paul, Trench, Trübner, 1911.
Mack, Frances, ed. *Seinte Marherete the Meiden ant Martyr*. EETS 193. London: Oxford University Press, 1934.
Missale ad usum insignis et praeclarae ecclesiae Sarum. Ed. Francis Dickinson. Burntisland: E. Prelo de Pitsligo, 1861.
Mustanoja, Tauno, ed. *The Good Wife Taught Her Daughter, The Good Wyfe Wold a Pylgremage, The Thewis of Gud Women*. Helsinki: Suomalaisen Kirjallisuuden Scuran, 1948.
Nevanlinna, Saara, and Irma Taavitsainen, eds. *St. Katherine of Alexandria: The Late Middle English Prose Legend in Southwell Minster MS 7*. Cambridge: Brewer, 1993.
Offord, M. Y., ed. *The Book of the Knight of the Tower, Translated by William Caxton*. EETS supplementary series 2. London: Oxford University Press, 1971.
Pahta, Päivi, "The Middle English Prose Legend of St. Faith in MS Southwell Minster 7." *Neuphilologische Mitteilungen* 94 (1993): 149–65.

Parker, Roscoe, ed. *Middle English Stanzaic Versions of the Life of St. Anne*. EETS 174. London: Oxford University Press, 1928.
Peter the Venerable. *Liber contra sectam sive haeresim Saracenorum*. In *Patrologia Cursus Completus: Series Latina*. Ed. J. P. Migne. Vol. 189. Columns 673b–720b.
Ragusa, Isa, and Rosalie Green, trans. *Meditations on the Life of Christ: An Illustrated Manuscript of the Fourteenth Century*. Princeton, N.J.: Princeton University Press, 1961.
Records of Early English Drama: Chester. Ed. Lawrence Clopper. Toronto: University of Toronto Press, 1979.
Records of Early English Drama: Coventry. Ed. R. W. Ingram. Toronto: University of Toronto Press, 1981.
Records of Early English Drama: Herefordshire, Worcestershire. Ed. David Klausner. Toronto: University of Toronto Press, 1990.
Records of Early English Drama: Somerset. Ed. James Stokes. Toronto: University of Toronto, 1996.
Records of Early English Drama: York. Ed. Alexandra Johnston and Margaret Rogerson. 2 vols. Toronto: University of Toronto Press, 1979.
The Register of the Gild of the Holy Trinity. Ed. Mary Dormer Harris. London: Oxford University Press, 1935.
Robbins, Rossell Hope, ed. *Historical Poems of the XIVth and XVth Centuries*. New York: Columbia University Press, 1959.
———, ed. *Secular Lyrics of the XIVth and XVth Centuries*. Oxford: Clarendon, 1952.
Savage, Anne, and Nicholas Watson. *Anchoritic Spirituality: Ancrene Wisse and Associated Works*. New York: Paulist Press, 1991.
Smith, Lucy Toulmin, ed. and trans. *English Gilds*. EETS o.s. 40. London: Oxford University Press, 1870.
Södergard, Osten, ed. *La Vie d'Edouard le Confesseur*. Uppsala: Almqvist & Wiksell, 1948.
Tanner, Norman, ed. *Heresy Trials in the Diocese of Norwich, 1428–1431*. Camden 4th series, 20. London: Royal Historical Society, 1977.
Thomas, A. H. and I. D. Thornley, eds. *The Great Chronicle of London*. London: G. W. Jones, 1938.
Tolkien, J. R. R., ed. *The English Text of the Ancrene Riwle: The Ancrene Wisse*. EETS o.s. 249. London: Oxford University Press, 1962.
Wallace, Kathryn Young, ed. *La Estoire de seint Aedward le Rei*. London: Anglo-Norman Text Society, 1983.
Wright, Thomas, ed. *The Book of the Knight of La Tour-Landry*. EETS 33. London: Paul, Trench, Trübner, 1868.

Secondary Texts

Aers, David. *Community, Gender, and Individual Identity: English Writing, 1360–1430*. London: Routledge, 1988.

---. "Whisper in the Ear of Early Modernists; or, Reflections on Literary Critics Writing the 'History of the Subject.'" In *Culture and History, 1350–1600.* Ed. Aers. Detroit: Wayne State University Press, 1992. 177–202.

Aers, David, and Lynn Staley. *The Powers of the Holy: Religion, Politics, and Gender in Late Medieval English Culture.* University Park: Pennsylvania State University Press, 1996.

Allen, Elizabeth. *False Fables and Exemplary Truth in Later Middle English Literature.* New York: Palgrave Macmillan, 2005.

Ames, Ruth. "The Feminist Connections of Chaucer's *Legend of Good Women.*" In *Chaucer in the Eighties.* Ed. Julian Wasserman and Robert Blanch. Syracuse: Syracuse University Press, 1986. 57–74.

Anderson, Benedict. *Imagined Communities: Reflections on the Origin and Spread of Nationalism.* London and New York: Verso, 1991.

Anderson, M. D. *Drama and Imagery in English Medieval Churches.* Cambridge: Cambridge University Press, 1963.

Anglo, Sydney. *Spectacle, Pageantry and Early Tudor Policy.* Oxford: Clarendon, 1969.

Armstrong, C. A. J. "The Piety of Cecily, Duchess of York." In *For Hilaire Belloc: Essays in Honour of His Seventy-Second Birthday.* Ed. Douglas Woodruff. New York: Greenwood Press, 1942. 68–91.

Ashley, Kathleen. "Historicizing Margery: The *Book of Margery Kempe* as Social Text." *Journal of Medieval and Early Modern Studies* 28 (1998): 371–88.

---. "Image and Ideology: Saint Anne in Late Medieval Drama and Narrative." In Ashley and Sheingorn. 111–30.

---. "The *Miroir des bonnes femmes*: Not for Women Only?" In Ashley and Clark. 86–105.

---. "Sponsorship, Reflexivity, and Resistance: Cultural Readings of the York Cycle Plays." In Paxson, Clopper, and Tomasch. 9–24.

Ashley, Kathleen, and Robert Clark, eds. *Medieval Conduct.* Minneapolis: University of Minnesota Press, 2001.

Ashley, Kathleen, and Pamela Sheingorn. *Interpreting Cultural Symbols: Saint Anne in Late Medieval Society.* Athens: University of Georgia Press, 1990.

Aston, Margaret. *Lollards and Reformers: Images and Literacy in Late Medieval Religion.* London: Hambledon Press, 1984.

Badir, Patricia. "Playing Space: History, the Body, and Records of Early English Drama." *Exemplaria* 9 (1997): 255–79.

Bainbridge, Virginia. *Gilds in the Medieval Countryside: Social and Religious Change in Cambridgeshire, c. 1350–1558.* Woodbridge, Suffolk: Brewer, 1996.

Baldwin, Elizabeth. "Review of 'The Theatre of Saints,' Sessions 1209 and 1309, International Medieval Congress, University of Leeds, 12–15 July 1999." *Early Theatre* 1 (1998): 114–16.

Baldwin, Frances. *Sumptuary Legislation and Personal Regulation in England.* Baltimore: Johns Hopkins University Press, 1926.

Balibar, Etienne. "The Nation Form." In Balibar and Immanuel Wallerstein, *Race, Nation, Class: Ambiguous Identities.* Trans. Chris Turner. London: Verson, 1991.

Barratt, Alexandra, "Margery Kempe and the King's Daughter of Hungary." In McEntire. 189–201.
Barron, Caroline. "The Parish Fraternities of Medieval London." In *The Church in Pre-Reformation Society*. Ed. Barron and Christopher Harper-Bill. Woodbridge, Suffolk: Boydell, 1985. 13–37.
Bartlett, Anne Clark. *Male Authors, Female Readers: Representation and Subjectivity in Middle English Devotional Literature*. Ithaca, N.Y.: Cornell University Press, 1995.
Baswell, Christopher. *Virgil in Medieval England: Figuring the Aeneid from the Twelfth Century to Chaucer*. Cambridge: Cambridge University Press, 1995.
Baum, Paull. "Chaucer's 'Glorious Legende.'" *Modern Language Notes* 60 (1945): 377–81.
Bayless, Martha. *Parody in the Middle Ages: The Latin Tradition*. Ann Arbor: University of Michigan Press, 1996.
Beckwith, Sarah. "Making the World in York and the York Cycle." In *Framing Medieval Bodies*. Ed. Sarah Kay and Miri Rubin. Manchester: Manchester University Press, 1994. 254–76.
———. "Ritual, Theater, and Social Space in the York Corpus Christi Cycle." In Hanawalt and Wallace. 63–86.
———. "A Very Material Mysticism: The Medieval Mysticism of Margery Kempe." In *Medieval Literature: Criticism, History, Ideology*. Ed. David Aers. Brighton: Harvester, 1986. 34–57.
Beidler, Peter. "Teaching Chaucer as Drama: The Garden Scene in the Shipman's Tale." *Exemplaria* 8 (1996): 492–93.
Bell, David. *What Nuns Read: Books and Libraries in Medieval English Nunneries*. Kalamazoo, Mich.: Medieval Institute Publications, 1995.
Bell, Susan Groag. "Medieval Women Book Owners: Arbiters of Lay Piety and Ambassadors of Culture." In *Women and Power in the Middle Ages*. Ed. Mary Erler and Maryanne Kowalski. Athens: University of Georgia Press, 1988. 149–87.
Bennett, H. S. *English Books and Readers, 1475–1557*. Cambridge: Cambridge University Press, 1952.
Bhabha, Homi. *The Location of Culture*. London and New York: Routledge, 1994.
Blake, F. N. *The Textual Tradition of the* Canterbury Tales. London: Arnold, 1985.
Blamires, Alcuin. *The Case for Women in Medieval Culture*. New York: Oxford University Press, 1997.
———. "Women and Preaching in Medieval Orthodoxy, Heresy, and Saints' Lives." *Viator* 26 (1995): 135–52.
Boffey, Julia. "Middle English Lives." In *The Cambridge History of Medieval English Literature*. Ed. David Wallace. Cambridge: Cambridge University Press, 1999. 610–34.
Bourdieu, Pierre. *Distinction*. Trans. R. Nice. Cambridge: Harvard University Press, 1984.
———. *The Field of Cultural Production*. New York: Columbia University Press, 1993.

———. *Outline of a Theory of Practice.* Trans. Richard Nice. Cambridge: Cambridge University Press, 1977.

Boureau, Alain. *La Légende dorée: le système narratif de Jacques de Voragine.* Paris: Les Editions du Cerf, 1984.

Breck, Allen. "John Wyclyf on Time." In *Cosmology, History, and Theology.* Ed. Wolfgang Yourgrau and Allen Breck. New York: Plenum Press, 1977. 211–18.

Brown, Carleton. "Lydgate's Verses on Queen Margaret's Entry into London." *Modern Language Review* 7 (1912): 225–34.

Brown, Peter. *The Cult of Saints.* Chicago: University of Chicago Press, 1981.

Brusendorf, Aage. *The Chaucer Tradition.* London: Oxford University Press, 1925.

Bryan, Jennifer. "Myself in a Mirror: Envisioning Interiority in Late Medieval England." Book in progress.

Burne, R.V. H. *The Monks of Chester: The History of St. Werburgh's Abbey.* London: S.P.C.K., 1962.

Butler, Judith. *Bodies That Matter: On the Discursive Limits of "Sex."* New York: Routledge, 1993.

———. *Gender Trouble: Feminism and the Subversion of Identity.* New York: Routledge, 1990.

Bynum, Carolyn Walker. *Holy Feast, Holy Fast.* Berkeley: University of California Press, 1987.

Cameron, Kenneth. *The Place-Names of Lincolnshire.* 6 vols. Nottingham: English Place-Name Society, 1985–97.

Cannon, Christopher. "Monastic Productions." In *Cambridge History of Medieval English Literature.* Ed. David Wallace. Cambridge: Cambridge University Press, 1999. 316–48.

Cavanaugh, Susan. "A Study of Books Privately Owned in England: 1300–1450." Ph.D. thesis, University of Pennsylvania, 1980.

Certeau, Michel de. *The Practice of Everyday Life.* Trans. Steven Rendall. Berkeley: University of California Press, 1984.

Chambers, E. K. *The Medieval Stage.* 2 vols. Oxford: Clarendon, 1903.

Clark, Robert L. A., and Claire Sponsler. "Queer Play: The Cultural Work of Crossdressing in Medieval Drama." *New Literary History* 28 (1997): 319–44.

Cleve, Gunnel. "Semantic Dimensions in Margery Kempe's 'Whyght Clothys.'" *Mystics Quarterly* 12 (1986): 162–70.

Clopper, Lawrence. "*Communitas*: The Play of Saints in Late Medieval and Tudor England." *Mediaevalia* 18 (1995): 81–109.

———. "Why Are There So Few English Saint Plays?" *Early Theatre* 1 (1998): 107–12.

Coletti, Theresa. "Genealogy, Sexuality, and Sacred Power: The Saint Anne Dedication of the Digby *Candlemas Day and the Killing of the Children of Israel.*" *Journal of Medieval and Early Modern Studies* 29 (1999): 25–59.

———. *Mary Magdalene and the Drama of Saints: Theater, Gender, and Religion in Late Medieval England.* Philadelphia: University of Pennsylvania Press, 2004.

———. "*Paupertas est donum Dei*: Hagiography, Lay Religion, and the Economics of Salvation in the Digby *Mary Magdalene.*" *Speculum* 76 (2001): 337–78.

Collette, Carolyn, and Vincent DiMarco. "The Matter of Armenia in the Age of Chaucer." *Studies in the Age of Chaucer* 23 (2001): 317–58.
Complete Peerage of England, Scotland, Ireland, Great Britain, and the United Kingdom. New ed. Ed. Vicary Gibbs. London: St. Catherine Press, 1910.
Cooper, Charles Henry. *Annals of Cambridge.* Vol. 1. Cambridge: Warwick, 1842.
Copeland, Rita. *Rhetoric, Hermeneutics, and Translation in the Middle Ages.* Cambridge: Cambridge University Press, 1991.
———. "Why Women Can't Read: Medieval Hermeneutics, Statutory Law, and the Lollard Heresy Trials." In *Representing Women: Law, Literature, and Feminism.* Ed. Susan Sage Heinzelman and Zipporah Batshaw Wiseman. Durham, N.C.: Duke University Press, 1994. 253–86.
Cowen, Janet. "Chaucer's *Legend of Good Women*: Structure and Tone." *Studies in Philology* 82 (1985): 416–36.
———. "Woman as Exempla in Fifteenth-Century Verse of the Chaucerian Tradition." In *Chaucer and Fifteenth-Century Poetry.* Ed. Julia Boffey and Janet Cowen. London: King's College, 1991. 51–65.
Crouch, David. Piety, *Fraternity and Power: Religious Gilds in Late Medieval Yorkshire, 1389–1547.* York: York Medieval Press, 2000.
Curtius, E. R. *European Literature and the Latin Middle Ages.* Trans. Willard Trask. Princeton, N.J.: Princeton University Press, 1983.
Davidson, Clifford. "British Saint Play Records: Coping with Ambiguity." *Early Theatre* 1 (1998): 97–106.
———. "The Middle English Saint Play and Its Iconography." In *The Saint Play in Medieval Europe.* Ed. Davidson. Kalamazoo, Mich.: Medieval Institute Publications, 1986. 31–122.
———. "Saint Plays and Pageants of Medieval Britian." *Early Drama, Art, and Music Review* 22 (fall 1999): 11–37.
———. "Saints in Play: English Theater and Saints' Lives." In *Saints: Studies in Hagiography.* Ed. Sandro Sticca. Binghamton, N.Y.: Medieval and Renaissance Texts and Studies, 1996. 145–60.
Deanesly, Margaret. "Vernacular Books in England in the Fourteenth and Fifteenth Centuries." *Modern Language Review* 15 (1920): 349–58.
Delany, Sheila. *Impolitic Bodies: Poetry, Saints, and Society in Fifteenth-Century England.* New York: Oxford University Press, 1998.
———. "Sexual Economics, Chaucer's Wife of Bath, and the *Book of Margery Kempe.*" In Evans and Johnson. 72–87.
D'Evelyn, Charlotte and Frances Foster. "Saints' Legends." In *A Manual of the Writings in Middle English, 1050–1500.* Ed. J. Burke Severs. Hamden, Conn.: Archon Books, 1970. 2. 410–649.
Dickman, Susan. "Margery Kempe and the Continental Tradition of the Pious Woman." In *The Medieval Mystical Tradition in England.* Ed. Marion Glascoe. London: Brewer, 1984. 150–68.
Dinshaw, Carolyn. *Chaucer's Sexual Poetics.* Madison: University of Wisconsin Press, 1989.

———. *Getting Medieval: Sexualities and Communities, Pre- and Postmodern.* Durham, N.C.: Duke University Press, 1999.

———. "Margery Kempe." In Dinshaw and Wallace. 222–39.

Dinshaw, Carolyn, and David Wallace, eds. *Cambridge Companion to Medieval Women's Writing.* Cambridge: Cambridge University Press, 2003.

Dobson, E. J. *The Origins of the Ancrene Wisse.* Oxford: Clarendon, 1976.

Doyle, A. I. "Books Connected with the Vere Family and Barking Abbey. *Transactions of the Essex Archaeological Society* 25 (1958): 222–43.

Driver, J. T. *Cheshire in the Later Middle Ages, 1399–1540.* Chester: Cheshire Community Council, 1971.

Driver, Martha. "Nuns as Patrons, Artists, Readers: Bridgettine Woodcuts in Printed Books Produced for the English Market." In *Art into Life: Collected Papers from the Kresge Art Museum Medieval Symposia.* Ed. Carol G. Fisher and Kathleen L. Scott. East Lansing: Michigan State University Press, 1995. 237–67.

Duffy, Eamon. *Stripping of the Altars: Traditional Religion in England, 1400–1580.* New Haven, Conn.: Yale University Press, 1992.

———. *Voices of Morebath: Reformation and Rebellion in an English Village.* New Haven, Conn.: Yale University Press, 2001.

Dutton, Anne. "Passing the Book: Testamentary Transmission of Religious Literature to and by Women in England, 1350–1500." In *Women, the Book and the Godly.* Ed. Lesley Smith and Jane Taylor. Cambridge: Brewer, 1995. 41–54.

———. "Piety, Politics and Persona: MS Harley 4012 and Anne Harling." In *Prestige, Authority and Power in Late Medieval Manuscripts and Texts.* Ed. Felicity Riddy. York: York Medieval Press, 2000. 133–46.

Eberly, Susan. "Margery Kempe, St. Mary Magdalene, and Patterns of Contemplation." *The Downside Review* 107 (1989): 209–23.

Edwards, A. S. G. "Fifteenth-Century Middle English Verse Author Collections." In *The English Medieval Book.* Ed. Edwards, Vincent Gillespie, and Ralph Hanna. London: British Library, 2000. 101–12.

———. "The Middle English Translation of Claudian's *De Consulatu Stilichonis.*" In *Middle English Poetry: Texts and Traditions.* Ed. A. J. Minnis. Woodbridge, Suffolk: York Medieval Press, 2001. 267–78.

———. "The Transmission and Audience of Osbern Bokenham's *Legendys of Hooly Wummen.*" In *Late Medieval Religious Texts and Their Transmission.* Ed. A. J. Minnis. Cambridge: Brewer, 1994. 157–67.

Elliott, Dyan. *Spiritual Marriage: Sexual Abstinence in Medieval Wedlock.* Princeton, N.J.: Princeton University Press, 1993.

Erler, Mary. "Margery Kempe's White Clothes." *Medium Aevum* 62 (1993): 78–93.

———. "Spectacle and Sacrament: A London Parish Play in the 1530s." *Modern Philology* 91 (1993–94): 449–54.

———. *Women, Reading, and Piety in Late Medieval England.* Cambridge: Cambridge University Press, 2002.

Escobedo, Andrew. *Nationalism and Historical Loss in Renaissance England.* Ithaca, N.Y.: Cornell University Press, 2004.

Evans, Ruth. "Body Politics: Engendering Medieval Cycle Drama." In Evans and Johnson. 112–39.
Evans, Ruth, and Lesley Johnson, eds. *Feminist Readings of Middle English Literature*. London and New York: Routledge, 1994.
Fradenburg, Louise. "We Are Not Alone: Psychoanalytic Medievalism." *New Medieval Literatures* 2 (1998): 249–76.
French, Katherine. "Maidens' Lights and Wives' Stores: Women's Parish Guilds in Late Medieval England." *Sixteenth Century Journal* 29 (1998): 399–425.
——. *People of the Parish*. Philadelphia: University of Pennsylvania Press, 2001.
Fyler, John. *Chaucer and Ovid*. New Haven, Conn.: Yale University Press, 1979.
Galloway, Andrew. "Chaucer's Legend of Lucrece and the Critique of Ideology in Fourteenth-Century England." *English Literary History* 60 (1993): 813–32.
Ganim, John. *Chaucerian Theatricality*. Princeton, N.Y.: Princeton University Press, 1990.
Garber, Marjorie. *Vested Interests*. New York: Routledge, 1992.
Garth, Helen Meredith. *Saint Mary Magdalene in Mediaeval Literature*. Baltimore: Johns Hopkins University Press, 1950.
Geary, Patrick. *Furta Sacra: Thefts of Relics in the Central Middle Ages*. Princeton, N.J.: Princeton University Press, 1978.
Gerould, Gordon Hall. *Saints' Legends*. Boston and New York: Houghton Mifflin, 1916.
Gibson, Gail McMurray. "Blessing from Sun and Moon: Churching as Women's Theater." In Hanawalt and Wallace. 139–54.
——. "Saint Anne and the Religion of Childbed: Some East Anglian Texts and Talismans." In Ashley and Sheingorn. 95–110.
——. *Theater of Devotion: East Anglian Drama and Society in the Late Middle Ages*. Chicago: University of Chicago Press, 1989.
Goodich, Michael. *Vita Perfecta: The Ideal of Sainthood in the Thirteenth Century*. Stuttgart: Anton Hiersemann, 1982.
Goodman, Anthony, and David Morgan. "The Yorkist Claim to the Throne of Castile." *Journal of Medieval History* 11 (1985): 61–69.
Görlach, Manfred. *Studies in Middle English Saints' Legends*. Heidelberg: C. Winter, 1998.
——. *The Textual Tradition of the South English Legendary*. Leeds: University of Leeds, 1974.
Le grand Robert de la langue française. 2d ed. Paris: Robert, 1985.
Gransden, Antonia. *Historical Writing in England*. 2 vols. London: Routledge, 1974, 1982.
Green, Richard Firth. *The Crisis of Truth*. Philadelphia: University of Pennsylvania Press, 1999.
Greene, Thomas. *The Light in Troy: Imitation and Discovery in Renaissance Poetry*. New Haven: Yale University Press, 1982.
Griffiths, Ralph A. *Reign of King Henry VI: The Exercise of Royal Authority, 1422–1461*. London: Ernest Benn, 1981.

———. "The Sense of Dynasty in the Reign of Henry VI." In *Patronage, Pedigree and Power in Later Medieval England*. Ed. Charles Ross. Totowa, N.J.: Rowman & Littlefield, 1979.

———. "The Trial of Eleanor Cobham: An Episode in the Fall of Duke Humphrey of Gloucester." *Bulletin of the John Rylands University Library* 51 (1969): 381–99.

Gumbrecht, Hans Ulrich, Ursula Link-Heer, and Peter-Michael Spangenberg, eds. *La Litterature Historiographique des Origines a 1500*. 3 vols. Heidelberg: Carl Winter, 1986.

Haigh, Christopher. *English Reformations: Religion, Politics, and Society under the Tudors*. Oxford: Clarendon, 1993.

Hampton, Timothy. *Writing from History: The Rhetoric of Exemplarity in Renaissance Literature*. Ithaca, N.Y.: Cornell University Press, 1990.

Hanawalt, Barbara. "Keepers of the Lights: Late Medieval English Parish Gilds." *Journal of Medieval and Renaissance Studies* 14 (1984): 21–37.

Hanawalt, Barbara, and David Wallace, eds. *Bodies and Disciplines: Intersections of Literature and History in Fifteenth-Century England*. Minneapolis: University of Minnesota Press, 1996.

Hanna, Ralph. "The Difficulty of Ricardian Prose Translation: The Case of the Lollards." *Modern Language Quarterly* 51 (1990): 319–40.

Harris, Kate. "Patrons, Buyers, and Owners: The Evidence for Ownership and the Role of Book Owners in Book Production and the Book Trade." In *Book Production and Publishing in Britain, 1375–1475*. Ed. Jeremy Griffiths and Derek Pearsall. Cambridge: Cambridge University Press, 1989. 163–99.

Hartog, François. *Régimes d'Historicité: Présentisme et Expériences du Temps*. Paris: Seuil, 2003.

Head, Thomas. "The Marriages of Christina of Markyate." *Viator* 21 (1990): 75–101.

Helgerson, Richard. *Forms of Nationhood: The Elizabethan Writing of England*. Chicago: University of Chicago Press, 1992.

Higgins, Anne. "Streets and Markets." In *A New History of Early English Drama*. Ed. John Cox and David Kastan. New York: Columbia University Press, 1997. 77–92.

Hilles, Carroll. "Gender and Politics in Osbern Bokenham's Legendary." *New Medieval Literatures* 4 (2001): 189–212.

Hodnett, Edward. *English Woodcuts, 1480–1535*. London: Oxford University Press, 1935.

Holzknecht, Karl Julius. *Literary Patronage in the Middle Ages*. Philadelphia, 1923.

Horobin, Simon. "The angle of oblivion" A Lost Medieval Manuscript Discovered in Walter Scott's Collection," *Times Literary Supplement*, November 11, 2005, 12–13.

Houlbrooke, R. A. "Women's Social Life and Common Action in England from the Fifteenth Century to the Eve of the Civil War." *Continuity and Change* 1 (1986): 171–89.

Hudson, Anne. *Premature Reformation: Wycliffite Texts and Lollard History*. New York: Oxford University Press, 1988.

Innes-Parker, Catherine. "Sexual Violence and the Female Reader: Symbolic Rape in the Saints' Lives of the Katherine Group." *Women's Studies* 24 (1995): 205–17.
Jambeck, Karen. "Patterns of Women's Literary Patronage: England, 1200–ca. 1475." In McCash. 228–65.
Jankowski, Eileen. "Chaucer's *Second Nun's Tale* and the Apocalyptic Imagination." *Chaucer Review* 36 (2001): 128–48.
———. "Reception of Chaucer's Second Nun's Tale: Osbern Bokenham's *Lyf of S. Cycle*." *Chaucer Review* 30 (1996): 306–18.
Jauss, Hans Robert. "The Alterity and Modernity of Medieval Literature." Trans. Timothy Bahti. *New Literary History* 10 (1979): 181–229.
Johnson, Ian. "*Auctricitas?* Holy Women and Their Middle English Texts." In *Prophets Abroad: The Reception of Continental Holy Women in Late-Medieval England*. Ed. Rosalyn Voaden. Cambridge: Brewer, 1996. 177–97.
———. "Tales of a True Translator: Medieval Literary Theory, Anecdote and Autobiography in Osbern Bokenham's *Legendys of Hooly Wummen*." In *The Medieval Translator 4*. Ed. Roger Ellis and Ruth Evans. Binghamton, N.Y.: Medieval and Renaissance Texts and Studies, 1994. 104–24.
Johnson, Lynn Staley. "Chaucer's Tale of the Second Nun and the Strategies of Dissent." *Studies in Philology* 89 (1992): 314–33.
Johnson, P. A. *Duke Richard of York, 1411–1460*. Oxford: Clarendon, 1988.
Jones, Sarah Reese. "'A Peler of Holy Cherch': Margery Kempe and the Bishops." In *Medieval Women: Texts and Contexts in Late Medieval Britain*. Ed. Jocelyn Wogan-Browne et al. Turnhout: Brepols, 2000. 377–91.
Jones, William. "English Religious Brotherhoods and Medieval Lay Piety: The Inquiry of 1388–89." *The Historian* 36 (1974): 646–59.
Keiser, George. "Patronage and Piety in Fifteenth-Century England: Margaret, Duchess of Clarence, Symon Wynter and Beinecke MS 317." *Yale University Library Gazette* (1985): 32–46.
Kelly, H. A. "St. Anne." *Chaucer Encyclopedia*. New Haven, Conn.: Yale University Press, forthcoming.
Kendall, Ritchie. *The Drama of Dissent: The Radical Poetics of Nonconformity, 1380–1590*. Chapel Hill: University of North Carolina Press, 1986.
Kendrick, Laura. *Chaucerian Play*. Berkeley: University of California Press, 1988.
Kennett, White. *Parochial Antiquities Attempted in the History of Ambrosden, Burcester, and Other Adjacent Parts in the Counties of Oxford and Bucks*. Oxford, 1695 [Early English Books microfilm].
Kettle, Ann, and A. P. Baggs. "Religious Houses." In *A History of the County of Cheshire*. Vol. 3. Ed. B. E. Harris. London: Institute of Historical Research by Oxford University Press, 1980. 132–44.
Kipling, Gordon. "The London Pageants for Margaret of Anjou: A Medieval Script Restored." *Medieval English Theatre* 4 (1982): 5–27.
———. *Triumph of Honor*. The Hague: Leiden University Press, 1977.
Kiser, Lisa. *Telling Classical Tales: Chaucer and the Legend of Good Women*. Ithaca, N.Y.: Cornell University Press, 1983.

Kolve, V. A. "Chaucer's *Second Nun's Tale* and the Iconography of Saint Cecilia." In *New Perspectives in Chaucer Criticism*. Ed. Donald Rose. Norman, Okla.: Pilgrim, 1981. 137–74.

Krueger, Roberta. *Women Readers and the Ideology of Genre in Old French Verse Romance*. Cambridge: Cambridge University Press, 1993.

Lagorio, Valerie. "*Defensorium Contra Oblectratores*: A 'Discerning' Assessment of Margery Kempe." In *Mysticism: Medieval and Modern*. Ed. Lagorio. Salzburg: Institut für Anglistik und Amerikanistik, 1986. 29–48.

Latham, R. E. *Revised Medieval Latin Word-List*. London, 1965.

Laurent, Sylvie. *Naître au Moyen Age: De la Conception à la Naissance: la Grossesse et l'Accouchement, XIIe–XVe siecle*. Paris: Léopard d'Or, 1989.

Lavezzo, Kathy, ed. *Imagining a Medieval English Nation*. Minneapolis: University of Minnesota Press, 2004.

Lawton, David. "Dullness in the Fifteenth Century." *English Literary History* 54 (1987): 761–99.

———. "Voice, Authority, and Blasphemy in the *Book of Margery Kempe*." In McEntire. 93–115.

Legge, Dominica. *Anglo-Norman Literature and Its Background*. Oxford: Clarendon, 1963.

Lerer, Seth. *Chaucer and His Readers: Imagining the Author in Late-Medieval England*. Princeton, N.J.: Princeton University Press, 1993.

———. "The Chaucerian Critique of Medieval Theatricality." In Paxson, Clopper, and Tomasch. 59–76.

Lewis, Katherine. *The Cult of St. Katherine of Alexandria in Late Medieval England*. Woodbridge, Suffolk: Boydell, 2000.

———. "Model Girls? Virgin-Martyrs and the Training of Young Women in Late Medieval England." In *Young Medieval Women*. Ed. Katherine Lewis, Noel Menuge, and Kim Phillips. Stroud: Sutton, 1999. 25–46.

Lindahl, Carl. *Earnest Games: Folkloric Patterns in the Canterbury Tales*. Bloomington: Indiana University Press, 1987.

Lindenbaum, Sheila. "Rituals of Exclusion: Feasts and Plays of the English Religious Fraternities." In *Festive Drama*. Ed. Meg Twycross. Cambridge: Brewer, 1996. 54–65.

Lochrie, Karma. *Margery Kempe and Translations of the Flesh*. Philadelphia: University of Pennsylvania Press, 1991.

Love, Rosalind. *Three Eleventh-Century Anglo-Latin Saints' Lives*. Oxford: Clarendon, 1996.

Lucas, Peter. *From Author to Audience: John Capgrave and Medieval Publication*. Dublin: University College Dublin Press, 1997.

———. "John Capgrave and the *Nova Legenda Anglie*: A Survey." *The Library*, 5th series, 25 (1970): 1–10.

Lumiansky, R. M., and David Mills. *The Chester Mystery Cycle: Essays and Documents*. Chapel Hill: University of North Carolina Press, 1983.

Lupton, Julia Reinhard. *Afterlives of the Saints: Hagiography, Typology, and Renaissance Literature*. Stanford, Calif.: Stanford University Press, 1996.

MacBain, William. "Anglo-Norman Women Hagiographers." In *Anglo-Norman Anniversary Essays*. Ed. Ian Short. London: Anglo-Norman Text Society, 1993. 235–50.

Maddern, Philippa. *Violence and Social Order: East Anglia 1422–1442*. Oxford: Clarendon, 1992.

Maddocks, Hilary. "Illumination in Jean de Vignay's Légende dorée." In *Sept siècles de diffusion, Actes du Colloque international sur la* Legenda Aurea. Ed. Brenda Dunn Lardeau. Montreal: Bellarmin, 1986. 155–62.

Mann, Jill. *Geoffrey Chaucer*. Atlantic Highlands, N.J.: Humanities Press International, 1991.

Margherita, Gayle. *Romance of Origins*. Philadelphia: University of Pennsylvania Press, 1994.

Marshall, Peter. *Reformation England, 1480–1642*. London: Arnold, 2003.

McCash, June Hall, ed. *The Cultural Patronage of Medieval Women*. Athens and London: University of Georgia Press, 1996.

McEntire, Sandra, ed. *Margery Kempe: A Book of Essays*. New York: Garland, 1992.

McGerr, Rosemarie. *Chaucer's Open Books*. Gainesville: University of Florida Press, 1998.

McRee, Benjamin. "Religious Guilds and Civic Order: The Case of Norwich in the Late Middle Ages." *Speculum* 67 (1992): 69–97.

———. "Religious Guilds and Regulation of Behavior in Late Medieval Towns." In *People, Politics and Community in the Later Middle Ages*. Ed. Joel Rosenthal and Colin Richmond. Gloucester: Alan Sutton, 1987. 108–22.

———. "Unity or Division? The Social Meaning of Guild Ceremony in Urban Communities." In *City and Spectacle in Medieval Europe*. Ed. Barbara Hanawalt and Kathryn Reyerson. Minneapolis: University of Minnesota Press, 1994. 189–207.

Meale, Carol. "'. . . Alle the Bokes That I Haue of Latyn, Englisch, and Frensch': Lay Women and Their Books in Late Medieval England." In *Women and Literature in Britain*. Ed. Meale. 128–58.

———. "'Gode Men / Wiues Maydnes and Alle Men': Romance and Its Audiences." In *Readings in Medieval English Romance*. Ed. Meale. Cambridge: Brewer, 1994. 209–25.

———. "Patrons, Buyers, and Owners: Book Production and Social State." In *Book Production and Publishing in Britain, 1375–1475*. Ed. Jeremy Griffiths and Derek Pearsall. Cambridge: Cambridge University Press, 1989. 201–38.

———. ed. *Women and Literature in Britain, 1150–1500*. Cambridge: Cambridge University Press, 1993.

Meyer, P. "Notice du MS Sloane 1611 du Musée Britannique." *Romania* 40 (1911): 541–48.

Middle English Dictionary (online). Ann Arbor: University of Michigan Humanities Text Initiative, 1999– .

Middleton, Anne. "The *Physician's Tale* and Love's Martyrs: "Ensamples Mo Than Ten" as a Method in the *Canterbury Tales*." *Chaucer Review* 8 (1973): 9–33.

Millet, Bella. "The Audience of the Saints' Lives of the Katherine Group." *Reading Medieval Studies* 16 (1990): 127–56.
Mills, David. *Recycling the Cycle: The City of Chester and Its Whitsun Plays.* Toronto: University of Toronto, 1998.
Minnis, Alastair. *Oxford Guide to Chaucer: The Shorter Poems.* Oxford: Clarendon, 1995.
———. "Repainting the Lion: Chaucer's Profeminist Narratives." In *Contexts of Pre-Novel Narrative: The European Tradition.* Ed. Roy Eriksen. Berlin: Mouton de Gruyter, 1994. 153–77.
Moore, Samuel. "Patrons of Letters in Norfolk and Suffolk, c. 1450." *PMLA* 27 (1912): 188–207; 28 (1913): 79–105.
Nelson, Alan. *The Medieval English Stage.* Chicago: University of Chicago Press, 1974.
Newbolt, M. R. *St. Werburgh and Her Shrine.* 3d ed. Chester: Phillipson & Golder, 1933.
Nissé, Ruth. "Grace under Pressure: Conduct and Representation in the Norwich Heresy Trials." In Ashley and Clark. 207–25.
———. "Prophetic Nations." *New Medieval Literatures* 4 (2001): 95–115.
———. "Reversing the Discipline: The *Tretise of Miraclis Pleyinge*, Lollard Exegesis, and the Failure of Representation." *Yearbook of Langland Studies* 11 (1997): 163–94.
Parsons, John Carmi. "Of Queens, Courts, and Books: Reflections on the Literary Patronage of Thirteenth-Century Plantagenet Queens." In McCash. 175–201.
Patterson, Lee. *Chaucer and the Subject of History.* Madison: University of Wisconsin Press, 1991.
———. "Chaucer's Pardoner on the Couch: Psyche and Clio in Medieval Literary Studies." *Speculum* 76 (2001): 638–80.
———. *Negotiating the Past: The Historical Understanding of Medieval Literature.* Madison: University of Wisconsin Press, 1987.
———. "On the Margin: Postmodernism, Ironic History, and Medieval Studies." *Speculum* 65 (1990): 87–108.
Paxson, James, Lawrence Clopper, and Sylvia Tomasch, eds. *The Performance of Middle English Culture: Essays on Chaucer and the Drama in Honor of Martin Stevens.* Cambridge: Brewer, 1998.
Percival, Florence. *Chaucer's Legendary Good Women.* Cambridge: Cambridge University Press, 1998.
Peters, Christine. *Patterns of Piety: Women, Gender and Religion in Late Medieval and Reformation England.* Cambridge: Cambridge University Press, 2003.
Pugh, T. B. "Richard Plantagenet (1411–60), Duke of York, as the King's Lieutenant in France and Ireland." In *Aspects of Late Medieval Government and Society.* Ed. J. G. Rowe. Toronto: University of Toronto Press, 1986. 107–41.
Reames, Sherry. *The Legenda Aurea: A Reexamination of Its Paradoxical History.* Madison: University of Wisconsin Press, 1985.
———. "A Recent Discovery Concerning the Sources of Chaucer's *Second Nun's Tale*." *Modern Philology* 87 (1990): 337–61.

Renna, Thomas. "Virginity in the *Life* of Christina of Markyate and Aelred of Rievaulx's *Rule*." *American Benedictine Review* 36 (1985): 79–92.

Rex, Richard. *Henry VIII and the English Reformation*. Houndmills, Basingstoke: Macmillan, 1993.

Rhodes, J. T. "Syon Abbey and Its Religious Publications in the Sixteenth Century." *Journal of Ecclesiastical History* 44 (1993): 11–25.

Riddy, Felicity. "Women Talking about the Things of God: A Late Medieval Sub-Culture." In *Women and Literature in Britain*. Ed. Meale. 104–27.

Robson, J. A. *Wyclif and the Oxford Schools*. Cambridge: Cambridge University Press, 1961.

Rosenthal, Joel. "Aristocratic Cultural Patronage and Book Bequests, 1350–1500." *Bulletin of the John Rylands University Library of Manchester* 64 (1982): 522–48.

Rosser, Gervase. "Communities of Parish and Guild in the Late Middle Ages." In *Parish, Church and People*. Ed. S. J. Wright. London: Hutchinson, 1988. 29–55.

———. "Going to the Fraternity Feast: Commensality and Social Relations in Late Medieval England." *Journal of British Studies* 33 (1994): 430–46.

———. "Parochial Conformity and Voluntary Religion in Late Medieval England." *Transactions of the Royal Historical Society*, 6th series, 1 (1991): 173–89.

Roth, Francis, O.S.A. *The English Austin Friars, 1249–1538* 2 vols. New York: Augustinian Historical Institute, 1966.

Salih, Sarah. *Versions of Virginity in Late Medieval England*. Cambridge: Brewer, 2001.

Sanok, Catherine. "Criseyde, Cassandre, and the *Thebaid*: Women and the Theban Subtext of Chaucer's *Troilus and Criseyde*." *Studies in the Age of Chaucer* 20 (1998): 41–71.

———. "Reading Hagiographically: Chaucer's *Legend of Good Women* and its Feminine Audience." *Exemplaria* 13 (2001): 323–54.

Scanlon, Larry. *Narrative, Authority, and Power: The Medieval Exemplum and the Chaucerian Tradition*. Cambridge: Cambridge University Press, 1994.

Scattergood, John. "Chaucer in the Suburbs." In *Medieval Literature and Antiquities*. Ed. Myra Stokes and T. L. Burton. Cambridge: Brewer, 1987. 145–62.

Schulenburg, Jane Tibbetts. *Forgetful of Their Sex: Female Sanctity and Society, ca. 500–1100*. Chicago: University of Chicago Press, 1998.

———. "Sexism and the Celestial Gynaeceum from 500 to 1200." *Journal of Medieval History* 14 (1978): 117–33.

Sikes, J. G., and Freda Jones. "Jesus College." In *History of the County of Cambridge and the Isle of Ely*. Vol. 3. Ed. J. P. C. Roach. Oxford: Oxford University Press, 1959. 421–28.

Simpson, James. "Ethics and Interpretation: Reading Wills in Chaucer's *Legend of Good Women*." *Studies in the Age of Chaucer* 20 (1998): 73–100.

———. *Oxford English Literary History Vol. 2: Reform and Cultural Revolution, 1350–1547*. Oxford: Oxford University Press, 2002.

Sklar, Ruth. "Cobham's Daughter: The *Book of Margery Kempe* and the Power of Heterodox Thinking." *Modern Language Quarterly* 56 (1995): 277–304.
Spiegel, Gabrielle. *The Past as Text.* Baltimore: Johns Hopkins University Press, 1997.
Sponsler, Claire. "The Culture of the Spectator: Conformity and Resistance to Medieval Performances." *Theatre Journal* 44 (1992): 15–29.
———. *Drama and Resistance: Bodies, Goods and Theatricality in Late Medieval England.* Minneapolis: University of Minnesota Press, 1997.
Staley, Lynn. *Margery Kempe's Dissenting Fictions.* University Park: Pennsylvania State University Press, 1994.
Stanbury, Sarah. "The Vivacity of Images: St. Katherine, Knighton's Lollards, and the Breaking of Idols." In *Images, Idolatry, and Iconoclasm in Late Medieval England.* Ed. Jeremy Dimmick, James Simpson, and Nicolette Zeeman. Oxford: Oxford University Press, 2002.
Stein, Robert. "Making History English: Cultural Identity and Historical Explanation in William of Malmesbury and Layamon's *Brut*." In *Text and Territory: Geographical Imagination in the European Middle Ages.* Ed. Sylvia Tomasch and Sealy Gilles. Philadelphia: University of Pennsylvania Press, 1998. 97–115.
Stevens, Martin. *Four Middle English Mystery Cycles: Textual, Contextual and Critical Interpretations.* Princeton, N.J.: Princeton University Press, 1987.
Stouck, Mary-Ann. "Saints and Rebels: Hagiography and Opposition to the King in Fourteenth-Century England." *Medievalia et Humanistica*, n.s., 24 (1997): 75–94.
Strohm, Paul. *England's Empty Throne: Usurpation and the Language of Legitimation, 1399–1422.* New Haven, Conn.: Yale University Press, 1998.
———. *Hochon's Arrow: The Social Imagination of Fourteenth-Century Texts.* Princeton, N.J.: Princeton University Press, 1992.
———. "Passion, Lyf, Miracle, Legende: Some Generic Terms in Middle English Hagiographical Narrative (Parts 1 and 2)." *Chaucer Review* 10 (1975): 62–76, 154–71.
———. *Social Chaucer.* Cambridge: Harvard University Press, 1989.
Summit, Jennifer. *Lost Property: The Woman Writer and English Literary History, 1380–1589.* Chicago: University of Chicago Press, 2000.
———. "Topography as Historiography: Petrarch, Chaucer, and the Making of Medieval Rome." *Journal of Medieval and Early Modern Studies* 30 (2000): 211–46.
Szell, Timea. "From Woe to Weal and Weal to Woe: Notes on the Structure of the *Book of Margery Kempe*." In McEntire. 73–91.
Taussig, Michael. *Mimesis and Alterity.* New York: Routledge, 1993.
Thrupp, Sylvia. *Merchant Class of Medieval London.* Chicago: University of Chicago Press, 1948.
Tolkien, J. R. R. "Ancrene Wisse and Hali Meidenhad." *Essays and Studies by Members of the English Association* 14 (1929): 104–26.
Tudor-Craig, Pamela, "Richard III's Triumphant Entry into York, August 29th, 1483." In *Richard III and the North.* Ed. Rosemary Horrox. Hull: University of Hull, 1986. 108–16.

Twycross, Meg. "'Apparell Comlye.'" In *Aspects of Early English Drama*. Ed. Paula Neuss. Cambridge: Brewer, 1993. 30–49.

———. "'Transvestism' in the Mystery Plays." *English Medieval Theatre* 5 (1983): 123–80.

Unwin, George. *The Gilds and Companies of London*. New York: Barnes & Noble, 1964.

Vickers, K. H. *Humphrey, Duke of Gloucester*. London: Archibald Constable, 1907.

Wallace, David. *Chaucerian Polity: Absolutist Lineages and Associational Forms in England and Italy*. Stanford, Calif.: Stanford University Press, 1997.

———. "Mystics and Followers in Siena and East Anglia: A Study in Taxonomy, Class and Cultural Mediation." In *The Medieval Mystical Tradition in England*. Ed. Marion Glascoe. London: Brewer, 1984. 169–91.

Warren, Nancy. *Spiritual Economies: Female Monasticism in Later Medieval England*. Philadelphia: University of Pennsylvania Press, 2001.

Watson, Nicholas. "Censorship and Cultural Change in Late-Medieval England: Vernacular Theology, the Oxford Translation Debate, and Arundel's Constitutions of 1409." *Speculum* 70 (1995): 822–64.

———. "Julian of Norwich." In Dinshaw and Wallace. 210–21.

Weinstein, Donald, and Rudolph Bell. *Saints and Society: The Two Worlds of Western Christendom, 1000–1700*. Chicago: University of Chicago Press, 1982.

Westlake, H. F. *The Parish Guilds of Mediaeval England*. London: Macmillan, 1919.

Wickham, Glynne. "The Staging of Saint Plays in England." In *The Medieval Drama*. Ed. Sandro Sticca. Albany: SUNY Press, 1972. 99–119.

Wilks, Michael. "Wyclif and the Great Persecution." In *Prophecy and Eschatology*. Ed. Wilks. Studies in Church History 10. Oxford: Blackwell, 1994. 39–63.

———. "Wyclif and the Wheel of Time." In *Wyclif: Political Ideas and Practice*. Ed. Anne Hudson. Oxford: Oxbow, 2000. 205–22.

Winstead, Karen. "Capgrave's Saint Katherine and the Perils of Gynecocracy." *Viator* 25 (1994): 361–76.

———. "Fear in Late-Medieval English Martyr Legends." In *More than a Memory: The Discourse of Martyrdom and the Construction of Christian Identity in the History of Christianity*. Ed. Johan Leemans. Louvain: Peeters Publishers, forthcoming.

———. *John Capgrave's Fifteenth Century*. Philadelphia: University of Pennsylvania Press, forthcoming.

———. "Piety, Politics, and Social Commitment in Capgrave's *Life of St. Katherine*." *Medievalia et Humanistica* 17 (1991): 59–80.

———. *Virgin Martyrs: Legends of Sainthood in Late Medieval England*. Ithaca, N.Y.: Cornell University Press, 1997.

Wogan-Browne, Jocelyn. "The Apple's Message: Some Post-Conquest Hagiographic Accounts of Textual Transmission." In *Late-Medieval Religious Texts and Their Transmission: Essays in Honour of A. I Doyle*. Ed. A. J. Minnis. Cambridge: Brewer, 1994. 39–53.

———. "'Clerc u lai, muïne u dame': Women and Anglo-Norman Hagiography in the Twelfth and Thirteenth Centuries." In *Women and Literature in Britain*. Ed. Meale. 61–85.

———. "Saints' Lives and the Female Reader." *Forum for Modern Language Studies* 27 (1991): 314–32.

———. *Saints' Lives and Women's Literary Culture, c. 1150–1300: Virginity and Its Authorizations*. Oxford: Oxford University Press, 2001.

———. "The Virgin's Tale." In Evans and Johnson. 165–94.

———. "Wreaths of Thyme: The Female Translator in Anglo-Norman Hagiography." In *The Medieval Translator* 4. Ed. Roger Ellis and Ruth Evans. Binghamton, N.Y.: Medieval and Renaissance Texts and Studies, 1994. 46–65.

Womack, Peter. "Shakespeare and the Sea of Stories." *Journal of Medieval and Early Modern Studies* 29 (1999): 169–87.

Yoshikawa, Naoë Kukita. "Veneration of Virgin Martyrs in Margery Kempe's Meditation: Influence of the Sarum Liturgy and Hagiography." In *Writing Religious Women*. Ed. Denis Renevey and Christiania Whitehead. Toronto: University of Toronto Press, 2000. 177–95.

Yuval-Davis, Nira. *Gender and Nation*. London: SAGE, 1997.

Zumthor, Paul. *Essai de Poétique Médiévale*. Paris: Seuil, 1972.

Index

actors, female, 163, 165
Adeldrid, Saint, 93
Aeneas, 20
Aers, David, 172, 175
Agatha, Saint, 2, 25, 34, 62, 79–80, 183 n.15
Agnes, Saint, 1, 25, 69, 96, 184 n.17; play of, 161, 222 n.70
Alceste, 43–44, 46–48, 50–51, 195 n.102, 196 n.2
Alcock, John (bishop of Ely), 30
Alexander the Great, 99, 209 n.49
Alexis, Saint, 40
Allen, Elizabeth, 183 n.16, 185 n.30
Anastasia, Saint, 8
anchoresses, 9–14
Ancrene Wisse, 9–11
Anderson, Benedict, 84, 102
Anglo-Normans: representation of, in *Life of Christina of Markyate*, 119–20; women, as patrons of saints' lives, 37
Anglo-Saxon saints, 55, 85–86, 92–93, 106, 110–11. *See also names of individual saints*
Anna, Saint, of East Anglia, 93
Anne, Saint, xx, 35, 40, 52, 202 n.55; feast of, 163; guild of (Lincoln), 153, 160. *See also* Bokenham, Osbern, Legend of St. Anne
Anne of Bohemia (queen of Richard II), 43, 46, 195 n.102, 196 n.1, 202 n.55
Anne of Denmark (queen of James I), 173
antifeminist literature, 42, 44–47, 194 n.90, 195 n.105, 196 n.2. *See also* antiphrasis
antiphrasis, 46–48, 195 n.105
Arthur (king), 98, 149, 151, 173
Arthur (Plantagenet; prince), 146, 147–49
Arundel, Archbishop, 137–38
Aschoghe, William (bishop of Salisbury), 61
Ashley, Kathleen, 135, 216 n.4, 218 n.30, 222 n.78

Assembly of Ladies, 41
Auchinleck legend of St. Margaret, 24
audience, feminine, 24–25, 28–33, 41–44, 46–49, 53, 63, 70, 89, 107, 183 n.14, 194 n.90, 203 n.60; as interpretive community, xii, 41, 48–49, 51, 53–54, 56–58, 70, 78, 106
Audry, Saint, of Ely. *See* Etheldreda, Saint
Augustinian friars, 67–68. *See also* Bokenham, Osbern; Capgrave, John

Babington, Katherine, 35
Badir, Patricia, 152, 162, 164, 222 n.75
Bainbridge, Virginia, 153, 158, 218 nn. 22, 31
Bale, John, 178
Barbara, Saint, 1, 38
Barclay, Alexander, 34, 86
Barron, Caroline, 154, 219 n.32, 220 n.55
Bartlett, Anne Clark, 48
Baxter, Margery, 15, 185 n.31
Beaufort, Lady Margaret, 36
Becket, Thomas, legends of, 86–87, 177
Beckwith, Sarah, 161, 215 n.48, 217 n.9, 223 n.82
Bede, 91, 92, 100, 209 n.56
Bedford, duke of, 60
Benedeit, 37
Benedictine order, 30, 86. *See also* Bradshaw, Henry; Lydgate, John
Bhabha, Homi, 85, 88, 113
Blunt, John Henry, 115
Bodleian Library MS Douce 114, 26, 125
body: female, 25, 88, 163, 165; male, 163, 171; saint's, x, xiii, 65–66, 96, 100; uncorrupt, as symbol of national community, 83, 85, 88, 102, 208 n.45. *See also* translation of saint's body

Index

Bokenham, Osbern, 3, 6, 28, 34, 38, 49, 83, 86, 188 n.6, 190 n.29, 201 n.44; and authorship of the *Gilte Legende,* 198 n.20; and the House of York, 54, 58, 68, 75–76, 197 nn.11–12, 201 n.46; Legend of Mary Magdalene, 34, 52–54, 56, 58, 62, 74–78, 129–31, 200 n.26; Legend of St. Agnes, 69, 79, 199 n.20; Legend of St. Anne, 54, 70–75, 80, 199 n.20, 202 n.56; Legend of St. Christine, 3, 62, 78; Legend of St. Faith, 62; Legend of St. Katherine, 34, 56–57, 62, 78–79; Legend of St. Margaret, 34, 54, 59, 60–61, 63–66, 69–70, 77, 79, 199 n.20; *Legends of Holy Women,* xv–xvi, 34, 35, 41, 51–58, 123, 125, 139–40, 182 n.1; *Mappula Angliae,* 55, 86

Bolingbroke, Roger, 68

Book of the Knight of the Tower, 6–10, 12, 16, 19, 24, 27, 41–42, 161, 165

books of hours, 3, 35, 42, 189 n.11

Bourchier, Henry, 56, 61,

Bourchier, Isabel (countess of Eu), 34, 51–54, 56, 58, 75–78, 80–81, 129–31

Bourdieu, Pierre, 39

Boureau, Alain, 23

Bradshaw, Henry, 49, 74; *Life of St. Werburge of Chester,* ix, x, xvi, 13, 41, 83–85, 88–110, 114–15, 123, 204 n.1, 207 n.28; *Lyfe of St. Radegunde,* 29–31, 38, 41

Breviarium ad usum insignis ecclesiae Sarum, 182 n.3

Bridget, Saint, of Sweden, 35, 110, 113–15, 124–25, 127, 213 n.24

British Library MS Additional 35298. See *Gilte Legende*

British Library MS Harley 4011, 198 n.19

British Library MS Harley 4012, 35

Brittain, F., 30

Brut, Walter, 15

Brutus, 20

Bulkeley family, 204 n.1

Burgh, Thomas, 34, 38, 63, 66–69, 197 n.6, 197 n.10

Bury St. Edmunds (Benedictine monastery), 34, 56, 61

Butler, Judith, xiv, 222 n.76

Cade, John, 59, 200 n.29

Cambridge, 35, 66–68, 201 n.44

Cambridge University Library Additional MS 3041. See Roscarrock, Nicholas

Canterbury Tales. See Chaucer, Geoffrey, *Canterbury Tales*

Capgrave, John, 3, 28, 38, 61, 82, 86, 188 n.6, 201 n.48, 206 n.16; *Life of St. Augustine,* 28, 38, 190 n.28; *Life of St. Gilbert of Sempringham,* 34, 86; *Life of St. Katherine,* 3, 35, 81, 189 n.17; *Life of St. Norbert,* 34

Catherine of Aragon, 146–52, 165, 172–73, 175

Catherine of Siena, Middle English life of, 26, 36, 125

Caxton, William, 86, 175

Cazelles, Bridget, 26

Cecilia, Saint, 1–9, 14–15, 27, 38, 62, 125, 133–37, 143, 162, 182 n.3, 183 n.15, 184 n.18; in the *Book of Margery Kempe,* 122, 125, 131, 133–37, 143; feast day of, 2; in Julian of Norwich, 3–6; in the *Life of Christina of Markyate,* 117–22, 125; in Nicholas Love, 16–19; in the *Second Nun's Tale,* 147, 165, 167–71

Certeau, Michel de, xiv, 22, 154, 159

Chad, Saint, 85, 93, 206 n.11, 208 n.37

Chaucer, Geoffrey, 25, 49; *Canterbury Tales,* 42, 43, 157, 166–67; *Legend of Good Women,* 42–48, 50–51; *Nun's Priest's Tale,* 46; *Roman de la Rose,* 43, 45, 195 n.99, 195 n.102; *Second Nun's Tale,* 166–72, 182 n.1, 203 n.62 ; *Troilus and Criseyde,* 42, 43, 45, 195 n.102; *Wife of Bath's Tale,* 166

Chester, 83–84, 102–5

Chester Play of the Assumption, 160, 163, 221 n.62

childbirth, 10, 31, 33, 125, 127, 213 n.32. See also procreativity, and literary production

Christ (Jesus), 2, 17, 69, 120, 126–30, 132–34, 141–44, 150, 171; as divine spouse, 1, 26, 57, 95–96, 100, 118, 147–48; feminized, 25–26; passion of, 5, 128

Christina the Astonishing, 26, 125

Christine, Saint, 3, 8, 52; play of, 161. See also Bokenham, Osbern, Legend of St. Christine

Christopher, Saint, guild of (Norwich), 154

Chronicle of London, 60, 145–46, 151–52, 158

Clare priory, 58

class. See social class

Index

classical past, xii–xiii, 43–44, 98, 177, 181 nn.2–3, 203 nn.62–63, 225 n.11
Cleopatra, 43, 47
Clopper, Lawrence, 216 n.3, 222 n.71
Clopton, John, 56
Clopton, William, 56
Cobham, Eleanor, 59–60, 68–69, 202 n.49
Coletti, Theresa, 134, 203 n.61, 213 n.27, 214 n.46, 216 n.4, 217 n.15, 220 n.53
conduct books, 6, 41, 193 n.89. See also *Book of the Knight of the Tower*
Constantine, 87, 179
conversion, 120, 136, 169, 215 n.56; in Anglo-Saxon history, 92, 94, 111–12, 209 n.56; in the *Book of Margery*, 127, 136; of Muslims, 209 n.56
Corpus Christi guild (York), 155, 160
Corpus Christi plays, 145, 147, 150, 153, 161
courtesy literature. *See* conduct books
courtly literature, 41, 43. *See also* Chaucer, Geoffrey, *Legend of Good Women*
cross-dressing, theatrical, xvii, 146, 163–65, 170–71
Crouch, David, 153, 157, 219 n.42
Curteys, William (abbot of Bury St. Edmunds), 34
Cuthbert, Saint, 85

Danish invasions, 83, 88, 91, 101–2
Davidson, Clifford, 216 n.2, 221 n.70
Delany, Sheila, 53, 59, 197 n.11, 200 n.25
Denston, Katherine, 34, 53, 54, 56–57, 70, 73–74, 80, 202 n.56
De sanctis Anglie, 86
Dido, 43, 47, 194 n.98
Digby plays: *Candlemas and Killing of Innocents*, 163; *Conversion of St. Paul*, 145; *Mary Magdalene*, 135, 145
Dinshaw, Carolyn, 132, 213 n.33, 214 n.44
Dorothy, Saint, 25, 34, 40, 52; play of, 161
Dunstan, Saint, 85, 206 n.11, 206 n.13
Dutton, Anne, 36

East Anglia, 58, 92–93, 123, 134
Edburga, Saint, 93, 205 n.10
Edith, Saint, of Wilton, 86
Edwards, A. S. G., 52, 197 nn. 4, 6, 201 n.46
Elizabeth I, 178–79

Elizabeth of Hungary, Saint, 6, 34, 51, 52, 62, 78, 125, 127
Elizabeth of Spalbeck, 26, 125
England: Anglo-Saxon history of, x, 37, 52, 91–95, 97, 102, 106, 110–12; fifteenth-century political culture, xv, 21, 27, 49, 54, 56, 58–61, 68–70, 198 n.19; as religious community, 5, 55–56, 84–85, 88–89, 95, 97–102, 105–7, 112, 114
eschatology, 92, 102, 176
Etheldreda, Saint (Audry), 93, 98, 100, 205 n.10
ethics. *See* exemplarity
exemplarity: as ahistorical, x, 106, 109; of female saints' lives, ix–xvii, 2–3, 5–23, 78, 83, 110, 145, 182 n.2, 184 n.19; and a gendered hermeneutics, 24, 32, 41–43, 46–48; and historical comparison, xv, 19–20, 49, 132, 172, 176, 179–80, 187 n.52; and narrative, 21–22, 185 n.30, 187 n.48; and national affiliation, 83, 85, 88, 105–6, 109, 110, 113–15; as a regulatory hermeneutics, xiv, 3, 26, 81, 177
exemplum, 19, 169

Faith, Saint, 38, 52, 62, 206 n.13
false steward, trope of, 97
female saints: incorruptible bodies of, 99–101, 108; as intercessors, 31–32, 63–64, 79–80, 177; as muses, 78–81, 203 nn.62–63; and national identity, 74, 84, 87–89, 99–102, 109, 115, 210 n.61. *See also individual saints*
female saints' lives, 39–41; Continental, 113–14, 124–26, 128; gendered address of, x–xiii, 13–14, 24, 28–29, 31–34, 42–44, 48, 53, 105, 107; as historical, ix–x, 91–94; male readers of, 38, 63; as misogynist, xiii, 26; as "narrative" literature, 28; as pornographic, 25, 27, 188 n.11; representations of public feminine spirituality in, 2, 6–7, 10–11, 17–18, 78, 120, 123–24, 128–31, 168–71; and/as social commentary, 81–82, 119–23, 135, 182 n.9, 212 n.12; violence in, x, xiii, 26, 64–65, 94, 188 n.11; as women's literature, xi–xiii, 26–27, 32, 54, 73–79. *See also* exemplarity, of female saints' lives; *individual saints' legends*; saints' plays and pageants
feminine audience. *See* audience, feminine

Flegge, Agatha, 34, 53, 79–80
The Floure and the Leafe, 41
Foxe, John, 178–80
France, xv, 55, 58, 60, 76, 206 n.13, 209 n.49, 222 n.70
French, Katherine, 153, 155, 160, 218 n.22, 219 n.34, 220 n.58, 221 n.63
Frideswide, Saint, 85, 205 nn.10–11

Garner, Stanton, 164
Gascoigne, Thomas, 115
gender: as a category of analysis, xi; as a category of identification, 13, 32, 37–38, 42, 48–49, 52–53, 56–58, 110, 163, 189 n.20; and history, xvii, 14, 20, 165; ideology, xiv, 22, 96, 123, 164, 166; performance of, xiv, 145, 147, 162–65, 170–71. *See also* exemplarity, and a gendered hermeneutics
genealogy, 75–76, 91–94, 111, 148–49, 207 nn.27–28, 217 n.12
Geoffrey of Vinsauf, 77
George, Saint, guild of (Norwich), 155–56. *See also* Barclay, Alexander; Lydgate, John, *Legend of St. George*
Gibson, Gail McMurray, 54, 198 n.13, 202 n.55, 212 n.17
Gilte Legende, 34, 39, 69, 85; authorship of, 198 n.20
Golden Legend. *See* Jacobus de Voragine
The Good Wife Taught Her Daughter, 41
Goscelin, 207 n.28
Green, Richard Firth, 156
Greene, Thomas, 177
Griffiths, Ralph A., 60, 200 n.37
guilds, parish. *See* parish guilds
Guillaume de Lorris. *See Romance of the Rose*

Hainault, Jacqueline of, 59–60
hagiography. *See* female saints' lives; male saints/saints' lives; native saints' lives
Hampton, Timothy, 177
Hanawalt, Barbara, 159
Hansen, Elaine Tuttle, 47
Harling, Anne, 35
Harris, Kate, 36
Hector of Troy, 98
Helen, Saint, 87, 152, 163; guild of (Beverly), 152, 163, 170–71; play of, 161, 222 n.70
Helgerson, Richard, 84
Henry IV, 68
Henry V, 61, 115, 156
Henry VI, 54, 56, 58–62, 69–70, 81, 187 n.52, 200 n.26, 201 n.44
heresy, xiv–xv, 15, 27, 44, 50, 94, 131, 137, 140, 159, 162, 166, 185 n.36
hermeneutics. *See* antiphrasis; exemplarity
Higden, Ranulf, 55, 91, 199 n.21
Higgins, Anne, 150
Hilton, Walter, 135
history: biblical, 98–99; English, 91–92, 94–95; literary, 24–25, 54; medieval ideas of, 20, 176–77; models of, and exemplarity, x, xii, xiv–xv, 14–19, 22, 83, 109–10, 116, 132, 143, 165; Renaissance ideas of, 176–77; saint defined against, 97–99. *See also* classical past; England, Anglo Saxon history of
Howard, John (duke of Norfolk), 56
Howard, Katherine, 34, 53, 56–57
Hudson, Anne, 137
Humphrey of Gloucester, 58–62, 69–70, 202 n.49
Hunt, Isabel, 34, 53

idols/idolatry, 93, 171, 177
imitatio, xvi, 3–5, 7, 9, 22, 78, 116–17, 182 n.2; and construction of gender, 14, 24; Lollard, 19, 186 n.37; and models of history, 15–16, 18, 74. *See also* exemplarity
Isabel (duchess of York), 75–76

Jacobus de Voragine, 17, 35, 36, 39, 55, 69, 79, 85, 125
Jambeck, Karen, 34
James, Mervyn, 150
Jean de Meun. *See Romance of the Rose*
Jesus. *See* Christ (Jesus)
John of Gaunt, 75, 148
John of Tynemouth, 86, 121
Johnson, Lynn Staley. *See* Staley, Lynn
John the Baptist, Saint, guild of (Baston), 163
Jourdemain, Margaret, 68–69, 202 n.49
Julian of Norwich, 3–6, 8, 11, 14, 25, 27, 140, 169, 172, 180; *imitatio* of St. Cecilia, 5, 14, 25, 167, 172

Index

Julius Caesar, 99, 208 n.46

Kalendre of the Newe Legende of Englande, 86–87, 110–15, 125
Katherine-Group Legends, 9, 193 n.84. See also *Seinte Marherete the Meiden ant Martyr*
Katherine of Alexandria, Saint, 1, 3, 8, 9, 12, 16, 25, 86, 96, 123–24, 125–26, 133, 141, 143, 183 nn. 7, 15; in the *Book of Margery Kempe*, 18, 124–25, 131, 135, 159; genealogy of, 87–88; guilds of, 157–58, 160; legends of, 35, 36, 38, 40, 86, 184 n.24; pageants/plays of, 145–52, 160–61, 165, 221 n.70
Kempe, John, 133–34
Kempe, Margery, xiii, xvi, 6, 14, 164, 169; *Book of Margery Kempe*, xiii–xiv, xvi, 97, 116–17, 122–44, 146, 172; and Continental holy women, 124–26; *imitatio* of female saints, 18, 22, 116–17, 122–36, 139–40; as object of interpretation, 140–44. See also *under* Cecilia, Saint; Mary Magdalene
Kenelm, Saint, 85, 206 n.11
Kipling, Gordon, 148, 216 n.6, 217 n.12
Knight of the Tower. See *Book of the Knight of the Tower*
Knighton, Henry, 16
Kolve, V. A., 169
Krueger, Roberta, 48

Lady Anne (countess of Stafford), 34, 36
Lady March, 27, 33–34
Lancastrian politics/representations, 58, 60, 68, 76, 140, 148–49, 198 n.19, 201 n.48
Lawton, David, 66, 213 nn. 24, 31
lay religion, 18, 135, 154, 159, 171, 172; public expression of, 162, 183 n.15
Legenda Aurea. See Jacopus de Voragine
legendaries, pastoral, 39–40, 188 n.6, 193 n.84
Leonard, Saint, fraternity of (Lynn), 159
Lerer, Seth, 55, 167
Lewis, Katherine, 2, 182 n.2, 183 n.15, 220 n.45
Life and Martyrdom of Saint Katherine of Alexandria (Harvard University Library, Richardson MS 44), 12, 39–40, 88
Life of Christina of Markyate, 117–22. See also Cecilia, Saint

Life of Edward the Confessor, 37
Life of St. Osith, 37
Life of St. Ursula, prose (Huntington MS 140), 86
Lindahl, Carl, 157
literacy, 6, 8, 27
Lollards/Lollardy, 15–16, 18–19, 131, 136–40, 162, 169, 185 n.31, 186 nn. 37, 42, 214 n.36. See also preaching, women's
London, 20, 103, 145, 147, 150
Love (God of), 42–46, 50, 73, 194 n.98, 195 n.102, 196 n.2
Love, Nicholas, 16–19, 162
Lucrece, 43, 47, 99
Lucy, Saint, 6, 25, 223 n.85; plays of, 161, 221 n.70
Lumiansky, R. M., 160
Lupton, Julia Reinhard, 175
Lydgate, John, 3, 27, 61, 188 n.6, 190 n.29; "Invocation to Seynte Anne," 34, 190 n.29; *Legend of St. George*, 34, 86; "Legend of Seynt Margarete," 27, 31, 33–34, 41; *Life of St. Alban and Amphibalus*, 34, 86, 87; *Life of St. Augustine of Canterbury*, 86; *Life of Sts. Edmund and Fremund*, 34, 86
Lyfe of Saynt Brandon, 87
Lyf of St. Katherin of Senis, 28, 50, 125
Lyfe of Saynt Edwarde Confessour and Kynge of Englande, 87
Lyf of Saynt Ursula, 87
Lyf of the Holy and Blessid Saynt Wenefryde, 86–87

male saints/saints' lives, 20–21, 38, 39–40, 52, 113
Margaret (duchess of Clarence), 38
Margaret, Saint, of Antioch, 1, 8, 9–11, 25, 31, 40, 124–25, 133, 160, 173; in the *Book of Margery Kempe*, 124–25; in pageant for Margaret of Anjou, 202 n.52; as patron of women in childbirth, 31, 68, 125, 190 n.25; plays of, 161, 223 n.85; vernacular legends of, 35, 86, 190 n.25, 202 n.51. See also Auchinleck legend of St. Margaret; Bokenham, Osbern, Legend of St. Margaret; *Seinte Marherete the Meiden ant Martyr*
Margaret of Anjou, 60, 69, 173

marriage, 104, 121, 147, 149, 214 n.39, 214 n.42; to Christ, 1, 26, 98, 106; holy woman's refusal/redefinition of, 8, 40, 118–19, 127, 133, 135, 184 nn.17–18
Mary. *See* Virgin Mary
Mary, Saint, Beverly fraternity of, 152
Mary de Bohun (wife of Henry Bolingbroke), 41
Mary d'Oignies, 26, 124–26, 128
Mary of Egypt, 213 n.26
Mary Magdalene, 8, 52, 62, 123, 130–31, 133; Margery Kempe's imitation of, 124–29, 131; plays of, 222 n.70. *See also* Bokenham, Osbern, Legend of Mary Magdalene
McRee, Ben, 154, 155–56
Meale, Carol, 41, 193 n.88
Mecthild of Hackeborn, 36
Medea, 43
Meditationes Vitae Christi, 17
Mercia, 91, 92, 93
Michael, Saint, guild of (Lincoln), 155, 157
Mildred, Saint, 85, 92, 205 n.10
Mills, David, 160
mimesis. *See imitatio*; exemplarity
Minerva, 76–77
Mirabilis, Christina. *See* Christina the Astonishing
Mirk, John, 85, 175, 186 n.42
mirrors for princes, 19, 27
misogyny, xiii, 24–27, 45, 195 n.107
Missale ad usum insignis et praeclarae ecclesiae Sarum, 182 n.3
Mowbray, John (duke of Norfolk), 58
muses, female saints as. *See* female saints as muses

national community, English, 55–56, 83–85, 106–7, 209 n.49. *See also* female saints, and national identity; native saints' lives
native saints' lives, 55, 85–87, 110–15. *See also* Bradshaw, Henry, *Life of St. Werburge of Chester*
Neville, Anne, of Stafford, 36
Nissé, Ruth, 185 n.34, 186 n.38
Norman conquest, 84, 102, 104–5
Northumbria, 92–93
Nova Legenda Anglie, 86–87
N-Town cycle. *See* Corpus Christi plays

Oswald, Saint, 55, 205 n.10, 206 nn. 11, 13
outlawry, 61–65, 201 n.41
Ovid, 77, 196 n.110, 208 n.38

pagans/paganism: as comparanda for late medieval persons/practices, 15–16, 116, 131, 137, 143, 170, 186 n.42; Saint Cecilia's preaching against, 171; as threat to virgin's body, 101, 184 n.17; women, who identify with female saint, 57
parish guilds, xvii, 146–47, 151–64, 166–67, 217 n.15; registration/requirements, 156; women's, 160, 221 n.63. *See also* social class/rank, and guild membership
Paston family, 58–59
patrons: female, xi, xiii, xv, 25, 28, 33–34, 37, 40–41, 42, 48, 51–54, 55–57, 62, 70, 74–78, 198 n.16, 202 n.56, 203 n.62; male, 34, 66, 190 n.29; as representative of female audience, 43, 63, 181 n.8
Patterson, Lee, 175, 177
Paxson, James, 149
Peasants' Revolt, 154
performance: of female sanctity, 145, 161, 166–72; of gender, xiv, 56, 75–76, 89–95, 97, 111, 146; of saints' plays/pageants, 146, 149–52, 161–65
Peter, Saint, guild of (Suffolk), 154
Peter the Venerable, 209 n.56
Pizan, Christine de, 27
Poor Clares, 17
preaching, women's, 2, 7, 9, 15, 75, 78, 130–31, 136, 168–69, 171. *See also* Lollards/Lollardy
procreativity, and literary production, 74–78, 81
Pugh, T. B., 58, 200 n.26
Pynson, Richard, 84, 86–87, 125, 204 n.1

question d'amour poems, 41, 196 n.111

Radegunde, Saint, legend of. *See* Bradshaw, Henry, *Lyfe of St. Radegunde*
Raymond of Capua, 28
Reames, Sherry, 169, 224 n.93
Reformation, 175–77
religious devotion: as feminine, 50, 72–73, 76; as historically specific, xii–xiii, xv, 117, 123, 135, 165, 170–71; as private/interior, 25–26, 73–74, 123, 129–31, 161–62; public

Index

expression of, 123–24, 133, 162, 163, 164, 166–69; as transhistorical, 74, 81, 95, 106–7, 109
Reysby, Nicholas, 34
Richard (duke of York), 54, 56, 58, 61–62, 68, 74, 76, 200 n.26
Richard II, 196 n.1, 202 n.55
romance, 41, 188 n.7, 193 n.88
Romance of the Rose, 43, 45
Rome, xvii, 2, 7, 99, 103, 119, 135, 170, 171, 209 n.49
Roscarrock, Nicholas, 121
Rosser, Gervase, 157, 159, 220 n.58
Royal Library MS Thott 517, 41

Sabina, Saint, 85; play of, 161, 222 n.70
St. Alban. *See* Lydgate, John, *Life of St. Alban and Amphibalus*
St. Radegund's abbey, Cambridge, 30
saints. *See* female saints; male saints/saints' lives
saints' lives. *See* female saints' lives, male saints/saints' lives; native saints' lives
saints' plays and pageants, 152–53, 161; historical record of, 145–46; in honor of English queens, 146–52, 172–73, 202 n.52, 216 nn. 6, 12; sponsorship of, 153, 160–61. *See also* cross-dressing, theatrical; performance, of saints' plays/pageants
St. Werburge's abbey, Chester, 84, 90, 95, 102, 108, 204 n.1
Salih, Sarah, 184 n.17, 214 nn. 41, 45, 215 n.58
Sampson, Saint, 85
Sarum breviary, 33, 182 n.3
Savage, Anne, 36
Scanlon, Larry, 187 n.48
Second Book of Homilies, 177
Seinte Marherete the Meiden ant Martyr (early Middle English legend of St. Margaret), 9–10, 12–13, 24
Sexburge, Saint, 93–94
Simpson, James, 18–19, 183 n.11, 195 n.104
Sklar, Ruth, 136
Smith, William, 16
social class/rank, xii, 29, 33, 41, 52, 107–9, 189 n.20; and guild membership, 155, 157–58
South English Legendary, 31, 35, 39, 69, 85, 182 n.1, 189 n.12, 192 n.78

Sponsler, Claire, 153, 181 n.7, 185 n.29, 194 n.91
Staley, Lynn, 122, 170, 212 nn.11–12, 224 n.96
Stanbury, Sarah, 16
Strohm, Paul, 183 n.11, 186 n.38, 194 nn.93–94, 196 n.1
Summit, Jennifer, 171, 175, 177, 190 n.26
Susana, Saint, play of, 161, 222 n.70

Talbot, C. H., 119
A Talking of the Love of God, 135
Taussig, Michael, 22, 187 n.54
Thomas of Walsingham, 121
Thorpe, William, 137–40
Thrupp, Sylvia, 157
translatio imperii et studii, 20, 120
translation of saint's body, 65–66, 100–101, 208 n.41
Trinity guild (Lynn), 155
Troy, 103
tyrants, 50, 63–64, 65, 139–40
Tudor drama, 147–52, 173

Unwin, George, 158
Urban (pope), 1, 119, 168, 171
Ursula, Saint: legends of, 40, 86, 173, 184 n.18, 206 n.13; in pageant for Catherine of Aragon, 146, 148–52, 165, 223 n.83

Vere, Elizabeth (countess of Oxford), 34, 51–54, 56, 58, 62, 81
virginity, 2, 8, 9; female saints as examples of, 10–11, 22, 118, 183 n.14; as metaphor for national identity, 88; as model for marital chastity, xiii, 8–9, 12, 22, 133, 184 n.18
virgin martyr legends. *See* female saints' lives
Virgin Mary, 73, 80, 98, 128, 152, 157, 164, 168; legend of, 41

Wales, 91. *See also* Welsh incursions
Wallace, David, 175, 196 n.1, 223 n.90
War of the Roses, 54
Warren, Nancy, 182 n.9, 197 n.12, 203 n.61
Watson, Nicholas, 27, 189 n.14
Welsh incursions, 88, 104

Werburge, Saint, of Chester, genealogy of, 92–93, 207 n.28. *See also* Bradshaw, Henry, *Life of St. Werburge of Chester*
Westlake, H. F., 163
Wetherby, Thomas, 155
Whethamstede, John (abbot of St. Alban's), 34
White, William, 15, 185 n.31
William de la Pole (marquess and duke of Suffolk), 58, 60
William of Malmsbury, 91
Winstead, Karen, 2–3, 33, 81, 124, 181 n.8, 182 n.2, 184 n.19, 189 n.17
witchcraft, 59–60, 68–69, 202 nn.49–51
Wogan-Browne, Jocelyn, 33, 38, 181 n.8, 188 nn. 3, 7, 192 n.73
women: as book owners, xi, xiii, 6, 34–37, 48; as readers/audience, xi, 22–23, 24, 28, 32–33, 37–38, 48, 53, 63, 195 n.102. *See also* audience, feminine; patrons, female

women's spirituality, defined against political/social concerns, 50–51, 54, 63, 70–71, 72–74, 76, 81–82, 182 n.9, 197 n.9
Woodville, Elizabeth (queen of Edward IV), 173
Wulfer (king of Mercia), 93–94, 97
Wulfric of Haselbury, legend of, 86
Wyclif, John, 15
Wycliffites. *See* Lollards/Lollardy; Wyclif, John
Wygnale, John (abbot of Derham), 34
Wynkyn de Worde, 87, 125
Wynter, Symon, 38

York plays. *See* Corpus Christi plays
York, house of, 53–54, 58, 68, 75–76. *See also* Bourchier, Isabel; Isabel (duchess of York); Richard (duke of York)

Acknowledgments

THIS PROJECT WAS BEGUN AT THE University of California at Los Angeles and my first thanks are to those who helped me when it was in its fledgling stage. Del Kolve is, as all his students know, exemplary in the best sense—at once inimitable and a model teacher, scholar, adviser, and colleague. I am grateful for all he has taught me. My thanks also to Chris Cannon, for asking hard questions and helping me see how they might be answered; to Andy Kelly, for helping me navigate the vast genre of hagiography; and to Eric Jager and Donka Minkova, for enthusiasm and support. This project also owes much to Claire Banchich, Jessica Brantley, and Jennifer Bryan, friends who continue to sustain my work in myriad ways. Jen has been an especially generous and astute reader (and rereader) of this book, and I am deeply grateful for the innumerable improvements in style and substance I owe to her.

I am very fortunate to have many supportive and inspiring colleagues at the University of Michigan. Sara Blair, Peggy McCracken, Josh Miller, Alisse Portnoy, Mike Schoenfelt, Viv Soni, Karla Taylor, Terri Tinkle, and Valerie Traub have all been perceptive readers of my work and generous colleagues. For advice, support, and energizing conversations about this and related projects, I thank Linda Gregerson, Anne Hermann, Steve Mullaney, Sid Smith, and Patsy Yaeger. I am also grateful to the Medieval Reading Group, the Premodern Colloquium, and the Women's Studies Program for the opportunity to present work from this book and for helpful feedback. Research leave from the Department of English gave me time to complete a draft of this book, and a wonderful year as a fellow at the Humanities Institute allowed me to make some final revisions and see it through production.

For especially helpful comments on individual chapters, I am grateful to Sarah Beckwith, Sara Blair, Catherine Brown, Barbara Fuchs, Claire Sponsler, and Karen Winstead. I am also eager to thank the two anonymous readers for the University of Pennsylvania Press for their generous engagement and many helpful suggestions. Other friends and colleagues have helped me think through questions, both local and large, or offered specific information or advice: among them, I want especially to thank Elizabeth Allen, Seeta Chaganti, Theresa Coletti, Lianna Farber, Bruce Holsinger, Simon Horobin, Kathy Lavezzo, Liz Scala, Fiona Somerset, Tom Toon, and Claire Waters. Thanks also to the members of the Medieval Writing Workshop, and especially its organizers, Rebecca Krug and Susie Phillips.

An earlier version of Chapter 6 appeared as "Performing Sanctity in Late Medieval England: Parish Guilds, Saints' Plays, and the *Second Nun's Tale*," *Journal of Medieval and Early Modern Studies* 32 (2002): 269–303. A much longer, and differently pointed, version of the reading of the *Legend of Good Women* that closes Chapter 2 is developed in "Reading Hagiographically: Chaucer's *Legend of Good Women* and Its Feminine Audience," *Exemplaria* 13 (2001): 323–54. My thanks to the editors and anonymous readers, and to the presses for permission to reprint. I am also grateful to the British Library for permission to reproduce the image in Chapter 4.

The publication of this book has been supported by a subvention from the Medieval Academy of America: I thank Richard Emmerson and the Academy for their generosity. I am grateful to Jerome Singerman and Erica Ginsburg at Penn Press for their guidance and help in seeing this book into print and to Kathryn Will and Rebecca Wiseman for their crucial assistance with the final preparation of the manuscript. The Office of the Vice President for Research at the University of Michigan also supported this project and its publication.

My final thanks are to Basil Dufallo, for the countless ways in which he has supported me and my work. This book is dedicated to him with love.